Office Milestones
Englisch für Büroberufe

Ruth Feiertag
Dr. Richard Hooton
Veronica Leary

Ernst Klett Verlag
Stuttgart · Leipzig

Office Milestones
Englisch für Büroberufe

Autoren: Ruth Feiertag; Dr. Richard Hooton; Veronica Leary (Fachteile Büro)

Berater: Robert Kanzog, Münster; Asiye Sezgin, Duisburg

Die Videos auf Seite 105 und 136 wurden von der Firma lingua tv
http://www.linguatv.com/ lizenziert.
Bei den Videos handelt es sich um Auszüge aus der LinguaTV-Reihe Business English.

Werkübersicht:
Schülerbuch, 978-3-12-808261-5
Lehrerhandbuch, mit Lehrer-Service-DVD-ROM und 3 Audio-CDs, 978-3-12-808267-7
Workbook mit 1 Audio-CD-ROM, 978-3-12-808265-3
Workbook mit Prüfungsvorbereitung KMK-Fremdsprachenzertifikat und 1 Audio-CD-ROM 978-3-12-808266-0
Office Milestones Online-Ergänzungen unter www.klett.de/online

1. Auflage   1   5   4   3   2   1 | 15   14   13   12   11

Alle Drucke dieser Auflage sind unverändert und können im Unterricht nebeneinander verwendet werden. Die letzte Zahl bezeichnet das Jahr des Druckes.
Das Werk und seine Teile sind urheberrechtlich geschützt. Jede Nutzung in anderen als den gesetzlich zugelassenen Fällen bedarf der vorherigen schriftlichen Einwilligung des Verlages. Hinweis §52 a UrhG: Weder das Werk noch seine Teile dürfen ohne eine solche Einwilligung eingescannt und in ein Netzwerk eingestellt werden. Dies gilt auch für Intranets von Schulen und sonstigen Bildungseinrichtungen. Fotomechanische oder andere Wiedergabeverfahren nur mit Genehmigung des Verlages.
Auf verschiedenen Seiten dieses Heftes befinden sich Verweise (Links) auf Internet-Adressen. Haftungshinweis: Trotz sorgfältiger inhaltlicher Kontrolle wird die Haftung für die Inhalte der externen Seiten ausgeschlossen. Für den Inhalt dieser externen Seiten sind ausschließlich die Betreiber verantwortlich. Sollten Sie daher auf kostenpflichtige, illegale oder anstößige Inhalte treffen, so bedauern wir dies ausdrücklich und bitten Sie, uns umgehend per E-Mail davon in Kenntnis zu setzen, damit beim Nachdruck der Verweis gelöscht wird.

© Ernst Klett Verlag GmbH, Stuttgart 2011. Alle Rechte vorbehalten. www.klett.de

Projektleitung: Matthias Rupp
Redaktion: Volker Wendland; Dr. Birgit Reinel, Tübingen
Herstellung: Angelika Lindner

Gestaltung: Marion Köster, Stuttgart
Umschlaggestaltung: Ulrike Wollenberg; Angelika Lindner
Grafiken: Jörg Mair, München
Satz: Marion Köster, Stuttgart
Reproduktion: Meyle + Müller Medien-Management, Pforzheim
Druck: Druckhaus Götz GmbH, Ludwigsburg

Printed in Germany
ISBN 978-3-12-808261-5

Vorwort

Das vorliegende Lehrwerk **Office Milestones** für die Englischklassen in den bürokaufmännischen Berufsschulen, Fachschulen und Berufsfachschulen sowie für auf Bürokaufleute ausgerichtete Englischkurse in der Erwachsenenbildung zeichnet sich insbesondere durch folgende Elemente aus:

- Berücksichtigung der Incoterms® 2010 (gültig ab 01.01.2011)
- Einbeziehung neuester Entwicklungen in der bürokaufmännischen Praxis, z. B. Textverarbeitung, Tabellenkalkulation, Präsentationen und Internetrecherchen
- Konsequente Berücksichtigung neuester Lehrpläne (Lernfelder) sowie durchgängiges Sprachkompetenztraining nach dem Gemeinsamen Europäischen Referenzrahmen (Sprachstufen B1 / B2)
- Möglichkeit zur Binnendifferenzierung durch gekennzeichnete Aufgaben mit höherem Schwierigkeitsgrad
- Umfangreiches Seh- / Hörverstehenstraining durch u. a. Originalvideos von der BBC sowie zahlreiche Audios
- Vokabelarbeit mit der „Word Bank" sowie mit den Vokabellernlisten, dem unitbegleitenden Vokabular und dem Glossar über Online-Link
- Vertieftes Vokabel-, Grammatik- und Hörverstehenstraining in den Workbooks 1 und 2, inklusive Audio-CD-ROM mit allen Schülerbuch- und Workbook-Audios
- Gezielte Prüfungsvorbereitung auf das KMK-Fremdsprachenzertifikat im Lehrwerk und in Workbook 2

Workbook 1:
Business Milestones Workbook mit Audio-CD-ROM,
978-3-12-808265-3

Workbook 2:
Business Milestones Workbook mit Prüfungsvorbereitung KMK-Fremdsprachenzertifikat und Audio-CD-ROM,
978-3-12-808266-0

Lernhilfen

WORDBANK Schlüsselvokabular
Info-Box Faktenwissen
Communicating across cultures Interkulturelle Kompetenz
Language and grammar Grammatik
Video lounge authentische Videos

Symbole

A 1.27   Audioverweis
V 4   Videoverweis
Phrases   Verweis auf Phrases
P, M, I, R   Produktion, Mediation, Interaktion oder Rezeption
Example: z. B. Beispieldialoge
Online-Link   Vokabellernlisten, unitbegleitendes Vokabular und Glossar über Online-Link
KMK   Aufgaben zur Vorbereitung auf die Prüfung zum KMK-Fremdsprachenzertifikat Englisch
  Internetrecherchen
✱   „Advanced"-Aufgaben

Inhaltsverzeichnis

1 Introducing yourself — 6

TOPICS / SKILLS Introducing yourself • Talking about your (future) profession
COMMUNICATING ACROSS CULTURES The German dual training system
LANGUAGE AND GRAMMAR Introducing and greeting people
OFFICE EXPERT Job profiles in offices • Streamlining office procedures

2 Taking care of visitors — 18

TOPICS / SKILLS Greeting visitors • Making conversation • Giving directions • Taking foreign visitors to a restaurant
COMMUNICATING ACROSS CULTURES Small talk • Describing German dishes • Going to restaurants in Britain
LANGUAGE AND GRAMMAR Will-future
OFFICE EXPERT Corporate entertainment • Preparing a conference

3 The company and its products and services — 38

TOPICS / SKILLS Describing a firm and its history • Describing products and services
COMMUNICATING ACROSS CULTURES Joint stock companies in the USA and Britain
LANGUAGE AND GRAMMAR Simple past and present perfect • Since and for
VIDEO LOUNGE BBC: Sport and leisure
OFFICE EXPERT Presenting your company online

4 The office — 51

TOPICS / SKILLS Describing the office / Computer terms • Catering in the office • Describing departments and responsibilities
COMMUNICATING ACROSS CULTURES Addressing people
LANGUAGE AND GRAMMAR Infinitive and gerund
OFFICE EXPERT Office suite applications • Working with spreadsheets

5 Telephoning — 63

TOPICS / SKILLS Appliances • Receiving and redirecting calls • Taking messages / Spelling • Making telephone calls • Messages for the answering machine
COMMUNICATING ACROSS CULTURES Telephoning in an English-speaking country
LANGUAGE AND GRAMMAR Tricky prepositions
OFFICE EXPERT Using mobile phones

6 Making arrangements — 84

TOPICS / SKILLS Booking flights, hotel rooms and exhibition stands / Hiring cars • Making appointments • Preparing a meeting • Taking the minutes
COMMUNICATING ACROSS CULTURES Tips for visitors to the UK
LANGUAGE AND GRAMMAR Continuous form
VIDEO LOUNGE BBC: Hospitality
OFFICE EXPERT Handling schedules • Arranging transportation

7 Making presentations — 100

TOPICS / SKILLS Preparing and delivering presentations • Describing graphs and diagrams
LANGUAGE AND GRAMMAR Line graphs, bar charts, pie charts
VIDEO LOUNGE Lingua TV: Presentations
OFFICE EXPERT Structuring presentations • Drawing graphs

Inhaltsverzeichnis

8 Form of written communication — 112

TOPICS / SKILLS Layout / Components of business correspondence • Writing e-mails, faxes, letters
COMMUNICATING ACROSS CULTURES The tone of English business correspondence
LANGUAGE AND GRAMMAR Typical mistakes in business correspondence
OFFICE EXPERT Word processing • E-mail flood in the office

9 Enquiries — 132

TOPICS / SKILLS Making enquiries • Discounts
LANGUAGE AND GRAMMAR Adjectives, adverbs
VIDEO LOUNGE Lingua TV: General enquiries

10 Offers — 142

TOPICS / SKILLS Making offers in writing and by phone • Comparing options • Incoterms® 2010
LANGUAGE AND GRAMMAR Some and any
OFFICE EXPERT Office supplies fairs • Comparing offers for office furniture

11 Orders — 159

TOPICS / SKILLS Placing orders
LANGUAGE AND GRAMMAR Capital letters
VIDEO LOUNGE BBC: Manufacturing
OFFICE EXPERT Ordering business cards

12 Transport and logistics — 171

TOPICS / SKILLS Modes of transport • Packing • Dispatch advice
LANGUAGE AND GRAMMAR False friends
VIDEO LOUNGE BBC: IT

13 Payment and reminders — 180

TOPICS / SKILLS Invoice • Means and terms of payment • Reminders and replies
LANGUAGE AND GRAMMAR How to translate "sollen"
OFFICE EXPERT Handling money • Writing a reminder

14 Complaints and adjustments — 196

TOPICS / SKILLS Making / Adjusting complaints
COMMUNICATING ACROSS CULTURES Complaining about products or services
LANGUAGE AND GRAMMAR Conditional clauses
OFFICE EXPERT Key account management • The copy machine • Licence agreements

15 Marketing products and services — 215

TOPICS / SKILLS Product life cycle and market research • Distribution channels • Advertising and public relations
LANGUAGE AND GRAMMAR Comparatives and superlatives
VIDEO LOUNGE BBC: Retailing
OFFICE EXPERT Purchasing incentives • Ergonomics in the office • Costs and calculations

16 Job applications in Germany and the EU — 229

TOPICS / SKILLS Job ads • Letters of application, CVs and job interviews • Employment in the EU
COMMUNICATING ACROSS CULTURES Job applications
VIDEO LOUNGE BBC: Travel and Tourism
OFFICE EXPERT Internship training abroad • Job fairs • Europass • Starting your own business

Appendix — 252

Role cards **252**
Alphabetical word list • Glossary • Acronyms • False friends • Countries, nationalities and languages • World map **257**
Unitbegleitendes Vokabular und Glossar zum Herunterladen über Online-Link 808261-0000

Unit 1
Introducing yourself

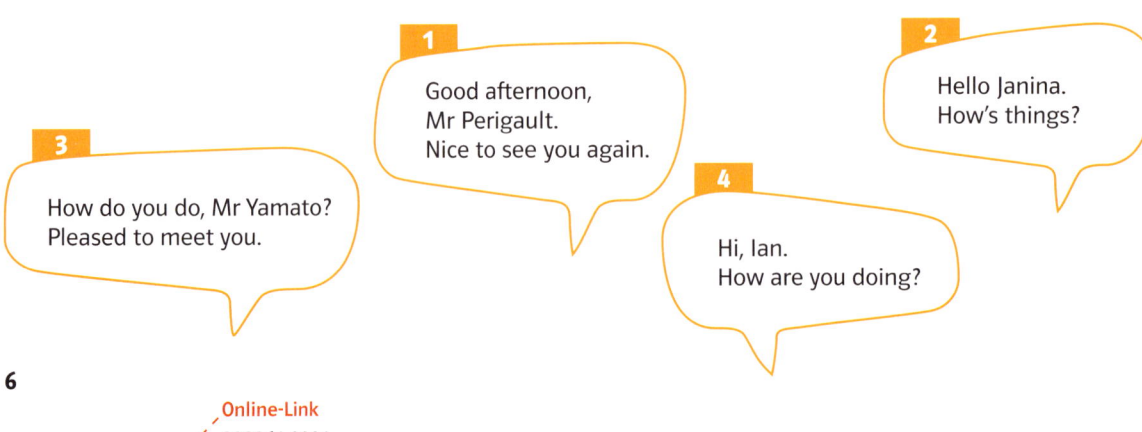

WORD BANK

I'm / my name is • I'm from • I was born in / on • to work as a … • to be a … • to work at / with / for … • to be interested in • to be into • trainee • apprentice • traineeship / apprenticeship • vocational school • to attend school • to be on a programme • to take part in • to train / to be training as a … • to train to be a … • to be training to become a … • to do a traineeship as a … • to qualify as a … • clerk • management assistant • consultant • specialist

In business it is often necessary to introduce yourself. It is therefore important to know what to say and what information to include. You may, for instance need to explain your professional role or duties in the firm. In a business situation introductions and greetings are often more formal than those among friends in a casual situation. It is important to choose the right style.

Decide which of the following phrases would be used in a formal and which in a casual situation. Match the phrases with the photos above.

1 Good afternoon, Mr Perigault. Nice to see you again.

2 Hello Janina. How's things?

3 How do you do, Mr Yamato? Pleased to meet you.

4 Hi, Ian. How are you doing?

Online-Link
808261-0001

A Talking about yourself

Students at a vocational school in Germany are asked to introduce themselves to a new English assistant who is to spend half a year at their school.

1 Take the roles of the assistant and the students and read the introductions.

Rona: Good morning. I'm Rona Mansfield. I come from Dulwich in South London and I'll be working here as an assistant teacher for the next six months. It would be good if a few of you could introduce yourselves so I can begin to learn your names. Perhaps you could tell me briefly what job you're training for and what your interests are. Hello, what's your name?

Stefanie: Hello. I'm Stefanie Krieger. I'm from Cologne but I was born in Hamburg. I'll be 17 next Monday. I'm doing a traineeship at Kabel AG in Leverkusen to become an office administration clerk. I'm very interested in computers and enjoy designing websites. I do quite a lot of sport, including aerobics and badminton.

Rona: Thank you, Stefanie, I'll remember the birthday! And what's your name?

Haris: Hi. My name's Haris Akbar. I'm from Cologne. I am 19 years old. I'm training at Schulz und Schmalenbach as an export clerk. I am very interested in football and support Werder Bremen. I work out regularly at a local gym. I love music. "The Devils" are my favourite group.

Rona: Thank you, Haris. My taste in music is a touch more traditional. Can you tell me something about yourself?

Antonella: My name is Antonella Piccolino but my friends call me Nella. Like Stefanie, I also work at Kabel AG but I'm training to be an Industrie-kauffrau, that's an industrial clerk or industrial business management assistant. I was born in Bergheim in 1992. Originally my family comes from Sicily. I'm very interested in the Italian language and Italian cooking. I also go to a fitness centre three times a week because I'm into body-building.

Rona: Gosh, I can see we'd better watch what we say. Right, we can continue with the introductions later. Could you make a plan of the classroom where everybody's sitting with names – first names and family names.

Unit 1 | Introducing yourself

2 Say whether the following statements from page 7 are TRUE or FALSE.
R

1. Stefanie Krieger was born in Cologne.
2. She is training to be an office administration clerk.
3. She doesn't like working with a computer.
4. Haris Akbar is doing a traineeship to become an industrial clerk.
5. He is between 20 and 30 years old.
6. He supports a football club from Bavaria.
7. Antonella Piccolino is at the same firm as Haris Akbar.
8. Her hobby is cooking Italian dishes.
9. She tries to keep fit.

3 Complete the following introduction using the words from the box.

at • from • in (3x) • near • to • on

I was born **2** Garforth **3** 23 March 1964. Garforth is a small town **5** Leeds **6** the UK. My family comes **7** the West Indies. I work **8** an advertising agency and I'm taking part **9** a training programme for advertising assistants. I regularly go **10** a gym for a work-out.

4 Listen to the following introductions and answer the questions.
R
A1.1

Thorsten

1. Where does Thorsten come from?
2. What is he training as?
3. What is his hobby?

Ludmilla

1. How long has Ludmilla been living in Germany?
2. How old is she?

Ayshe

1. When was Ayshe born?
2. What is she training to become?
3. What does she do in her free time?

Introducing yourself | Unit 1

5 Work in groups and make up similar introductions with the help of the
P   following hints.

> Phrases

Training or working as:	industrial clerk/industrial business management assistant, office administration clerk/office management assistant, wholesale and export clerk/management assistant in wholesale and foreign trade, bank clerk/bank business management assistant, management assistant in advertising, freight forwarding and logistics services clerk/management assistant in freight forwarding, IT specialist, management assistant in retail business, publisher's assistant/management assistant in publishing, insurance clerk/insurance business management assistant
Firms:	ENKA AG, Schuster & Schneider, Taufrisch OHG, Kohlhaas & Söhne, Globistik-Transport KG, Sportsmarketing GmbH, Online-Consulting
Hobbies:	Swimming, reading fantasy novels, cycling, volleyball, Sci-Fi films, buying clothes, computer games, horses, snowboarding, clubbing

Language and grammar
Work in groups of four. Introduce yourself briefly in writing.
You may use imaginary details if you wish. Read the introduction
out to your group.

> Phrases

Language and grammar: Introducing yourself

Antonella sagt: I **was** born in Bergheim in 1992.	Auf Deutsch hätte sie gesagt: Ich **bin** 1992 in Bergheim geboren.
Im Englischen werden Geburtszeitpunkt und Geburtsort mit simple past angegeben:	
My father **was** born in Italy. Haris **was** born on 7 July 1992.	Mein Vater ist in Italien geboren. Haris ist am 7. Juli 1992 geboren.
Außerdem wird im Englischen erst der Ort genannt und danach der Zeitpunkt: I was born **in Bergheim in 1992**.	Im Deutschen ist die Reihenfolge umgekehrt: Ich bin **1992 in Bergheim** geboren.
Haris sagt: I'm training as **an** export clerk. She's **a** travel consultant. He works as **a** programmer.	Auf Deutsch hätte er gesagt: Ich mache eine Ausbildung als Exportkaufmann. Sie ist Reiseverkehrskauffrau. Er arbeitet als Programmierer.
Im Englischen steht zur Angabe des Berufes der unbestimmte Artikel: **a travel consultant.** Im Deutschen steht kein Artikel: **Reiseverkehrskauffrau.**	
I am **a** publisher's assistant. I am training as **a** bank clerk or bank business management assistant.	Ich bin Verlagskaufmann. Ich mache eine Ausbildung als Bankkaufmann.

9

Unit 1 | Introducing yourself

> **Communicating across cultures: Introducing and greeting people**
>
> In English-speaking countries people often give only their first name when introducing themselves - "Hi, I'm Jonathan". In more formal contexts they give their first name and surname but never just their surname as is usual in Germany - "I'm Jennifer Ashton". Often people add; "Please call me Jennifer".
> "How do you do" is a formal greeting which is nowadays rarely used. The other person also says "How do you do" and will probably add "Pleased to meet you".
> A usual greeting is "Hello, how are you?" The other person says something like "Fine, thanks / not so bad / so-so" and immediately adds "How are you?" Friends usually say something like "Hi, Justin. How are you doing?" or "Hello, Sarah, how's things?"
> Sarah might reply: "Fine, how's things with you?"

B Young people talk about their (future) professions

Rona Mansfield meets more students at the vocational college and asks them to introduce themselves and tell her what training programme they're on:

Oliver:	Hello, I'm Oliver: I'm training to become an office management assistant.
Jeannine:	My name's Jeannine: I'm on the trainee programme of a high street bank.
David:	I'm David: I'm an insurance business management assistant.
Jennifer:	Hi, I'm Jennifer: I want to train as an advertising assistant.
Antje:	I'm Antje: I hope to be a restaurant manager.
Rosa:	Hi, I'm Rosa: I am interested in qualifying as a foreign language correspondent.
Dennis:	I'm Dennis: I want to get on to a training programme for retail management assistants.
Niko:	I'm Niko: I want to train as an event management assistant.
Simone:	Hi, I'm Simone: I'm applying to train as an IT specialist.
Janina:	Hello, my name's Janina: I work for a wholesaler in the electrical goods industry.
Mike:	I'm Mike: I'm a trainee export clerk.
Dragan:	I'm Dragan: I'm training to be a management assistant in publishing.
Hasan:	Good morning. I'm Hasan: I am planning to train as an industrial clerk or industrial business management assistant.

My name's Samira. I am taking part in an ITC programme.

Hello, I'm Sabrina. I'm training to be a travel consultant.

Introducing yourself | Unit 1

1 Read the introductions on page 10 and match the German occupations with their English paraphrases.

1. Kauffrau für Tourismus und Freizeit
2. Kaufmann im Einzelhandel
3. Fremdsprachenkorrespondentin
4. Kaufmann für Spedition und Logistikdienstleistung
5. Veranstaltungskauffrau
6. Industriekauffrau
7. Automobilkaufmann
8. Kaufmann für Bürokommunikation
9. Kauffrau für Marketingkommunikation
10. Kaufmann im Groß- und Außenhandel
11. Kauffrau für Versicherung und Finanzen
12. Informatikkaufmann
13. Bankkaufmann

a. advertising assistant / management assistant in advertising
b. bank clerk / bank business management assistant
c. automobile sales management assistant
d. management assistant in event organisation
e. management assistant for freight forwarding and logistics
f. industrial clerk / industrial business management assistant
g. insurance clerk / insurance business management assistant
h. IT consultant / management assistant in informatics
i. management assistant in office communication
j. retail business management assistant
k. secretary with foreign languages / foreign language correspondent
l. management assistant for tourism and leisure
m. wholesale and export clerk / management assistant in wholesale and foreign trade

2 Übertragen Sie die folgenden Aussagen ins Englische.

1. Ich habe eine Ausbildung als Industriekaufmann gemacht.
2. Ich möchte eine Ausbildung als Automobilkaufmann machen.
3. Ich möchte als Fremdsprachenkorrespondentin ausgebildet werden.
4. Ich will Versicherungskaufmann werden.
5. Ich nehme an einem IT-Weiterbildungsprogramm teil.
6. Ich bewerbe mich um einen Ausbildungsplatz als Bürokauffrau.
7. Ich mache eine Ausbildung als Kauffrau im Einzelhandel.
8. Ich arbeite bei einem Großhändler.
9. Ich möchte gerne eine Ausbildung als Werbekaufmann machen.

Unit 1 | Introducing yourself

3 Work in groups of three. Act out the following conversation, inserting your own names and training courses.
I/P

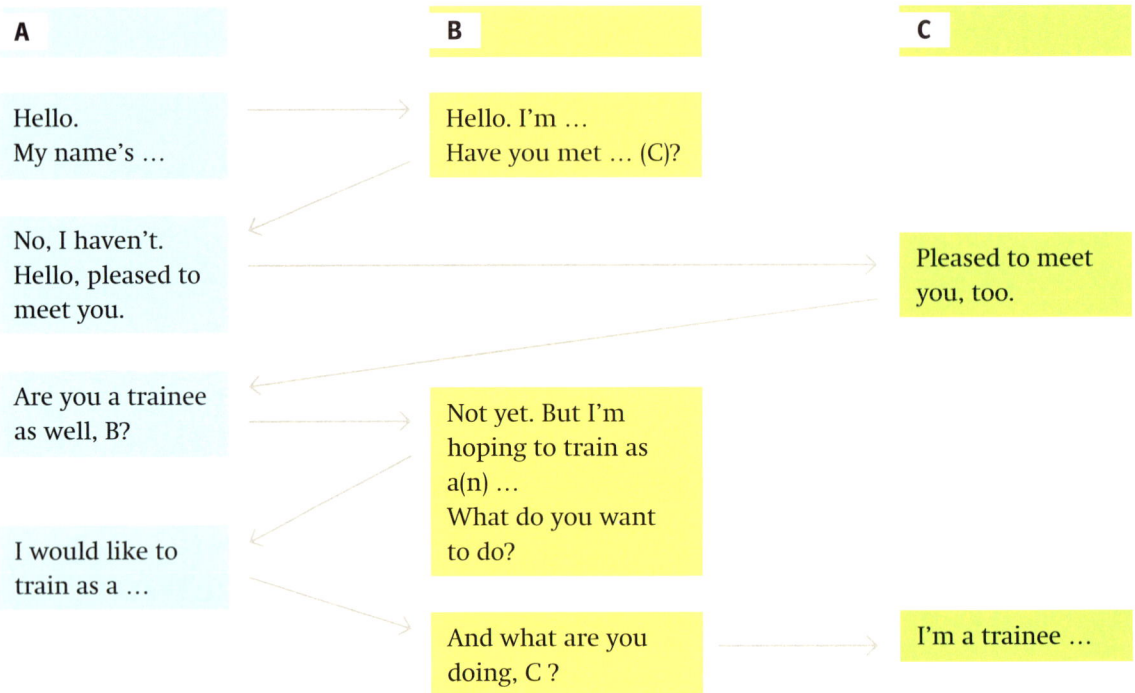

4 Work in groups of three. Use the phrases from the conversation above and make similar dialogues.
I/P

Phrases

5 Listen to the following dialogue and say which of the following statements are true for Patrick and Janina.
R
A 1.2

1. I'm training to become an industrial clerk.
2. I want to train as an export clerk.
3. I'm in the electrical goods industry.
4. There are good prospects of promotion.
5. I'm allowed to advise customers.
6. I get on well with the people I work with.
7. I can use my English.
8. I can work on my own.

6 Work in groups of two. Introduce yourselves and say what you do. Ask each other what you like or dislike in your job.
I

Phrases

7 Search the Internet for two of the following international job titles. Note down the details of one job ad. Compare and discuss your findings with the group.

freight forwarding clerk • trainee advertising assistant • insurance clerk •
IT assistant • trainee assistant events • bilingual secretary / secretary or PA with
foreign languages • trainee tourism assistant / tourism clerk

12

Communicating across cultures: The German "dual training" system

The German "dual training" system combining on the job apprenticeships / traineeships with vocational school has no direct systematic equivalent in Britain and the USA. This is also true of the large number of protected job titles with a prescribed course of training in Germany. However, in Britain, for example, there are many training programmes, traineeships and apprenticeships in more traditional skilled occupations (plumber, electrician, etc.), also vocational courses leading to an NVQ (National Vocational Qualification). Most trainee programmes (except traditional apprentices) are shorter than in Germany and people often do additional courses later (e.g. in CLAIT = computer literacy and information technology) leading to a national or international qualification.

As a result of these differences German job titles can often not be translated literally. It is necessary to paraphrase them in such a way that a foreign employer can get a realistic idea of the range of activity covered.

The statement "Ich mache eine Ausbildung zum Industriekaufmann bei der ENCOR AG" could be paraphrased as follows: "I am on a 3-year training programme with ENCOR AG to qualify as an industrial clerk / industrial business management assistant specialising in the commercial side of an industrial business. During the training programme I have to attend courses at vocational school either two days a week or in blocks of several weeks at a time. At the end of the training period I sit for an examination before the local chamber of commerce."

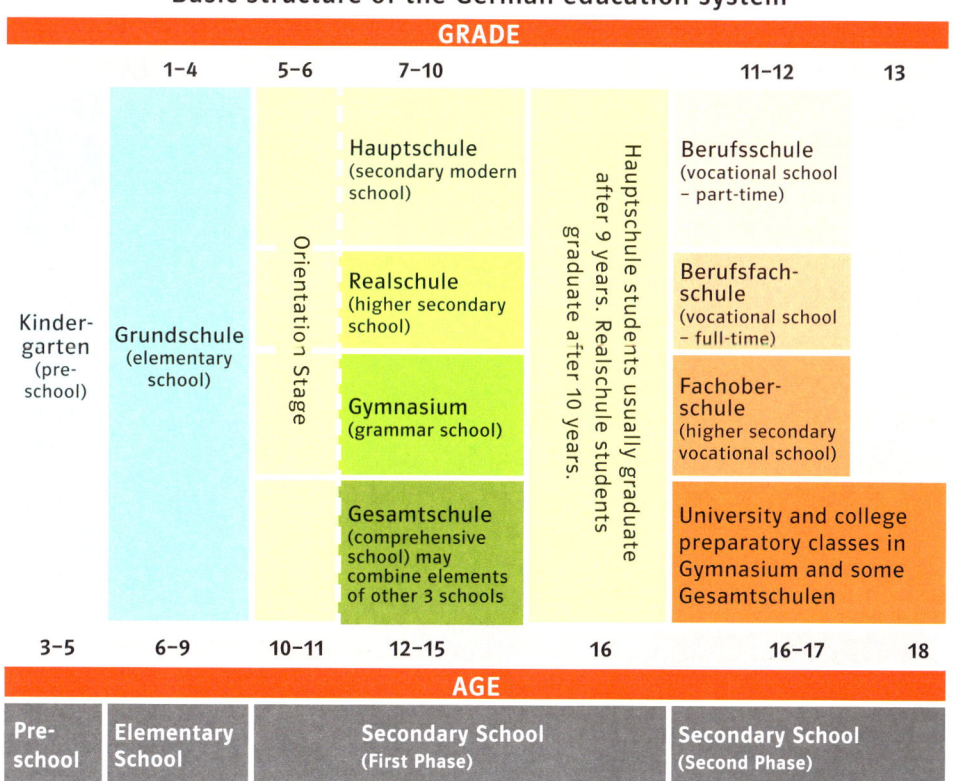

Basic structure of the German education system

Unit 1 | Introducing yourself

Office expert

1 Job profiles in offices

1 Many different verbs are used to describe job tasks in an office. Look at Exercise 2 and match the following English verbs (1.–10.) to their German equivalents (a.–j.).

1. to complete
2. to conduct
3. to deal with
4. to maintain
5. to make computations
6. to process
7. to place
8. to post
9. to route
10. to screen

a. aufgeben
b. Berechnungen durchführen
c. (durch)führen, leiten
d. pflegen
e. sich befassen mit
f. überprüfen, aussondern
g. verarbeiten
h. (per Post) verschicken
i. vervollständigen
j. weiterleiten

2 The duties performed by office assistants may include a combination of tasks.
R/M First assign the jobs (A.–E.) to the appropriate job duties (1.–15.). Some duties may apply to more than one job. Then use a dictionary and translate the job duties into German.

A. Secretary with foreign languages
B. Personal assistant
C. Human resources assistant
D. Accounting assistant
E. Office administration clerk

Job duties
1. Answer telephones, direct calls and take messages.
2. Prepare graphics, statistics and tables for presentations.
3. Answer enquiries (phone, e-mail, in person) concerning payments.
4. Organise application and contract documents.
5. Conduct plant tours for foreign visitors.
6. Process information by maintaining/updating filing, database systems, etc.
7. Create and design texts with the computer.
8. Translate company advertising material.
9. Screen applicant profiles and job adverts.
10. Complete schedules, manage diaries and arrange appointments.
11. Deal with English language correspondence and documents.
12. Make computations for balancing and maintaining accounts.
13. Open, sort and route incoming mail and prepare outgoing mail.
14. Create and place job adverts corresponding to relevant requirements.
15. Post payments and refunds to appropriate account or cost centre.

Introducing yourself | Unit 1

3 Complete the description of key soft skills with the words from the box.

> command • communicator • detail • discretion • individual • intercultural •
> meeting • member • multi-task • organisational • pressure • professional

A personal assistant needs to be a good **1** in speech and writing with an excellent **2** of English. The ability to prioritise work and to **3** – which means being able to work on several tasks at any given time – are equally important. Accuracy and attention to **4**, as well as good **5** skills are also required. Personal assistants are often assigned to a group, not just an **6**, and, therefore, need to be able to work independently and as a **7** of a team. The position of an executive secretary or office management assistant requires **8** because such persons often have to deal with confidential information. A friendly, **9** manner, being able to work under **10** and **11** deadlines are essential criteria for all types of assistants. **12** awareness is a key factor when working for a company that deals with foreign customers.

4 Create a job profile for each of the five jobs (A.–E.) in Exercise 2. You can use the list of job duties on page 14 and add your own ideas.

> Phrases

2 Streamlining office procedures

1 Complete the following definitions with suitable words from the box.

> characters • combination • downloaded • located • pre-formatted • storage

Tools for saving time
Templates are **1** files that serve as a starting point for creating new documents. They can be **2** and are available for letters, business forms, etc.
A **keyboard shortcut** is a key **3** that performs a certain command. Most shortcuts are **4** in a programme's menu. **Auto text** is a **5** location for text or graphics you want to use again. The selections have to be at least five **6** long and each is recorded as an auto text entry and assigned a unique name.

2 Match the recommendations (1.–4.) with the examples (a.–d.).

1. Automate processes
2. Replicate repetitive tasks
3. Reuse information
4. Use shortcuts

a. Create and print labels and envelopes for mass mailings.
b. Learn keyboard shortcuts, such as pressing SHIFT + F10, to display the shortcut menu for the selected item.
c. Save time by using professional templates or create your own templates for text elements you use frequently.
d. Think about how you can automate tasks you do regularly.

3 Discuss which streamlining techniques you are already familiar with and you can recommend. Which ones would you like to try?

Unit 1 | Introducing yourself

Phrases: Introducing yourself and others

To introduce yourself

I'm Peter./My name is Henry Myers.	Ich heiße Peter./Ich heiße Henry Myers.
Please call me Henry.	Nennen Sie mich doch Henry.
My surname is Hillary, my first name is Tom.	Mein Familienname ist Hillary, mein Vorname Tom.
How are you? (How are you doing?)	Wie geht es Ihnen/Dir? (informelle Begrüßung)
I'm from Berlin, and I am 20 years old.	Ich stamme aus Berlin und bin 20 Jahre alt.
I'm British/Irish.	Ich bin Brite/Ire.
I **was** born in Cyprus on 7 August 1982.	Ich bin am 7. August 1982 in Zypern geboren.
Have you met Mr Martens?	Kennen Sie Herrn Martens?
May I introduce Dr. Bolt to you?	Darf ich Ihnen Herrn Dr. Bolt vorstellen?
Pleased/Nice to meet you.	Ich freue mich, Sie kennen zu lernen.
And how are you?	Und (wie geht es) Ihnen?
Didn't we meet at the Boat Fair?	Haben wir uns nicht schon auf der Boot-Messe kennen gelernt?
I've heard a lot **about** you **from** Mr Winter.	Herr Winter hat mir schon viel von Ihnen erzählt.

To talk about your hobbies and interests

I am interested in computers.	Ich interessiere mich für Computer.
I love travelling more than anything else.	Ich reise schrecklich gern.
I like to go clubbing.	Ich gehe gern in die Disco.
I'm **into** body-building.	Ich interessiere mich für Bodybuilding.
I do a lot of diving.	Ich gehe oft tauchen.

To talk about your training or your work

I'm a trainee export clerk.	Ich mache eine Ausbildung zum Exportkaufmann.
I'm training to become	Ich mache eine Lehre als
an industrial clerk/industrial business management assistant	Industriekaufmann/-frau
a wholesale and export clerk/management assistant in wholesale and foreign trade	Kaufmann/-frau im Groß- und Außenhandel

an office administration clerk/office management assistant	Kaufmann/-frau für Bürokommunikation
a freight forwarding and logistics services clerk/management assistant in freight forwarding and logistics	Kaufmann/-frau für Spedition und Logistikdienstleistung
a bank clerk/bank business management assistant	Bankkaufmann/-frau
a retail clerk/management assistant in retail business	Kaufmann/-frau im Einzelhandel
a management assistant for tourism and leisure	Kaufmann/-frau für Tourismus und Freizeit
a publisher's assistant	Verlags-/Medienkaufmann/-frau
an insurance clerk/insurance business management assistant	Kaufmann/-frau für Versicherungen und Finanzen
a management assistant in advertising	Kaufmann/-frau für Marketing-kommunikation
a management assistant in event organisation	Veranstaltungskaufmann/-frau
an automobile sales management assistant	Automobilkaufmann/-frau
I'm taking part in an ITC programme.	Ich nehme an einem ITC-Ausbildungsprogramm teil.
I'm in the catering **industry**.	Ich bin in der Cateringbranche.
I work **at** SITCOM Ltd.	Ich arbeite bei SITCOM Ltd.
I **attend** vocational school.	Ich besuche die Berufsschule.
What are you doing job-wise, Nina?	Nina, was machst du beruflich?
What are you training to be, Timo?	Was machst du für eine Ausbildung, Timo?
What do you like **about** your job?	Was gefällt dir an deiner Arbeit?
What industry are you in?	In welcher Branche arbeitest du?

To say what you like or dislike about your training or your work

I like my job because I get on well with the people I work with.	Ich mag meine Arbeit, weil ich mich mit meinen Kollegen gut verstehe.
I can work **on** my own.	Ich kann selbstständig arbeiten.
There are good prospects **of** promotion.	Die Aufstiegschancen sind gut.
I have to key in data all day long.	Den ganzen Tag muss ich Daten eingeben.
I have to work a lot of overtime.	Ich muss viele Überstunden machen.

Unit 2 | Taking care of visitors

A

B

C

D

Unit 2
Taking care of visitors

WORD BANK
visitor • visit • refreshments • to greet • to receive • to welcome • to meet • flight • hotel • weather • hobbies • sports • to entertain • to chat • directions • floor plan • map • layout • premises • to go • to turn • to follow • restaurant • menu • meal • dish • to invite • to choose

Greeting visitors to your company and making them feel welcome may be an important part of your job. You should always be friendly and helpful as first impressions are often very important. You may have to entertain them until the person they want to see appears. The language in which both you and they can communicate will often be English, even when the visitors do not come from an English-speaking country. English is rapidly becoming a lingua franca in Europe.

1 Match the phrases with the photos above.

1 Welcome to Schneider GmbH. Did you have any trouble finding us?

2 Have you met Ms Reuter? She is our marketing manager.

3 Go along the corridor. The conference room is the second door on the right.

4 Did you have a pleasant flight?

Online-Link
808261-0002

2 Translate the following statements from the introductory text into German.

1. Greeting visitors may be an important part of your job.
2. First impressions are often very important.
3. You may have to entertain visitors until the person they want to see appears.
4. The language in which both you and they can communicate will often be English.

A Greeting visitors

Marcel Krenz, an export clerk at International Snacks GmbH, a German food processing company, has been asked by his boss, Markus Diepholz, to receive Kirsty Burnham and Kevin Sears who represent a major British catering chain. They are interested in the wide range of snacks and lunch boxes the company produces.

1 Read the above text, listen to the dialogue and answer the following questions.

1. Who is Marcel Krenz?
2. What are his visitors from Britain interested in?
3. What refreshments do Kirsty Burnham and Kevin Sears prefer?
4. What is Kevin's position?
5. What is Frau Wieland in charge of?
6. Where have Kirsty Burnham and Frau Wieland met before?
7. Why has Marcel Krenz been asked to receive the visitors?

2 Match the expressions on the left with those on the right.

1. a food processing company
2. a major chain
3. a wide range of snacks
4. I'll let him know you're here
5. a couple of minutes
6. a sparkling mineral water
7. she's on the export staff
8. she's in charge of sales to the EU
9. I'd like you to meet Frau Wieland
10. we've already met

a. a large assortment of snacks
b. she is responsible for sales to the EU
c. a few minutes
d. we already know each other
e. water with gas bubbles
f. a company using raw materials to make food products
g. an important company with many branches
h. I would like to introduce you to Frau Wieland
i. she is a member of the export sales personnel
j. I will inform him that you have arrived

Unit 2 | Taking care of visitors

B Making conversation

Marcel and the visitors from Britain chat while waiting for Herr Diepholz.

1 Listen to the CD and complete the following dialogue on a separate sheet of paper.

R
A1.4

Marcel: Did you have a pleasant flight?
Kirsty: Oh yes, the flight was very straightforward – **1**. There was a bit of turbulence, though. I'm afraid I don't like that.
Marcel: **2** does the flight from Manchester take?
Kevin: It only takes about one and a half hours. But we **3** as a result of the time difference.
Marcel: Of course. What was **4** in Manchester? Was it as good as it is here?
Kirsty: Surprisingly, yes. We have been having **5** lately. It's almost like summer. But generally Manchester gets a lot of rain. From the Atlantic – it's on the west side, you know.
Marcel: Yes, I've heard it gets a lot of rain. **6** is Manchester United doing?
Kitsty: No idea, I'm afraid. I'm **7** a football person. Kevin is, aren't you? Ask him.
Kevin: They're still among the top teams and **8** in the Champions' League quarter finals.
Marcel: I know, they may be playing Bayern Munich next … ! I've heard that Manchester is a very vibrant place.
Kirsty: It certainly is. It's become a **9** city. Lots of gigs and clubs. All the old industry has gone and the old buildings have been renovated. You'd like it. You ought to come some time.
Marcel: I'd like to. Are there any **10**?
Kevin: Definitely. It's amazing how cheap they are if you book **11**. If you search the internet you can save a lot of money.
Marcel: Well, that's really … Ah, here comes Herr Diepholz …

2 Complete the following conversations with the words from the boxes.

Dialogue 1

afraid • doing • flight • like • proud • time

You: How was your **1**?
Visitor: Rather bumpy, I'm **2**.
You: I'm sorry to hear that. What was the weather **3** in Glasgow?
Visitor: Oh, it was the same as here, overcast and windy. But that's nothing unusual for this **4** of the year.
You: How are Glasgow Rangers **5**?
Visitor: They play in the UEFA Europa League, we're rather **6** of them. I support Celtic, though.

Dialogue 2

apart • by • for • from • how • there

You: Where do you come **1**, Miss Spears?
Visitor: I'm from South Africa. Just now I've come from Berlin **2** train.
You: **3** was the train ride? Was the train punctual?
Visitor: Actually, the train was 10 minutes late, **4** from that the ride was quite pleasant, though.
You: South Africa must be a wonderful country. At least that's what everybody here says who's been **5**.
Visitor: You should come and see **6** yourself. There's a lot to see and do for tourists.

3 Match the questions with the answers.

1. Can I offer you a cold drink? h
2. Is this your first visit to Germany? f
3. Did you have a good flight? g
4. Would you like something to read? c
5. What was the weather like in Portugal? d
6. May I take your coat? a
7. Do you take milk and sugar? b
8. Are you interested in tennis? e

a. No, thank you. I'll keep it on. I'm cold.
b. No, thanks. I'm on a diet.
c. Yes, please. Perhaps your company brochure?
d. Very sunny. We could do with some rain.
e. No, it's not my thing. I prefer cycling.
f. Yes, it is.
g. Oh no. There was a lot of turbulence.
h. Thank you. An apple juice would be fine.

4 Restore the correct order of this jumbled dialogue.

1. Barmaid (in pub): Yes, it's freezing, isn't it? And this awful drizzle.
2. Customer: It's not like June at all.
3. Barmaid: They say its going to improve for the weekend, though.
4. Customer: Isn't the weather dreadful!

Communicating across cultures: Small Talk

In Britain the weather is very changeable, which makes it a constant topic of conversation:

The weather is wonderful, superb, lovely, very good. The weather is awful, ghastly, dreadful, terrible.

Example:
Newsagent: Good morning. How are you today?
Customer: Fine. Isn't it a beautiful day?
Newsagent: Wonderful. Let's hope it stays like this.
Customer: I'm afraid the weather forecast says rain.

Unit 2 | Taking care of visitors

5 Role play: Work in pairs. Make up dialogues using the following prompts and the phrases at the end of the Unit.

> **Student A:** How was your trip?
>
> **Student B:** Rather tedious, there was a tailback on the motorway from Frankfurt.

Student A asks about:	Student B replies using these expressions:
flight/trip/journey	pleasant, rather tedious, lots of turbulence, tailback on the motorway, long delay at the airport, etc.
weather	sunny, overcast, slight drizzle, fog, gale-force winds, snow, is going to improve, cold for the time of the year, quite warm, pouring rain, windy, etc.
first visit to …	oh yes, many times, once before, but not much time to see anything, no never, long been wanting to visit …, etc.
hotel	nice and quiet, service first-class, a bit far from the exhibition centre, rather noisy, excellent restaurant, etc.
visitor's home town	small place in Wisconsin, has changed a lot in recent years, many tourists visit it, has vibrant business centre, scenic village in the mountains, busy port in India, etc.
sports events	not very interested in golf, watch as many tournaments as possible, would like to see the match, support XYZ club, etc.

Taking care of visitors | Unit 2

C Giving directions

Kirsty Burnham has lost her way in the office building. She is standing at the reception desk. The receptionist directs her to Herr Diepholz' – the managing director's – office.

1 Take the role of the receptionist. Use the floor plan, the phrases below and the phrases at the end of the unit.

Phrases

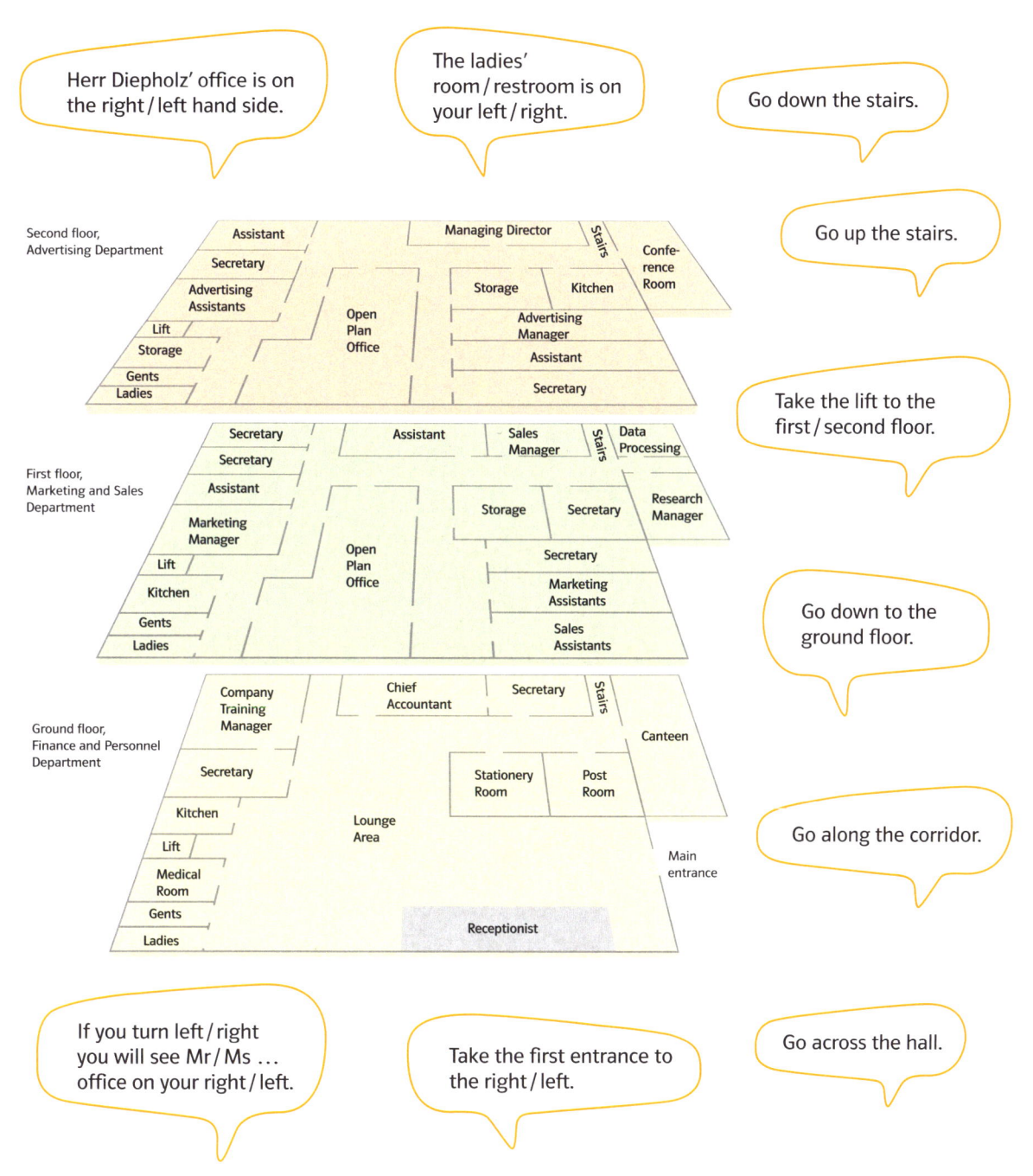

> Herr Diepholz' office is on the right / left hand side.

> The ladies' room / restroom is on your left / right.

> Go down the stairs.

> Go up the stairs.

> Take the lift to the first / second floor.

> Go down to the ground floor.

> Go along the corridor.

> Go across the hall.

> If you turn left / right you will see Mr / Ms … office on your right / left.

> Take the first entrance to the right / left.

Second floor, Advertising Department: Assistant, Secretary, Advertising Assistants, Lift, Storage, Gents, Ladies, Open Plan Office, Managing Director, Storage, Kitchen, Stairs, Conference Room, Advertising Manager, Assistant, Secretary

First floor, Marketing and Sales Department: Secretary, Secretary, Assistant, Marketing Manager, Lift, Kitchen, Gents, Ladies, Open Plan Office, Assistant, Sales Manager, Storage, Secretary, Secretary, Marketing Assistants, Sales Assistants, Stairs, Data Processing, Research Manager

Ground floor, Finance and Personnel Department: Company Training Manager, Secretary, Kitchen, Lift, Medical Room, Gents, Ladies, Chief Accountant, Secretary, Lounge Area, Stationery Room, Post Room, Stairs, Canteen, Main entrance, Receptionist

23

Unit 2 | Taking care of visitors

2 Work in pairs. Explain to each other the way to certain rooms.

1. Your partner is at the main entrance. He asks you: "Could you tell me the way to the Sales Manager's office?"
2. You are in the canteen. You ask your partner:" Where is the conference room, please?"
3. Your partner is leaving the Advertising Manager's office. He asks you: "Would you mind telling me where the medical room is?"
4. You are in the Marketing Assistants' room. You ask your partner: "I need to freshen up a bit. Could you tell me the way to the ladies'/the men's toilets/restroom (Am)?"

3 The visitors from England want to see some of the famous sights in Munich. Use the map on page 25 and direct them from the station (Hauptbahnhof) to the following destinations:
Hofbräuhaus [1], Frauenkirche [2], Englischer Garten [3].

Phrases

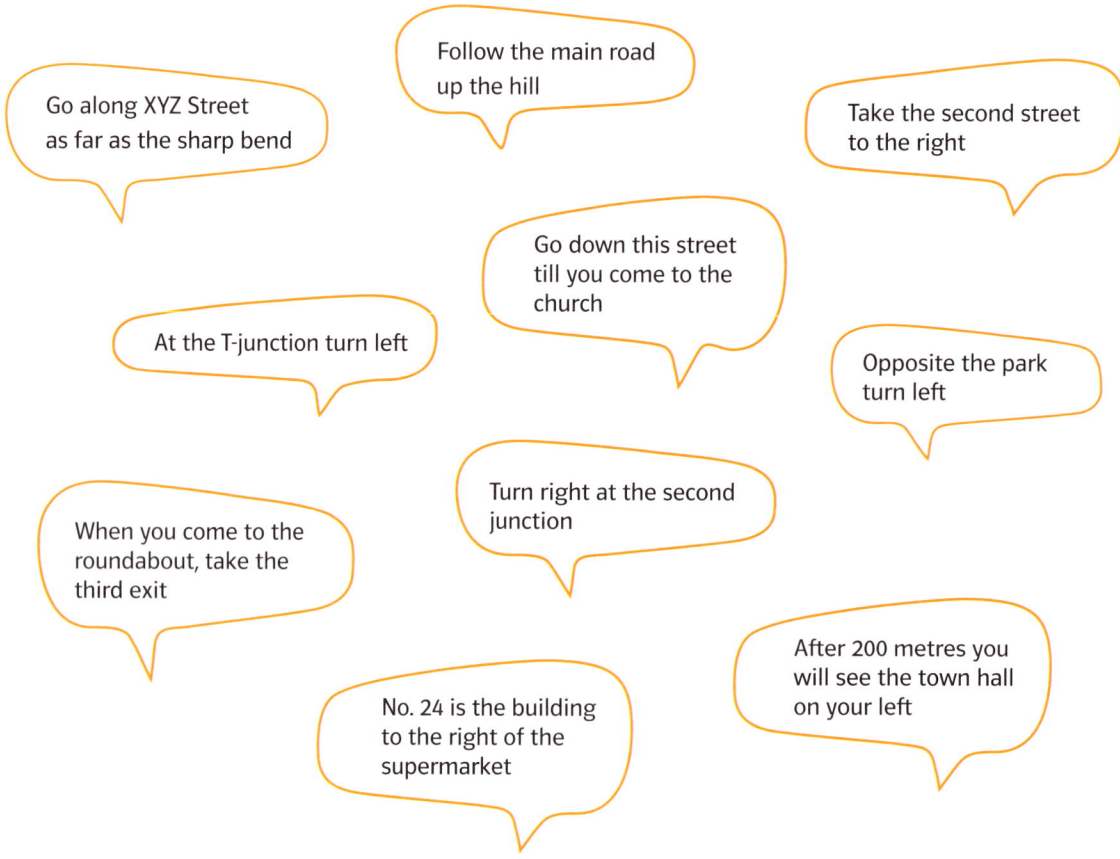

Go along XYZ Street as far as the sharp bend

Follow the main road up the hill

Take the second street to the right

Go down this street till you come to the church

At the T-junction turn left

Opposite the park turn left

Turn right at the second junction

When you come to the roundabout, take the third exit

After 200 metres you will see the town hall on your left

No. 24 is the building to the right of the supermarket

Taking care of visitors | Unit 2

4 Listen to the explanations given by the Tourist Information assistant and find out which famous sights the visitors will be seeing during their stroll through the town centre of Munich.

1

2

3

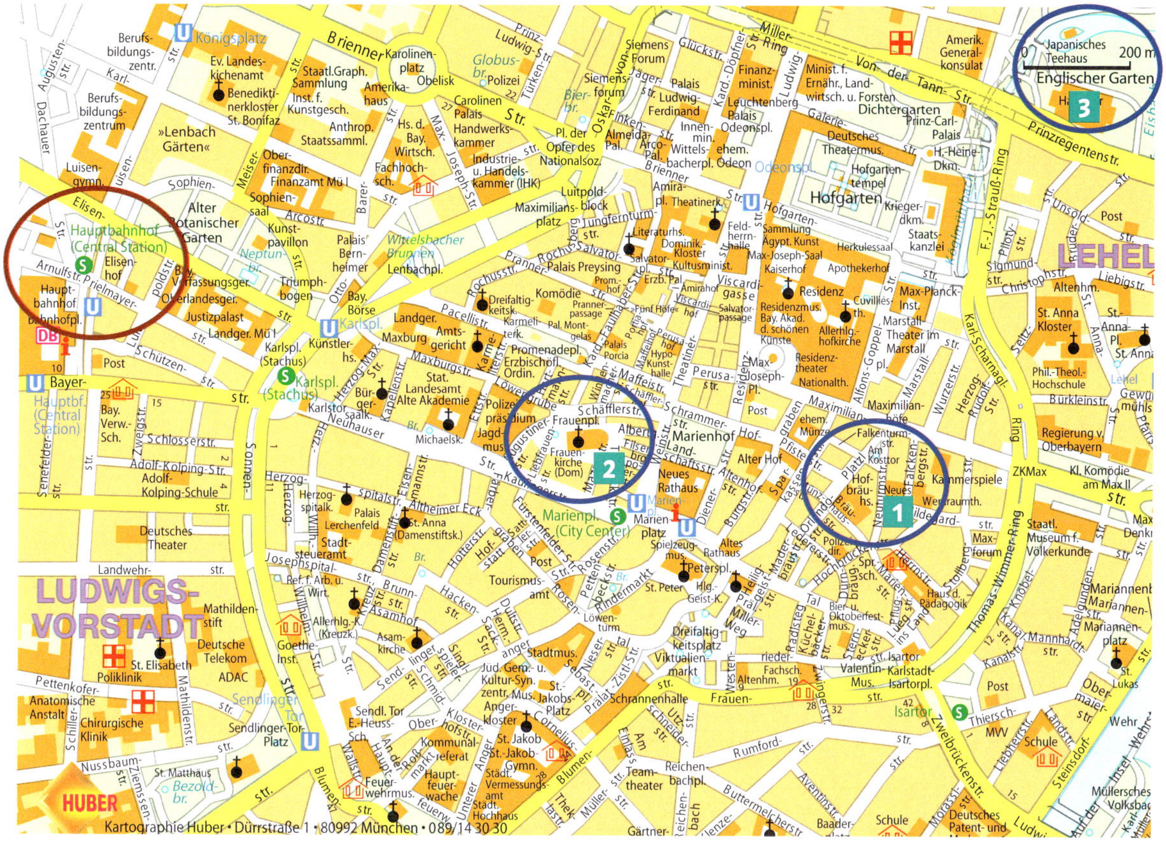

5 David Stedman has been visiting your headquarters in Berlin. He now has an appointment at your offices in Inselstraße, Düsseldorf. He has been told that the office is within walking distance of the main station. As he has some time on his hands before his appointment he would like to have instructions how to get there on foot.

Click on to a map of Düsseldorf on the internet and e-mail the instructions to him (davidstedman@aol.com).

Unit 2 | Taking care of visitors

D Describing the layout of the premises and carrying out a tour of the firm for visitors

Markus Diepholz and Marcel Krenz take Kirsty Burnham and Kevin Sears on a tour of the company's premises.

1 Listen to the dialogue and decide whether the following statements are TRUE or FALSE.
R
A1.6

1. All the administrative work is dealt with at the offices.
2. The senior staff also work in the open-plan offices.
3. Marcel Krenz' office has a nice view of the surrounding countryside.
4. The canteen also provides vegetarian snacks.
5. Herr Diepholz and his visitors cross the car park to reach the kitchen facilities.
6. Freshness and hygiene are the most important considerations.
7. International Snacks are planning to do some market research on what people feel about their packaging.

2 You are Kevin Sears. Write a memo in English on the tour of the premises of International Snacks.
P
Remember: A memo has to be brief, clear and to the point.

```
+ + MEMO + + MEMO + + MEMO + + MEMO + + MEMO + +

To:       Michael Kent, General Manager
From:     Kevin Sears, Assistant to Kirsty Burnham
Date:     Wednesday, 23 March 201_
Subject:  Our tour of the Premises of International Snacks,
          Düsseldorf
```

3 Sie sind Marcel Krenz. Verfassen Sie eine kurze Aktennotiz in Deutsch über die
KMK Betriebsbesichtigung und die Reaktionen der britischen Besucher.

MEMO

```
Für:     Geschäftsleitung
Von:     Marcel Krenz, Exportsachbearbeiter
Datum:   20.03.201_
Betreff: Betriebsbesichtigung mit Kirsty Burnham und Kevin
         Sears von Global Catering, Manchester, UK
```

E Taking foreign visitors to a restaurant

Herr Diepholz invites Kirsty and Kevin to lunch and asks Marcel to join them and interpret.

1 Listen to the dialogue and write down what Kirsty and Kevin order (starter, main course, dessert, drinks).

Speisekarte

Vorspeisen
Pikante Brokkoli-Pastetchen
Gefüllte Steinpilze
Kraftbrühe mit Ei
Lauchcremesuppe
Avocado-Kaltschale

Hauptgerichte
Schweinebraten mit Rotkohl und Salzkartoffeln
Rinderrouladen mit Blumenkohl und Kartoffelpüree
Rheinischer Sauerbraten mit Rotkohl und Kartoffelklößen
Wiener Schnitzel mit Pommes frites und Salat
Wildgulasch mit Speckknödeln und Preiselbeeren
Forelle Müllerin-Art
Lauch-Soufflé
Gemüsebratlinge

Nachspeisen
Gemischtes Eis
Rote Grütze mit Sahne
Bayerische Creme
Käseplatte

Unit 2 | Taking care of visitors

2 Find the correct equivalents.

1. Bockwurst — m
2. Bratkartoffeln — e
3. Bratwurst — f
4. Erbsensuppe — i
5. Frikadellen — h
6. Gurkensalat — c
7. Kartoffelbrei — g
8. Kartoffelsuppe — j
9. Pommes frites — d
10. Rinderbraten — k
11. Rindfleischbrühe — a
12. Schokoladenpudding — b
13. Schweinebraten — l

a. beef broth
b. chocolate pudding
c. cucumber salad
d. French fries
e. fried potatoes
f. grilled sausage
g. mashed potatoes
h. meatballs
i. pea soup
j. potato soup
k. roast beef
l. roast pork
m. large frankfurter

Communicating across cultures: Describing dishes

For a number of typical German dishes there are no direct translations. You will have to describe them to your visitors from abroad. These expressions may help you:

Which part of the meal is it?
It's a starter.
It's the main course.
It's a dessert.

What kind of food is it?
It's meat (pork, beef, veal, lamb).
It's poultry (chicken, turkey).
It's fish (salmon, trout, plaice, haddock).
It's game (venison, rabbit).
It's a sort of pasta (spaghetti, noodles).
It's a vegetable (peas, beans, carrots, green peppers, cauliflower, cabbage, Brussels sprouts, asparagus).

How is it made?
It's made of mashed potatoes, ground / minced meat, chopped onions.
It's filled / stuffed with (rice, minced meat, vegetables).
It's boiled (baked, stewed, grilled, fried, smoked).

What does it taste like?
It's hot / spicy.
It's sweet / sour.
It's tart.
It's savoury.
It tastes a bit like (yoghurt, veal, mousse au chocolat).

Taking care of visitors | Unit 2

3 Study the explanations and find out which of the German dishes they refer to.

Jägerschnitzel • Kopfsalat • Rote Grütze • Semmelknödel • Spätzle

1. It's a dessert. It's a jelly made of red berries thickened with corn starch. It's not too sweet. Quite tart, in fact.
2. They go with a main course. They're dumplings made of white bread with eggs and parsley. They're rather filling, though.
3. It's a schnitzel, a sort of pork escalope with sauce and mushrooms.
4. It's a kind of home-made pasta, typical of the South West of Germany.
5. It's lettuce with oil and vinegar dressing.

4 Ask the amateur chefs among you to explain two of the following dishes in English to your group. Use the expressions at the end of the unit.

Zigeunerschnitzel • Sauerkraut • gemischter Salat • gefüllte Paprikaschoten • Milchreis • Hackbraten • Linseneintopf

`Phrases`

5 Choose a starter, a main course and a dessert from the menu on page 27 and explain it to a foreign visitor. Use the phrases at the end of the unit.

`Phrases`

6 Work in groups. Explain your favourite dishes to the group.

**Communicating across cultures:
Going to restaurants in Britain**

You may have to wait to be seated. A waiter will ask how many you are and indicate a table. Of course, you can say something like: "Couldn't we sit over there in the window?"

The waiter/waitress may ask you whether you want to order drinks straight away. After you have had time to study the menu, the waiter or waitress will say: "Are you ready to order, madam?" If you are not, you could say: "We're not quite ready. We need a moment or two."

When the food comes, he/she will probably say: "Enjoy your meal" or sometimes just "Enjoy!" However, there is nothing like "Guten Appetit" that you can say to your companions/guests.

Complaining is very difficult. You should at all costs avoid being aggressive or loud – this will not get you anywhere. Be nice, understanding, humorous if possible.

Finally, when you want to pay, you say: "Could I have the bill, please."

Unit 2 | Taking care of visitors

Language and grammar 1
Choose the correct form of the verbs.

1. I `give` you a ring towards the end of the week.
2. We `let` you `know` as soon as possible.
3. If you `wash` the dishes, I `dry`.
4. I `ask` Joanna if she `want` to come.
5. You `chop` the mushrooms and I `cook` the pasta.
6. I `pass` on the message when I `see` her on Friday.
7. I `pick` him up at the station if you `want`.
8. He `help` you with your move if you `give` him a ring on Wednesday.
9. I `give` you a lift if you like.
10. David `stand` in for you if necessary.

Language and grammar 2
Translate the following text.

Wir übergeben die Sendung morgen früh der Spedition Fuhrmann Logistik und hoffen, dass die Ware übermorgen wohlbehalten bei Ihnen ankommt. Wir helfen Ihnen gerne, wenn Sie noch weitere Fragen haben. Wir sind sicher, dass unsere exquisiten Schuhe Ihren Kunden gefallen und dass sich diese Artikel in Großbritannien gut verkaufen lassen.

Language and grammar: Will-future

Die "will"-Zukunftsform (meistens in der abgeschwächten Form I'll, we'll) wird im Englischen bei spontanen Entscheidungen benutzt und entspricht dem Präsens im Deutschen.

Marcel Krenz says:	I'll give Herr Diepholz a ring and let him know you're here.
Kevin Sears says:	I'll have black coffee.
Marcel Krenz says:	I'll just ring through and order them.
Sit down and I'll make some coffee.	= Setz dich hin. Ich koche Kaffee.
You keep an eye on the spaghetti and I'll make the salad.	= Pass du auf die Spaghetti auf. Ich mache den Salat.
Allerdings wird "will" nicht in Nebensätzen der Bedingung und der Zeit verwendet.	
I'll fetch the newspapers if you make the tea.	= Ich hole die Zeitungen, wenn du Tee machst.
I'll tell him as soon as he arrives.	= Ich sage es ihm, sobald er ankommt.

Office expert

1 Corporate entertainment

1 You work in the public relations department of an international company.
R/P In groups discuss and decide which event (A–D) below and on page 32 to invite which of the people to (1.–4.).

1. The annual company outing for your staff of 125 and their spouses.
2. Members of the Executive Women's Forum, a group of your global concern's most influential female executives.
3. The CEO of your biggest customer with his two teenage sons.
4. An international team of engineers, researchers and managers who have successfully completed a multi-billion dollar project.

A

FIFA World Cup

Hospitality packages for corporate customers or individuals (minimum purchase per match or series of four), comprising:
- FIFA World Cup™ premium match ticket
- Match-day hospitality benefits at the stadium such as:
  - high-end catering
  - bar-service
  - free parking
  - entertainment and gifts
- Access to travel packages (flight/bus transfers to matches and accommodation)

B

Dancing and Dining on a Danube River Cruise Boat

Roll out the red carpet for your guests and treat them to an evening of dancing and dining on this exclusive river cruise. To the music of the Evergreen Big Band your guests can waltz the night away on the Blue Danube.
Included in the package are a banquet of delicious finger food, salads and canapés. The boat offers two dance floors, one above deck with live music and a disco below deck, all for just €35 per person (minimum of 200 guests, maximum 275).

Unit 2 | Taking care of visitors

C

Chelsea Flower Show

The Chelsea Flower Show is a special occasion to mark in your corporate calendar. Enjoy the best in British hospitality at the most famous flower show in the world.
Experience this spectacular show together with delicious cuisine and fine wines in the Hospitality Village. Included is the entrance ticket to the show, the show catalogue, morning coffee, champagne and canapé reception as well as a four-course dinner with selected first-class wines.

Date	Price
Tuesday 25th May	£ 489 + VAT
Wednesday 26th May	£ 445 + VAT
Thursday 27th May	£ 389 + VAT
Friday 28th May	£ 269 + VAT

D

Edinburgh Military Tattoo

The Edinburgh Military Tattoo is a spectacular performance suited for every age, nationality or taste, making it an ideal event for your corporate entertainment. Early booking is recommended for watching the pipes and drums and other performances from around the world.
The hospitality package includes:
- Private table in the Queen Anne Room, exclusive hire options available
- Early access to Edinburgh Castle grounds
- Champagne and canapé reception
- Three-course banquet dinner with selected wines
- After-dinner coffee and dessert
- Castle-facing premier seating

Price: £ 385 + VAT per person

2 Find the English equivalents in the brochures (A.–D.) above and on page 31
M   for the following German terms.

1. Paket(angebot)
2. Firmenkunden
3. Luxusbewirtung
4. kostenloses Parken
5. Sektempfang
6. der rote Teppich
7. Cocktailhappen
8. frühzeitige Buchung
9. Mietmöglichkeit
10. Festessen

3 Decide on a small gift to present to each of your guests. Report back to the
P   class and give reasons for your choices.

Taking care of visitors | Unit 2

2 Preparing a conference

1 You have been given the task of preparing the annual company Technical Day which is going to take place this year in the Czech Republic. About 50 engineers, managers and technicians from around the world are expected to attend. You had a brainstorming session with your boss about the things you need to do. Unfortunately, your notes from the meeting got mixed up.

Complete the *To do* list below with the right verbs from the box. Then put the tasks in the correct order, i.e. decide which things need to be done first, second, third, etc.

arrange (5) • choose (2) • draw up (3) • make (8) • prepare (7) • send (6) • send out (4) • set (1)

TO DO
- 1 ☐ ... dates for conference
- 5 ☐ ... accommodation for participants
- 8 ☐ ... final arrangements
- 2 ☐ ... a suitable conference venue
- 4 ☐ ... the invitations
- 3 ☐ ... conference schedule
- 7 ☐ ... conference bags / folders
- 6 ☐ ... documentation with directions and details

2 Choosing the right venue is a key factor contributing to the success of a conference. Make up the questions you need to ask yourself to help in your choice – we've provided some possible answers.

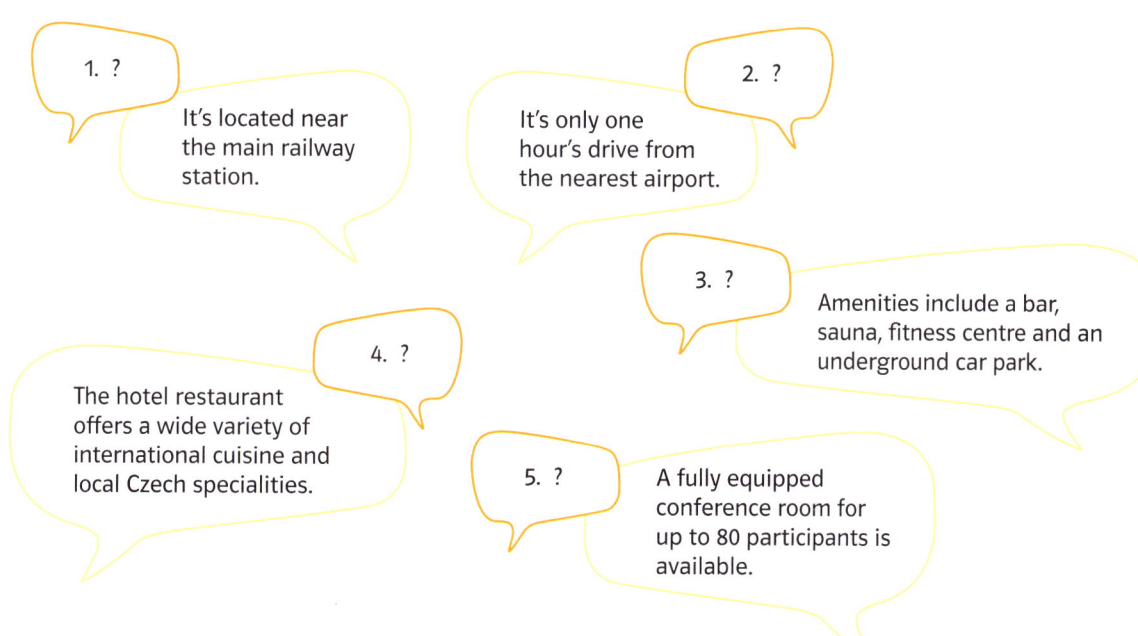

1. ? — It's located near the main railway station.
2. ? — It's only one hour's drive from the nearest airport.
3. ? — Amenities include a bar, sauna, fitness centre and an underground car park.
4. ? — The hotel restaurant offers a wide variety of international cuisine and local Czech specialities.
5. ? — A fully equipped conference room for up to 80 participants is available.

33

Unit 2 | Taking care of visitors

3 Read the extracts from a hotel website and find answers to your questions
R   in Exercise 2 on page 33, if possible.

Mamaison Imperial Hotel ★★★★

Located only a few steps from the main square Masarykovo, the 4-star **Mamaison Imperial Hotel Ostrava** offers luxury accommodation in downtown Ostrava, Czech Republic, minutes away from the famous Stodolni Street, full of bars, pubs and clubs, and from all of Ostrava's major tourist attractions.

Offering hospitality for more than 100 years, this extraordinary hotel prides itself on providing friendly and personal service to all its guests at a reasonable price. The Mamaison Imperial Hotel Ostrava is an ideal choice for business travellers, couples and families alike. This luxury hotel offers outstanding services, such as a stylish sport bar, an elegant restaurant, a 24-hour front desk, wireless internet connection, a completely equipped conference centre as well as a wellness area with indoor swimming pool, sauna and different kinds of massages and beauty treatments.

Prices range from € 120 – 160 per single room but discounts are available for preferred customers and corporate bookings of 20 or more.

Clarion Congress Hotel

The **Clarion Congress Hotel Ostrava** in Ostrava-Zábřeh can be easily reached from the centre and the railway station. It is the nearest hotel to the Leoš Janáček airport in Ostrava-Mošnov. Arrangements for a pick-up service (24 hours) at no extra charge can be made.

You will spend peaceful nights in the nicely furnished rooms and start every new day at the rich and complimentary breakfast buffet. In each of the two buildings there are two floors which are completely non-smoking.

The Harmonie Restaurant offers tasty Czech, Moravian and international cuisine and a wide selection of quality wines. During meetings and conferences a wide choice of refreshments can be enjoyed in the Atrium Piazza D'Oro as well. These include hot and cold food, salads and confectionery and are included in our conference package. Prices for the conference package range from € 150 – 200 per participant, depending on the size of the group (minimum 10 participants).

In the vicinity of the Clarion Congress Hotel Ostrava you can find the Vitkovice Sports and Culture Palace, the ČEZ Arena, sports grounds and tennis courts. Next to the hotel there is a partially covered and permanently supervised car park.

✱ 4 Schreiben Sie einen Kurzbericht für Ihre Chefin in Englisch, in dem Sie **Phrases**
KMK Argumente für und wider die beiden oben beschriebenen Veranstaltungsorte darlegen und eine Empfehlung für eines der beiden Hotels aussprechen. Berücksichtigen Sie dabei die folgenden Punkte:

- Verkehrsanbindung (Nähe zum Bahnhof/Flughafen, Parkmöglichkeiten)
- Verpflegung
- Konferenzeinrichtungen und Dienstleistungen
- Freizeiteinrichtungen (Sauna, etc.)
- Preise und Rabatte

Phrases: Taking care of visitors

To welcome visitors

Good afternoon. Can I help you?/What can I do for you?	Guten Tag. Was kann ich für Sie tun?
Please take **a seat**.	Bitte nehmen Sie Platz.
Can I offer you some refreshments?	Darf ich Ihnen etwas anbieten?
Coffee with milk and sugar, tea, herbal tea, fruit juice, sparkling/still mineral water, coke?	Kaffee mit Milch und Zucker, schwarzer Tee, Kräutertee, Fruchtsaft, Mineralwasser mit/ohne Kohlensäure, Cola?
Frau Sievers **is expecting** you.	Frau Sievers erwartet Sie.
I'm afraid, Frau Sievers is still in a meeting.	Frau Sievers ist leider noch in einer Besprechung.
She will be **with** you in a few minutes.	Sie wird in ein paar Minuten da sein.

To make conversation

Did you have a pleasant flight?	Hatten Sie einen angenehmen Flug?
How was the **journey**?	Wie war die Fahrt?
Have you ever been to Oldenburg before?	Waren Sie schon einmal in Oldenburg?
Where do you come **from**?	Wo kommen Sie her?
What was the weather **like** in Belfast?	Wie war das Wetter in Belfast?
Would you like to see something **of** Bonn?	Möchten Sie in Bonn etwas besichtigen?
Are you satisfied with your hotel?	Sind Sie mit dem Hotel zufrieden?
I'll have an orange juice.	Ich nehme einen Orangensaft.
No thanks, I don't take milk or sugar.	Nein danke, ich nehme weder Milch noch Zucker.
The flight was rather bumpy.	Der Flug war ziemlich unruhig.
The trip was very pleasant. Thank you.	Danke. Die Fahrt war sehr angenehm.
Actually, I have been to Oldenburg twice, in 1999 and in 2002.	Ich war tatsächlich schon zweimal in Oldenburg, 1990 und 2002.
The weather was fine. Not a cloud **in** the sky.	Das Wetter war schön. Kein Wölkchen am Himmel.
We've had a lot of rain lately.	In der letzten Zeit hat es bei uns viel geregnet.
I'd like to visit Beethoven's house.	Ich möchte mir gerne das Beethoven-Haus ansehen.

Unit 2 | Taking care of visitors

The hotel will do. It's **on** a rather noisy street, though.	Das Hotel geht einigermaßen. Es liegt allerdings an einer ziemlich lauten Straße.
The hotel is excellent. Very quiet.	Das Hotel ist ausgezeichnet. Sehr ruhig.

To give directions

GB	USA	Germany
second floor	third floor	2. Etage
first floor	second floor	1. Etage
ground floor	first floor	Erdgeschoss
basement	basement	Untergeschoss/Keller

Take the lift to the third floor.	Fahren Sie mit dem Aufzug in den dritten Stock.
Go up/down (the stairs) to the 2nd floor.	Gehen Sie (die Treppe) hinauf/hinunter zum 2. Stock.
Herr Diepholz' office is on the **right hand** side.	Das Büro von Herrn Diepholz ist auf der rechten Seite.
At the junction **turn** right/left.	Gehen/Fahren Sie an der Kreuzung nach rechts/links.
Go **straight ahead** to …	Gehen/Fahren Sie gerade aus bis …
Go down this street till you come to the …	Gehen/Fahren Sie auf dieser Straße weiter bis Sie zu … kommen.
When you come to the roundabout, take the 3rd exit.	Am Kreisverkehr nehmen Sie die dritte Ausfahrt.
Follow the main road up the hill.	Fahren Sie die Hauptstraße weiter bergauf.
After 200 yards you will see the church **to** your left.	Nach (ca.) 200 m sehen Sie die Kirche auf der linken Seite.

To take visitors on a tour of your firm's premises

We would like to show you **round** the company's premises.	Wir möchten Ihnen unsere Firma auf einem Rundgang zeigen.
We have two open-plan offices.	Wir haben zwei Großraumbüros.
These are our production facilities.	Hier sehen Sie unsere Fertigungsanlagen.
We'll go through this door which leads to the canteen.	Wir gehen durch diese Türe, die zur Kantine führt.

The canteen looks very modern and airy.	Die Kantine wirkt sehr modern und luftig.
We leave this building and **cross** the car park.	Wir verlassen jetzt dieses Gebäude und gehen über den Parkplatz.
I think we had better be getting back to our office now.	Ich glaube wir sollten jetzt lieber ins Büro zurückgehen.
Our visit has certainly been very interesting.	Unser Besuch war wirklich sehr interessant.

To take visitors to a restaurant

This is a typical German restaurant.	Das ist ein typisch deutsches Restaurant.
Let's have a look **at** the menu?	Wollen wir uns die Speisekarte ansehen?
What **about** you? What are you having?	Wie ist es mit Ihnen/Dir? Was nehmen Sie/was nimmst Du?
Are you having a starter?	Nimmst Du/Nehmen Sie eine Vorspeise?
I think I'll just have a main course.	Ich nehme nur ein Hauptgericht.
Could I have a starter as a main course?	Kann ich eine Vorspeise als Hauptgericht nehmen?
It's a sort of pasta.	Es sind Teigwaren.
It's cabbage stuffed with minced meat.	Es ist Kohl mit einer Hackfleischfüllung.
It tastes a bit like mushrooms.	Es schmeckt ein bisschen wie Pilze.
I'm not hungry enough for a 3-course meal.	Ein Menü mit 3 Gängen ist mir zuviel.
I'd like a German beer.	Ich möchte ein deutsches Bier.
Would you like a salad as a starter?	Möchten Sie einen Salat als Vorspeise?
I'll have the lamb cutlets with beans.	Ich nehme die Lammkoteletts mit Bohnen.
I prefer chicken **to** fish.	Ich esse lieber Geflügel als Fisch.
I'm **a** vegetarian.	Ich bin Vegetarier/in.
My wife would like the trout with almonds.	Meine Frau möchte die Forelle mit Mandeln.
What about some ice cream as a dessert?	Wie wär's mit Eis als Nachtisch?
I'd **rather** have some cheese.	Ich hätte lieber etwas Käse.
It was delicious but I'm afraid I can't eat any more.	Es hat sehr gut geschmeckt, aber ich bin leider schon satt.
I'm going to do without a dessert.	Ich verzichte auf eine Nachspeise.

Unit 3 | The company and its products and services

UNIT 3
The company and its products and services

WORD BANK
image • history • range of products • company brochure • global player • start-up business • family-owned firm • workforce • manufacturing • provision of services • business idea • stock corporation • public limited company • private limited company • to found • to establish • to manufacture • to provide • old-established • modern • traditional • leading • small • medium-sized • state-of-the-art

When companies describe themselves in their sales literature they generally attempt to create a particular image. They may refer to the firm's history to emphasise qualities such as experience and reliability. If they do not have a long history behind them, they may prefer to emphasise that they are a young, dynamic, forward-looking company, providing new products and services.

1 List the adjectives and expressions from the box under the categories given below:

old-established • flexible • dynamic • reliable • with many years' experience • young • forward-looking • taking advantage of the new media • solid • state-of-the-art

Example:

traditional

old-established

modern

state-of-the-art

2 Find examples of traditional and young companies in Germany and other countries.

3 Choose the adjectives from the box on page 38 which best describe the company you are training at. Is it a traditional or a young company? Give details.

A Introducing a firm and giving a brief history

While waiting for an interview at Herkules AG, Sandra Kohl studies the company brochure in English. It begins with an article on the history of the firm.

Herkules – the global sports brand

Back in 1922 the shoemaker Heinrich Schuster made the first sports shoes for the local sports club, the TSV Neustadt. Very soon sportsmen from neighbouring clubs ordered sports shoes from Mr. Schuster and two years later he employed a staff of 25. In 1927 he rented a factory building and bought the machinery required for industrial manufacturing. The company continued to prosper until World War II. In 1948 Heinrich Schuster's son Helmut took over and changed the company's name to Herkules. At the Olympic Games in Melbourne in 1956 several of the athletes competing wore Herkules shoes.

A few years later Helmut Schuster added footballs and other types of ball to Herkules's range of products and in the early 70s took up the production of sports bags. Meanwhile Herkules employed 3400 people and its products featured in all the Olympic Games and World Championships.

By 2010 the workforce had risen to 12,500 and Herkules had become the market leader in the EU and a global player with production sites in Germany, Portugal, Morocco, Malaysia and Taiwan.

Olympic Games

Unit 3 | The company and its products and services

1 Read the text on page 39 and ask the questions which would produce the
R following answers.

Example:
Question:
1. Who founded the company?

Answers:
1. The company was founded by **Heinrich Schuster**.
2. Mass production began **in 1927**.
3. **Olympic Games and World Championships** are of particular importance for the company.
4. Apart from shoes the company produces **bags and balls**.
5. Herkules has got production sites in **Germany, Portugal, Morocco, Malaysia and Taiwan**.

2 Find the missing prepositions from the box with the help of the text on page 39.
R

> by • from • in (2x) • of • over • until • up • to (2x) • with

Back **1** 1922 Heinrich Schuster made the first sports shoes.
Sportsmen **2** neighbouring clubs ordered sports shoes.
Two years later he was employing a staff **3** 25.
The company prospered **4** World War II.
In 1948 Schuster's son Helmut took **5** and changed the name **6** Herkules.
In the early 70s Herkules took **7** the production of bags.
Herkules' products featured **8** all the Olympic Games.
9 1990 the number of staff had risen **10** 9,500.
Herkules is a global player **11** production sites in several countries.

3 Read the text on Herkules again and find words or phrases that mean the same as
R the following expressions.

1. people employed by a firm
2. production on a large scale
3. an assortment of articles
4. the company that has a dominant position in a given market
5. a company that is active worldwide

✱ 4 Sandra Kohl informiert eine Freundin über die Firma Herkules.
KMK Verfassen Sie hierfür eine schriftliche Zusammenfassung der wichtigsten Fakten in Deutsch, die ca. 80 Wörter umfasst. Gehen Sie dabei kurz auf folgende Punkte ein:

- Entwicklung des Unternehmens
- Produkte
- gegenwärtige Stellung des Unternehmens

40

The company and its products and services | Unit 3

5 Read the introduction below, then listen to Martha Dinsdale describing her firm and complete the following text.

Christian Kleine, an IT specialist, is interested in doing a short practical abroad. At a job fair he meets Martha Dinsdale, managing director of Smartmart Ltd, who describes the development of her firm.

"Our company, Smartmart Ltd., was **1** in 1999. Our business **2** was to provide an online market for private individuals or **3** companies with something to **4** who do not want to spend a lot of **5** online selling it themselves. This, as we all **6**, can be very time-consuming! It's not everybody's idea of an **7** way to spend an evening! Some people do not feel sufficiently secure with the **8** to do their own buying and selling. But, it is amazing how many **9** have things to sell and how many potential **10** there are. After we had completed a feasibility study, we **11** through the local chamber of commerce for financial and other **12** in establishing a start-up business. Our **13** expenditure was for designing and setting up an attractive and efficient **14** which would be capable of dealing with a large **15** of hits. There's no point in opening up **16** on the internet with an inadequate or badly designed website. We were quite overwhelmed by the amount of **17**. Our business has grown in line with the other big **18** marts. We charge a commission of 10% on sales completed, i.e. the **19** pays. We are now making a healthy **20** and in two or three years' time we will be thinking in terms of going public."

6 Match the English expressions with their German equivalents.

1. private individuals
2. time-consuming
3. sufficient
4. amazing
5. feasibility study
6. apply through the local chamber of commerce
7. financial support
8. start-up business
9. expenditure
10. inadequate
11. overwhelmed
12. online mart
13. charge a commission of 10%
14. go public

a. 10% Provision verlangen
b. Auslagen, Ausgaben
c. ausreichend, genügend
d. bei der örtlichen IHK beantragen
e. erstaunlich
f. finanzielle Unterstützung
g. Machbarkeitsstudie
h. neugegründetes Unternehmen
i. Online-Markt
j. Privatpersonen
k. sich in eine Aktiengesellschaft umwandeln
l. überwältigt
m. unzureichend, unzulänglich
n. zeitraubend

Unit 3 | The company and its products and services

7 Answer the following questions on Martha's talk.
R
1. When was the company founded?
2. What was their business idea?
3. Why did they think people would use their services?
4. What was their most expensive investment?
5. How does the company earn its living?

8 Christian Kleine fasst die Informationen, die ihm Martha Dinsdale über ihre Firma
KMK gegeben hat, auf Deutsch in einer Gesprächsnotiz für seine Personalabteilung zusammen. Bitte übernehmen Sie seine Rolle.

Gesprächsnotiz

Empfänger: *Personalabteilung*

Verfasser: *Christian Kleine, IT-Support*   Datum:

Gesprächspartner: *Martha Dinsdale von Smartmart Ltd.*

Betreff: *Vorstellung von Smartmart Ltd.*

9 Describe your own company in writing. Model your description on the
P descriptions of other companies in this unit.

> **Communicating across cultures:**
> **Joint stock companies** *(Kapitalgesellschaften)* **in the USA and Britain**
>
> The British **Public Limited Company** (abbreviated to **PLC** or **plc** after the company name) and the American **Stock Corporation** (abbreviated to **Inc.** or **Corp.**) are roughly comparable to the German Aktiengesellschaft. The British **Private Limited Company** (abbreviated to **Ltd**) and the American **Closed Corporation** are approximately equivalent to the German GmbH. British and American joint stock companies are managed by a **Board of Directors** under the leadership of a Chief Executive Officer (CEO) (chairman of the board or managing director), who may also hold the title of Chairman or President. The head of a **Private Limited Company** is generally called the Managing Director.

10 Search the Internet for some of the following global players. Make notes on their products or services in English. Compare your notes with the group.

> Tata Group • GlaxoSmithKline • Arcelormittal • Antofagasta • RWE Group •
> Berkshire Hathaway • Verizon • De Beers • China Mobile • Rio Tinto Zinc • HSBC •
> Selesio AG • Sir Robert McAlpine

The company and its products and services | Unit 3

B Describing products and services

At home Sandra Kohl looks at Herkules' homepage on the internet. Sandra clicks on the button "about us" to learn more about the company. The following website appears.

Herkules
the global sports brand
www.herkules.com

Herkules is Europe's leading manufacturer of state-of-the-art sports shoes, balls and bags. Innovative technology and minute attention to detail provide products that successfully fuse the creative energies of the world of sport, lifestyle and fashion.

Herkules concentrates its efforts on the three big fields of football, athletics and tennis. For decades our superb shoes, balls and bags have helped world-class athletes to win gold medals at Olympic Games and prestigious cups at World Championships and Tournaments.

www.herkules.com

about us | login | join | shopping cart | track your order | delivery | contact | customer service | FAQ | imprint | disclaimer

Herkules
ALL PRODUCTS
FOOTBALL
BAGS
TENNIS
RUNNING

NEW! Wimbledon II
NEW! Sports Mate
NEW! Turbostar
NEW! Air Lift 2000

We accept Visa, Mastercard and Switch / Delivery is free for orders worth € 250 or more.

For further information click here

1 Which buttons do you click on if you want to find out more about the following?

1. the firm
2. all their products
3. particular product groups
4. individual products
5. details about delivery
6. frequently asked questions
7. how to place an order
8. repairs

2 Replace the adjectives in brackets with appropriate expressions from the box.

excellent • the most modern • very careful • highly regarded

1. Herkules is Europe's leading manufacturer of (state-of-the-art) **1** sports shoes.
2. Innovative technology and (minute) **2** attention to detail provide products that fuse the creative energies of the world of sport, lifestyle and fashion.
3. For decades our (superb) **3** shoes and bags have helped world-class athletes to win gold medals at Olympic Games and (prestigious) **4** Cups at World Championships and Tournaments.

Unit 3 | The company and its products and services

3 Match the German statements on the next page with the following English statements.
R / M

Janine: I work for a small upmarket advertising agency. We specialise in media companies.

Patrizia: I work for a medium-sized company manufacturing organic cosmetic preparations.

Tatjana: The company I work for is a leading manufacturer of precision instruments.

Sinan: I work for a small family firm making a wide range of high quality furniture.

Markus: My company are IT consultants providing customised solutions for corporate clients.

Holger: I work for a small catering company specialising in providing lunches for local companies. We offer a lot of vegetarian dishes. We're basically a small start-up.

Jörg: My company is a wholesaler stocking a wide range of electrical products.

Claudia: The company I work for is a major retailer of food and some non-food products. I work in the admin section.

V1 Video lounge Sport and leisure

BBC Motion Gallery

You are about to see a video on the sport and leisure industry. While watching the video, keep the following questions in mind:

1. How are the three presenters dressed? Which do you find most natural and convincing? Why?
2. Which different fitness club products does the video mention?
3. What does the first presenter mean when she says fitness has become a lifestyle business?
4. According to the video what is the overall economic situation of the fitness and leisure club industry?

Discuss your answers with the class.

The company and its products and services | Unit 3

1. Ich arbeite für ein mittelständisches Unternehmen, das Biokosmetik herstellt.
2. Meine Firma ist eine IT-Beratungsgesellschaft und bietet Firmenkunden maßgeschneiderte Lösungen an.
3. Die Firma, bei der ich arbeite, ist ein bedeutender Einzelhändler für Lebensmittel und Non-Food-Produkte.
4. Ich arbeite bei einem kleinen Partyservice, der sich auf Mittagessen für die Firmen in der Umgebung spezialisiert hat.
5. Meine Firma ist ein führender Hersteller von Präzisionsinstrumenten.
6. Ich arbeite bei einem Familienunternehmen, das hochwertige Möbel herstellt.
7. Ich arbeite bei einer kleinen exklusiven Werbeagentur.
8. Bei meiner Firma handelt es sich um eine Großhandlung mit einem breiten Sortiment von Elektroartikeln.

4 Write similar descriptions of two firms' products or services with the help of the following hints.

Types of firms	medium-sized enterprise, import/export company, large manufacturer, start-up company, wholesaler, retail chain, family-owned firm, IT consultancy, publishing house, advertising agency, catering firm, Public Limited Company, Private Limited Company, Stock Corporation
Products/services	household appliances, IT services, exotic fruit, steel tubes, creation of advertising material, groceries, silk fabrics, audio books, clocks and watches, cleaning services, office software
Descriptions	modern, upmarket, high-quality, fresh, in demand, excellent, unique, interesting, attractive, reliable, thorough, long-lasting, state-of-the-art, customised, inexpensive

We specialise in …

Our products/services are …

We are …

We offer …

I work for …

Example:
I work for a family-owned firm specializing in the manufacture of state-of-the-art steel tubes.

5 Work in groups. Describe the firm you are training at and its products and/or services to your group. Use the phrases at the end of the unit.

Phrases

45

Unit 3 | The company and its products and services

6 Dolmetschen Sie folgende Aussagen:
M

1. „Ich arbeite bei einer mittelgroßen Werbeagentur. Wir stellen attraktives Werbematerial für eine Lebensmittel-Einzelhandelskette her."

2. „Meine Firma ist auf die Herstellung einzigartiger Seidenstoffe höchster Qualität spezialisiert."

3. „Wir bieten maßgeschneiderte Lösungen für Bürosoftware an."

4. „Wir sind ein junger Musikverlag mit einem anspruchsvollen Sortiment von Titeln."

★ 7 Project work: Work together with two other students to set up your own company. See Exercise 5 for useful expressions.
I/P

Phrases

Step 1: Discuss the following questions:
- What is your business idea?
- How can you find out whether your idea is any good?
- Where can you get help, financial or otherwise?
- What are the most essential investments to enable you to begin trading?

Step 2: Think up a good name for your company.

Step 3: Divide the work among yourselves:
- Student A creates an eye-catching logo.
- Student B designs a business card incorporating the logo.
- Student C designs a company letterhead also incorporating the logo.

Step 4: Present the result to the class.

Language and grammar 1
Find out whether the periods of time mentioned in the following sentences are entirely in the past or whether they continue to the present. Then choose the correct tense for the verbs in brackets.

1. It all (begin) in 1975.
2. Two years later he (launch) the new product.
3. The company (be successful) for many years now.
4. Since 2002 we (offer) these unique marketing services.
5. By now Herkules (become) a global player.
6. Last September Robert Hanks (start) a new business in the USA.
7. In the past there (be) a big demand for such systems.
8. But in the meantime they (be replaced) by faster systems.
9. So far we (have) no complaints.
10. I (speak) to him only yesterday.

The company and its products and services | Unit 3

> **Language and grammar: Simple Past and Present Perfect**
>
> Wird ein Zeitraum genannt, der vollständig in der Vergangenheit liegt, steht "simple past".
>
> Back **in 1922** Heinrich Schuster **made** the first sports shoes.
> **At the Olympic Games** several athletes **competed** wearing Herkules shoes.
> **A few years later** he **added** footballs to the range of products.
> Our company **was founded in 1999**.
>
> Wenn ein Zeitraum genannt wird, der bis in die Gegenwart reicht, steht "present perfect".
>
> **For decades** our superb shoes **have helped** athletes to win gold medals.
> **In the meantime** ACE **has become** the market leader in Germany.
> **Since the beginning** of the 90s **we have specialised** in real-time solutions.
> I **have been** in my present department **for three months**.

Language and grammar 2
Decide which of the alternatives in brackets are correct.

1. I (am/have been) a trainee (for/since) 4 months.
2. We (see/have seen) a number of employees leave (for/since) 1998.
3. We (have specialised/specialise) in providing networking systems (for/since) more than a year.
4. She (wants/has wanted) to live in Berlin (since/for) she was 17 years old.
5. We (have known/know) the company (since/for) it was founded in 1983.
6. I (am thinking/have been thinking) of changing my job (since/for) a long time.
7. We (place/have placed) orders with this company (since/for) its foundation.

> **Language and grammar: "since" and "for"**
>
> "since" bezieht sich auf den Anfang des Zeitraums
> since Christmas
> since 24 June
> since my last report
>
> "for" bezieht sich auf den Zeitraum selbst
> for 3 weeks
> for several days
> for a couple of years
>
> **Merke: Im Deutschen wird „seit" mit der Gegenwart verwendet, "since" und "for" stehen im Englischen mit "present perfect".**
>
> Ich **bin seit** drei Jahren bei Topline-Computers beschäftigt.
> **Seit** Januar **bin** ich der Abteilungsleiter.
>
> I **have been** employed with Topline-Computers **for three years** now.
> **Since January I have been** head of the department.

Office expert

Presenting your company online

1 Micron company, specialists for automotive solutions, has decided to present itself online. Before listening to a discussion between the website designer and a company representative match the English verbs (1.–12.) to their German equivalents (a.–l.).

1. to access
2. to appear
3. to set up
4. to enable
5. to finalise
6. to include
7. to insert
8. to provide
9. to refer to
10. to stand for
11. to suggest
12. to update

a. abschließen
b. aktualisieren
c. anbieten
d. aufnehmen
e. betreffen, sich beziehen auf
f. einfügen
g. einrichten
h. ermöglichen
i. erscheinen
j. stehen für, repräsentieren
k. vorschlagen
l. Zugriff haben

2 Now listen to the discussion about the desired features and options and answer the questions below.

R
A 2.15

1. Name **three elements** the company wants to include on their website.
2. How many **categories** are suggested for the main menu of the homepage?
3. What does **PDF** stand for according to the text?
4. What happens if you click on a **hyperlink**?
5. What **kinds of information** are included under the category **Contact**?
6. What **category** can you click on if you want information about **copyright**?

3 Listen again and decide if the following statements are TRUE or FALSE.

R
A 2.15

1. The company wants to be able to add newer information at a later date.
2. The homepage of a website is also called "home".
3. Clicking on a sub-category opens up a drop-down menu.
4. A drop-down menu includes different options or sub-categories.
5. Downloads and Support are to be included under General Services.
6. Privacy Policy and Terms of Use are types of legal information.

The company and its products and services | Unit 3

4 Discuss in groups what sort of website you would need for a specific purpose
P (for example, a club, your company). One person leads the discussion, making sure all questions are asked and everyone contributes. Another member should take notes and a third member reports back to the class.

> Phrases

1. What is the aim of the online presentation? To provide information? To sell products or services?
2. What sorts of content should be included? Text? Graphics? Pictures? Animation? Contact information?
3. Should the website include downloads?
4. Do you want to include hyperlinks within the website (internal) and/ or to other websites (external)?
5. Do you have any ideas about the basic design, colours and layout?

✱ **5** Ihr Unternehmen Dataexchange bereitet sich auf eine Internetpräsentation
KMK vor, um seine Dienstleistungen vorzustellen. Zu diesem Zweck wurden Sie gebeten, die Auftaktseite der Firmenwebsite ins Englische zu übertragen.

Dataexchange
Datenbanksysteme

einfach + innovativ + individuell

News   Zum Support Center   Suche

- Home
- News und Presse
- Lösungen
- Dienstleistungen
- Online Services
- Unternehmen
- Referenzen
- Kontakt

Willkommen bei der Dataexchange Datenbanksysteme AG – Ihr Partner für integrierte Softwarelösungen

✔ Sie benötigen ein System, das es nicht von der Stange gibt?
✔ Sie suchen für Ihre Datenbank zusätzliche Auswertungsmöglichkeiten, die Ihnen Ihr eingesetztes System nicht bietet?
✔ Sie möchten die Anforderungen für ein neues Projekt ermitteln?
✔ Dann sind Sie hier richtig!

Unsere Kernkompetenz ist die Entwicklung individueller Softwarelösungen für Datenbankanwendungen. Dazu gehören neben der Erstellung von schlüsselfertigen Komplettsystemen unter anderem auch die Weiterentwicklung vorhandener Datenbanken und die Entwicklung von Bedieneroberflächen zur einfachen Auswertung von Datenbankinhalten.

Glossar | Impressum | Datenschutz | Nutzungsbedingungen

© 2011 Dataexchange Datenbanksysteme AG | Stand 01/2011

Unit 3 | The company and its products and services

Phrases: The company and its products and services

To introduce your firm

Our company was founded in 1972.	Unsere Firma wurde 1972 gegründet.
Our business idea was …	Unsere Geschäftsidee bestand darin …
In 1998 we were taken over by …	1998 wurden wir von … übernommen.
We are a leading manufacturer **of** …	Wir sind ein führender Hersteller von …
I work for an upmarket advertising agency.	Ich arbeite bei einer exklusiven Werbeagentur.
We are a **medium-sized** family firm.	Wir sind ein mittelständisches Familienunternehmen.
We are a wholesaler **specializing in** …	Wir sind ein Großhandelsunternehmen und sind spezialisiert auf …
My company is a major food retailer.	Meine Firma ist ein bedeutender Lebensmitteleinzelhändler.
We are a start-up company offering customized solutions.	Wir sind ein junges Unternehmen, das maßgeschneiderte Lösungen anbietet.
We are a chain of organic cosmetics suppliers.	Wir sind eine Kette von Anbietern biologischer Kosmetikprodukte.
The legal form of our company is a public limited company.	Juristisch gesehen ist unsere Firma eine (britische) Kapitalgesellschaft, vergleichbar einer deutschen Aktiengesellschaft.
FastTrack Inc. is a stock corporation.	FastTrack Inc. ist eine (US-)Kapitalgesellschaft.

To describe your firm's products / services

We manufacture state-of-the-art solutions.	Wir bieten Lösungen nach dem neuesten Stand der Technik an.
Our high-quality products are well-known **all over** the world. They are unique.	Unsere erstklassigen Produkte sind weltbekannt. Sie sind einzigartig.
Our instruments are both reliable and long-lasting.	Unsere Instrumente sind zuverlässig und haben eine lange Lebensdauer.
The software we offer is carefully adapted to suit your requirements.	Unsere Software wird Ihren Bedürfnissen sorgfältig angepasst.
We make a wide range of high-quality furniture.	Wir stellen ein breites Sortiment hochwertiger Möbel her.
We import exotic fruit **from** South America.	Wir importieren tropische Früchte aus Südamerika.
The travel agency I work for **specialises in** upmarket package tours.	Das Reisebüro, bei dem ich arbeite, ist auf exklusive Pauschalreisen spezialisiert.

Unit 4
The office

Offices may be spacious open-plan, purpose-built areas in a major company, individual small rooms to accommodate two to three people, or elegant premises at a prestigious address in a converted building. They may be back offices where employees have no contact with the public, or front offices to which the public have access.

> **WORD BANK**
> front office • back office • open-plan office • office supplies • furniture • electronic equipment • internet access • catering equipment • organization chart • department • business unit • head • assistant • superior • colleague • to be in charge of • to be responsible for • to report to

1 Match the following types of office with the pictures above.

1. front office
2. back office
3. manager's office
4. open plan

2 Tell your group in which type of office you would prefer to work and give reasons for your preferences.

> I'd like to work in a(n) … office because …

> I'd prefer to work in a(n) … office because …

Online-Link
808261-0004

Unit 4 | The office

A   The office environment

1 Match the following pieces of office equipment with the numbered items above.

a. calculator
b. scotch tape/sellotape
c. biro
d. desk
e. note pad
f. trays
g. filing cabinet
h. aluminium briefcase
i. keyboard
j. memory stick
k. monitor
l. desk tidy
m. pair of scissors
n. wastepaper bin
o. ruler
p. punch
q. rubber/eraser
r. pot plant
s. desk lamp
t. mobile phone
u. stapling machine/stapler
v. swivel chair
w. mouse
x. elastic band

2 Use the following prepositions and describe the position of the equipment you see in the picture.

The keyboard is
The …

on • under • behind • between • in front of • next to • on the right of • opposite • near • on top of

the desk.
the …

The office | Unit 4

3 List the items shown on page 52 under the following categories:

Office supplies / Stationery	Furniture	Electrical equipment / Hardware
rubber	desk	computer

4 How many computer terms and abbreviations can you find in the puzzle below? Make a list. Compare your lists in class.

Computer terms puzzle

	A	B	C	D	E	F	G	H	I	J
1	I	B	M	O	D	E	M	Q	R	H
2	T	O	E	S	L	A	N	P	X	A
3	D	O	M	T	C	D	R	O	M	R
4	E	T	O	O	L	B	A	R	O	D
5	S	B	R	O	W	S	E	T	N	D
6	K	E	Y	B	O	A	R	D	I	I
7	T	E	R	M	I	N	A	L	T	S
8	O	S	C	A	N	N	E	R	O	K
9	P	C	C	C	U	R	S	O	R	M
10	D	O	W	N	L	O	A	D	X	B

5 Work in groups. Make up similar puzzles with other computer terms and abbreviations. Ask the other groups to find the terms and abbreviations.

P/I

Unit 4 | The office

6 Listen to Anita, Ali and Nadine describing the office environment in which they work and take notes. Work in pairs and compare your notes.
R
◎ A 1.9

7 Draw a grid like the following. Use your notes and fill in the grid. Then listen to the dialogue again, complete the grid and answer the questions below.
R
◎ A 1.9

	Office (front office – open plan or back office?)	Office equipment (PC? Photocopier? Scanner? …?)
Anita	…	…
Ali	…	…
Nadine	…	…

1. What does Anita like about her office?
2. What does Ali like about his office?
3. What does Nadine like about her office?

8 Translate the following statements from the dialogue into German.
M
1. I work in a large open-plan office with about 20 other people. It is spacious and airy with large windows. Fortunately, there is air-conditioning.
2. Our offices are situated in an old villa in the centre of Hanover. The office I work in is a front office.
3. The view from the windows is not very exciting – the office looks out on to the car park.
4. Our office has a wide range of equipment. We all have PCs with internet access.
5. I like the privacy of a small office – you don't get the feeling there's somebody looking over your shoulder the whole time. We all get on very well together.

9 Describe your own office.
P

10 Check out the latest products of three manufacturers of photocopiers and scanners, including any innovative features. Make notes and compare your findings with the group.

The office | Unit 4

B Catering in the office

1 Übertragen Sie die Aussagen von Anita, Nadine und Ali ins Deutsche.
KMK

Anita We have a small kitchen attached to the office with a fridge and tea and coffee making facilities. Our official coffee break is a quarter of an hour at 10.30 am and 3 pm.
At lunchtime we go to the canteen. There is quite a good range of hot and cold snacks, some of them vegetarian. My friend Alexandra is a vegetarian so we usually have a fresh vegetable soup and a salad with fruit as a dessert. We both watch our figures and the canteen is very good about giving calorie counts.

Nadine We have a tea and coffee machine in the office and a kitchen at the end of the corridor with a microwave. We don't have a set coffee break but lunch is from 12.30 to 1.15 pm. Our company is too small to have a canteen so we either bring sandwiches or convenience food that we can warm up in the microwave. There is an upmarket supermarket nearby with an interesting range of good quality convenience food with things like fresh soups and Chinese and Thai dishes. We sometimes go out to a pub but the lunch break is really too short for that.

Ali We have a small kitchen with a coffee machine and fridge. Only Amelie is allowed to touch it. We have an hour lunch break.
We don't have a canteen either. So we usually bring sandwiches or go out. There's a snack bar nearby that has quite an interesting range of snacks and a pub with not very appetising meatballs and filled rolls. Quite often, when we're working to a deadline, we just eat a sandwich at our desks and an apple.

2 Match the words on the left with the explanations on the right.

1. calorie count
2. coffee making facilities
3. convenience food
4. snack bar
5. upmarket supermarket

a. equipment for making coffee
b. pre-prepared food
c. small restaurant/shop producing light/quick food
d. high-quality supermarket
e. energy content

Unit 4 | The office

3 What are the catering arrangements like at your firm? Work in pairs to produce a brief description in writing that you can read out to the other students.

Phrases

C The company's organization chart

1 Study the organization chart below and complete the following text.

R

Nadine works for a car sales company. The **1** is Jochen Küppers who is one of the two owners of the firm. His personal assistant is his elderly **2** Eva Cebulla. Nadine's superior, Jessica Rathsmann, a trained accountant, is the head of the **3** Department, and a motor-car mechanic, Markus Nehring, is in charge of **4**. The **5** manager is Natalie Hoffmann, the managing director's sister-in-law. Eddy Gerstenberg, an engineer, is the head of the **6** Department. André Fontaine, who is training to become a car sales management assistant, reports to him.

The car sales company is organized like this:

Managing Director
Jochen Küppers

Secretary
Eva Cebulla

Administration and Finance	**Purchasing**	**Sales**	**Customer Service**
Jessica Rathsmann	Natalie Hoffmann	Eddy Gerstenberg	Markus Nehring
Nadine Boedeker		André Fontaine	

> **Info: Large companies**
>
> The larger a company is the more complex its organisation tends to be. Large companies are headed by a chief executive officer (CEO) or a chairman of the board. They have many different business units and departments, such as a personnel, legal or marketing department. The scope of an individual employee's responsibilities will also be smaller and his or her duties more specialised in a large company than in a small one.

2 Study the above texts and find the equivalents of the German titles.

R

Geschäftsführer • Einkaufsleiter • Vorstandsvorsitzender •
Automobilkaufmann • Leiter des Kundendienstes • Personalchef •
Leiter des Rechnungswesens • Persönliche Assistentin

56

The office | Unit 4

3 Work in pairs. Partner A asks Partner B about his/her current department. Then change roles.

> Which department are you in?

> I work in the … department.

Partner A

Who is your boss?
What is he/she responsible for?
Who does she report to?
What's your general manager's name?
Who are your colleagues?
What are you responsible for?

Partner B

The head of our department is …
She is in charge of …
Her superior is …
Our general manager is called …
My colleagues are …
I process/I'm in charge of …

4 Listen to five trainees describing to their friends what they or their colleagues do in the departments they are in. Find out which departments they are working in.

A 1.10

	Christine	Harun	Annette	Simon	Christos
Department?	…	…	…	…	…

Language and grammar 1
Translate the following sentences.

1. Unsere Firma ist zu klein für einen eigenen Parkplatz.
2. Diese Frage zu beantworten ist für mich zu kompliziert.
3. Nun ist es zu spät für eine Bewerbung.
4. Es ist noch zu früh, darüber zu entscheiden.
5. Sie kam als Letzte zu der Besprechung.
6. Unser Unternehmen ist das einzige, das diese Lösung anbietet.

Language and grammar 2
Choose the correct form of the verbs in brackets.

1. We are having problems (find) qualified programmers.
2. We look forward to (get) your comments on this matter.
3. It is no use (buy) a new one, if it is still the same model.
4. They are having difficulties (meet) the deadline.
5. I am not used to (drive) big cars like this.
6. I object to (have) my work criticised when it's not justified.

Unit 4 | The office

Language and grammar: Infinitive and gerund

Nach "too …", "the first", "the last", "the only one" steht im Englischen der Infinitiv:

Our company is	too small	**to have** a canteen.
This problem is	too difficult for us	**to solve** without help.
It is	too late for you	**to apply** for the job.
She was	the first	**to come.**
He was	the last	**to arrive.**
He was	the only one	**to take part.**

In folgenden Fällen sind deutsche Sprecher auch versucht, einen Infinitiv zu benutzen.

Es steht aber das Gerund:

I am looking forward **to receiving** your reply.
I am looking forward **to being shown** their new flat.
I am not used **to speaking** in public.
I object **to being forced** to work overtime.
I am having problems **understanding** him.
We had no difficulty **persuading** him.
It is no use **waiting** for the new regulations.

Communicating across cultures: Addressing people

In English-speaking countries hierarchical differences may be less pronounced than in German companies. Certainly, they are not so obvious from the way people address each other as first names are generally used. Immediate superiors are also usually addressed by their first name. Where there is a considerable difference in status the titles Mr / Mrs / Miss and surname may be used when addressing a superior.

In Britain or the USA business contacts will very quickly address you by your first name and try to establish an informal atmosphere. When introducing yourself to English-speaking people, always give both your first name and your surname. If they firstname you, you should, of course, do the same.

In schools students usually address teachers with the title (Mr / Mrs / Miss) and surname and in shops and restaurants customers may be addressed as sir / madam, e.g.: Are you ready to order, sir? Can I help you, madam? It is important simply to recognise this – you will not have to use it yourself.

Note:
As we have already seen there is often no one-to-one equivalent to German job titles. Similarly there is no direct equivalent to the much used German word "Sachbearbeiter". It may correspond to "the person dealing with the case / our order" or "the person in charge of …".

Office expert

1 Office suite applications

1 Work in groups and make a mind map of the different types of programmes that are typically part of office suite applications.

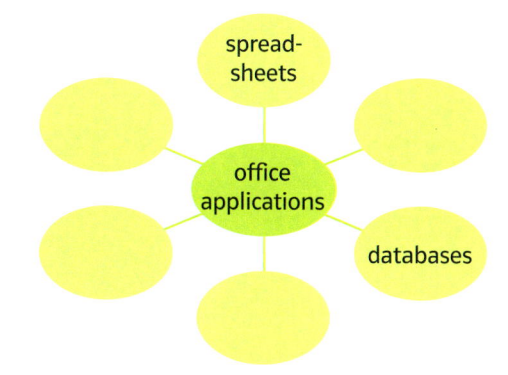

2 Choose the correct word in brackets to complete the following sentences.

1. A(n) (record/item/folder) in a database is the collection of information about a certain person or product. *(Datensatz)*
2. If I want to get information from a database I have to (call/delete/retrieve) it. *(abrufen)*
3. Excel is an example for (database/spreadsheet/mailing) software. *(Tabellenkalkulation)*
4. Another word for "values" is "(figures/words/money)". *(Werte)*
5. (Mail merge/multi-tasking/blogging) makes it easy for you to send a personal letter to a number of people at the same time. *(Serienbrief)*
6. Another word for "e-mail" is "electronic (post/message/memo)". *(Nachricht)*
7. To write a letter means to (compare/contain/compose) it. *(erstellen)*
8. You use an (edition/editor/addition) to change and improve, for example, graphics. *(Editorprogramm)*
9. I need a (remainder/remember/reminder) in order not to forget something. *(Erinnerung)*
10. Notes taken at a meeting are called (protocol/minutes/lists). *(Protokoll)*

3 What can you do with which applications? Use the words below to form sentences describing the functions and features of the different applications.

Example: **Database:** changes/any number of records/at one time/information/easily/retrieve → With a database changes can be made in any number of records at one time and information can easily be retrieved.

1. **Spreadsheets:** change/width of columns/calculate/display/values
2. **Word processors:** a. create/edit/print/documents/texts; b. check spelling/mail merge/create and send/personalised letters
3. **Presentation programmes:** prepare/slide show/add/animation/graphics
4. **E-mail clients:** store/manage/compose/receive/messages
5. **Graphics suites:** include/bitmap graphics editor/vector graphics editor
6. **Note-taking programmes:** record/information/take/minutes/meetings

Unit 4 | The office

2 Working with spreadsheets

1 Find the English equivalents for the German words (1.–10.) in the following spreadsheet.

1. Gehaltsliste, Löhne
2. Zinsen
3. Ausgaben
4. Verkauf
5. Quartal
6. Werbung, Öffentlichkeitsarbeit
7. Honorarkosten, Gebühren
8. Erlös, Einnahmen
9. Betriebskosten
10. Verwaltung

	A	B	C	D	E
1		1st quarter	2nd quarter	3rd quarter	4th quarter
2	Sales	$890	$982	$1,200	$799
3	Fees	$420	$400	$432	$630
4	Dividends	$430	$760	$720	$870
5	Interest	$182	$60	$55	$66
6	Total revenue	$1,922	$2,202	$2,407	$2,365
7					
8	Payroll	$899	$904	$904	$904
9	Publicity	$390	$451	$350	$250
10	Administration	$232	$230	$256	$240
11	Operations	$550	$420	$399	$402
12	Total expenses	$2,071	$2,005	$1,909	$1,796
13					
14	Total	– $149	+ $197	+ $498	+ $569

2 Decide if the following statements are TRUE or FALSE.
R

1. In only one quarter did the company spend more than they earned.
2. The revenue of fees and dividends increased from the first to the second quarter.
3. Less money was spent on publicity in the second half of the year.
4. Cell D5 shows that $55 was spent on interest in the third quarter.
5. Cell B8 shows the money paid to staff in the first three months of the year.
6. Over the year the company earned more but also spent more money.

3 Now look at the spreadsheet again and answer the questions.
P

1. What items contributed to the total earnings or revenue of the company?
2. What types of expenses did the company have?
3. How many months altogether are represented by this spreadsheet?

Phrases: The office

To describe the office

I work in an open-plan office.	Ich arbeite in einem Großraumbüro.
I work in a small office for two people.	Ich arbeite in einem kleinen Büro für zwei Personen.
She works in the back office.	Sie arbeitet in einem Büro ohne Publikumsverkehr.
I prefer working in a front office.	Ich arbeite lieber in einem Büro mit Publikumsverkehr.
My office is spacious and airy.	Mein Büro ist geräumig und luftig.
The office looks **out on to** the car park.	Vom Büro sieht man auf den Parkplatz.
We all have PCs with internet access.	Wir haben alle einen PC mit Zugang zum Internet.
There is a photocopier, a fax machine and file shredders.	Wir haben einen Kopierer, ein Faxgerät und Aktenvernichter.
The senior staff use the computer projectors for presentations.	Die leitenden Angestellten verwenden die Beamer für ihre Präsentationen.

To introduce the people in the office

He is the overall **boss**, the managing director.	Er ist der oberste Chef, der Geschäftsführer.
Mr Kent is the chief executive.	Herr Kent ist der Vorstandsvorsitzende.
She is **head** of department.	Sie ist die Abteilungsleiterin.
He **reports to** Frau Niemeyer.	Er untersteht Frau Niemeyer.
Frau Niemeyer is our superior.	Frau Niemeyer ist unsere Vorgesetzte.
She is assistant/secretary **to** Mr Kent.	Sie ist Herrn Kents Assistentin/Sekretärin.
I am **in charge of** exports.	Ich bin Exportsachbearbeiterin.
I am responsible for sales to the EU.	Ich bearbeite/bin zuständig für den Verkauf in die EU-Länder.
He deals with/processes/handles complaints.	Er bearbeitet Mängelrügen.
He makes sure that instalments are paid **on** time.	Er kümmert sich um den pünktlichen Eingang der Ratenzahlungen.
Robert is one of the partners of our firm.	Robert ist einer der Partner in unserer Firma.
I hope to be **taken on** after I've finished my course.	Ich hoffe nach der Ausbildung übernommen zu werden.

Unit 4 | The office

To talk about catering in the office

Our official coffee break is a quarter of an hour.	Offiziell haben wir eine Viertelstunde Kaffeepause.
We have a small kitchen with a fridge, a coffee machine and a microwave.	Wir haben eine kleine Küche mit Kühlschrank, Kaffeemaschine und Mikrowelle.
At lunchtime we go to the canteen.	Zum Mittagessen gehen wir in die Kantine.
We either bring sandwiches or convenience food.	Wir bringen entweder belegte Brote oder ein Fertiggericht mit.
The canteen caters for vegetarians, too.	Die Kantine bietet auch Gerichte für Vegetarier.

To describe your company's organization chart

He is our **chief executive officer**.	Er ist der Chef unserer Firma.
The department Administration and Finance is subdivided into five units.	Die Abteilung Verwaltung und Finanzen besteht aus fünf Bereichen.
The Marketing Department is part of Sales.	Die Marketing-Abteilung gehört zum Verkauf.
IT Support is responsible for all our IT equipment.	IT-Support ist zuständig für alle IT-Anlagen.
We are an international company and our **personnel** department is called "human resources".	Wir sind ein internationales Unternehmen und unsere Personalabteilung heißt „Human Resources".
The head of our legal department is a lawyer specializing in company law.	Der Leiter unserer Rechtsabteilung ist ein Fachanwalt für Gesellschaftsrecht.
Our company is divided **into** five business units.	Unsere Firma ist in fünf Geschäftsfelder unterteilt.

Telephoning | Unit 5

UNIT 5
Telephoning

WORD BANK

telephone • number • extension • handset • landline • answering machine • mobile / cell phone • mailbox • text message • telephone alphabet • symbols • codes; to put through • to hold • to catch • to spell • to repeat • to take down • to read back; slowly • clearly • precisely

The telephone has long been an essential tool of business communication but in the past few years it has been revolutionised by the privatisation of state telecom companies and the advent of mobile telephony. People can call and be called wherever they happen to be. Even if a person is not available to take calls a text message can be sent or a message can be left on their voice-mail.

1 Read the text and match the expressions on the left with the explanations on the right.
R

1. essential tool　　　　a. telephoning without fixed lines
2. privatisation　　　　 b. arrival
3. advent　　　　　　　c. selling state-owned enterprises to the public
4. mobile telephony　　d. mailbox
5. voice-mail　　　　　 e. important instrument

2 Describe the telephone situations above.
P

Online-Link
808261-0005

63

Unit 5 | Telephoning

A Appliances and components

1 Read the following sentences and translate them into German. Use the words below.

- Handy
- Telefonbuch
- Festnetztelefonanlage
- Hörer
- Besetztzeichen
- Onlineverzeichnis
- Telefonauskunft
- Anrufbeantworter
- Freizeichen
- Festnetzleitung

1. My fixed line handset includes an answering machine.
2. It is important to replace the receiver carefully otherwise anyone ringing will get the engaged signal.
3. When you pick up the receiver you hear the dialling tone.
4. The latest innovation is to combine landline and mobile phones – when you leave your home the landline becomes a mobile.
5. My telephone handset can also be used to send and receive fax messages.
6. Most people have a copy of the old-fashioned local telephone directory with a business section. Sometimes the Yellow Pages are in a separate book.
7. However, post offices no longer keep a complete nationwide set of telephone directories.
8. Many people have online directories.
9. The traditional Directory Enquiries has been replaced by a number of competing companies.
10. The applications of mobile phones/cell(ular) phones are increasing all the time.

2 Work in groups. Describe to your group the telephoning equipment you have at the office, at home and for mobile communication.

B Receiving and redirecting calls

1 Restore the correct order of the two jumbled dialogues and write them out.

Dialogue 1

1. Receptionist:	Delphi Materials. Good afternoon. How can I help you?
2. Caller:	No, thanks. I'll call back later.
3. Receptionist:	Just a moment, Mr Martin. I'll put you through to Louisa Bates … Oh, I'm sorry, her extension is engaged at the moment. Would you like to hold?
4. Caller:	Hello. This is Robert Martin from Komplettbau in Erfurt, Germany. I'd like to speak to someone in accounts, please.

Dialogue 2

1. Receptionist:	May I ask what it's about?
2. Caller:	It's about the dreadful beds we had to sleep in. My back is still aching.
3. Receptionist:	Could you give me your name please?
4. Caller:	My name is Jakob Grailing and I need to speak to your general manager.
5. Receptionist:	Just a second. I'll connect you to Customer Relations.
6. Caller:	Hi. The reason I'm calling is …
7. Receptionist:	Florida Leisure Park. Good morning. What can I do for you?

2 Listen to the following telephone conversation between Marcel Krenz of International Snacks GmbH and Jennifer Glover, a receptionist at Global Catering in Manchester and say whether the following statements are TRUE or FALSE.

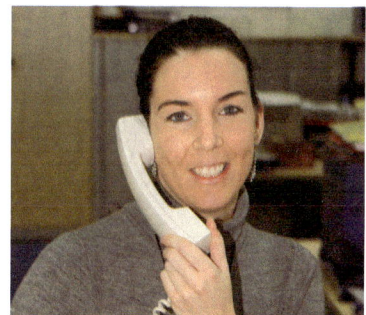

1. Jonathan Ashley works for Omnipolis Research Consultants Ltd.
2. Marcel Krenz wishes to speak to Jennifer Glover.
3. Jennifer Glover knows for certain that Kirsty Burnham is not in.
4. Marcel Krenz prefers to be put on hold.
5. Marcel Krenz has got Kirsty Burnham's mobile phone number.
6. Marcel Krenz does not want to be put through to Kevin Sears.

Unit 5 | Telephoning

3 Hören Sie sich die Dialoge noch einmal an und finden Sie heraus, wie Folgendes auf Englisch formuliert wird.
KMK
A 1.11

1. Was sagt Jonathan Ashley, als das Telefon klingelt?
2. Was sagt Marcel Krenz, als er sich verwählt hat?
3. Wie stellt sich Marcel Krenz bei Ms Glover vor?
4. Was sagt Jennifer Glover, während Sie Marcel Krenz durchzustellen versucht?
5. Was antwortet Marcel Krenz auf die Frage, ob er jemand anderen sprechen möchte?
6. Was sagt Jennifer Glover, als sie wissen will, ob Marcel warten möchte oder ob sie zurückrufen soll?
7. Mit welchen Worten schlägt Jennifer Glover vor, Kirsty auf ihrem Handy anzurufen?
8. Wie formuliert Marcel die Bitte, zu Kevin Sears durchgestellt zu werden?

4 Beantworten Sie die Fragen zu nachstehendem Text schriftlich auf Deutsch.
KMK

1. Warum schicken viele Menschen einem Geschäftspartner lieber eine E-Mail als ihn anzurufen?
2. Wovor haben wir Angst, wenn wir ein Auslandsgespräch führen sollen?
3. Welche Aspekte der Kommunikation fehlen bei einem Telefongespräch?
4. Was soll man tun, wenn man nicht versteht, was der Gesprächspartner sagt?

> **Info:**
> **Telephoning in a foreign language**
>
> Telephoning in a foreign language can be rather frightening. No wonder people often prefer to send an e-mail where they can plan what they want to say and need not fear immediate comeback. However, a telephone call is sometimes unavoidable and one wonders: Will I understand what they are saying? What do I say if I can't? Can I just hang up in embarrassment? Will I be able to express what I want to say? Will they laugh if I make some awful mistake? We all know these kinds of fears when we have to ring someone abroad. And, to some extent, the fears are justified. The non-verbal side of communication is missing. We can't see the person's face, their lips and gestures. They can't see our gestures and the look of despair on our faces! It's best to remain calm and ask them to speak slowly and repeat anything that is not clear.

Telephoning | Unit 5

5 In her first week at Herkules Sandra Kohl finds herself alone in the office and it is precisely then that the telephone rings.

R
A 1.12

Work with a partner. Listen to the telephone conversation twice. Partner A makes a note of the phrases Sandra uses to ensure that she understands what Jim Farquhar is saying. Partner B makes a note of the strategies and phrases Jim Farquhar uses to make Sandra understand him and feel good about her English. Then compare your findings.

6 Complete the telephone phrases below using words from the box. Then translate
R / M the phrases into German.

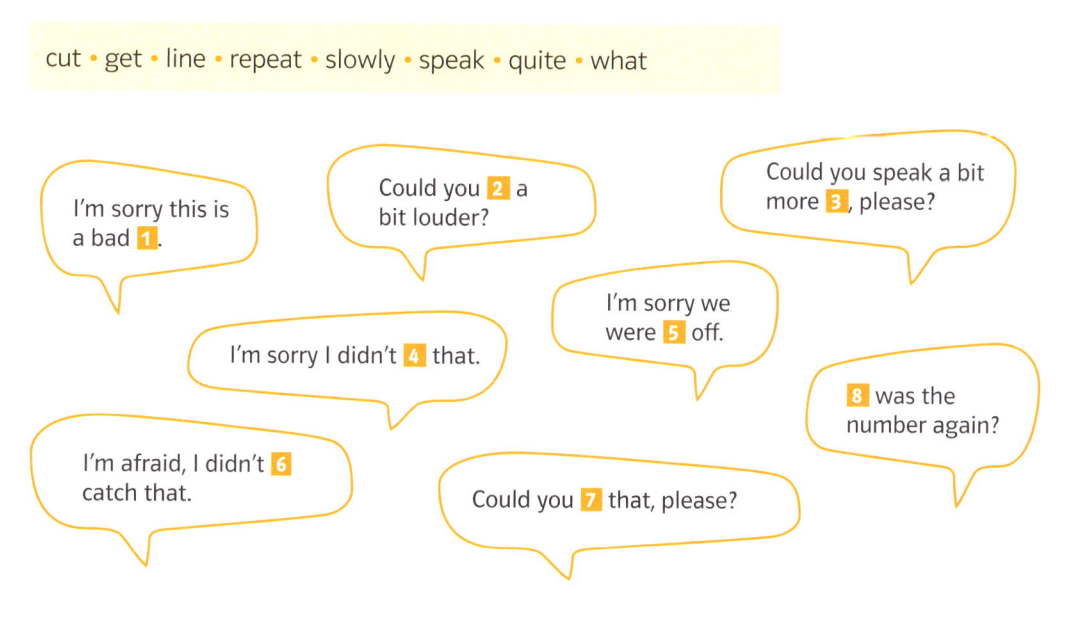

cut • get • line • repeat • slowly • speak • quite • what

I'm sorry this is a bad **1**.

Could you **2** a bit louder?

Could you speak a bit more **3**, please?

I'm sorry I didn't **4** that.

I'm sorry we were **5** off.

8 was the number again?

I'm afraid, I didn't **6** catch that.

Could you **7** that, please?

67

Unit 5 | Telephoning

7 Roleplay this telephone conversation with a partner. Use the phrases at the end of the unit. `Phrases`

Firma: Heinz GmbH, Dresden

Nehmen Sie den Anruf entgegen.

Sagen Sie, dass Sie den Anrufer schlecht verstehen und bitten Sie ihn, etwas lauter zu sprechen.

Es ist jetzt besser.
Fragen Sie, worum es geht.

Bitten Sie den Anrufer einen Moment zu warten und verbinden Sie ihn mit Frau Lange.

Sagen Sie, dass die Leitung leider im Moment besetzt ist und fragen Sie, ob der Anrufer warten möchte.

Die Durchwahl ist 23. Frau Lange wird bis 16 Uhr im Büro sein.

Wiederholen Sie die vorherige Information.

Antworten Sie und verabschieden Sie sich.

Company: Baltic Car Supplies, Tallinn, Estonia

Nennen Sie Ihren Namen und den Namen der Firma. Sie möchten Frau Lange sprechen.

Sprechen Sie etwas lauter und fragen Sie, ob Sie jetzt besser zu verstehen sind.

Es geht um eine Rechnung.

Bedanken Sie sich.

Sagen Sie, dass Sie lieber später zurückrufen möchten und fragen Sie nach der Durchwahl.

Sie haben das nicht richtig verstanden und bitten um Wiederholung.

Bedanken Sie sich und verabschieden Sie sich.

8 Work in pairs. Sit back to back. Use your notes from Exercise 5 and the phrases at the end of the unit. Then act out a similar dialogue. `Phrases`

C Taking messages

1 Übertragen Sie den folgenden Text ins Deutsche.

> **Info: How to take a message**
>
> When taking messages it is important to make sure that you take down all the relevant details. You should first make sure that you take down the name of the caller. It is usually necessary to ask him/her to spell names and addresses. Be sure to get the postcode.
>
> It is essential to note down telephone numbers accurately. Failure to do so will lead to a lot of problems. Read back telephone numbers to check that you have got them right. Telephone numbers are often read differently in different countries. In Britain numbers are simply given in the order they occur, eg: 0044 020 363 2991 = oh oh four four – oh two oh - three six three – two nine nine one. Instead of **oh** Americans usually say **zero**. People often say: double oh or: two double nine one. If necessary, ask the caller to repeat the number more slowly.
>
> Get callers to spell e-mail addresses precisely. Even the slightest mistake results in e-mails being sent back. @ is pronounced at, (.) is read as dot, (cf "dotcoms" = internet companies), (/) is pronounced slash and (–) is read as hyphen or dash or minus.
>
> Your company may have a special form for recording telephone messages.

2 There are different international telephone alphabets but people very often make up their own as they go along. Spell the following names and addresses using the international telephone alphabet on page 70. Then listen and check.

Brian Urquart • Jonathan McEwan • Trevelyan Networking Ltd • Peterborough • Heidi Schlösser • Detlev Jaegermeyer • Jörg Eyrich • Silberstein • Chemnitz • Ditzhuizen • Mbamali • Werchojansk • Ian McWhirter • Appletreewick in Wharfedale • Georg Süsterhenn • Bad Oeynhausen

3 Spell the following names and addresses using your own telephone alphabet.

Mississippi • Philadelphia • Rhondda • Le Havre • Eyjafiallajökull • Energize Ltd. • Joachim • Fort Myers • Wolfgang Somborn • Kiel • Mississauga Enterprises Inc. • Maldives Travel Lounge

Unit 5 | Telephoning

International telephone alphabet

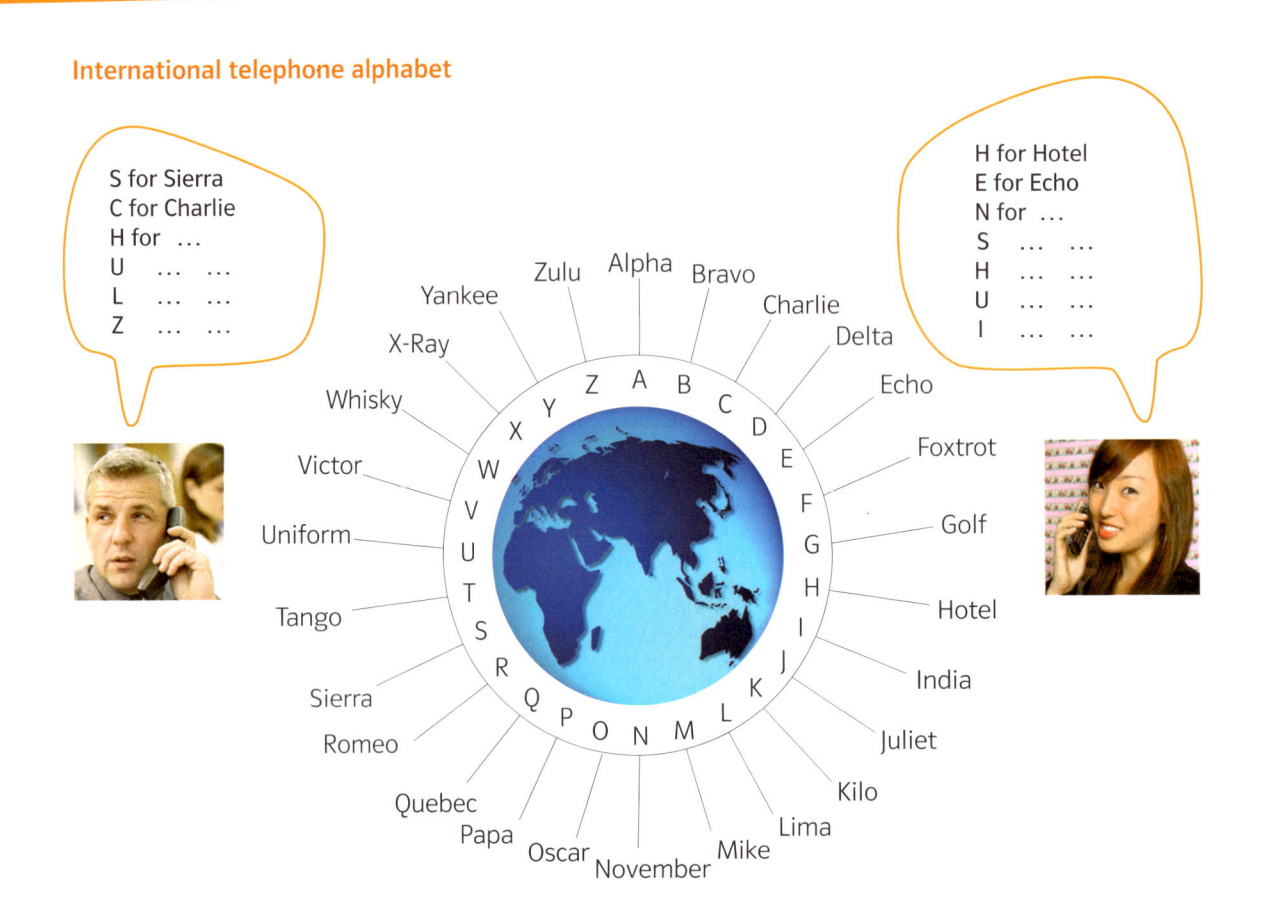

S for Sierra
C for Charlie
H for …
U … …
L … …
Z … …

H for Hotel
E for Echo
N for …
S … …
H … …
U … …
I … …

Alpha, Bravo, Charlie, Delta, Echo, Foxtrot, Golf, Hotel, India, Juliet, Kilo, Lima, Mike, November, Oscar, Papa, Quebec, Romeo, Sierra, Tango, Uniform, Victor, Whisky, X-Ray, Yankee, Zulu

4 Work in pairs: Sit back to back and spell your name and the name and address of your company using the international telephone alphabet. Then change roles and check the results.

Phrases

Symbol:	Name:	Example:
'	apostrophe [apostrofi]	O'Connor
@	at	info@
A/a	capital letters/small letters	USA/asap
-	hyphen/dash/minus	t-online
Ö	o-umlaut/oe/o with 2 dots	Möller
:	colon	http:
/	slash/stroke	org/gla/
\	backslash	\docs.nt\
.	dot	.de
_	understroke	tourist_org.

Telephoning | Unit 5

Codes / numbers:

+49	(0)711	664376-0	34
country code	area code	office number	extension
04275	Leipzig		
post/zip code	city		

5 Work in groups. Group A uses the role card below and dictates the following
KMK telephone numbers, e-mail addresses and websites. Group B uses the role card
on page 252 and dictates the information given there. Then check your results.

Role card: Partner A	Role card partner B ⇨ page 252
1. +44 (1234) 687791	
2. (0203) 4670976	
3. (051) 27 81 13 - 12	
4. (0171) 25333980	
5. info@terstegen.com	
6. dieter.wilhelmsen@abconsulting.de	
7. www.mittelpunkt.de/abo	
8. info@sykescottages.com	

6 First copy the form below. Then listen to the conversation and take the message.
R/P
A 1.14

```
TELEPHONE MESSAGE

Message for:

Message taken by:              Date:

Caller:

Subject:
```

7 You are David Verhoeven. You receive a telephone call from the UK. See on
R/P page 72 for what you yourself say in the conversation with Mr Jones.
A 1.15

First copy the form below. Then listen to the conversation and make a note of the
message in German.

```
TELEFONNOTIZ

Nachricht für:

aufgenommen von:              am:

Anrufer:

Betreff:
```

71

Unit 5 | Telephoning

David Verhoeven:	Anton Hein GmbH, Erkelenz, guten Tag.
David Verhoeven:	Good morning, Mr Jones. I'm afraid Mrs van Steuben is away on a business trip. She is not due back before the beginning of next week. Is there anyone else you'd like to speak to?
David Verhoeven:	Certainly. No problem.
David Verhoeven:	Right. Could you give me your name and your boss's name again, please?
David Verhoeven:	It's David Verhoeven. I'd better spell my second name: V for Victoria, E for egg, R for Richard, H for happy, O for ox, E for Egg, V for Victoria, E for egg and N for nice. I hope you got that alright.
David Verhoeven:	I'll make sure she gets your message. The name of your company was CyberWorld, wasn't it? I didn't catch the name of the town, though.
David Verhoeven:	Thank you and thank you very much for ringing. Goodbye.

8 Work in pairs. Copy the English and the German forms for telephone messages. Sit back to back. Partner A "rings" partner B and leaves a short message. Partner B takes down the message, either in German or in English – depending on the recipient. Then change roles. Use the role card on page 252.   `Phrases`

Example:

Partner A: "This is Pavel Banka speaking. I've got a message for Herr Meister, your purchasing manager. Please tell him that the MP3 Player C27 is again in stock and that I could ship them tomorrow morning. Ask Herr Meister to ring me as soon as possible."

Partner B takes down the message on a form.

```
TELEFONNOTIZ

Nachricht für:      Herrn Meister, Einkauf
aufgenommen von:   (Ihr Name)                    am:
Anrufer:            Pavel Banka
Betreff:            MP3 Player C27 wieder vorrätig
Herr Banka könnte die C27-Player morgen früh absenden.
Bittet möglichst bald um Rückruf.
```

9 Work in pairs. Sit back to back and practise taking messages. Use the phrases at the end of the unit.   `Phrases`

D Making telephone calls

**Communicating across cultures:
Telephoning in English-speaking countries**

It is important to use suitable polite phrases when ringing people in English-speaking countries. If you know the person you are ringing it is usual to ask how they are getting on etc. before you get down to business (Example: How are you doing? I haven't spoken to you for a long time etc.).

If you are about to mention a problem or difficulty, you should begin with "I'm afraid …"
A request often begins with "Could you possibly …?" (Could you possibly repeat the address?) or "I would be grateful if you would / could …".

When someone does you a service, it is usual to say something like: "Excellent!", or "Brilliant!"

When someone thanks you for your help you can say, "You're welcome" or "Not at all".

Don't just say "yes" or "no". Say: "Yes, I think so"; "No, I'm afraid not".

❗ The problem for German speakers is that short answers which are NOT impolite in German come across in English as unfriendly or impolite.

1 Listen to the conversation and note down the missing expressions on a separate sheet of paper.

R
A 1.16

Voice:	Good morning. Cardboard Box Company, John Hough speaking.
Nadine Pfeiffer:	Good morning. **1** your packaging materials. My boss **2** your sales literature.
John Hough:	Certainly, **3** you our literature. **4** the name and address of your company.
Nadine Pfeiffer:	The name of the company is Hülshoff GmbH.
John Hough:	**5** , please.
Nadine Pfeiffer:	H for Harry, **6** , L for lemon, S for sugar, H for Harry, O for Otto, double F for Frederick, and then G m b H. The street is Zülpicher Str 131, 50001 Köln, that's Cologne and it's spelt K for knock, O for Otto with two dots, L for lovely and N for nice.
John Hough:	Oh dear, **7** the street as well.
Nadine Pfeiffer:	Z for Zoe; U for ugly with two dots; L for lovely; P for princess; **8** ; C for carrot; H for Henrietta; E for egg and R for Ritz.
John Hough:	Brilliant. I will send you the sales literature immediately and **9** you again. By the way, **10** name?
Nadine Pfeiffer:	Yes, Huff. **11** ?

Unit 5 | Telephoning

John Hough: I'm afraid not. It's spelt H O U G H, that is H for Henry, O for orange, U for united, G for Green and H for Henry again. My first name's John **12**!
Nadine Pfeiffer: Thank you very much. Goodbye.
John Hough: Thank you. **13** the literature in a couple of days. Goodbye.

2 First copy the form below. Then listen to the telephone conversation between Lucy Batt and Chloe Stott and fill in the form Chloe has prepared for her boss's information.
R
A 1.17

Contact person:

Days of arrival and departure:

Size and location of the cottage:

Charge per week:

Additional charges:

Half the total rent plus booking charges to be paid by:

Balance to be paid by:

Modes of payment:

Mode of booking:

Telephoning | Unit 5

3 Roleplay this telephone conversation with a partner.

KMK

Phrases

Employee at Form und Raum GmbH (eigener Name)	British customer John Willoughby, Exclusive Interiors, London
Melden Sie sich am Telefon.	
	Stellen Sie sich vor. Sie haben die neuen Lampen der deutschen Firma auf einer Ausstellung gesehen und möchten eventuell einige bestellen.
Sie sind gerade allein im Büro. Fragen Sie, ob der Anrufer eine Nachricht hinterlassen möchte.	
	Sie möchten, dass jemand so bald wie möglich zurückruft. Sie geben Ihre Telefonnummer in London an: (020 897 3884).
Sie bitten den Anrufer, die Telefonnummer langsam zu wiederholen. Den Namen haben Sie auch nicht verstanden. Er soll ihn bitte buchstabieren.	
	Buchstabieren Sie den Namen und wiederholen Sie die Telefonnummer langsam und deutlich. Sie sind heute bis 18.00 Uhr britischer Zeit im Büro.
Es wird auf jeden Fall jemand im Laufe des Nachmittags anrufen.	
	Sie bedanken sich und verabschieden sich.
Sie verabschieden sich ebenfalls.	

E Leaving a message on an answering machine

> **Info: A message on an answering machine**
> 1. Begin by saying "Good morning" etc. Do not say your name first as the first few words may get "lost".
> 2. Pronounce your name very clearly, give your company's name as well and mention the place / country you are calling from, if necessary.
> 3. Be as concise and polite as possible when leaving the message.
> 4. Repeat figures and spell names, if necessary.
> 5. At the end repeat your name and dictate the telephone number slowly.

Kopieren Sie den Vordruck, hören Sie die Nachricht ab und fassen Sie sie auf Deutsch in einer Telefonnotiz zusammen.

KMK

```
TELEFONNOTIZ

Nachricht für:

aufgenommen von:                   am:

Anrufer:

Betreff:
```

Language and grammar
Choose the correct prepositions.

1. The meeting will be held from 2 pm (until/**to**) 4 pm.
2. Thank you for your letter (from/**of**) 9 December.
3. We are prepared to wait (**until**/by) next Friday.
4. We enclose a description of our facilities (**by**/of) an independent expert.
5. We have received numerous enquiries (of/**from**) start-up companies.
6. The tickets will have to be confirmed (**by**/until) the middle of next week.
7. We haven't heard (of/**from**) him recently.
8. The book (of/**by**) a well-known writer is available in paperback.
9. We expect to receive the consignment (**by**/until) Friday at the latest.
10. I've never heard (**of**/from) the firm. Are you sure you've got the name right?
11. It's a study (**of**/by) the CBI (Confederation of British Industry).
12. He has to get to the airport (until/**by**) 4 pm.

Language and grammar: Tricky prepositions – getting the wrong one may change the meaning

by / until   bis
I need the report **by** Monday means that you must get it on Monday (or sooner) because from then on you will need it for your work. Example: The goods must reach us **by** the end of next week.

I need the report **until** Monday means that you need it only until Monday and will then be finished with it.
Example: The import licence is valid **until** 31 August. (You say: until **the thirty-first of** August.)

from … to   von … bis
This year's shoe fair will take place **from** 30 June **to** 4 August. (You say: … from **the thirtieth of** June to **the fourth of** August.)
Wrong: from 30 June ~~until~~ 4 August

from, of, by   von / vom
The date of a communication is preceded by "of" or "dated":
Example: We refer to your offer **of** 2 November. (You say: … of **the second of** November.)
Wrong: We refer to your offer ~~from~~ 2 November.

Where the communication came from is expressed by "from":
Example: We received a complaint **from** one of our customers.
Wrong: We received a complaint ~~of~~ one of our customers.

The author is introduced by means of the preposition "by":
Example: This is shown in a report **by** an independent study group.
Wrong: This is shown in a report ~~of~~ an independent study group.

Office expert

Mobile madness

With their often shrill ring tones and callers talking loudly, mobile phones, Blackberries and I-phones are everywhere: on buses, trains, on the street, at parties. What can you do to be a more polite mobile phone user?

1 Match the rules for mobile phone etiquette (1.–8.) to the texts (A.–H.).

1. Keep private conversations private
2. Lights out, phone off
3. Modulate your voice
4. Observe the proximity rule
5. KISS = Keep it short and simple
6. Don't talk and drive
7. Use common sense
8. Love the one you're with

A. Phoning while driving can cause accidents and is outlawed in many countries. Studies show that using a hands-free device doesn't solve the problem. Either wait or pull over to the side of the road.
B. Leave your phone off at funerals and job interviews or places such as libraries and places of worship where a quiet atmosphere is called for.
C. Keep your voice low, don't shout or argue if other people are nearby.
D. Keep your call brief if you're in a public place – arrange to call back later.
E. In public places such as restaurants or on buses avoid private conversations. Put the ringer on vibrate or silent mode and let the call roll over to voicemail. If the call is important, step outside or move off to the side to return it.
F. It's impolite to take a call in the middle of a conversation – after all if the caller were present they wouldn't just interrupt the conversation.
G. Move at least ten feet away from other people when talking on your mobile.
H. You should turn off your phone in the theatre, the cinema and at concerts – people are paying money to be entertained, not to listen to your ring tones.

2 Match the display indicators (1.–6.) with the correct description of the mobile phone functions (a.–f.).

a. Appears when you receive a new message. It flashes when SIM card is full.
b. Camera function is activated.
c. Choose to customise your settings.
d. Indicates the strength of the signal.
e. Internet connection.
f. Scroll backward one page.

Unit 5 | Telephoning

3 **KMK** In Ihrer Firma macht man sich Gedanken über den sicheren Umgang mit Mobilgeräten und Ihre Chefin hat Sie damit beauftragt, die wichtigsten Aspekte zusammenzufassen. Im Intranet Ihrer internationalen Firma finden Sie die folgenden Sicherheitshinweise für den Umgang mit Mobiltelefonen in Englisch vor. Geben Sie die wesentlichen Inhalte auf Deutsch wieder.

Safety information

Important: Read this information before using your wireless mobile phone.

Exposure to radio frequency signals
Your wireless mobile telephone is a low power radio transmitter and receiver. When it is ON, it receives and also sends out radio frequency (RF) signals. International agencies have set standards and recommendations for protection against RF electromagnetic energy.

Phone operation
Do not operate your mobile telephone when a person is within 4 inches (10 centimetres) of the antenna. A person or object within 4 inches (10 centimetres) of the antenna could impair call quality and may cause the phone to operate at a higher power level than necessary and expose that person to RF energy.

Driving
Observe the following guidelines when using your phone while driving:
- Give full attention to driving – driving safely is your first responsibility.
- Use hands-free phone operation, if available.
- Pull off the road and park before making or answering a call if driving conditions so require.

Electronic devices
Most modern electronic equipment is shielded from RF signals. However, certain equipment may not be shielded against the RF signals from your wireless phone.

Vehicles
RF signals may affect inadequately installed or shielded electronic systems in motor vehicles. Check with the manufacturer or its representative regarding your vehicle.

Posted facilities
Turn your phone OFF in any facility where notices so require or in areas posted "Turn off two-way radio", such as blasting areas and potentially explosive atmospheres. Obey all signs and instructions. Sparks from your battery in such areas could cause an explosion or fire resulting in bodily injury or even death.

Phrases: Telephoning

To make friendly remarks at the beginning of a telephone conversation

Oh, hello Nadine. Nice to hear **from** you. How are things **over there**?	Hallo Nadine. Schön von Dir zu hören. Wie geht's denn so?
Good morning Mrs Glover. I hope you had a pleasant holiday.	Guten Morgen Mrs. Glover. Ich hoffe, Sie hatten einen angenehmen Urlaub.
Good afternoon Mr McEwan. **What's** the weather in Scotland **like**?	Guten Tag Mr. McEwan. Wie ist das Wetter in Schottland?

Reactions

Fine, thank you. And how are you?	Gut, vielen Dank. Und wie geht es Ihnen?
Thank you, it was really very relaxing.	Danke, es war wirklich sehr erholsam.
We've had an awful lot of rain recently, I'm afraid. What's it like in Germany?	Es hat in der letzten Zeit leider schrecklich viel geregnet. Wie ist das Wetter in Deutschland?

To ask the caller to speak more slowly, to spell sth., to repeat sth.

Oh sorry. I didn't quite catch that. Could you repeat it more slowly, please?	Es tut mir Leid, das habe ich nicht verstanden. Könnten Sie es etwas langsamer wiederholen?
Could you possibly spell that? Is that the name of the town?	Könnten Sie das vielleicht buchstabieren? Ist das der Name der Stadt?
I'm afraid I didn't get the telephone number. Could you give me it again, please?	Leider habe ich die Telefonnummer nicht mitbekommen. Würden Sie sie bitte wiederholen?

To ask for somebody

Could I speak **to** Ms Burnham, please?	Könnte ich bitte Ms. Burnham sprechen?
Could you put me **through** to Mr Hough?	Könnten Sie mich mit Mr. Hough verbinden?
Could you give me his/her extension, please?	Könnten Sie mir bitte seine/ihre Durchwahl geben?
I'd like to speak to someone from the sales department.	Ich möchte gern jemanden im Verkauf sprechen.

To say that someone is not available

I'm afraid Kirsty Burnham is not in the office at the moment.	Kirsty Burnham ist z. Zt. leider nicht in ihrem Büro.
… is in a meeting.	… ist in einer Besprechung.
… has someone **with** her.	… hat Besuch.

Unit 5 | Telephoning

… is **on** a business trip.	… ist auf Geschäftsreise.
… is out **at** lunch.	… ist zu Tisch.
… is no longer **with** the company.	… ist nicht mehr bei unserer Firma.

To offer to ring back or take a message

I'm afraid Mr Hough is speaking **on** the other line. Would you prefer to hold or shall I ask him to ring back?	Mr. Hough spricht leider gerade auf der anderen Leitung. Möchten Sie warten, oder soll er Sie zurückrufen?
Can he call you back this afternoon?	Kann er Sie heute Nachmittag zurückrufen?
Can I give him a message?	Kann ich ihm etwas ausrichten?
Would you like to leave a message?	Möchten Sie eine Nachricht hinterlassen?

Reactions

Thank you. I'll ring back later.	Danke sehr. Ich rufe später zurück.
I'm afraid I won't be in the office this afternoon. I'll give you my mobile number.	Ich bedaure, ich bin heute Nachmittag außer Haus. Ich gebe Ihnen meine Handy-Nummer.
Yes, please. Could you tell him that …?	Ja bitte. Könnten Sie ihm ausrichten, dass …?

To refer someone to someone else

I'm afraid … I don't know the details.	Leider … kenne ich mich damit nicht aus.
… I am not familiar **with** this order.	… weiß ich über diesen Auftrag nicht Bescheid.
… I am not in charge of this transaction.	… bearbeite ich diesen Vorgang nicht.
I'll put you through to Mr Sears.	Ich stelle Sie zu Mr. Sears durch.
Shall I put you through **to** his secretary?	Soll ich Sie mit seiner Sekretärin verbinden?
Would you like to speak **to** somebody in the accounts department?	Möchten Sie mit jemandem aus der Abteilung Rechnungswesen sprechen?

Reactions

Yes, please. She may be able to help.	Ja bitte. Sie kann mir vielleicht helfen.
No thanks, I really need to speak **to** the export manager.	Nein danke. Ich muss unbedingt mit dem Exportleiter sprechen.

To ask for/about something

Would you please let me know if …?	Ich möchte gern wissen, ob …?
I'd like to ask **whether** it would be possible to …	Wäre es möglich, dass …

Could you possibly …?	Könnten Sie/Könntest Du …?
Do you think you could …?	Könnten Sie/Könntest Du vielleicht …?
You'd be doing us a great favour if you could …	Sie täten uns einen großen Gefallen, wenn Sie …
Please **make sure** that …	Bitte sorgen Sie dafür, dass …
I would really appreciate **it** if you could …	Ich wäre Ihnen sehr dankbar, wenn Sie …

Reactions

Certainly.	Ja, natürlich.
I see no reason why not.	Natürlich. Warum nicht.
Certainly. No problem.	Klar. Kein Problem.
I will certainly do my very best.	Ich werde bestimmt mein Bestes tun.
Definitely. I'll see to it myself.	Ganz bestimmt. Ich werde mich selbst darum kümmern.

To refuse something

I'm afraid we can't agree **to** your proposal.	Leider können wir uns mit Ihrem Vorschlag nicht einverstanden erklären.
We find this level of service quite unacceptable.	Für uns ist diese Art von Kundendienst absolut inakzeptabel.
This is unfortunately not what we had in mind.	Leider hatten wir uns das nicht so vorgestellt.

Reactions

That is a pity.	Das ist wirklich schade.
That is most regrettable.	Das ist überaus bedauerlich.
I can quite understand. We are trying hard to improve things.	Das kann ich verstehen. Wir bemühen uns nach Kräften um eine Verbesserung.
There must have been a misunderstanding.	Hier muss ein Missverständnis vorliegen.

To apologise

I'm terribly sorry but …	Es tut mir schrecklich Leid, aber …
I really must apologise for the inconvenience we've caused you.	Ich möchte mich für die Ihnen entstandenen Unannehmlichkeiten vielmals entschuldigen.
I'm very sorry. Thank you for being so understanding.	Es tut mir sehr Leid. Vielen Dank für Ihr Verständnis.
I can only repeat that I'm very sorry **for** the delay.	Ich kann mich nur nochmals für die Verzögerung entschuldigen.

Unit 5 | Telephoning

Reactions

It could happen to anyone.	Das hätte jedem passieren können.
It's a mistake that is very easily made.	So ein Fehler kommt oft vor.
Don't worry. The main thing is that the mistake has been rectified.	Machen Sie sich keine Gedanken. Hauptsache, der Fehler ist behoben.
Well, let's just hope it doesn't happen again.	Hoffen wir nur, dass es nicht noch einmal geschieht.
It has caused us a lot of embarrassment.	Es war für uns sehr peinlich.

To play for time

Can I ring you back? I need to look **at** the file.	Kann ich Sie zurückrufen? Ich muss erst die Unterlagen einsehen.
I'll have to have a word with the line manager.	Ich muss die Sache erst mit dem Bereichsleiter besprechen.
I'm afraid I can't access the file **on** my monitor at the moment. Can I ring you back?	Leider habe ich im Moment auf meinem Computer keinen Zugriff auf die Datei. Kann ich Sie zurückrufen?
I'm afraid I can't give you a definitive answer **at** the moment. I'll get back to you this afternoon if that's OK.	Leider kann ich Ihnen z. Zt. keinen endgültigen Bescheid geben. Wenn es Ihnen recht ist, rufe ich Sie deswegen heute Nachmittag zurück.

Reactions

I'm afraid you said that the last time I rang. I'm not prepared to be put **off** again.	Das haben Sie schon beim letzten Mal gesagt. Ich lasse mich nicht noch einmal so abspeisen.
Certainly, but please give me your extension so that I can ring you direct if necessary.	Natürlich, geben Sie mir aber doch bitte Ihre Durchwahl, damit ich Sie nötigenfalls direkt anrufen kann.
I wish to settle the matter now. I should be grateful if you would put me through to the person responsible.	Ich möchte die Angelegenheit jetzt klären. Bitte stellen Sie mich zu dem entsprechenden Sachbearbeiter durch.
Fine. I look forward to hearing from you. I leave the office **at** 4 pm your time.	Schön. Ich erwarte Ihren Anruf. Ich bin bis 4 Uhr Ihrer Zeit im Büro.

To insist that something is done by a certain date

We need the goods **by** Wednesday **at** the very latest.	Wir benötigen die Ware bis spätestens Mittwoch.
We definitely need the documents **by** 3 May.	Wir müssen die Unterlagen unbedingt bis zum 3. Mai erhalten.
Can we rely **on** that?	Können wir uns darauf verlassen?
Please make sure it arrives **no** later **than** the end of April.	Bitte sorgen Sie dafür, dass es spätestens Ende April eintrifft.
Monday 31 July is the final deadline.	Montag, der 31. Juli ist der letzte Termin.

To promise something

We promise you that …	Wir versprechen Ihnen, dass …
You have my word. The documents will reach you **by** Monday.	Ich gebe Ihnen mein Wort. Die Dokumente treffen spätestens Montag bei Ihnen ein.
We will certainly **ensure** that …	Wir werden bestimmt dafür sorgen, dass …
The goods will be definitely dispatched tomorrow.	Die Ware wird mit Sicherheit morgen abgeschickt.

To end the conversation

Goodbye Miss Pfeiffer. Thank you for calling.	Auf Wiederhören, Frau Pfeiffer. Vielen Dank für Ihren Anruf.
Thank you. Goodbye. Have a nice weekend.	Danke schön. Auf Wiederhören. Schönes Wochenende!
Sorry, I must have got a wrong number.	Entschuldigung, ich habe mich verwählt.

Reactions

Goodbye Mr Hough. You'll be hearing from us again soon.	Auf Wiederhören Mr. Hough. Sie werden bald wieder von uns hören.
Goodbye. You too.	Auf Wiederhören. Gleichfalls.

UNIT 6
Making arrangements

WORD BANK

arrangements • booking • reservation • flight • destination • departure • arrival • hotel • accommodation • ensuite bathroom • diary • appointment • conference • meeting • topic • agenda • minutes • fair • exhibition • application • stand • to organise • to book • to hire • to attend • to record

An important part of the job of secretarial or clerical staff is to make arrangements on behalf of management. This may include managing the boss's diary and making or rescheduling appointments, booking flights or train tickets, making hotel reservations and hiring cars.
A secretary may be required to organise meetings and conferences and to take part in order to keep a record of what is said and decided. It is her job to generally facilitate proceedings, making sure that the participants have everything they need. Many companies take part in trade fairs and exhibitions and it may be the task of the secretary to book stand space and help organise the company's participation. Finally, the secretary will be responsible for welcoming visitors, often from abroad. Obviously, a good command of foreign languages is an absolute must.

Study the text and answer the following questions.

1. Why may a secretary be asked to be present at a meeting?
2. What are the various duties of a secretary as given in the text? Make a list and translate it into German.

Making arrangements | Unit 6

A Flights and accommodation

1 Global Catering in Manchester has meanwhile taken over a German company
R   and renamed it Global Catering München GmbH. Executives from the German,
A 1.19 British and American companies are to meet for a conference in Munich before
flying on to Madrid to attend an international food fair.

Melanie Schmiedel, personal assistant (PA) to Udo Moersen, manager of Global Catering München GmbH, has been asked to organise the conference from 5th to 7th September at the company's premises in Munich. She decides to start by ringing her opposite number at the company's headquarters in Manchester.

Listen to the dialogue and complete the following sentences:

1. The conference is to take place in **1** on **2**
2. The sales manager is going **3**
3. Melanie Schmiedel will book rooms for **4** at **5**
4. Jackie Rowland asks whether the Munich hotel caters for **6**
5. Lunch will be provided by **7**
6. Jackie Rowland will book the flights from **8** to **9**
7. Melanie Schmiedel sends Jackie Rowland a copy of **10**

2 Taking the role of Melanie Schmiedel send two e-mails confirming the hotel
P   reservation at Zum Goldenen Ochsen, Wittelsbacher Allee 57, 81220 München to Naomi Rodgers at the American company on Rodgers.GlobalCateringusa@aol.com and to Jackie Rowland on Rowland.GlobalCateringuk@aol.com answering Jackie Rowland's query and asking whether the Americans have any special wishes as far as catering is concerned. Executives will be picked up at the airport. You require flight times and the names of the American executives.

To:	Rowland.GlobalCateringuk@aol.com	**Cc:**
From:	schmiedel.GlobalCateringmunich@aol.com	**Date:**
Subject:		

85

Unit 6 | Making arrangements

3 Melanie Schmiedel then rings the Hotel Granada in Madrid to make arrangements
R   for the six executives attending the International Food Fair from 7 to 9 September.
A1.20

Listen to the conversation twice and answer the following questions:

1. What rooms does Melanie want to book?
2. What are the special features of the rooms she is offered?
3. What are the nationalities of the executives?
4. What meal will the executives receive automatically?
5. What arrangements are there for the evening meals?
6. What special catering arrangements are necessary for Kirsty Burnham?
7. How will the executives get to the exhibition grounds?
8. Why are they advised against hiring a car?

Flight	Departure Time	Arrival Time	Destination
ZY 207	8.45 am	11.30 am	Madrid
ZY 213	6.30 pm	9.15 pm	Munich

Melanie has meanwhile booked the flights from Munich to Madrid. The flight ZY 207 leaves Munich at 8.45 am on 7 September and arrives in Madrid at 11.30 am. Return flight ZY 213 is at 6.30 pm on 9 September.

4 Taking the role of Melanie Schmiedel send an e-mail to the Granada Hotel   Phrases
P   informing them of the flight number and times and giving the names of the
     six executives. Ask them to confirm that the executives will be picked up at the
     airport.

5 In your role as Melanie Schmiedel send an e-mail to Naomi Rodgers cc Jackie   Phrases
P   Rowland giving information about the flight from Munich to Madrid and the hotel
     booking in Madrid.

86

6 Work with a partner. Act out the following dialogue with the help of the prompts.

James Critchley	**Jennifer Ainsworth**
SmartMart Ltd	
	Saskatchewan Airlines
book flight/O'Hare airport Chicago	
	date/one-way/return?
return/start 25 June/return 30 June	
	one moment/look monitor/flight 2pm 25 June/London Heathrow/ return O'Hare 9 am 30 June
OK/price?	
	Business/Economy?
Business	
	£837 return/book?/pay credit card
book/pay Visa	
	number/expiry date
4731 5026 7100 5314/9 July 2014	
	address?
James Critchley 136 Brunswick Avenue Brighton BN3 1NA	
	thank you/flight SA324/booking reference SA7XP2/send confirmation/ticket/I forgot – aisle or window?
window	
	anything else?
book car/recommend company	
	work with Excelsior Limos/20% discount/ mention us/booking reference/telephone number/New York Office/001.201.4338301
thank you/will ring	
	thank you/choose Saskatchewan/goodbye

7 Your boss asks you to check out times and prices of business class flights to Mumbai, India (direct flights from your nearest airport). Make notes on the options.

Unit 6 | Making arrangements

＊ 8 Work with a partner. Act out the following dialogue with the help of the role cards.

`Phrases`

> **Role card: Partner A**   **Role card partner B ⇨ page 253**
>
> Sie sind Ivor Friedmann von der Mietwagenfirma Excelsior Limos Inc. in Chicago und erhalten einen Anruf von James Critchley von der britischen Firma SmartMart Ltd. **Nehmen Sie den Anruf entgegen.**
> - Mietwagen verschiedener Kategorien (Kompakt- bis Luxusklasse) zur Abholung am Flughafen bereit
> - Preis für Kompaktklasse $200 pro Woche, Preis pro Tag $50
> - keine Beschränkung der Anzahl der gefahrenen Meilen
> - Versicherung im Preis enthalten, bei Unfall muss der Kunde allerdings 10% der Kosten selbst tragen
> - Zusatzversicherung zur Deckung der 10% Selbstbeteiligung (excess coverage): $60 pro Woche
> - 20% Rabatt für Kunden der Saskatchewan Airlines
> - Gesamtpreis: $200 plus $60 Zusatzversicherung minus $40 Rabatt = $220
> - Zahlung per Kreditkarte erwünscht unter Angabe der Kreditkartennummer und des Verfallsdatums sowie der Adresse des Kunden

B   Meetings, conferences and fairs

1   Making an appointment

Melanie Schmiedel's boss Udo Moersen is to go to Manchester for one day to discuss the integration of the German company into the group and the new product range with Kirsty Burnham. He asks his PA to arrange a day to fit in with Ms Burnham's agenda. He would arrive about 9.30 and stay till 2.45. He would prefer Wednesday.

Melanie Schmiedel has Herr Moersen's diary in front of her and rings Jackie Rowland, who likewise refers to Ms Burnham's diary. They try to decide which day it would be possible to meet. Kirsty Burnham would like to invite Udo Moersen out to a pub for a working lunch, if he would like that.

Making arrangements | Unit 6

1 Sit back to back with your partner (Role card B) and act out the dialogue between them in which they arrange an appointment in Manchester and cover the other points mentioned.

Phrases

Role card: Partner A	Role card partner B ⇨ page 253
Terminkalender von Udo Moersen	
Montag 9 Uhr: Treffen mit Lieferanten Pauli & Co; 11.30 Ad.Slot Internetwerbung Frau Franzen	**13. Juni**
Dienstag Einzelhändler im Großraum München ab 9 Uhr bis ca 15.30 Uhr	**14. Juni**
Mittwoch	**15. Juni**
Donnerstag 16. Juni Geburtstag meiner Frau, 20.00 Uhr Tisch bei Da Pino reserviert	
Freitag 17. Juni 11 Uhr: Besprechung der Produktplanung mit Xaver; 13–14 Uhr Mitarbeiterbesprechung	

Communicating across cultures: Tips for visitors to the UK

Trains:
There are no supplementary charges for faster trains in Britain (the Eurostar to Brussels and Paris is more expensive!). Trains that stop at many stations are obviously slower than those that rarely stop. How often and where they stop is given on the indicator and timetables. It is very important to make sure that the train stops where you want to get off! Do not assume that all trains will stop at the same station on your return journey. Each train may stop at a different selection of stations.

Pubs:
Pubs are an important institution in Britain and are a popular venue at lunchtime for an informal meal. Many provide food at lunchtime, less often in the evening. As a rule there is no waiter service. You go to the bar to buy drinks where turn-taking is observed although there is no visible queue. If the pub is crowded it may be a good idea to discreetly wave a 10 pound note to let the barman/barmaid know you are waiting. Often English people buy rounds, saying things like "What's yours?" or "What are you having?".

Unit 6 | Making arrangements

> Everybody is in principle expected to buy a round. If you don't, there may be an embarrassed silence. Food is also ordered and paid for at the bar and is brought to the table where you are sitting. All drinks and food are paid for straight away.
>
> **Tipping (taxis and restaurants):**
> In Germany you frequently tip by rounding up the amount of the bill. If the taxi fare is Euro 8.10 you might say Euro 8.50 or Euro 9.00. In Britain a taxi driver would not know what you meant. If the fare is £5.30 you could give the driver a £10 pound note and say "please give me change for £6". In restaurants the bill is generally brought on a little tray. You put enough money on the tray to pay the bill. The waiter returns, takes the tray away and comes back again with your change on the tray. You then decide what to put on the tray as a tip. It does not have to be a percentage of the bill.

2 Ihr Chef muss geschäftlich zum ersten Mal nach England. Geben Sie ihm einige
KMK Tipps. Fassen Sie dazu die Informationen in der Box (Communicating across cultures) zusammen.

2 Preparing the agenda

1 Übertragen Sie die Agenda ins Deutsche.
KMK
Melanie Schmiedel has now received the draft agenda of the conference in Munich on 6 and 7 September as drawn up by her boss.

Agenda

1. Welcoming guests
2. Minutes of the last conference in Boston, USA
3. Report on the Munich company and its integration in the group by Xaver Ertl
4. Presentation by Kirsty Burnham on the development of Global Catering's sales
5. Report by Kevin Sears on the development of Global Catering's European business
6. Consumer health concerns – from obesity to organic food – recent market research presented by Jeanne-Anne Taylor
7. Presentation on the role of international trade fairs in Global Catering's marketing strategy by Udo Moersen
8. Other business

2 In your role as Melanie Schmiedel send an e-mail to Jackie Rowland at Global
P   Catering UK and Naomi Rodgers at Global Catering USA enclosing the above draft agenda as an attachment, requesting notification of any additions or modifications in the course of the following week.

Phrases

Making arrangements | Unit 6

3 Preparing a meeting

Read the following text and make a list of the most important points.

As PA to Udo Moersen Melanie Schmiedel has been asked to assist at the conference in Munich.

This involves supervising the preparation of the room, making sure that there is an adequate supply of tea, coffee, soft drinks and mineral water (sparkling and still) available.

Any equipment required such as a computer projector, whiteboard or flip chart with a supply of board markers must be available and in working order.

Her boss may require files, additional information, or he may need to make telephone calls etc.

She must be on hand to provide any assistance necessary. Some of the German executives' English leaves much to be desired and so she may be asked to interpret or translate.

Video lounge Hospitality

BBC Motion Gallery

This video deals with the hotel and catering trade.
Keep the following questions in mind while watching the video:

1. Does Judith like her job? What are the disadvantages?
2. What problem does the sector face that is highlighted several times in the course of the video?
3. What – mentioned towards the end of the video – is the sector doing to solve this problem?
4. What is Wayne Spencer's job title? Describe his appearance.
5. What particular skills do people working in this industry require?

Discuss your answers with the class.

Unit 6 | Making arrangements

4 Taking the minutes

✱ Translate fhe first three paragraphs of the following text.
M

The minutes

It is important for an accurate written record of the transactions of a meeting or conference to be kept. It is essential for those involved to be able to refer back to the minutes and see what was said and, in particular, what was agreed. The minutes are evidence in law of the proceedings of the meeting.

The names of those present and any apologies for non-attendance must be recorded. In this case there are the six executives with Udo Moersen acting as chairman or chair and a number of other employees of the Munich company and finally, Melanie Schmiedel.

Especially in a discussion it is difficult to keep a word for word account of what is being said. The person taking the minutes may be able to note down only the most important points. It is particularly important that any figures or dates should be recorded accurately.

The minutes have to be presented to those present at a later date for approval or corrections.

Melanie Schmiedel has also been asked to take the minutes. As most of the topics on the agenda are presentations which will be available in written form her minute-taking will be largely restricted to the questions and answers following the presentations.

5 Booking an exhibition stand

Melanie now has to ring the exhibition authorities in Madrid to check that their order for a stand is OK. After checking her records she sees that she returned the application about two months ago.

Melanie Schmiedel:	Good morning. Melanie Schmiedel from Global Catering in Munich speaking. I'm afraid I don't speak Spanish. Do you speak English or German?
Exhibition authorities:	I do speak English. What can I do for you? By the way my name's Rosa de la Fuente.
Melanie Schmiedel:	I'd like to check our stand reservation for the International Food Fair. I sent off the application form two months ago but I have not received confirmation yet.
Rosa de la Fuente:	Just a second. Let me check my monitor. Yes, here it is. Global Catering. A corner stand, 25m^2, with kitchenette and conference area. Is that OK?
Melanie Schmiedel:	Excellent. When will you be sending out the confirmations?
Rosa de la Fuente:	In a couple of weeks at the latest, I should think. But you can assume that everything's OK.
Melanie Schmiedel:	We shall need an interpreter with English and German. Can you recommend anyone?
Rosa de la Fuente:	I would get in touch with the Multilingua Agencia by e-mail under multilinguaservices@aol.com or send them a fax. The telephone number is 0034 91 4022468 and the fax number is the same with a 9 at the end instead of the 8. I'm sure they'll be able to recommend someone suitable.
Melanie Schmiedel:	Brilliant. I'll get in touch with them right away. Thank you very much. Goodbye.
Rosa de la Fuente:	Thank you for ringing. Bye.

1 Lesen Sie den Dialog, decken Sie den Text dann ab und drücken Sie Folgendes auf Englisch aus.

1. Sie sprechen kein Spanisch.
2. Sie möchten die Standreservierung überprüfen.
3. Sie haben einen Eckstand von 25 m^2 mit Teeküche und Besprechungsraum gebucht.
4. Sie wollen wissen, wann die Bestätigungen herausgeschickt werden.
5. Sie brauchen eine Dolmetscherin für Englisch und Deutsch.

Unit 6 | Making arrangements

2 Write a fax as Melanie Schmiedel to the Multilingua Agencia (see page 93) giving
P   details of your requirements. Set out your fax as in the form below.

TELEFAX TRANSMISSION
Global Catering München GmbH

Nymphenburger Allee 93
80335 München
Tel.: (0049) (0)89277183
Fax: (0049) (0)89277190

To:	Attention:
From:	Fax: (0034) (91)4022469
Date:	Pages (incl. this one):
Subject:	

Language and grammar
Translate the following sentences.

1. Als Anhang senden wir Ihnen unsere neueste Preisliste.
2. Gestern habe ich von 13:00 Uhr bis 16:30 Uhr auf Ihren Anruf gewartet.
3. Pro Woche versenden wir zwischen 20 und 30 Angebote.
4. Wir investieren regelmäßig 5 % unseres Gewinns in neue Technologien.
5. Leider warten wir noch immer auf Ihre Überweisung.
6. Zur Zeit versuchen unsere Mitbewerber eine Firma in USA zu übernehmen.
7. Wegen des Booms in China steigen die Stahlpreise weltweit.
8. Er organisiert die Konferenz, die nächste Woche stattfindet, und wir buchen die Hotelzimmer.

Language and grammar: Continuous form (Verlaufsform)

Die Verlaufsform (he is writing an e-mail) dient zur Beschreibung einer gerade vor sich gehenden Handlung sowie einer allmählichen Entwicklung, häufig markiert durch **now, just, still, when, while, since, for** etc.	Our competitors **are trying** to undercut our prices. They **are** still **waiting** for a reply. Prices **have been rising** in the last few months. We **are thinking** of buying a house.
Da die einfache Verbform (he writes 50 e-mails a day) ausdrückt, dass etwas immer so ist oder immer wieder geschieht, ist die Verwendung der Verlaufsform in bestimmten Fällen unerlässlich, um klar zu machen, dass etwas nur von vorübergehender Natur ist.	They **are having** problems with their suppliers (= at the present time). They **have** problems with their suppliers (= often / always). I **am living** with my parents at the moment (= but I'm looking for a flat of my own). I **live** in Dresden (= permanently).
Die Verlaufsform kann für feste Planungen und Abmachungen auch für die Zukunft benutzt werden.	He is giving a presentation at the conference. I am picking him up at the airport next Friday (= this has been arranged).

Making arrangements | Unit 6

Office expert

1 Handling schedules

P You work for an international company in Berlin and your boss, who is on a business trip, has asked you to arrange a meeting for the week of 9 to 13 May with Ms Link, head of the logistics department, and Mr Brunner, head of production. Your boss needs at least two hours and would prefer a meeting early in the week.

Phrases ▶

After looking at Ms Link's and Mr Brunner's schedules, write an e-mail to your boss (m.desai@mail.com) proposing two alternative dates for the meeting and asking which she would prefer. Explain why a meeting early in the week is not possible.

Ms Link's calendar

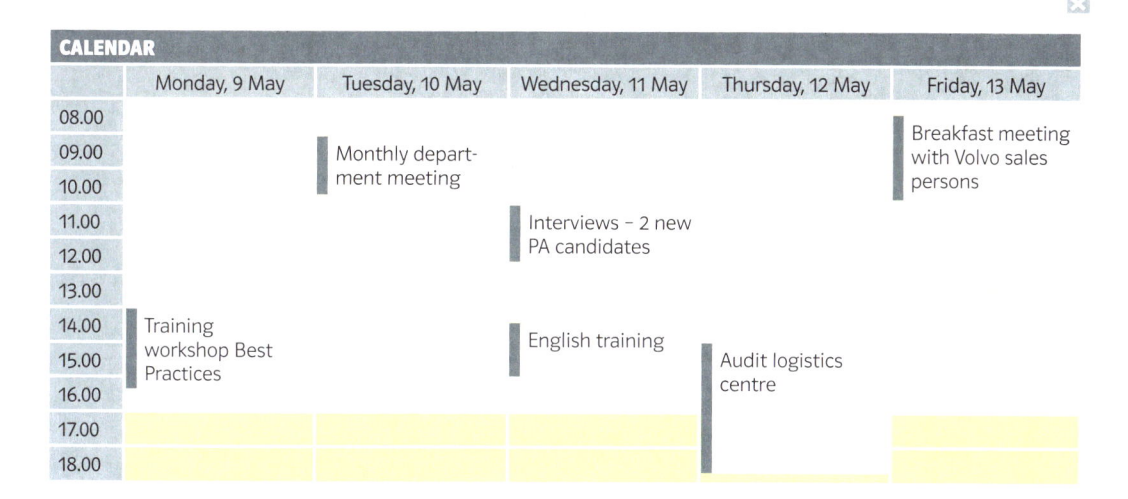

CALENDAR	Monday, 9 May	Tuesday, 10 May	Wednesday, 11 May	Thursday, 12 May	Friday, 13 May
08.00					Breakfast meeting with Volvo sales persons
09.00		Monthly department meeting			
10.00					
11.00			Interviews – 2 new PA candidates		
12.00					
13.00					
14.00	Training workshop Best Practices		English training	Audit logistics centre	
15.00					
16.00					
17.00					
18.00					

Mr Brunner's calendar

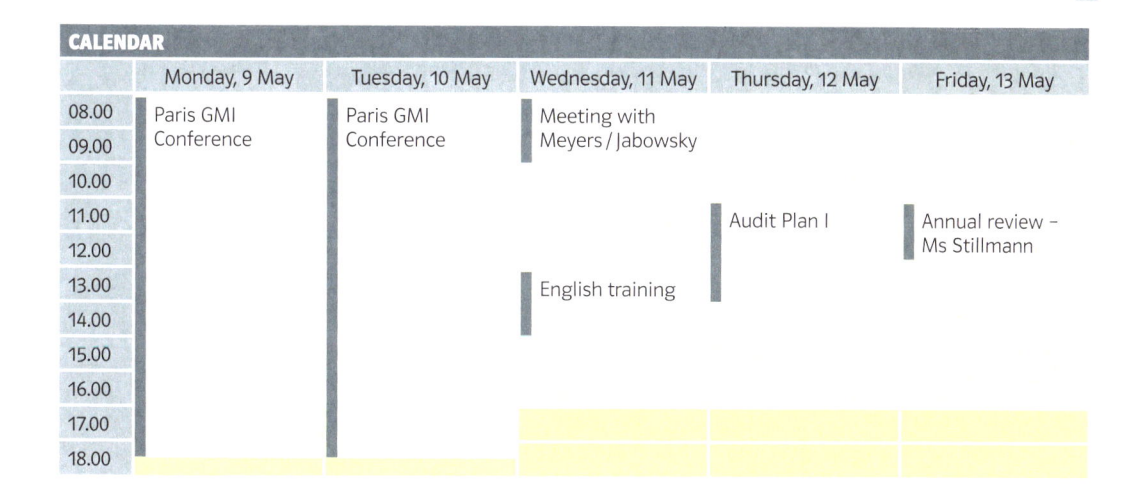

CALENDAR	Monday, 9 May	Tuesday, 10 May	Wednesday, 11 May	Thursday, 12 May	Friday, 13 May
08.00	Paris GMI Conference	Paris GMI Conference	Meeting with Meyers / Jabowsky		
09.00					
10.00					
11.00				Audit Plan I	Annual review – Ms Stillmann
12.00					
13.00			English training		
14.00					
15.00					
16.00					
17.00					
18.00					

2 Arranging transportation

You need to arrange for transportation from Stansted Airport to London and return for two members of your international sales team, Gary and Claudia who will be staying at the Hastings Hotel in 42 New Broad Street. Their flight arrives at 11:05 pm on Sunday evening.

Phrases

Study the information from the Stansted Express website and the map. Write an e-mail to the team (garysmith@mail.com, claudiaheft@mail.com) informing them about the following:

- earliest and latest possible departure times for the train to London
- why you have decided to book the train tickets online
- destination point in London
- directions from the train station to the hotel
- total costs for the return tickets

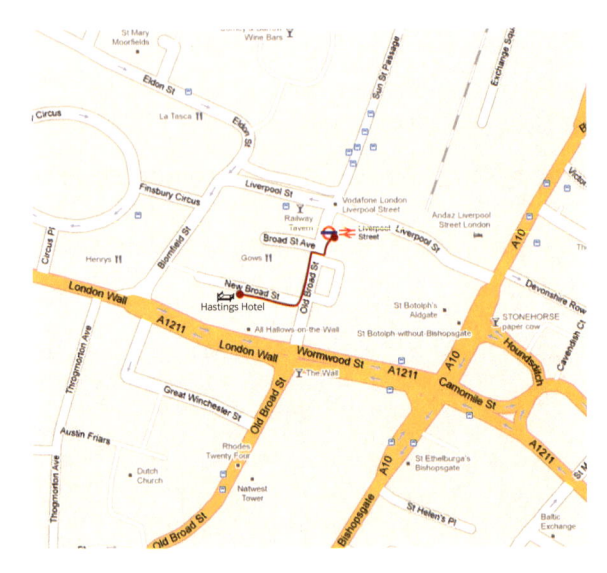

Stansted Express offers great value – save up to £2 on the full ticket office price. The discount is only available for online bookings.

Sunday	From	Until	Minutes past each hour
Departs Stansted Airport	05.30 06.00 06.30 07.00	23.45 23.59 00.30 01.00 01.30	00 – 15 – 30 – 45

Ticket name	Adult fare	Child fare	
Express Class Open Single From ticket machine/office	£18.00 £19.00	£9.00 £9.50	Book now
Express Class Open Return From ticket machine/office	£26.70 £28.70	£13.35 £14.35	Book now
First Class Open Single From ticket machine/office	£29.50 £30.50	£14.75 £15.25	Book now
First Class Open Return From ticket machine/office	£44.00 £46.00	£22.00 £23.00	Book now

Please note: Passengers MUST buy their tickets before boarding the train. Passengers will not be allowed through the barrier without a valid ticket. Open tickets can be used on any train: return travel must be within 30 days of the outward journey.

Phrases: Making arrangements

To book flights or trains

Please reserve a window/aisle seat **on** the 8.30 am flight to Munich.	Bitte reservieren Sie einen Platz am Fenster/Gang für den Flug um 8:30 Uhr nach München.
Are you travelling economy or business class?	Fliegen Sie Economy- oder Business-Class?
I would like to reserve a window seat on the 9.15 ICE train to Hamburg.	Ich möchte einen Fensterplatz des ICE um 9:15 Uhr nach Hamburg reservieren lassen.
Is that first or second class, one way or return?	Erster oder zweiter Klasse? Einfach oder hin und zurück?
Is there a supplementary charge for the InterCity to Edinburgh?	Muss für den Intercity nach Edinburgh ein Zuschlag bezahlt werden?
There is no supplementary charge.	Es wird kein Zuschlag erhoben.
You are booked **on** flight no ZY 652 **on** 23 March, departing London Gatwick **at** 7.30 am, arriving Munich 10.15 am.	Sie sind am 23. März für Flug Nr. ZY 652 gebucht, Abflug London Gatwick um 7:30 Uhr, Ankunft München 10:15 Uhr.
You should check in two hours before departure to allow **for** security.	Sie sollten wegen der Sicherheitsüberprüfung zwei Stunden vor Abflug einchecken.

To book hotel or conference rooms

We require a single/double room with **ensuite** bathroom.	Wir benötigen ein Einzel-/Doppelzimmer mit Bad.
I should like to book an executive suite for three nights **from** 3 **to** 6 March with Internet access.	Ich möchte eine Präsidentensuite mit Internetzugang für drei Nächte vom 3. bis 6. März buchen.
We require a conference room **to seat** 25–30 people.	Wir brauchen ein Besprechungszimmer für 25–30 Personen.
For our annual general meeting we need an assembly hall **of** at least 500 square metres equipped with a stage and a big screen.	Für unsere Jahreshauptversammlung brauchen wir einen Versammlungssaal von mindestens 500 Quadratmetern mit Bühne und Großbildschirm.
I should be grateful if you could confirm the booking **in** writing/**by** e-mail/**by** fax.	Wir wären für eine Bestätigung der Buchung per Brief/E-Mail/Fax dankbar.
Is it possible to order a buffet lunch?	Besteht die Möglichkeit ein Mittagsbuffet zu bestellen?
We regret that we have to cancel the reservation. We realise that it is very short notice.	Wir bedauern, diese Reservierung stornieren zu müssen. Wir sind uns dessen bewusst, dass dies sehr kurzfristig geschieht.

Unit 6 | Making arrangements

To make appointments

I'm afraid I'm engaged all day on Wednesday.	Leider bin ich am Mittwoch den ganzen Tag besetzt.
Friday would suit me fine.	Freitag würde mir gut passen.
I'd prefer Thursday morning.	Donnerstag Morgen wäre mir lieber.
It's Monday **at** 11, then.	Also bleibt es bei Montag um 11 Uhr.
Could we meet **on** Monday 17 at 10 am?	Könnten wir uns am Montag, den 17. um 10 Uhr vormittags treffen?
– Certainly. Monday at 10 am is fine.	– Ja, sicher. Montag 10 Uhr ist o.k.
Would Tuesday suit you?	Würde Ihnen Dienstag passen?
– Not so good. My diary's full, I'm afraid. Wednesday would be better.	– Eigentlich nicht. Mein Terminkalender ist leider voll. Mittwoch wäre besser.
I'm free all day Wednesday.	Am Mittwoch geht es den ganzen Tag.

To prepare the agenda

A draft agenda has already been drawn up.	Ein Entwurf für die Tagesordnung ist bereits erstellt worden.
Notification of any additions or changes is requested within a week.	Es wird gebeten, eventuelle Zusätze oder Änderungen innerhalb einer Woche anzugeben.

To prepare and assist at a meeting

He/She is chairing the meeting.	Er/Sie leitet die Sitzung.
He is the chairman, he/She is the chairperson.	Er/Sie ist der/die Vorsitzende.
Perhaps you could each introduce **yourself** briefly indicating your role in the company.	Vielleicht könnten Sie sich kurz vorstellen und dabei auf Ihre Stellung in der Firma eingehen.
Has everyone got a copy of the agenda?	Haben alle eine Kopie der Tagesordnung bekommen?
We shall adjourn **for** lunch **at** …	Um … unterbrechen wir für das Mittagessen.
Lunch will be provided by our own caterers.	Unser eigener Versorgungsbetrieb wird das Mittagessen liefern.
Are there any further comments?	Gibt es noch Wortmeldungen?
Shall we take a vote?	Sollen wir nun abstimmen?
The proposal is accepted.	Damit ist der Vorschlag angenommen.

Making arrangements | Unit 6

To book an exhibition stand

We are interested in displaying our products **at** the Madrid Motor Show.	Wir sind daran interessiert, unsere Produkte auf der Automobilmesse in Madrid auszustellen.
Our company wishes to reserve floor space for a stand **covering** 8 x 15 metres.	Unsere Firma möchte die für einen Stand von 8 x 15 Metern benötigte Ausstellungsfläche reservieren lassen.
We are interested in introducing our software solutions at this years's Computer Fair and would like to ask you to send us your information package with application forms.	Wir sind daran interessiert, unsere Software-Lösungen bei der diesjährigen Computermesse vorzustellen und möchten Sie bitten, uns Ihre Messe-Information mit Anmeldeformularen zu schicken.
We wish to book a stand in the main exhibition hall.	Wir möchten einen Stand in der Hauptausstellungshalle buchen.

To organise the necessary equipment

Our stand must have internet access and it must be equipped with telephone lines.	Unser Stand muss Internetzugang haben und er muss mit Telefonleitungen ausgestattet sein.
First-class catering services will also be required.	Wir benötigen ebenfalls erstklassigen Catering-Service.

To write invitations

The chairman will be pleased to welcome you **at** our annual dinner **at** the Park Hotel.	Der Vorsitzende gibt sich die Ehre, Sie zu unserem alljährlichen festlichen Abendessen im Park Hotel begrüßen.
The reception will be held in our main hall **between** 10 am **and** 3 pm.	Der Empfang findet zwischen 10 und 15 Uhr in unserer Haupthalle statt.

To have a stand built and dismantled

Are you in a position to design an eye-catching stand for us and erect it before 15 March?	Sind Sie in der Lage, für uns einen ins Auge fallenden Stand zu entwerfen und vor dem 15. März aufzubauen?
Can you help us remove the heavy exhibits and dismantle the stand?	Können Sie uns dabei helfen, die schweren Ausstellungsstücke zu entfernen und den Stand abzubauen?

UNIT 7
Making presentations

WORD BANK

presentation • audience • delivery • content • prompt cards • key words • points • introduction • main body • conclusion • visual aids • eye-contact • body language • handout • to prepare • to rehearse • to deliver • statistics • developments • degree • percentage • comparisons • rankings • graphs • diagrams • bar chart • line graph • pie chart • to visualise • to describe • to rise • to fall • to remain unchanged • to fluctuate • to account for • slight • steady • dramatic

You may be required to present your company and its products – either informally or on a more formal level. This may range from the introduction of a specific product or products to presenting the company as a whole. Although many may feel a bit scared of standing up before an audience, the ability to make good oral presentations is a key skill. However, it is a skill that can be acquired and improved by practice. It is important, above all, to remember that the style and manner of delivery is as important as the content.

Translate the following sentences into German.

M

1. You may feel scared of standing up before an audience.
2. Making a good oral presentation is a key skill.
3. This skill can be acquired and improved.
4. Style of delivery is as important as content.
5. You may be required to make a presentation on your company and its products.

A Preparing a presentation

You have been asked to give a presentation of your company and its products. The presentation will be brief. You have a maximum of 5 minutes at your disposal. The following hints should help you to prepare.

Start by deciding what you want to include and what your objectives are. Remember that there are limits to the number of facts your audience can absorb. The following are intended as helpful hints:

How to make a presentation

- Do not write out your presentation in full. Use numbered prompt cards with key words. They are the best way to avoid forgetting important points.
- Your presentation should have an introduction, main body and conclusion.
- First give a brief overview of points to be covered.
- Divide up the main body according to the number of important points.
- Finish with a conclusion.

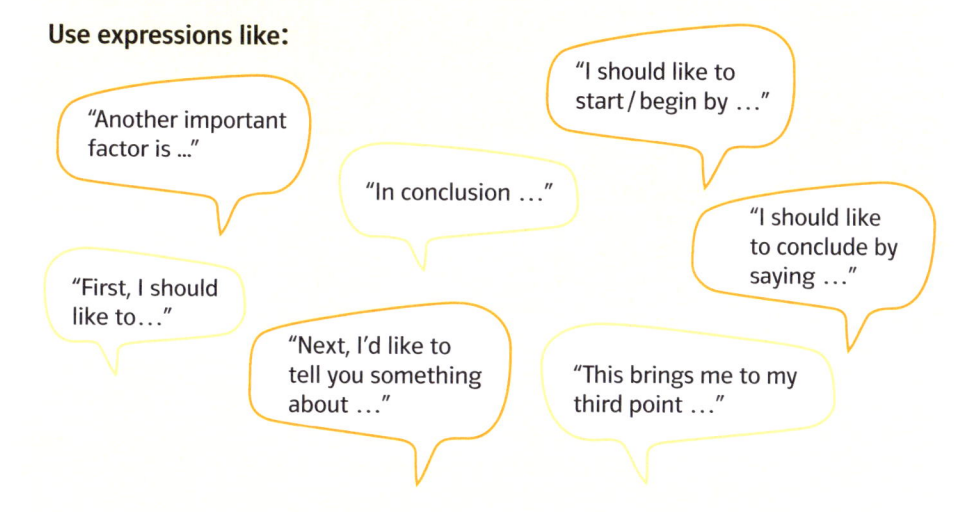

Use expressions like:

- "Another important factor is …"
- "I should like to start/begin by …"
- "In conclusion …"
- "I should like to conclude by saying …"
- "First, I should like to…"
- "Next, I'd like to tell you something about …"
- "This brings me to my third point …"

in order to signal the different sections of your presentation.

Reinforce what you say by **visual aids**, such as powerpoint slides. Visual aids help you to explain complicated ideas more easily and arouse and hold the interest of your audience and make your presentation look more professional. If you print them out they may double as a handout.

Visual aids may take the form of overhead transparencies or computer files showing graphs, pictures, flowcharts, brief statements/cues (e.g. the key words from your prompt cards). Here are a few helpful hints:

- Limit the text to six lines.
- Use no more than six words per line.
- Print the text in large letters, using upper and lower case letters.
- Use dark colours, such as black, red, blue or green.

Unit 7 | Making presentations

1 Fassen Sie den Text über die Vorbereitung einer Präsentation unter Beantwortung folgender Fragen auf Deutsch zusammen.

1. Warum soll eine Präsentation nicht schriftlich ausformuliert werden?
2. Wie soll eine Präsentation gegliedert sein?
3. Welche Vorteile bietet Anschauungsmaterial?
4. Wie müssen Folien aussehen, damit sie wirken?

2 Now listen to a presentation by Udo Moersen from the German subsidiary of Global Catering and complete the following text.

A 1.21

Good morning, ladies and gentlemen. **1** a few words about our company. Since last January we have been a part of Global Catering Manchester but we are an old-established Munich company producing a range of Bavarian specialities.

We have now entered the rapidly growing market for convenience foods, **2** a range of freshly prepared dishes to quality supermarkets and delicatessens and **3** the catering for company board meetings, conferences etc.

In Munich and internationally **4** of young business people (male and female) who do not have the leisure to cook but who still demand high-quality, imaginative, prepared meals which they can quickly pop into their briefcases on their way home.

Our sales figures show that this is a growth market (I don't want to bore you **5** which I hope you have all received). We are also exporting Bavarian specialities to Britain and the USA via Global Catering and its subsidiaries. At the same time we are importing British and American specialities to Germany.

6 that we look forward to rapid growth in these markets. Catering is a modern industry with massive potential whose importance is still underestimated in Germany **7**.

3 Udo Moersen used the following prompt cards for his presentation. Listen again and restore the correct order of his jumbled prompt cards.

A 1.21

(1) conclusion: growth industry

(2) part of Global Catering but old Munich company. Bavarian specialities!

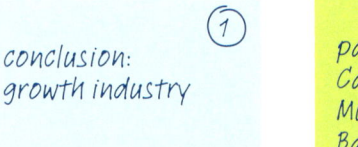

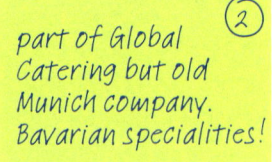

(3) target group: busy young professionals

(4) supermarkets / delicatessens / corporate catering

(5) sales figures (see handout!) exports to USA/UK; imports

Making presentations | Unit 7

✱ 4 Having studied the above information, hints and examples now start preparing
P   your presentation of your company and its products. Write your prompt cards and
     decide which visual aids you are going to use.

Content of your presentation:
- size, type, location, activities of company
- products in general, selection of products, services
- main markets, domestic/export
- sales figures
- special features of products e.g. state-of-the-art, environmentally friendly

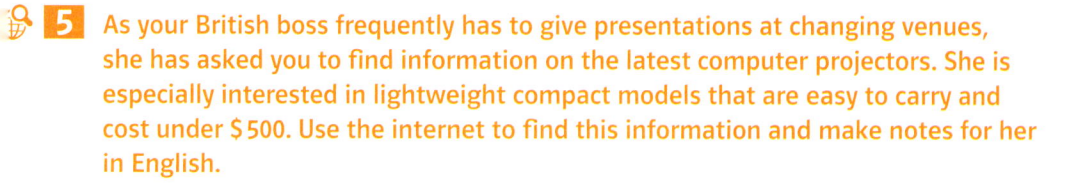

5 As your British boss frequently has to give presentations at changing venues, she has asked you to find information on the latest computer projectors. She is especially interested in lightweight compact models that are easy to carry and cost under $500. Use the internet to find this information and make notes for her in English.

B Delivering a presentation

Useful tips

It is a good idea NOT to read out a prepared text. It is easy to bore your audience. You make a much more lively impression if you speak freely using prompt cards and visual aids to remind you of the various points. This also helps to ensure that your body language is natural. If you are planning to use equipment such as an overhead projector or a computer projector, make sure a) they are working and b) you know how to operate them. Practise and rehearse your presentation, preferably with real people as an audience.

- Do not speak too quickly (in order to get the whole thing over as quickly as possible!)
- Speak clearly – make sure everybody can hear you.
- Do not speak monotonously – you will sound as if you are boring yourself and will bore your audience!
- Do not wave your arms around mechanically – your gestures should be appropriate.
- Look at your audience, establish eye contact.
- Look happy and confident. Smile.

It is very helpful for the person making the presentation to be given constructive, concrete and detailed feedback. Only in this way can they become aware of how they come across and how this can be changed. This is a prerequisite for developing skills in oral presentation.

1 Ein Kollege muss eine Präsentation halten und hat Sie um Rat gebeten.
KMK Schreiben Sie ihm eine E-Mail auf Deutsch und geben Sie ihm Hinweise für eine Präsentation unter Verwendung der Informationen in „Useful tips".

Unit 7 | Making presentations

★ 2 Now give your presentation on your company and its products to your fellow
P/I students. The other students listen to the presentation and assess it according to the following evaluation scheme. The audience should award points out of ten under each heading (on a separate sheet of paper).

Evaluation of presentation/checklist:

		Points
Preparation	evidence of careful preparation	▪
Structure	introduction, main body – clear emphasis on small number of important points – conclusion	▪
Content	relevance, well-substantiated with facts and figures	▪
Visual aids	appropriate use of simple, easy-to-understand visual aids	▪
Delivery	not too fast, eye contact, appropriate body language, confident, relaxed	▪
Language	no jargon, straightforward, use of signalling expressions like: "I should like to begin/conclude by …"	▪
Overall impression	lively, humorous, easy to follow, right length	▪

★ 3 The following is an example of a more ambitious presentation using visual
R aids. At an investment seminar Daniela Webb gives a brief presentation on the Limpopo Mining Company and its products, using a computer projector. Make a list of expressions that would be useful in any presentation.

"Good morning, ladies and gentlemen. I should like to give a brief presentation on our company and its products in the context of this investment seminar.

I'll begin by showing you a graph illustrating the rising demand for zinc and copper worldwide and the development of production at our sites in Asia and Africa. As a result of the strength of the world economy and particularly rapid growth in China and India demand for our products has soared dramatically over the last two years.

At the same time we are investing strongly in the development of our sites. This is a photograph of construction work on our new site in Kazakhstan. As you can see from this graph, production there jumped by 20% last year. We are also spending a large slice of our profits on exploration.
The pie chart shows what proportion of our expenditure goes on the construction and development of sites and the exploration of new sites.

In conclusion, I should like to emphasise that demand for our products is expected to be strong in the foreseeable future. I am sure that this brief presentation will have shown you that Limpopo Mining shares will add some excitement to your investment portfolio.

Thank you very much indeed for your time. I shall be very pleased to answer any questions you may have."

Making presentations | Unit 7

Language and grammar:
Describing graphs and diagrams

Statistics are easier to read if they are presented in the form of bar charts, line graphs or pie charts. When making a presentation, you may have to describe graphs. The expressions given on the following pages will be helpful.

1 Developments over time can be visualised by line graphs

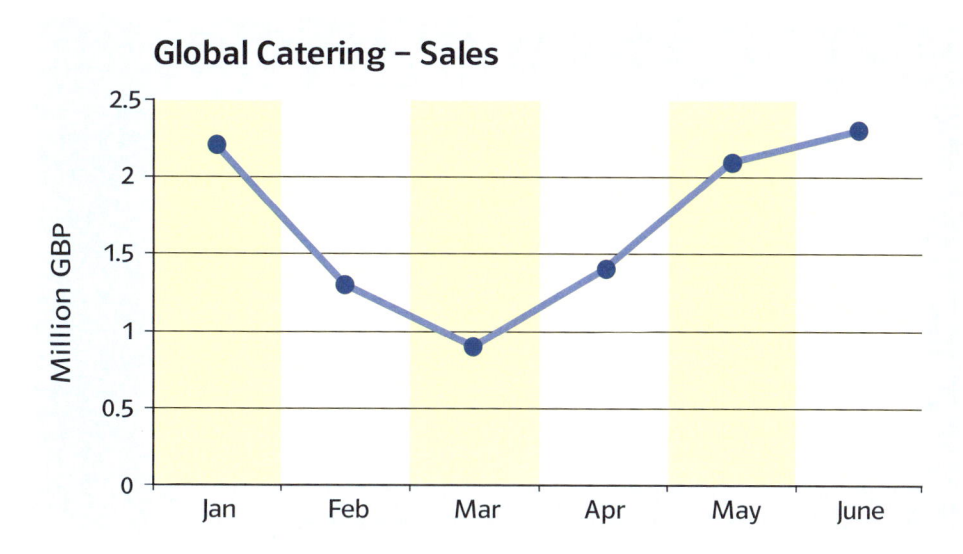

Global Catering – Sales
(Million GBP, Jan–June)

Video lounge Presentations

lingua tv

This video shows a presentation given by a senior Purple Fashion executive. After watching it answer the following questions:

1. Does the presenter make a natural impression?
2. Do you find her gestures and smile convincing?
3. Why is it not necessary to take notes?
4. When does she plan to answer questions?
5. When and where was Purple Fashion founded?
6. Is this her actual presentation?
7. What in her view is Purple Fashion's "obsession"?

105

Unit 7 | Making presentations

To describe developments

1. upwards	
to rise / increase / go up / jump **by ... from ... to ...** to reach a peak / maximum **of ...**	Between May and July exports rose by 5% from 10,000 units to 10,050 units. In June prices reached a peak of €75.
2. unchanged	
to remain / stay unchanged / stable / flat **at ...** to fluctuate **between ... and ...**	Sales remained unchanged at 750m units. In the second quarter oil prices fluctuated between 42 and 61 dollars per barrel.
3. downwards	
to fall / decline / go down / drop / slump **by ... from ... to ...** to reach a low / minimum **of ...** / the lowest point **at ...**	Last year the average price dropped by 2% from € 100 to €98. In March the lowest point was reached at 28 dollars.

At a meeting Kirsty Burnham from Global Catering in Manchester presents her company to a gathering of potential customers. She refers to the last half year's sales and to the line graph on the preceding page.

1 Read her description and find the correct prepositions from the box.

at • by • from • of • of • to • to • to

In January sales stood **1** 2.2 million pounds. Then there was a dramatic decline **2** GBP 1.3m in February. Sales continued to fall steadily and reached the minimum **3** 0.9m in March. Between March and May, however, sales jumped **4** 0.9m **5** 2.1m. In June sales had risen **7** around 9% **6** the peak **8** 2.3 million pounds.

2 Choose the correct adjective or adverb. See *Language and grammar* in Unit 9.

1. In January imports fell (sharp / sharply).
2. Sales remained (constant / constantly) for three months.
3. A (slight / slightly) increase in prices had been expected.
4. There was a (gradual / gradually) fall in turnover.
5. Oil prices have been rising (dramatic / dramatically).

To describe the speed or degree of change

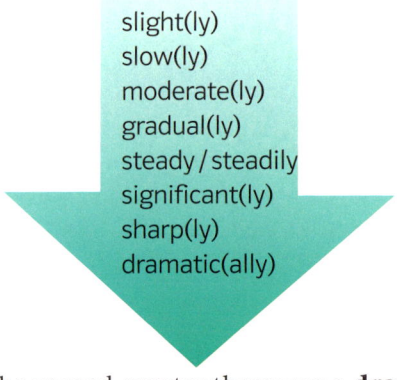

> slight(ly)
> slow(ly)
> moderate(ly)
> gradual(ly)
> steady / steadily
> significant(ly)
> sharp(ly)
> dramatic(ally)

In the second quarter there was a **dramatic** increase in sales. In June imports rose **sharply**.

Making presentations | Unit 7

2 Comparisons and rankings are visualised by means of bar charts

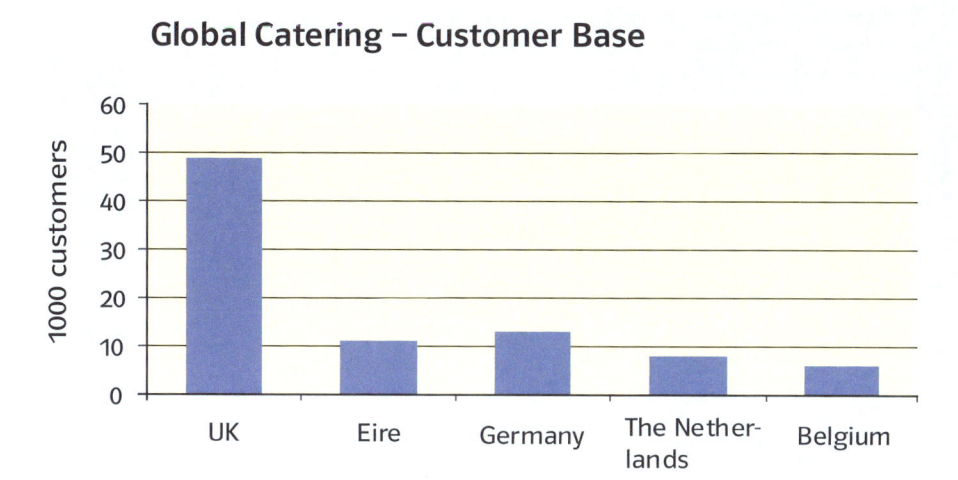

Global Catering – Customer Base

[Bar chart showing 1000 customers by country: UK ~49, Eire ~11, Germany ~13, The Netherlands ~8, Belgium ~6]

To describe comparisons and rankings

to be higher/lower/bigger/smaller/more/less expensive **than** …	Petrol prices in Germany are higher than in Austria.
to be **as** high/low/expensive **as** …	French cars are just as expensive as German cars.
to be the biggest/lowest/most expensive **of** …	This is the most expensive model of all.
to be/come first/second/last **with**	Spain comes first with 45 million tourists.
to be/follow **in** first/fifth/last place	Norway is in fourth place behind France and the UK.
to be followed **by** …	Sweden is followed by Denmark which exports 56 % of its production.
to be **at** the bottom/top/of the list/table	Germany is at the bottom of the table with just 17%.

At the same meeting Kirsty Burnham presents the above bar chart indicating the company's customer base.

> **Study the bar chart above and her description below and complete the description as appropriate.**

Naturally most of our **1** are based in the UK, close to 50,000. Our next biggest **2** is Germany, where we have approx. 13,000 customers, closely **3** by The Irish Republic with more **4** 10,000 customers. The Netherlands and Belgium are **5** fourth and fifth place **6** around 8,000 and 6,000 customers, respectively.

107

Unit 7 | Making presentations

3 Shares and percentages can be visualised with the help of **pie charts**

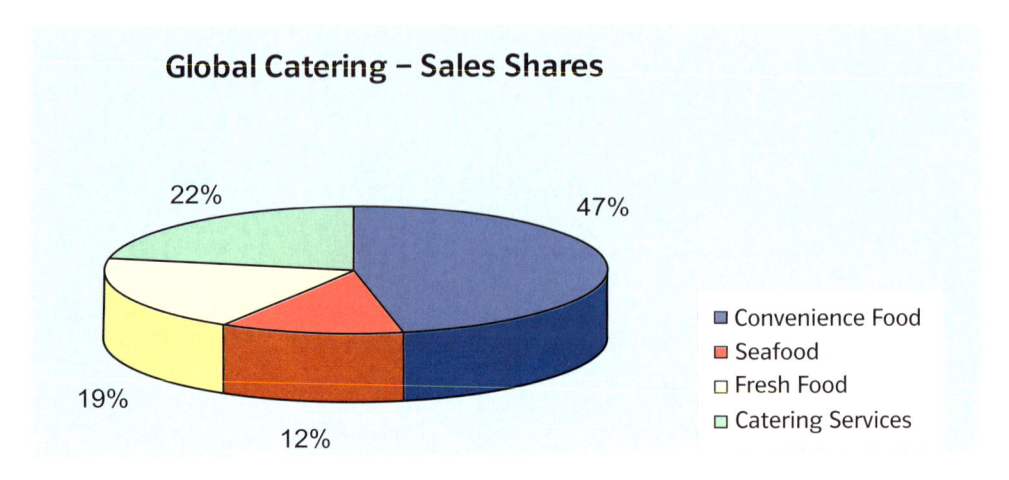

Global Catering – Sales Shares

- Convenience Food: 47%
- Seafood: 12%
- Fresh Food: 19%
- Catering Services: 22%

To describe shares (percentages)

to make **up** …/to account **for** …	Nail varnish makes up 20% and lipsticks account for half of the total.
to have a share/percentage/slice **of** …	Hairspray has a share of only 10 per cent.

1 Write down what Kirsty Burnham might say to describe the above pie chart on Global Catering's sales shares.

★ 2 Two years ago your company installed solar panels on the roof of an office building. As a number of your business partners are interested in this project, you are preparing a presentation in English for them. Describe the monthly electricity output in kWh generated by the solar panels in the first year. Note that in that year April was particularly sunny and July exceptionally wet.

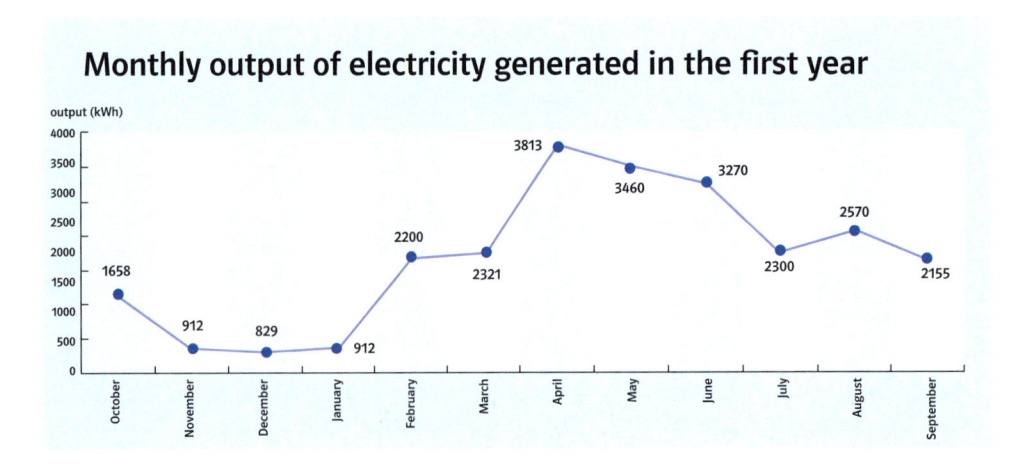

Monthly output of electricity generated in the first year

output (kWh)

- October: 1658
- November: 912
- December: 829
- January: 912
- February: 2200
- March: 2321
- April: 3813
- May: 3460
- June: 3270
- July: 2300
- August: 2570
- September: 2155

108

Office expert

1 Structuring presentations

1 Read the following guideline and summarise the main points as a list of dos and don'ts to keep in mind when preparing presentations.

The first step in preparing a talk or presentation is to think about **what you want to achieve**. Is the point to share information, convince your audience of something or motivate them?

Once you have set your goals, you have to think about **your audience** so you can customise your presentation to their needs. Will you be talking to experts or will your audience have little knowledge or experience about your topic? What are their expectations? What kind of questions might they ask?

After determining the focus of your presentation, you will need to **line up the facts** to support your point of view. Your data – whether as text or in graphical form – should be accurate and complete to portray you as a reliable source of information.

You have to consider your priorities, **your key points** and just how much detail you want to include. Finding the right balance here isn't always easy; too much information and you'll overwhelm your audience, too little will leave them feeling they haven't been adequately informed.

One of the most essential aspects is not to ramble but to outline your talk and give it **a clear structure**. The general rule is to tell them what you're going to tell them (forecast), tell them, and then tell them what you told them (summary). A point that is sometimes overlooked but which is also important is the need to signpost your talk. This means indicating clearly to your audience what point in the presentation you are currently at (for example, "My first point …", "In conclusion …").

As any successful speaker will tell you, **rehearsing your presentation** is an absolute must. Experts often recommend practising out loud in front of a mirror or even videotaping your practice sessions, keeping eye contact, body language and pace in mind.

Last but not least, it's not a good idea to leave anything to chance. Make sure you know how to use the **equipment** without any problems and that it is set up and ready to run when you need it.

Unit 7 | Making presentations

2 Read the following advice and use it to prepare a software presentation with a
P   partner about this topic. You may also include the guideline from Exercise 1 on
    page 109 in your presentation. Present the results in class.

> ### Rules to keep in mind when designing a presentations
>
> First, you need to think about the **background**. Contrast and consistency are the two most important criteria, i.e. you should choose a background that is different from the fonts and stick to one background. For projections a light text on a semi-dark background is better as the eye is attracted to light. Select a simple textured background to make the text easier to read.
> The **bullet points** should be placed along the left margin of the page, one above the other to give a neat appearance and provide more room for the text.
> **Graphics** should be placed off centre, generally on the left. They should also match the message and not just be for decoration.
> **Capitalization rules** and your **choice of fonts** are important. You should not write everything in capital letters because such text is hard to read and aggressive. It is a good idea to just capitalize the first word of the title and of each bullet point. Exceptions are, of course, proper nouns, such as names of companies, people, places, etc. If you capitalize the first words of the bullet points on one page, you should do so throughout your presentation. When translating from German into English, remember that nouns are not normally capitalized in English. Also remember to proofread the entire text carefully.
> You should use just one type of font (e.g. Arial), two at the most, per presentation. The fonts should be easy to read and at least 14pt large.
> **Colours** should be used sparingly and consistently. For example, you might choose one colour for the fonts of all your titles and a somewhat darker or lighter shade of the same colour for the rest of your text. Avoid the colour red because it is aggressive and difficult to read.
> The mistake many people make is to place too much text on the screen. You should try and **shorten your message**, keep it easy to understand and not write everything out in complete sentences. A good idea is to try and follow the "7 x 7" rule, i.e. to create pages with a maximum of seven words across and seven lines down.

2 Drawing graphs

1 Label the following diagrams (1.–5.) with the English terms (a.–e.).

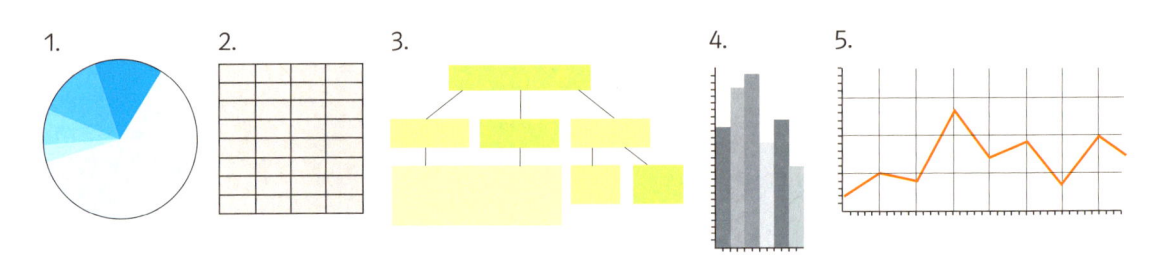

1.   2.   3.   4.   5.

a. bar chart   b. line graph   c. organigram   d. pie chart   e. table

2 Listen to two descriptions of economic developments and draw the graphs.
R
A 2.16

Phrases: Making presentations

To make a presentation

I should like to start **by** telling you something about my company/organisation.	Zunächst möchte ich Ihnen etwas über meine Firma/mein Unternehmen sagen.
First, I should like to introduce my company briefly.	Als Erstes möchte ich Ihnen mein Unternehmen kurz vorstellen.
My presentation will deal **with** …	Meine Präsentation behandelt …
I intend to keep my presentation as brief as possible.	Ich möchte meine Präsentation so kurz wie möglich halten.
I would like to focus **on** the following points/areas/products/services:	Ich möchte mich auf folgende Punkte/Gebiete/Produkte/Dienstleistungen konzentrieren:
I would welcome any questions **at** the end of my presentation.	Ich wäre gern bereit, etwaige Fragen am Ende meiner Präsentation zu beantworten.
Has everyone received a copy of the handout?	Haben alle den Handzettel bekommen?
The handout summarises the main points and gives an overview of the relevant figures and statistics.	Der Handzettel enthält die Hauptpunkte und gibt einen Überblick über die entsprechenden Zahlen und Statistiken.

To structure the main part of your presentation

Now my second point is …	Ich komme nun zu Punkt 2 …
Thirdly, let me give you some basic statistics.	Drittens darf ich Ihnen ein paar grundlegende Statistiken zeigen.
The gist of the matter/central issue is …	Der Kernpunkt/die zentrale Frage ist …
I should now like to move **on** to the next topic.	Ich möchte nun gern zum nächsten Thema kommen.
An excellent example **of** this is …	Ein hervorragendes Beispiel dafür ist …
I should like to give you an example to illustrate this point.	Ich möchte diesen Punkt mit einem Beispiel erläutern.
A distinct trend emerges **from** the figures.	Aus den Zahlen geht ein deutlicher Trend hervor.
In this connection it is worth mentioning …	In diesem Zusammenhang sollte man erwähnen, …

To conclude your presentation

To sum **up** we can say that …	Zusammenfassend kann man sagen, dass …
I should like to finish **by** saying/thanking the organisers/pointing out …	Ich möchte schließen mit der Bemerkung/dem Dank an die Organisatoren/dem Hinweis …

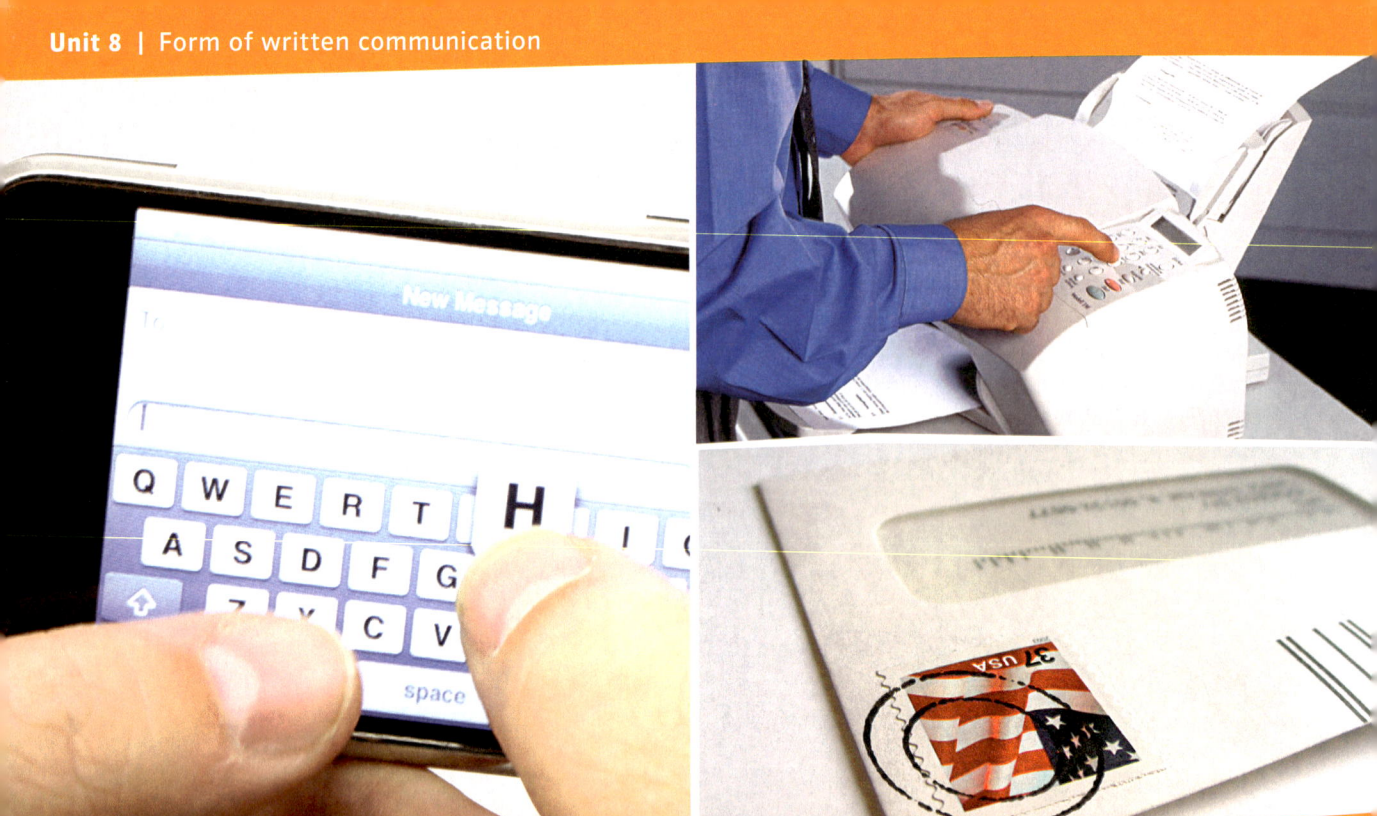

Unit 8
Form of written communication

WORD BANK
e-mail • facsimile message • letter • sender • letterhead • addressee • recipient • attention line • reference line • date • attachment • subject • salutation • initials • complimentary close • signature • covering page • enclosure • structure • paragraph • style • linking words • to attach • to delete • to forward

Written communication plays an essential role in business in cases where documentation in writing is required. It may, for instance, also be used to ensure that misunderstandings cannot arise. However, in recent years the traditional letter has increasingly been replaced by new, quicker and frequently less formal media. In business correspondence the letter has now largely been replaced by e-mails and to a lesser degree by faxes.

1 Work with a partner. Make a grid for yourself like the one below. Then read the text that follows and fill in your grid. Compare the result with your partner's information in the grid.

	Advantages	Disadvantages
E-Mail		
Letter		
Fax		

Online-Link
808261-0008

The advantages of **e-mails** are too well-known to require explanation here. However, there are a number of disadvantages. Spam is a major time waster. According to one source 95% of e-mails sent worldwide are spam. Hence the need to install spam filters. Security is also a major issue. E-mails and attachments may be used to transfer spyware and other viruses. Privacy is also a problem – you cannot be sure that your e-mails are not being read by an unauthorised third party. Finally, authenticity – who is the e-mail really from? – is a further issue undermining the reliability and safety of e-mails which can be addressed by installing digital signatures. Sometimes one might feel it's safer to entrust one's important message to the old-fashioned snail-mail!

In international business transactions **faxes** are used to communicate with partners in countries where the e-mail system is still unsatisfactory or unreliable. Faxes are also preferred to e-mails whenever business people want their partners to have some written (and possibly signed) evidence of a transaction. Faxes, like e-mails, may also be used where speed is essential, e.g. for offers. Signatures on faxes are nowadays recognised as evidence even by the courts.

The business **letter** is still widely used in legal contexts, in connection with formal contracts and complaints. Such letters are often "faxed and posted", i.e. sent by fax and by post. Only a letter ensures that the communication is not read by an unauthorised person. Letters also serve as covering letters when a catalogue or similar enclosure is to be sent.

2 Translate the following English sentences into German.

M

1. Letters have largely been replaced by e-mails.
2. E-mails can be addressed to several people at the same time.
3. Worms and viruses may make it necessary to instal protective software.
4. It is a disadvantage that e-mails cannot easily be signed.
5. In some countries the e-mail system is unsatisfactory or unreliable.
6. It may sometimes be necessary to have written evidence of a transaction.
7. Business letters are still widely used in connection with formal contracts.
8. A letter is less likely to be read by unauthorised persons.

Unit 8 | Form of written communication

A Layout and components of business correspondence

1 E-Mails*

From:	stella.starr@shineandsparkle-uk.com
To:	info@sunshineflights.co.uk
Cc:	f.pluto@shineandsparkle-usa.com
Sent:	201_-08-14 15:18
Attachments:	
Subject:	Package tours to the Dominican Republic

Dear Sunshine Flights — salutation

As an incentive we wish to offer a one-week package tour to the Dominican Republic to our most successful sales representatives. Please make us preliminary offers for at least three price categories. — body of e-mail

Kind regards — complimentary close

Stella Starr
Marketing Manager — signature block

Shine and Sparkle UK Ltd.
143 High Street
Starminster
BS34 1BU
Tel. 01420 562 265 — signature footer

---

* Both ways of spelling are acceptable, **e-mail** and **email**.

114

Info: E-mails

From:	Your e-mail address will appear automatically.
To:	Be careful not to make the slightest mistake when entering the recipient's address, or else the e-mail will be returned.
Cc:	The abbreviation stands for "carbon copy". With old-style typewriters copies used to be made by inserting carbon paper between the blank sheets of paper. This is where you enter the addresses of the persons to whom you wish the message to be forwarded.
Bcc:	Addresses listed under "Blind Carbon Copy" do not appear in the message header of the other recipients.
Sent:	Instead of "Sent" you may find the word "Date". The correct date and time will be entered automatically.
Attachments:	Any kind of file, such as word documents (.doc), excel sheets (.xls), pictures (e.g. .jpg), etc. can be attached to an e-mail.
Subject:	You should always mention the precise subject matter of your correspondence. Firstly it will help your business partner to deal with your mail and secondly it will prevent him/her from deleting it for fear of viruses.
Salutation:	Very formal salutations like "Dear Sirs" or "Gentlemen:" are not used in e-mails. Use "Dear …" instead. In the English-speaking world correspondence is personalised whenever possible: Dear Fiona Dear Ms Starr or even (to avoid "Dear Sirs"): Dear Sunshine Flights
Body of the e-mail:	Note that the first word starts with a capital letter.
Complimentary close:	There is a range of expressions to choose from, like: With best/kind regards Kind/Best regards Regards Best wishes or (very formal in e-mails) Yours sincerely
Signature block:	Write your title or department below your name. In Britain women often add (Miss) or (Mrs) in brackets after their name, e.g. Janine Smith (Miss), if they wish to be addressed in this way.
Signature footer:	Add your company's full name, address and telephone number to all e-mails you send to persons or companies who may not know you or your firm.

Do not use special characters like ß, ä, ö or ü. They may come out very strangely at the other end! Use ss, ae, oe and ue instead.

Unit 8 | Form of written communication

1. Choose the appropriate alternative from the brackets.

1. You may (enclose/**attach**) files to an e-mail. *anhängen*
2. You should always watch out for (**viruses**/germs). *Viren*
3. Make sure that you (wipe out/**delete**) suspicious e-mails. *entfernen / löschen*
4. E-mails can be (passed on/**forwarded**) to third parties. *weiterleiten*
5. Do not forget to mention the (theme/**subject**) of your e-mail. *Anlass / Betreff*
6. E-mails always start with the (complimentary close/**salutation**). *Anrede*
7. The recipient or (**addressee**/sender) is the person the e-mail is sent to. *Adressant*

2. Study the example e-mail on page 114. Then restore the correct order of the jumbled elements below and rewrite the e-mail.

(1) **Sent:** 201_-11-09

(2) **Cc:** walter-elliot@kellynchhall.ie

(3) Thank you.
Kind regards
Nancy

(4) **From:** nancy.steele@jenningsfood.com

(5) Jennings Food Ltd.
Delaford Industrial Estate
Barton
GU7 3AB
Tel. 01430 37968

(6) Sorry to inform you that the 150 picnic hampers as per yesterday's order have not yet arrived. Please make sure that we get them by tomorrow 11 a.m. at the very latest.

(7) Dear Kitty

(8) **To:** k.bennet@longbourne.co.uk

(9) **Subject:** Late delivery

Form of written communication | Unit 8

3 Search the Internet and find out about "netiquette" and "texting abbreviations". Make notes and compare your findings with the group. Send a text message in English using appropriate abbreviations to one of your classmates.

> **Info: How to write e-mails**
>
> - Keep messages short and to the point.
> - Focus on one subject per message and include a relevant subject title for the message.
> - Include your signature footer when communicating with persons who may not know you personally.
> - Capitalize words only to highlight an important point. Capitalizing is generally felt to be like SHOUTING!
> - Be sparing in your use of exclamation marks.
> - Never send chain letters through the Internet.
> - Be professional and be careful what you say. E-mails are easily forwarded.
> - Be careful when using sarcasm and humour.
> - Never assume that your e-mails will be read only by you and the recipient.
> - Emoticons like :-) for "happy" or ;-) for "only joking" should be reserved for communication with business partners with whom you are on a familiar footing.
> - Use abbreviations sparingly as you cannot be sure that your partner in a foreign country is familiar with them.

4 Your colleague does not speak English. Explain the above information to him in German.

You might begin like this:
„Ich habe im Internet interessante Hinweise über das, was man bei E-Mails beachten soll, gefunden. Der Text beginnt mit der Ermahnung E-Mails kurz und präzise zu formulieren. Man soll sich auf ein Thema pro Mail beschränken und einen passenden Betreff wählen …"

2 Faxes

There is no established layout for faxes (facsimile messages). Firms are free to design their own covering page. A typical one could look like this:

Herkules
the global sports brand

Ziegelberg 8–12
89331 Neustadt
Tel. +49 8358 888-0
Fax +49 8358 88820
www.Herkules.com

Telefax Message

To:	India Sports 112 Delhi Road, Meerut-250 001 Uttar Pradesh, India	**Attention:** **Fax:**	Mr. Kunal Mahajan +91 121 2512275
From:	Laura Bayerle, Purchasing Department		
Date:	1 Feb 201_	**Pages:**	(incl. this page) 1
Subject:	Our order No. ABF / 16 of 20 January		

Dear Mr. Mahajan

If it is possible, we should like to increase our order for item 345 (plain navy T-shirts) from 1750 to 2000 units for the sizes L and XL.

Please let me know by return whether you are in a position to dispatch the extra articles together with the rest of our order.

Thank you very much.

Regards

Laura Bayerle
Laura Bayerle

If you do not receive all the pages, please advise us as soon as possible.

Form of written communication | Unit 8

Info: Fax

The **names, addresses, telephone** and **fax numbers** of both the sender and the addressee should be recorded on the fax. The **date** is also essential as well as an appropriate **subject line**. As fax transmissions are sometimes interrupted, the **number of pages** is mentioned to show the recipient whether any pages are missing. If you send a business letter by fax, write the recipient's fax number below the inside address and refer to the total number of pages on the first page.

1 Use the fax on page 118 as an example and rewrite the following fax using the correct spacing and punctuation.
P

> Getränke König Am Sprudelbach 17 06122 Halle Tel. 0345 785634 Fax 0345 785635 Telefax To BIG Beverages Ltd 38 Cromwell Road Chipping OX7 5SR UK Fax +44 1608 647919 Attention Ms Maggy Lane From Nicole Sachse Import Department Date 31 Jan 201_ Pages incl. this one 1 Subject Our order for 500 bottles of Tropicana Fruit Juice of 28 Jan Dear Ms Lane I am sorry to cause you trouble but our client has just informed us that he needs the fruit juice as early as Friday next week I trust you will be able to bring forward delivery by three days Thank you for your co-operation Best wishes *Nicole Sachse* Nicole Sachse

2 Study the fax on page 118. Then restore the correct order of the jumbled elements
R / P below and rewrite the fax.

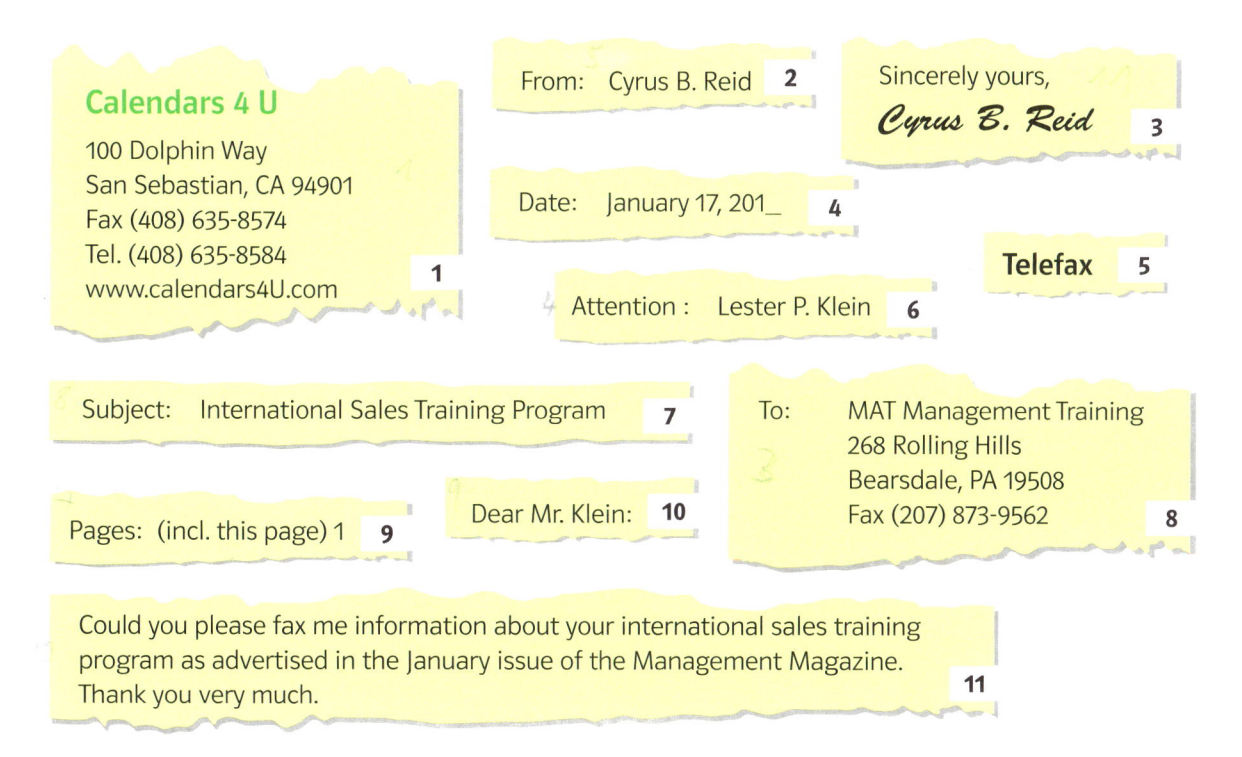

Calendars 4 U
100 Dolphin Way
San Sebastian, CA 94901
Fax (408) 635-8574
Tel. (408) 635-8584
www.calendars4U.com   **1**

From: Cyrus B. Reid   **2**

Sincerely yours,
Cyrus B. Reid   **3**

Date: January 17, 201_   **4**

Telefax   **5**

Attention :   Lester P. Klein   **6**

Subject: International Sales Training Program   **7**

To: MAT Management Training
268 Rolling Hills
Bearsdale, PA 19508
Fax (207) 873-9562   **8**

Pages: (incl. this page) 1   **9**

Dear Mr. Klein: **10**

Could you please fax me information about your international sales training program as advertised in the January issue of the Management Magazine. Thank you very much.   **11**

119

Unit 8 | Form of written communication

3 Business letters

1 Match the numbers (1–11) in the following business letter with the letters (A–K)
R   in the definitions given on the following pages.

International Snacks GmbH (1)   Fürstenstr. 19
                                                      40547 Düsseldorf
                                                      Tel. 0211 577563
                                                      Fax 0211 577566
                                          E-Mail info@internationalsnacks.de
                                                   www.internationalsnacks.de

RH / rf   (2)

14 August 201_   (3)

Global Catering   (4)
17 Nelson Square
Manchester
MA17 3DF
UK

Attention: Ms Kirsty Burnham   (5)

Dear Ms Burnham   (6)

Brochure on rules and regulations   (7)

As promised on the occasion of your recent visit to our company I am sending you enclosed the translation of the brochure on the German rules and regulations for food processing in the catering industry.

May I take this opportunity of thanking you and Mr. Sears for your visit.
My colleagues and I greatly enjoyed meeting you in person.   (8)

Yours sincerely   (9)
International Snacks GmbH   (10)

Markus Diepholz

Markus Diepholz
Export Manager

Enc.   (11)

120

A **Letterhead** shows a company's logo, name and address, its telephone, fax and e-mail numbers and its Internet address.

B **Reference line** may show the initials of the signatory and the secretary or references to files or departments.

C **Date**
As 07/08/12 would mean 7 August 2012 for an Englishman and 8 July 2012 for an American, it is advisable to write out the month. The following ways of writing the date are recommended:
7 August 2012   or   7 Aug 2012   or   August 7, 2012
Note that the year is written out in full.
Giving the year first, then the month and then the day is rapidly becoming accepted worldwide: 2012-08-07.

D **Inside address**

British usage   **North American usage**

Messrs J. McDream & Co.   Samantha Duvet
91 Malvern Road   The Mattress Corporation
Ashford   1386 Munras Avenue
Kent   Monterey, CA 93940
CA3 6AH   USA
UK

Note that in British business letters Messrs, Mr, Mrs, Ms and Miss are written on the same line as the name. In the USA they are often omitted altogether. Messrs is only used for smaller firms, such as partnerships. Do not write Messrs if the company's name is followed by "Ltd", Plc", "Inc." or "Corp.". Ms should be used whenever the marital status of the female addressee is not known.

Note that in Great Britain the postal code is written on its own line below the place name, whereas in USA and Canada it is placed after the place name on the same line.

When letters are written to foreign countries, the name of the country should be shown on the final line of the inside address.

E **Attention line** ensures that the letter is dealt with by a specific person. You may write **Attention:**, **For the attention of ...:**, or (less formal) **FAO:**
As an alternative the person's name may be included in the inside address. This is a must if the recipient is addressed by name in the salutation.

Global Catering   Ms Kirsty Burnham
17 Nelson Square   Global Catering
Manchester   17 Nelson Square
MA17 3DF   Manchester
UK   MA17 3DF
                                           UK
Attention: Ms Kirsty Burnham

Unit 8 | Form of written communication

F Salutation (UK)

Dear Sirs, Dear Sir/Madam

Dear Ms Burnham
Dear Customer
Dear Margaret

Salutation (USA and Canada)

(Ladies and) Gentlemen:
To whom it may concern:
Dear Mr O'Reilly:
Dear Sean:

G Complimentary close (UK)

Yours faithfully/sincerely
(Yours faithfully is rarely used now)
Yours sincerely, Kind regards
Yours sincerely
Best regards, Kind regards,
Best wishes

Complimentary close (USA and Canada)

Sincerely, Very truly yours,
Sincerely, Sincerely yours,
Yours truly, Sincerely, Sincerely yours,
Regards, Cordially,

If at all possible you should address the person you are writing to by name. "Dear Sirs" or "Gentlemen:" is only used when you do not have a name to write to. Traditionally salutation and complimentary close should be in line with each other.

H Body of the letter
Note that in English the first word of a business letter starts with a capital letter.

I Subject line
may be preceded by the words "Subject" or "Re" and should be as specific as possible. Do not just write **"Your offer"** but **"Your offer for mouse pads of 23 May"**. In the UK subject lines are normally written below the salutation, in the USA above the salutation. They may be either underlined or typed in capital letters or **bold** type.

vorausgegangen

fett

J Enclosure
Whenever enclosures are sent with a letter, a reference to the enclosure is required at the bottom of the letter. You may write "Enclosure(s)" or "Enc(s)".

K Signature block
In the UK – but not in the USA – the signature block often begins with the company's name. The signatory's name and title (or department) are typed below the signature. If somebody signs the letter on behalf of another person, the other person's name is typed below the signature, preceded by the word **"for"** or by the abbreviation **pp.** meaning "on behalf of".

Namen

NetOrbiter Ltd.
Maria Bertram
pp. Henry Crawford
Chief Information Officer

Fred Parry
for Betty Bickerton
Credit Manager

2 Work with a partner. Find the right order for these jumbled addresses. Then dictate them to your partner.

UK
Woodbridge
Messrs Frost & Winter
22 James Street
Suffolk
IP3 7KL
Managerial Skills Training

Ultimate IT Solutions Inc.
USA
Denver, CO 80121
Barbara Goodyear
1280 Mayflower Drive

Attention: Tom Finch
4 Tamar Industrial Estate
UK
Finch Electronics Ltd.
PL3 7CT
Plymouth

3 Seven elements are missing from this traditional business letter. Copy the letter
R/P and add the missing elements using your own imagination for details.

Superdress GmbH

Fritz-Walter-Str. 28, 80469 München
Tel. +49 89 4677524, Fax +49 89 4677625
www.superdress.munich.de

TS / is

Mr Tony Shaw
Wilson and Thatcher Ltd.
2 Brook Lane
Bristol
BS9 2ET

We are pleased to enclose our Spring Catalogue showing our absolutely fabulous range of shirts. We feel sure that they will appeal to your young customers. If you place an order within the next two weeks, you will be granted 3% early order discount.

We look forward to welcoming you as a customer.

Resi Martl

Unit 8 | Form of written communication

B Structure and style of business correspondence

1 Beginning, main part and end

Business correspondence must be well organised. The body of the correspondence should consist of three separate parts: the beginning, the main part and the end.

The **beginning** is either a single sentence or a short paragraph that states the reason why you are writing the correspondence. Example: I am going to be in Boston on May 20, and would like to meet you, if possible.

The **main part** contains the details. There should be a separate paragraph for every new idea. Example: Every now and then the new software does not provide the degree of protection against spam that we had expected. That is why I would like to discuss the problem with you personally.
A morning meeting would be best for me. Would 9 a.m. be convenient for you?

In the end section the writer sums up and underlines what he/she would like the recipient to do. Alternatively he/she may add a remark designed to create goodwill. Example: If this fits in with your schedule, please leave a message with my secretary. I look forward to seeing you in Boston.

Especially when you are writing to a customer it is advisable to end the communication on a friendly note.

Business correspondence should meet the so-called ABC specifications:
Accurate correct and complete as to facts
Brief short sentences, simple expressions, plain English
Clear easy, natural style, without formality or familiarity

R/P Put the eight jumbled elements of this correspondence into the correct order and write it out.

1. Furthermore, we would like to draw your attention to our latest development, small wind turbines for commercial and domestic use. Please see page 3 of our catalogue.

2. Yours sincerely

3. Should you need any further information please contact us at any time.

4. As an attachment we are sending you our catalogue and price list. These already include a 25% trade discount. We also offer quantity discounts for major orders. Our terms of payment are 30 days net.

124

| 5 | Dear Mr Wyndham |

| 6 | We look forward to receiving your first order which will be given top priority. |

| 7 | Your e-mail enquiry of 18 June |

| 8 | Thank you for your interest in our solar panels. |

2 Linking words

Business correspondence is often made up of standard phrases. In order for the correspondence to read smoothly such individual text-building blocks ought to be connected by **linking words** like **also**, **as well as**, **both** … **and**, **in addition**, **moreover**, **further**, **firstly**, **secondly**, **finally** etc. which suggest a list. Example: **Finally**, we should like to confirm the date for next year's fashion show.

Other linking words imply a contrast: **whereas**, **while**, **in contrast to**, **however**, **although** etc. Example: Last month sales of DVD players rose by 3.5 per cent **whereas** sales of TV sets fell by 2.8 percent.

The following linking words indicate that an explanation is being given: **this is why**, **therefore**, **thus**, **as**, **because** etc. Example: We are most dissatisfied with your services. **This is why** we have decided to instruct a different company.

Translate the following sentences into German. Note particularly the linking words in bold type.

1. He is very unhappy with the service. **This is why** he has stopped going to that restaurant.
2. Last year wages increased **whereas** retail sales stagnated.
3. **First,** delivery by road is quicker and **second**, it is more flexible.
4. We have decided not to place further orders **as** there have been so many delays.
5. **Both** our company **and** our suppliers have experienced strong growth this year.
6. We are prepared to place an order for 1000 notebooks. **However**, we expect a substantial quantity discount.
7. There has been severe flooding in this part of the country. **In addition**, we have been faced with prolonged electricity cuts.
8. **Although** we were not entirely satisfied with the execution of our previous order, we are prepared to give your company another chance.
9. Our canteen offers three different menus. We **also** serve vegetarian dishes.
10. **Finally**, we would like to thank you once more for making this concession.

Unit 8 | Form of written communication

Language and grammar 1
Decide which of the alternatives in brackets is correct.

1. I suggest (that you wait/to wait) for the outcome of the inspection.
2. We would appreciate (if you could/it if you could) let us have your confirmation by return.
3. We would appreciate (receiving/to receive) your prompt reply.
4. We would like to (excuse us/apologize) for not having reacted earlier.
5. Please (excuse/apologize) the inconvenience caused by this incident.
6. We look forward (to doing/to do) business with you.
7. We hope (to be entrusted/to being entrusted) with your order.
8. I would appreciate (to hear/hearing) from you soon.
9. We would suggest (to ring/ringing) Fisher's bookshop in Cambridge.
10. I would appreciate (it if you sent/if you sent) a driver to the airport.

Language and grammar 2
Find the English equivalents of the following German phrases.

1. Wir möchten uns für die entstandenen Unannehmlichkeiten entschuldigen.
2. Wir sehen Ihrer baldigen Antwort mit Interesse entgegen.
3. Bitte entschuldigen Sie dieses Versehen.
4. Wir hoffen, bald wieder von Ihnen zu hören.
5. Wir schlagen vor, die Teile per Luftfracht zu schicken.
6. Wir möchten Ihnen vorschlagen, die Sache mit der Geschäftsleitung zu besprechen.
7. Wir wären Ihnen für eine ausführliche Beschreibung sehr dankbar.
8. Ich würde vorschlagen, ein Taxi zu nehmen.
9. Wir freuen uns, Ihren Auftrag in Kürze zu erhalten.
10. Für diese Verzögerung bitten wir um Entschuldigung.

Language and grammar:
Typical mistakes in business correspondence

Wer diese Verben korrekt verwendet, vermeidet die häufigsten Fehler, die Deutschen beim Verfassen englischer Geschäftskorrespondenz unterlaufen.

suggest (vorschlagen)
We suggest **repeating** the test.
We suggest **that you (we) repeat** the test.
falsch: We suggest ~~to repeat~~ the test.

appreciate (schätzen, begrüßen, dankbar sein, anerkennen)
(a) We would appreciate **it** if you could assist us.
("**it**" is absolutely necessary here!)
(b) We would appreciate **receiving** the unit as soon as possible.
falsch: We would appreciate ~~to receive~~ the unit as soon as possible.

apologize (sich entschuldigen)
We **apologize for** the delay.
falsch: We ~~excuse us~~ for the delay.

excuse (verzeihen, entschuldigen)
Please **excuse** the delay.
falsch: Please ~~apologize~~ the delay.

look forward to (entgegensehen, sich freuen auf)
We look forward to **hearing** from you soon.
falsch: We look forward to ~~hear~~ from you soon.

hope (hoffen)
We hope **to hear** from you soon.
falsch: We hope to ~~hearing~~ from you soon.

Communicating across cultures:
The tone of English business correspondence

What is considered polite differs in different cultures. For example, one-word answers such as "ja", "nein" are not impolite in German. If I say: "Sollen wir ins Kino gehen?", you could answer "Ja" in German. In English people would be more inclined to say "Yes, that would be nice / great". Thus, German business correspondence tends to be factual and to the point. Polite phrases are often considered superfluous. While this abrupt tone is generally accepted in Germany, it may seem rude to English-speaking people or sound as though you are not interested. That is why you ought to aim to make frequent use of expressions like: **We would like to** (inform you); **I would be grateful** (if you could help me), **I am afraid** (the system is not running smoothly); **We are very sorry** (to inform you); **Would you be so kind as** (to inform us in time) in your English correspondence. Do not forget to insert the word **please** whenever you make a request, e.g.: If we can be of further assistance **please** do not hesitate to contact us.
Note: Please do not say: ~~We kindly ask you~~ …, say **We would like to ask you** … instead.

Office expert

1 Word processing

1 Complete the following text with the terms in the box.

> Cut and paste • hard copies • hyphenation • insert • justification • margins • Search • word processor • word wrap

With a **1** you can not only create and store documents, but also change them. Though there are different word processors, they all support a row of basic features. Probably the most useful one is their ability to delete or **2** characters, words, paragraphs or even whole sections of a text. If you make a typo, you just back up the cursor and correct it. **3** allows you to cut out or remove part of the text from one place in the document and insert or paste it in where you want to have it. You can also copy a section of the text by simply highlighting it. With a printer you can make **4** of your text.

With a word processor you can also determine different page sizes and **5** so that the text fits the page. **6** and replace is another useful feature that has the software look through the whole text for a certain word or phrase to either delete or replace it. With **7** the word processor moves from one line to the next as they are filled with text. To give your document a professional appearance, word processors also generally feature automatic hyphenation and justification. Using a comprehensive dictionary, the automatic **8** constantly checks words as you input them. If a word is too long when you come to the end of a line, it is split, a hyphen is added and the rest of the word is placed on the next line. **9** spaces your words evenly across a line so that the text is in line with the margin.

2 Match the word processing terms (1.–8.) to the descriptions (a.–h.).

1. graphics
2. headers and footers
3. mail merging
4. page numbering
5. spell checker
6. thesaurus
7. windows
8. word completion

a. lets you insert text from one file into another for mass mailings
b. finds words with similar meaning
c. highlights misspelt words and offers alternatives
d. the right one automatically appears on each page
e. finishes longer words
f. let a text or graphic appear at the top or bottom of each page
g. allow you to work on two documents at a time
h. lets you insert or create your own illustrations

3 Find the English equivalents for the following German terms (1.–12.) in the exercises on page 128.

1. ausschneiden und einfügen
2. automatischer Zeilenumbruch
3. Kopf- und Fußzeile
4. Rechtschreibprüfung
5. Seitennummerierung
6. Seitenrand
7. Serienbrief
8. Silbentrennung
9. suchen und ersetzen
10. Synonymwörterbuch
11. Textverarbeitung
12. Wortvervollständigung

2 E-mail flood in the office

KMK Lesen Sie den folgenden Text über die Flut von E-Mails in Büros und beantworten Sie die untenstehenden Fragen auf Deutsch.

Surveys made in Germany and abroad show that office workers are overwhelmed by a daily flood of e-mails. Users in large companies receive and send an average of 85 e-mails per day. Experts estimate that some 60 billion e-mails are sent daily.

How important are these e-mails? The answer is: not very. Just 15% of the e-mails received are critical and another 38% important. The other half are made up of 20% bulk mail, 16% spam and 11% office chat.

The biggest problem, ironically, is that many – more than 50% of those surveyed – feel the need to check their e-mails every few minutes or at least a few times every hour. This leads to lost productivity with the pressure to answer any received e-mails as quickly as possible. Experts talk of information addiction because over 50% of those polled admit accessing their e-mail accounts at home in the evening and at the weekend.

What to do? Don't send copies to just anyone and everyone and limit checking your mail to four or five times a day.

1. Wie viele E-Mails werden täglich in Deutschland versandt?
2. Wie hoch ist der Prozentsatz an unerwünscht zugesandten E-Mails zu Werbezwecken?
3. Welche negative Auswirkung hat das ständige Abrufen und Beantworten von E-Mails?
4. Wie viel Prozent der befragten Personen rufen ihre E-Mails auch abends und am Wochenende ab?
5. Welche Ratschläge werden für den Umgang mit E-Mails gegeben?

Unit 8 | Form of written communication

Phrases: Correspondence – E-mail, Letter, Fax

To refer to previous communication

Thank you very much for your letter **of** …	Wir danken Ihnen für Ihren Brief vom …
Many thanks for your e-mail/e-mail.	Vielen Dank für Ihre E-Mail.
We refer to your fax **of** …	Wir nehmen Bezug auf Ihr Fax vom …
Further to our discussion **on** 2 May …	Im Anschluss an unser Gespräch am 2. Mai …

To ask for something

Please let us have …	Wir bitten Sie um …
Would you please send us …	Bitte schicken Sie uns …
Please be so kind **as** to send us …	Wir bitten Sie höflich uns … zu schicken.
We **would** like to ask you for …	Wir möchten Sie um … bitten.
Please make sure that …	Bitte sorgen Sie dafür, dass …

To communicate good news

We are pleased to inform you that …	Wir freuen uns Ihnen mitteilen zu können, dass …
You will be pleased to hear that …	Sie werden sich bestimmt darüber freuen, dass …
It is particularly gratifying that …	Besonders erfreulich ist, dass …

To refuse something

I'm afraid I cannot agree **to** this proposal.	Leider muss ich diesen Vorschlag ablehnen.
I'm afraid that sounds quite unacceptable **to** us.	Das ist für uns leider völlig inakzeptabel.
Much as we regret it, we have to say no.	Zu unserem großen Bedauern müssen wir eine abschlägige Antwort geben.
We regret that we are unable to assist you.	Wir bedauern, Ihnen nicht behilflich sein zu können.

To apologize

We are very sorry but …	Es tut uns sehr leid, aber …
We **would** like to apologize for the delay.	Wir möchten uns für die Verspätung entschuldigen.

| Please accept our apologies for this. | Wir entschuldigen uns dafür. |
| Please excuse the mix-up. | Bitte entschuldigen Sie die Verwechslung. |

To make a suggestion

We would suggest that you send us a copy.	Wir schlagen Ihnen vor, uns eine Kopie zu schicken.
May we suggest that you inform the supplier.	Wir möchten vorschlagen, den Lieferanten zu benachrichtigen.
It would be advisable to send the details **by** fax.	Es wäre gut, wenn Sie uns die näheren Angaben faxen könnten.

To request that something is done by a certain date

We need the components **by** Friday **at** the very latest.	Wir benötigen die Teile spätestens Freitag.
Please make sure that they arrive **no** later **than** the end of April.	Bitte sorgen Sie dafür, dass sie spätestens Ende April ankommen.
Monday, 31 July, is the final deadline.	Montag, der 31. Juli, ist der letzte Termin.

To end a correspondence on a friendly note

We **look forward to hearing** from you.	Wir sehen Ihrer Antwort mit Interesse entgegen.
We **hope to hear** from you soon.	Wir hoffen, bald von Ihnen zu hören.
We look forward to a long and fruitful business relationship.	Wir freuen uns auf lange und lohnende Geschäftsbeziehungen mit Ihrer Firma.
We look forward to serving you again.	Wir freuen uns darauf, Ihnen wieder zu Diensten sein zu können.
We look forward to welcoming you as our customers.	Wir würden Sie gerne als neuen Kunden begrüßen.
We hope this proposal will be of interest **to** you.	Wir hoffen, dieser Vorschlag findet Ihr Interesse.
We hope this information **will** help you.	Wir hoffen, dass diese Auskunft hilfreich für Sie ist.
Thank you for your assistance.	Wir danken Ihnen für Ihre Bemühungen.

Unit 9
Enquiries

WORD BANK

enquiries • transactions • supplier • source of information • website • quotation • cost estimate • brochure • price list • terms and conditions • samples • trade discount • quantity discount • cash discount • introductory discount

Business transactions often start with enquiries. **General enquiries** are requests for brochures, pricelists etc. and for information about business terms. **Specific enquiries** give particulars about the goods/services requested and ask for detailed **quotations**.

The internet is now the most convenient way of locating possible suppliers and this is facilitated by the use of search engines. Traditional sources of information, such as chambers of commerce, yellow pages and trade associations have their own websites offering links to many potential suppliers. Trade fairs and exhibitions, visits by agents and advertising campaigns also provide information on new products.

Read the text above and translate the German sentences into English.

1. Die Suche nach Lieferanten im Internet wird durch Suchmaschinen sehr erleichtert.
2. Industrie- und Handelskammern, Gelbe Seiten und Branchenverbände geben auch über das Internet Auskunft.
3. Auch auf Messen und Ausstellungen sowie durch Werbekampagnen und den Besuch eines Vertreters werden neue Produkte bekannt gemacht.

Enquiries | Unit 9

A Enquiries in writing

Sarah Brookfield, purchasing manager at SPORTS ISLAND, a British sports equipment chain, is interested in the latest running shoes presented by Herkules, the German manufacturers, on their website. She decides to make further enquiries by e-mail.

1 Study Sarah's e-mail enquiry and say which of the prepositions in brackets are correct.

From:	sarah.brookfield@sportsisland.co.uk
	Sarah Brookfield, purchasing manager, SPORTS ISLAND
To:	exports@herkules.com **Cc:**
Sent:	201_-09-25 **Attachments:**
Subject:	Enquiry about Herkules Turbostar running shoes

Dear Sir/Madam — *appropriate salutation*

We saw your presentation of the new Turbostar On and Off Road Running Shoe (**1** on/in) your website and would like to ask you (**2** for/of) further details. — *source of address*

We are a chain of sports equipment retailers with outlets (**3** at/in) 12 major cities in the UK. For further information (**4** on/of) our firm please see our website www.sportsisland.uk. — *introduction of your company*

Please inform us (**5** of/about) your export prices and possible discounts as well as your terms of payment and delivery. We may be placing regular orders (**6** about/for) 300 to 400 pairs of each size. We assume that you will be able to deliver (**7** from/off) stock.

request to send
- catalogues and price lists
- a quotation or cost estimate

request for information on
- prices and discounts
- terms of payment and delivery
- delivery periods

In conclusion may we ask you to send us samples (**8** for/to) test purposes.

further requests (if applicable)
- samples

Thank you for your attention (**9** at/to) our enquiry. We look forward to hearing (**10** of/from) you. — *closing phrase*

Best regards — *complimentary close*

Sarah Brookfield
Purchasing Manager

SPORTS ISLAND
41 Bryant Road
London W7 9QB
Tel. 020 74127333
Fax 020 74127334

Unit 9 | Enquiries

2 Cover up Sarah Brookfield's e-mail and complete these sentences on your own
R/P sheet of paper.

1. Sarah Brookfield saw a presentation of …
2. SPORTS ISLAND is a …
3. They would like to be informed about …
4. Their regular orders might comprise …
5. For test purposes they would like to have …
6. They look forward to …

3 Restore the correct order of these jumbled elements and rewrite the
R/P correspondence on your own sheet of paper.

1. We look forward to your early reply.

2. Please send us your price list and information on quantity discounts, terms of payment and delivery and indicate your shortest delivery time.

3. Subject: Topsweets Mint Bars

4. We are a German wholesaler specialising in confectionery for young people and are very interested in your Mint Bars as there is a rapidly growing market for British-type sweets here in Germany.

5. Yours sincerely
Zuckermann & Sacher GmbH

   Dieter Sacher

6. We would appreciate it if you could send us samples for test purposes.

7. Dear Topsweets Ltd

8. We would then place a trial order. If the mint bars sell well, we expect to place regular orders in future.

9. We saw the advertisement for your Topsweets Mint Bars in the March issue of the International Confectionery Journal and our general manager tasted them at a reception in the British Embassy in Berlin.

4 Copy the e-mail form below. Use the above correspondence and the phrases at
P the end of the unit and write a detailed e-mail enquiry about the new innovative generation of tablet PCs. You saw their advertisement in the computer journal "IT.COM!". Address your e-mail to IT.COM, ITcom@aol.com, using your own name and a company name of your choice. Use your imagination for any details you may need.

Phrases

From:

To: Cc:
Sent: Attachments:

Subject:

134

Enquiries | Unit 9

5 Sie arbeiten bei Getränke König, Am Sprudelbach 17, 06122 Halle, Tel. 03 45
KMK 78 56 34, Fax 03 45 78 56 35 im Einkauf. Ihre Firma möchte ihren guten Kunden zu Weihnachten ein besonderes Geschenk machen. Ihre Chefin, Nicole Sachse, hat auf der Hompage des irischen Glasherstellers Wexford Crystal plc, 1 Wexford Avenue, Sanditon, County Cork, Republic of Ireland, farbige Kristallgläser für Long Drinks im Geschenkkarton zu je drei Stück gesehen.

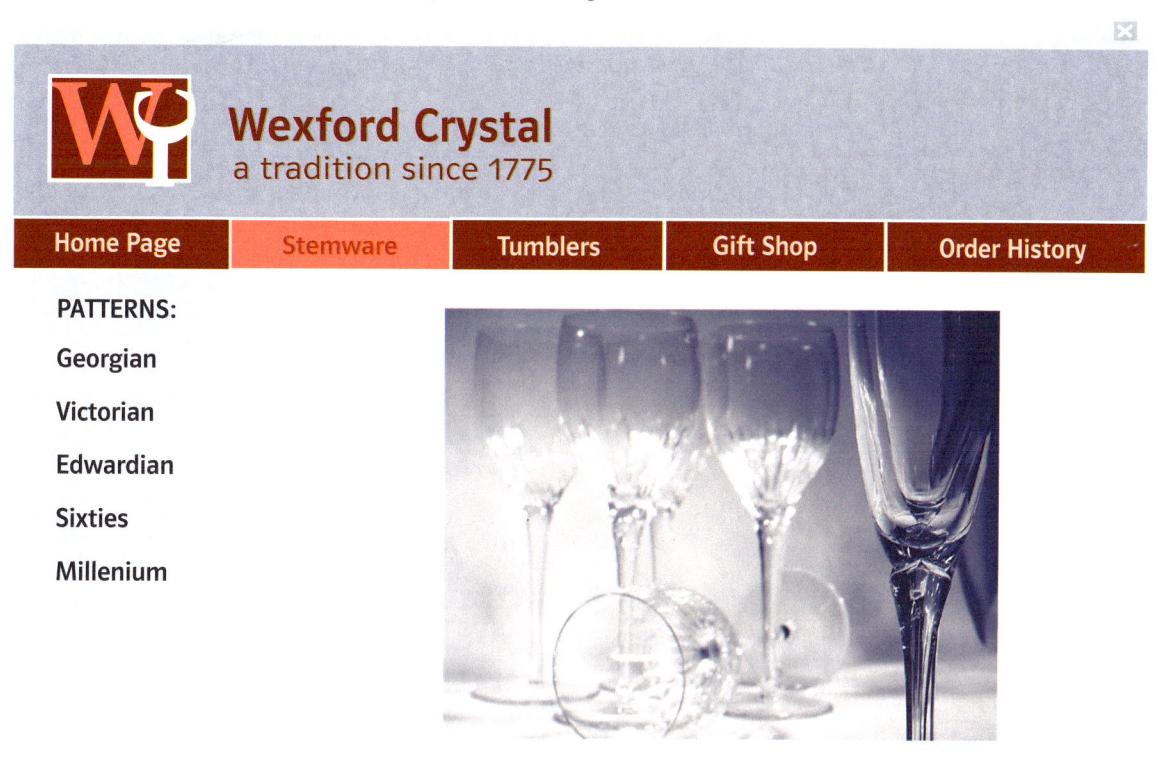

Wexford Crystal
a tradition since 1775

| Home Page | Stemware | Tumblers | Gift Shop | Order History |

PATTERNS:
Georgian
Victorian
Edwardian
Sixties
Millenium

Sie bittet Sie eine Anfrage, die sie selbst unterschreiben wird, zu verfassen und dabei folgende Punkte zu berücksichtigen:

- Datum 1. September
- Betreff
- Bezug auf Internetseiten von Wexford Crystal
- Vorstellung Ihrer Firma als einer führenden Getränkegroßhandlung, Firmenbroschüre liegt bei
- Grund Ihrer Anfrage
- Bitte um Zusendung von Prospekten und Preislisten
- Bitte um Angabe der Lieferzeit
- Bitte um Angabe der Liefer- und Zahlungsbedingungen
- Sonderwunsch: nur je zwei Gläser pro Geschenkpackung
- Umfang eines möglichen Auftrags: 3 000 Sets
- Bitte um baldige Antwort
- Anlage: Firmenbroschüre

> Phrases

Unit 9 | Enquiries

6 Your stressed out boss, a Canadian, feels he is in desperate need of a wellness holiday on a Caribbean island. Check out wellness holidays on the Caribbean Commonwealth island of Santa (or Saint) Lucia and make notes for him in English. Your boss is very demanding and only the best is good enough for him.

B Enquiries by phone

1 Restore the order of this jumbled dialogue. Match the numbers with the letters.

1. Calendars 4 U. Michael Bennet speaking. How can I help you?
2. Certainly. Please let me have your address.
3. Thank you. I'll post it today.
4. Yes of course. And full details of our generous discounts for volume orders.
5. My pleasure. Thank you for calling.

a. That's good. Thank you.
b. It's 30, Netherfield Road, Winchester SO2 9LZ. And my name is Jonathan Denny.
c. I take it the brochure contains a price list?
d. Hello. My name is Jonathan Denny. I'm interested in your animal calendars. Could you send me a brochure?
e. Goodbye.

2 Listen to the dialogue and check your work.
R
A 1.22

V4 Video lounge General enquiries

This video shows an enquiry by telephone. Look out for the answers to the following questions:

1. Compare the appearance of the two women. Which do you find more appropriately/appealingly dressed?
2. What seems to be the secretary's main activity apart from answering the phone?
3. What is Purple Fashion enquiring about?
4. What kind of order does she wish to place first?
5. What discount does the manufacturer offer her? What discount does she want?
6. What is the final discount offered?
7. What is the total amount of the invoice?
8. How long does delivery take?

Enquiries | Unit 9

3 Working with a partner now create and act out a similar dialogue along the
I/P   following lines.

Phrases

A

Linda/Larry Lawson from the British language school Business Speak in Brighton gets a call.

Linda/Larry Lawson offers to send a detailed brochure and asks for the caller's address.

Linda/Larry Lawson promises to send the brochure by post the next morning and thanks the caller for his/her interest in their courses. He/she adds that he/she is convinced that the caller will find the appropriate course.

B

The caller introduces him/herself as Stefan/Stefanie Merz from Rostock, Germany. He/she is interested in crash courses in business English in the summer.

Stefan/Stefanie Merz spells his/her name and address, Ostseeallee 27, 66123 Rostock, Germany.

Stefan/Stefanie Merz thanks Linda/Larry Lawson and says Good-bye.

4 Work with a partner, sit back to back and act out the following telephone
I   conversation with the help of the role cards.

Phrases

Role card: Partner A   **Role card partner B ⇨ page 254**

Torsten/Tanja Kirchner, Auszubildende/r bei Hammer Werkzeughandel, Remscheid, ruft auf Bitten des Chefs bei Powertools plc, Cardiff, UK, an. Torsten/Tanja bittet um Auskunft über die Werkzeugsätze für Heimwerker (household tool kits) von Powertools.
Die E-Mail-Adresse lautet: imports@hammerwerkzeughandel.de. Vor allem möchte man Näheres über Lieferzeiten und Mengenrabatte erfahren.
Torsten/Tanja beendet das Gespräch und dankt für die Bemühungen.

Info: Discounts

Granting discounts is an effective means of winning new or retaining old customers.
Trade discounts are granted to retailers.
Introductory discounts are granted to facilitate the introduction of new products or services.
Quantity discounts are granted for volume orders.
Early order discounts are granted for bookings/purchases made well in advance.
Cash discount is granted for early payment.

Unit 9 | Enquiries

5 Copy the sentences and complete them on your own sheet of paper, inserting the
R   appropriate type of discount.

1. In view of the size of your order we are prepared to grant you a **1** of 15%. *quantity d.*
2. We are prepared to launch your new product on the Greek market, if you grant us a substantial **2**. *introductory d.*
3. For payment within 7 days we grant 2% **3**. *cash discount*
4. Only registered businesses qualify for a **4**. *trade d.*
5. On bookings made 3 months in advance you will be granted 10% **5**. *early order d.*

6 Work with a partner. Partner A wishes to place an order with partner B, provided
I   he/she is granted a discount. Use the ideas from the grid below to negotiate the
    granting of a discount. Then change roles.

> Phrases

Example:

A

I'd be quite willing to introduce your new software package CP36-97 to the German market. But I'm afraid that won't be so easy. There are a lot of competing programs. That's why I'd have to offer customers at least a 20% introductory discount.

I'm afraid we will have to offer **some** incentive to our customers. What would you say to 10% introductory discount?

B

Well, actually the package isn't exactly new. It's just an updated version of the previous one. So there isn't any real reason for granting an introductory discount.

I'd have to get back to my boss for that. I'll let you know in a few minutes.

Order for	Discount requested	Arguments	
		for	against
Hotel room for 3 nights	20% early order discount	booking made 2 months in advance	granted on bookings made 3 months in advance
200 Topsweets Mint Bars	30% trade discount	buyer is a retailer, has a small shop	quantity too small, trade discount only for business-size volumes
50 CD/radio/cassette stereo players	3% cash discount	payment made within 10 days	normally only 2%
75 kgs of Norwegian Smoked Salmon	5% quantity discount	price high compared to competitors' prices	quantity discounts start at 100 kgs.

Language and grammar

Copy the sentences and fill in the correct form, either the adjective or the adverb, and underline the word the adjective or adverb refers to.

Example:
(clear) We wish to point out **1** that this is the deadline.
We <u>wish to point out</u> *clearly* that this is the deadline.

(prompt) We would be grateful for a **2** reply.
(prompt) Thank you for replying **3** to our inquiry.
(strict) This information is given in **4** confidence.
(relative) This is a **5** minor problem.
(immediate) We must insist on **6** delivery.
(immediate) Please contact our representative **7**.
(comparative) Last year they placed **8** small orders with us.
(high) We are **9** dissatisfied with your services.
(fair) Their customers receive updates **10** regularly.
(considerable) Prices have increased **11** in the last few months.
(considerable) They have **12** funds at their disposal.
(approximate) What is the **13** arrival date of the vessel?
(approximate) We have received **14** seventy enquiries.
(definite) This car is **15** too small for me.
(definite) We will let you have our **16** decision by Wednesday.

Language and grammar: Adjectives and adverbs

Mit Adjektiven werden Substantive und das Verb "to be" näher bestimmt.

We expect to place **regular orders** in future.
"regular" ist ein Adjektiv und kennzeichnet das Substantiv "orders".

We **will be glad** to receive information on your discounts.
"glad" ist ein Adjektiv und gehört zu "will be", einer Form von "to be".

Mit Adverbien (adjective +ly) werden Verben, Adjektive und Adverbien näher bestimmt.

We assure you that your order **will be executed promptly**.
"prompt**ly**" ist ein Adverb und kennzeichnet das Verb "to execute".

There is a **rapidly growing** market for British sweets in Germany.
"rapid**ly**" ist ein Adverb und kennzeichnet das Adjektiv "growing".

There is an **extremely rapidly** growing market for British sweets in Germany.
"extreme**ly**" ist ein Adverb und kennzeichnet das Adverb "rapidly".

Unit 9 | Enquiries

Phrases: Enquiries

To mention the source of address

We saw your advertisement for laser printers in the October issue of PC World.	Wir haben Ihre Anzeige für Laserdrucker im Oktoberheft der Zeitschrift PC World gesehen.
We have obtained your address **from** the Anglo-German Chamber of Commerce.	Wir erhielten Ihre Anschrift von der Deutsch-Britischen Handelskammer.
Your services have been recommended to us **by** a business partner, …	Ihre Dienstleistungen wurden uns von einem Geschäftspartner empfohlen, …
We have visited your website and …	Wir haben Ihre Webseite angeklickt und …

To introduce your company

We are a young and rapidly growing firm **specialising** in …	Wir sind ein junges, rasch wachsendes Unternehmen und sind auf … spezialisiert.
We are well-established manufacturers **of** …	Wir sind ein gut eingeführter Hersteller von …
Our firm is a leading importer of tools with excellent contacts **all over** the EU.	Unsere Firma ist ein führender Importeur von Werkzeugen mit ausgezeichneten Kontakten in der gesamten EU.

To say what you require

We are interested in …	Wir interessieren uns für …
Could you please let us have a brochure and a price list **for** the services you offer.	Wir bitten um einen Prospekt und eine Preisliste für die von Ihnen angebotenen Dienstleistungen.
Please enclose a catalogue **of** your latest products.	Bitte fügen Sie einen Katalog für Ihre neuesten Produkte bei.
Please send us a quotation **for** …	Bitte machen Sie uns ein (Preis-)Angebot über …
We would be grateful for a cost estimate **for** …	Für einen Kostenvoranschlag für … wären wir dankbar.
Please quote your lowest prices for …	Bitte nennen Sie uns Ihre günstigsten Preise für …
We need a further shipment **of** …	Wir benötigen eine weitere Lieferung …

To ask for further information

We would be grateful for information **on** your terms of payment and delivery.	Wir bitten um nähere Angaben zu Ihren Liefer- und Zahlungsbedingungen.
Do you grant any quantity discounts? … any early order discount? … trade discount? … introductory discount? … cash discount?	Gewähren Sie Mengenrabatt? … Frühbucherrabatt? … Wiederverkaufsrabatt? … Einführungsrabatt? … Skonto?
Can you deliver ex stock?	Können Sie ab Lager liefern?
Please state your earliest delivery date.	Bitte geben Sie uns Ihr frühestes Lieferdatum an.
What is the minimum quantity **for** a trial order?	Was ist die Mindestmenge für einen Probeauftrag?

To ask for other services, if applicable

We would welcome a presentation of your services on our premises.	Wir wären dankbar für eine Präsentation Ihrer Dienstleistungen in unseren Geschäftsräumen.
A visit **by** your representative would be appreciated.	Wir wären dankbar für einen Besuch Ihres Vertreters.

To close the communication with a standard phrase

We look forward to hearing from you soon.	Wir freuen uns darauf, bald wieder von Ihnen zu hören.
If your prices are competitive, we may be able to place substantial orders in future.	Wenn Ihre Preise konkurrenzfähig sind, werden wir Ihnen bald größere Aufträge erteilen können.
If the goods **meet with** our customers' approval, your products should sell well in this market.	Wenn die Ware unseren Kunden zusagt, dürften sich Ihre Erzeugnisse auf unserem Markt gut verkaufen lassen.
We hope to hear from you shortly.	Wir hoffen, bald wieder von Ihnen zu hören.

Unit 10
Offers

WORD BANK
offer • quotation • cost estimate • catalogue • brochure • price list • stock • sample • terms of delivery • INCOTERMS • terms of payment • options • solicited • unsolicited • valid • to offer • to quote • to process • to enclose • to attach

Offers are sent either in reply to an enquiry **(solicited offers)** or on the seller's own initiative in the form of sales communications to individuals or companies likely to be interested in the goods or services offered **(unsolicited offers)**. Detailed, specific offers are often called **quotations**. Offers for work to be done take the form of **cost estimates**.

By making an offer the seller declares his willingness to sell certain goods or perform certain services at a certain price and on certain terms.

Offers are binding on the person or firm making the offer unless it is expressly stated in the offer that

- the prices are subject to change without notice or that the offer is either
- without engagement or
- valid until a certain date or
- valid as long as stocks last.

Note that all enquiries should be answered, even those for goods or services your firm does not provide. Where possible, recommend an alternative supplier.

Offers | Unit 10

1 Study the text on offers on page 142 and match the expressions on the left with their German equivalents on the right.

1. solicited offer
2. unsolicited offer
3. without engagement
4. valid until 31 May
5. as long as stocks last
6. prices are subject to change without notice
7. cost estimate

a. freibleibend
b. gültig bis 31. Mai
c. Preisänderungen vorbehalten
d. Kostenvoranschlag
e. solange Vorrat reicht
f. unverlangtes Angebot
g. verlangtes Angebot

2 Übertragen Sie folgende Sätze ins Englische.

KMK

1. Ein verlangtes Angebot wird als Reaktion auf eine Anfrage abgegeben.
2. Viele Firmen schicken unverlangte Angebote an mögliche Interessenten für ihre Produkte.
3. Ein Kostenvoranschlag ist ein Angebot für eine Arbeit, die ausgeführt werden soll.
4. Dieses Angebot ist freibleibend.
5. Unsere Preise gelten nur bis zum 31.07.201_.
6. Preisänderungen bleiben vorbehalten.
7. Solange der Vorrat reicht, bieten wir Ihnen wie folgt an: …

> **Info: Successful offers**
>
> Effective offers are decisive for the success of your business. When making an offer you should
> - answer an enquiry promptly
> - whenever possible personalise the salutation
> - thank the enquirer for his interest in your goods or services
> - if you cannot provide all the information right away let the prospective customer know that his enquiry will be processed as soon as possible
> - be as helpful and polite as possible
> - give all the information required
> - provide additional information that might be useful
> - refrain from making promises you cannot keep
> - say something positive about your firm and / or your products
> - conclude your offer with a phrase designed to make the customer feel positive towards your firm

3 Work in pairs. Close the book. Write down as many of the above recommendations as you remember. Then compare your list with your neighbour's list.

P

A Offers in writing

In reply to her enquiry about running shoes Sarah Brookfield from SPORTS ISLAND has received the following e-mail offer from Herkules.

1 Study the e-mail offer and find the missing nouns from the box.

attachment • business • delivery period • discount • enquiry • orders • position • sample • stock

---

From: exports@Herkules.com, Philipp Schäfer, export department
To: sarah.brookfield@sportsisland.co.uk, Sarah Brookfield, purchasing manager, SPORTS ISLAND
Cc:
Attachments: Price List, Test Report, Brochure
Sent: 201_-09-26

Subject: Your enquiry about Herkules Turbostar running shoes

Dear Ms Brookfield [personal salutation]

Thank you very much for your **1** of 25 September. [expression of thanks for the enquiry]

We are sending our brochure and price list as an **2**. On orders exceeding 200 pairs in one size we grant a quantity **3** of 5 per cent. Our prices are quoted EXW Neustadt. For orders exceeding 1000 pairs of one size each we require a **4** of 3 weeks. Smaller orders can be delivered from **5**.
[description of goods/services offered]
[prices (unit and total) and discounts]
[terms of delivery and delivery period]

Normally we do business on the basis of cash with order for first orders. For regular **6** we are prepared to grant open account terms with quarterly settlement. [terms of payment]

We are also attaching a Test Report, published by the British Consumers' Association, which puts Herkules running shoes in top **7** in the categories of both comfort and durability. [additional information]

Five **8** pairs of the new Turbostar have been despatched to you this morning and should reach you in the next few days. [reference to samples, etc.]

We look forward to establishing regular **9** relations with you. [goodwill phrase]

Yours sincerely
Herkules [complimentary close]

Philipp Schäfer
Export Department

Offers | Unit 10

2 Restore the correct order of these jumbled elements and rewrite the correspondence on a piece of paper.

R/P

1 We look forward to welcoming you as our customers.

2 Topsweets Mint Bars

3 For first orders our terms of payment are cash with order. For regular customers our terms are 30 days net.

4 Our prices are quoted DAP to your premises. On orders for more than 100 kgs we grant 10% discount. The mint bars can be delivered within 2–4 weeks from receipt of order, depending on the volume of the order.

5 We are pleased to send you enclosed our brochure describing our whole range of products and our special folder on Topsweets Mint Bars as well as our latest price list.

6 Dear Mr Sacher

7 To enable you to convince yourself of the superior taste of Topsweets Mint Bars we are sending you by separate post samples together with an assortment of our other products. We are sure that you will be delighted with our sweets that are very popular among discerning customers all over the world.

8 Encls. Brochure, folder, price list

9 Yours sincerely
Topsweets Ltd.

Martha Creams

10 Thank you very much for your recent enquiry.

145

Unit 10 | Offers

3 You work in the export department of a German wholesaler for electronic equipment. Your boss, Cornelia Klinkenberg, has received the following e-mail enquiry. Reply to this enquiry taking your boss's notes into account.

Phrases

From: james.leigh@leigh.co.uk
To: cornelia.klinkenberg@topelektronik.de
Cc:
Sent: 201_-08-02   **Attachments:**
Subject: SomeThing Mp3 Players

Dear Ms Klinkenberg

Please quote us your best prices for the following SomeThing Mp3 players:

500 units   article No. 487-13, 8 GB, with backlit LCD display
(vorrätig, Stückpreis EURO 83,50)

700 units   article No. 487-26, 16 GB 3D, USB, extremely compact in size
(nur 400 vorrätig, Stückpreis EURO 32,80. Lieferzeit für die restlichen 300 Stück 6 Wochen. als Ersatz Artikel 487-15 vorschlagen, gleiches Modell, aber Lebensdauer der Batterie 30 statt 24 Stunden, Stückpreis EURO 45,90)

300 units   article No. 487-45, 1.5 GB, with SD-card slot
(vorrätig, Stückpreis EURO 85,30)

As the goods are urgently required for a new store to be opened by the end of next month, we would ask you to indicate your earliest date of delivery.
(20 % Mengenrabatt für gesamten Auftrag einräumen)
(Versand kann drei Tage nach Auftragseingang erfolgen)

We assume that the usual terms of payment and delivery will apply.
(richtig)

Thank you for your prompt attention to our enquiry.

Yours sincerely

James Leigh
Leigh & Co. Ltd.
17 Camden Place
Bristol
BS6 6HR
Tel. 0117 4430030

(bitte meinen Namen darunter setzen)

Danke Klinkenberg

✱ 4
KMK Sie sind Susan/James Vernon und arbeiten im Verkauf bei Powertools plc, Snowdon Industrial Estate, Cardiff CA4 9ZB. Torsten/Tanja Kirchner von der Firma Hammer Werkzeughandel, Lehmkuhle 104, 42896 Remscheid, hat um eine schriftliche Bestätigung des Angebots gebeten, das Sie ihm/ihr heute früh telefonisch gemacht haben.

Verfassen Sie dieses Schreiben (in englischer Sprache) und berücksichtigen Sie dabei Folgendes:

- Datum von heute
- Betreff: Angebot Nr. TK/234
- Bezug auf Telefongespräch
- Angebot für 1000 Stück 9-teiliger Haushalts-Werkzeugsatz (9-piece household tool kit), Artikel Nr. HTK-9
- Listenpreis pro Stück: € 4,99, FCA Cardiff, Incoterms 2010, einschließlich Verpackung, abzüglich 30 % Händlerrabatt
- Gesamtpreis nach Abzug des Händlerrabatts: € 3.493,00.
- Zahlungsbedingungen: innerhalb von 30 Tagen netto, innerhalb von 10 Tagen 2 % Skonto (cash discount)
- Lieferzeit: 3 Wochen
- 2 Muster-Werkzeugsätze werden heute an Hammer Werkzeughandel zu Testzwecken geschickt
- Dank für das Interesse an den Produkten von Powertools plc
- Zusicherung sorgfältiger Ausführung des Auftrags

B Offers by phone

1 Edward Ferrars from Norland Industries in Southampton, Great Britain, gets a phone call from an overseas customer.
R
A1.23 Read the statements first. Then listen to the dialogue and mark on your own sheet of paper whether the statements are TRUE or FALSE.

1. Tom De Boer is calling from South America.
2. He has no Norland colour printers left in his stock.
3. He wishes to order 200 units of the colour printer CP 150.
4. The terms of delivery are FOB Durban.
5. Last year's model CP 100 cost GBP 72.50.
6. There is increasing competition from Japan.
7. 30% trade discount will be granted on all future orders.
8. The customer asks for an offer in writing.

2 Copy Mr Ferrars' quotation and insert the missing expressions from the box.
R

> from receipt of order • look forward to • pleased to • Referring to • within 30 days

Dear Mr De Boer

Norland Colour Printers CP 100 and 150 – Quotation no. CP-2024

1 your enquiry of 2 Feb. 201_ we are **2** inform you that we can quote as follows

Quantity	Description	Unit Price	Total
500	Norland Colour Printer CP 100	GBP 75.50	GBP 37,750.00
200	Norland Colour Printer CP 150	GBP 85.20	GBP 17,040.00
			GBP 54,790.00
	less 30% trade discount		GBP 16,437.00

TOTAL   GBP 38,353.00

Delivery: within four weeks **3** , CIF Durban.

Payment: net cash **4** from receipt of invoice.

We **5** receiving your order.

Yours sincerely
Edward Ferrars
Norland Industries

C Comparing options

1 KMK Ihre Firma plant, 5 Mitarbeiter aus dem Export für eine Woche zu einem Intensiv-Sprachkurs nach England zu schicken. Zwei Angebote wurden in die engere Wahl gezogen. Verschaffen Sie sich einen Überblick über diese beiden Angebote, indem Sie die Tabelle auf Seite 150 (kopieren und) in deutscher Sprache vervollständigen.

THE DORSET SCHOOL OF ENGLISH

The DORSET SCHOOL OF ENGLISH offers you a tailor-made study programme for your staff at any time you wish, except in August. Our offer includes a one-week intensive course, 6 hours of tuition a day (except Sundays), focussing on general business English and on specific export terminology.

Our language school is situated in Lyme Regis, the pearl of Dorset, a traditional seaside resort on the English Channel, made famous by the celebrated novelist Jane Austen.

Your staff will be placed with English business and professional families and there will never be another student of your native language in the same family.

The sports programme (tennis, swimming, surfing and sailing), which is free of charge, takes the learning experience outside the classroom.

Lyme Regis is rich in fossils. We offer fossil hunting trips as a special treat for our students.

Excursions to Exeter, Dartmoor and Bath can be booked at short notice.

Tuition fees: £400 per week
For more than 10 participants from one firm we offer a 15 % discount.
Accommodation and full board in host families: £490 per week.

Booking fee, to be paid when booking: £50. Full payment to be made 6 weeks before the course begins.

Contact: Brian Hill, THE DORSET SCHOOL OF ENGLISH, The Cobb, Lyme Regis, EX3 5AN

Unit 10 | Offers

BUSINESS SPEAK

BUSINESS SPEAK is an international language school for business people, located in Brighton on the South Coast. Brighton is a vibrant seaside resort and conference centre, just one hour's train journey from London.

Our business English intensive courses which take place four times a year (September 2–8, October 14–20, February 10–16 and May 21–27) would suit your staff's needs admirably. These intensive courses consist of 5 hours of tuition in the mornings and four study visits to British firms in the afternoons.

Maximum number of participants: 8.

Our students live either at an exclusive private hotel or with carefully selected English host families.

We offer a wide range of sports activities, such as golf, riding, surfing, sailing and fishing. Equipment can be hired at a small charge.

Course fees: £480 per week
Accommodation and half board:
Private hotel: £90 per day
Host family: £450 per week

To confirm the booking a deposit of £75 per person must accompany the booking form. The balance is required no later than eight weeks before the course commencement date.

Please contact:
Mrs Pam Robinson • BUSINESS SPEAK • 120, Brunswick Square • Brighton • BN1 9PH

	Anbieter A	Anbieter B
Veranstalter	Dorset School of English	
Kursort		
Teilnehmerkreis und -zahl	speziell unsere Gruppe	
Schwerpunkt		
Unterrichtsstunden pro Tag		
Unterbringung		
Exkursionen		
Freizeitangebot		
Kurstermine		
Preis für Unterkunft und Verpflegung		
Kursgebühren		
Anzahlung		
Auskunft		

✶ 2 Make up your mind which of these two offers you would prefer to accept. Then write a short memo for your US parent company's personnel department, giving at least two reasons for your choice.

MEMO
From: (your own name)   Date:
To: Personnel Department, Headquarters USA
Subject: Intensive language course in the UK

3 Your boss has asked you to look up Business English courses in Poole / Bournemouth on the south coast of England. Make notes on two or three that seem suitable and write a memo in English giving names and important details.

D INCOTERMS® (Terms of delivery)

The Incoterms are a set of nationally and internationally accepted rules defining the obligations of the seller and the buyer as regards the tasks, costs and risks involved in the transport of goods. They were first drawn up by the International Chamber of Commerce in Paris in 1936 and were last updated in 2010.

The Incoterms 2010 are grouped in two categories:
- rules for any mode or modes of transport
- rules for sea and inland waterway transport

The Incoterms 2010 consist of 11 rules, two of which are new:
- DAT (Delivered at Terminal) replaces the former DEQ rule
- DAP (Delivered at Place) replaces the former rules DAF, DES and DDU

Incoterms 2010

Seller — Carrier — Port of Shipment (Quay) — Ship — Ship — Port of Destination (Quay) — Container Terminal — Carrier — Buyer

I. Any mode or modes of transport

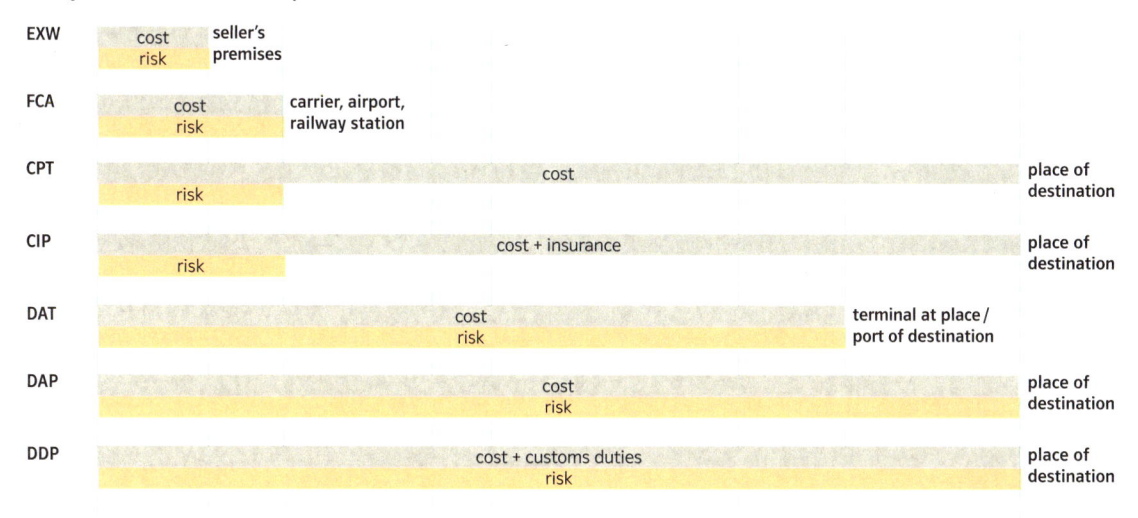

Term	Cost	Risk	Location
EXW	cost	risk	seller's premises
FCA	cost	risk	carrier, airport, railway station
CPT	cost	risk	place of destination
CIP	cost + insurance	risk	place of destination
DAT	cost	risk	terminal at place / port of destination
DAP	cost	risk	place of destination
DDP	cost + customs duties	risk	place of destination

II. Sea and inland waterway transport

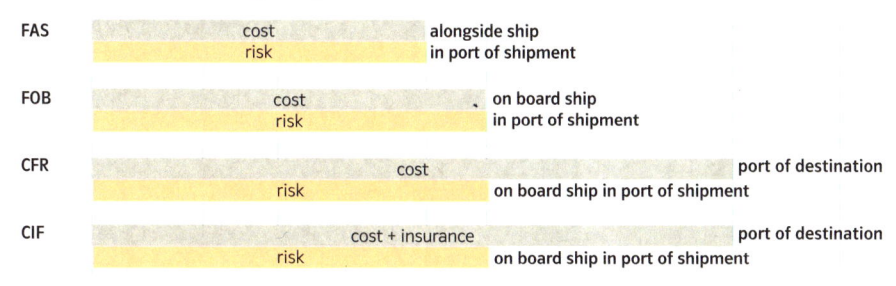

Term	Cost	Risk	Location
FAS	cost	risk	alongside ship in port of shipment
FOB	cost	risk	on board ship in port of shipment
CFR	cost	risk	port of destination / on board ship in port of shipment
CIF	cost + insurance	risk	port of destination / on board ship in port of shipment

® International Chamber of Commerce, ICC

Rules for any mode or modes of transport

Incoterms® 2010

Incoterm	Designation	Seller's obligations	Passing of risk from seller to buyer
EXW	Ex Works Ab Werk	place the goods at the disposal of the buyer at the seller's premises (factory, warehouse etc.)	at the seller's premises
FCA	Free Carrier Frei Frachtführer	deliver the goods to the carrier named by the buyer	when the goods are handed over to the carrier
CPT	Carriage Paid to Frachtfrei	deliver the goods to the carrier and pay the cost of carriage to the named place of destination	when the goods are handed over to the carrier
CIP	Carriage and Insurance Paid to Frachtfrei versichert	deliver the goods to the carrier, pay the cost of carriage and take out insurance to the named place of destination	when the goods are handed over to the carrier
DAT	Delivered at Terminal Geliefert Terminal	place the goods at the buyer's disposal, unloaded, at a named terminal at a named place/port	when the goods have been unloaded at the terminal
DAP	Delivered at Place Geliefert benannter Ort	place the goods at the buyer's disposal, ready for unloading, at the named place of destination	at the place of destination
DDP	Delivered Duty Paid Geliefert verzollt	place the goods at the buyer's disposal, ready for unloading, at the named place of destination, carry out all customs formalities and pay import duty, if any	at the place of destination

Rules for sea and inland waterway transport

Incoterms® 2010

Incoterm	Designation	Seller's obligations	Passing of risk from seller to buyer
FAS	Free Alongside Ship Frei Längsseite Schiff	deliver the goods alongside the ship named by the buyer at the named port of shipment	when the goods are alongside the ship in the port of shipment
FOB	Free on Board Frei an Bord	deliver the goods on board the ship named by the buyer at the named port of shipment	when the goods are on board the ship in the port of shipment
CFR	Cost and Freight Kosten und Fracht	deliver the goods on board the ship and pay the costs and freight to the named port of destination	when the goods are on board the ship in the port of shipment
CIP	Cost, Insurance and Freight Kosten, Versicherung und Fracht	deliver the goods on board the ship; pay the costs and freight to the named port of destination and take out insurance for the transport	when the goods are on board the ship in the port of shipment

® International Chamber of Commerce, ICC

Offers | Unit 10

Under all clauses the seller must deliver the goods to the buyer at the named place and the buyer must take delivery of the goods *(Ware abnehmen)*. The seller must procure *(beschaffen)* or help to procure the transport documents and pack the goods, if customary *(handelsüblich)*.

Note that under the Incoterms CPT, CIP, CFR and CIF the seller bears the risks only up to the place of delivery, i.e. until the goods are handed over to the (first) carrier or have been loaded on board ship in the port of shipment. Under these terms the seller must, in addition, contract *(Vertrag abschließen)* and pay for the carriage to the place or port of destination.

1 Read the business transactions and complete them with the right Incoterms.
R

1. Jennings Food Ltd. has bought five colour printers from Norland Industries. Jennings Food's driver picks up the colour printers at Norland Industries' production plant. The printers have been sold on the basis of …?

2. Powertools plc, Cardiff, has received a large export order from a Brazilian customer. Powertools plc pays for the goods to be taken to the docks in Cardiff and for the loading on board the vessel "Southern Cross". The terms of delivery are …?

3. International Snacks GmbH, a German food processing company, usually delivers its snacks by lorry to Global Catering's premises in Manchester, assuming all costs and risks for the entire transport and dealing with any border formalities that may arise. Their terms of delivery are most likely …?

4. Herkules is processing a major order for running shoes and tennis shoes from a Japanese customer. Herkules arranges and pays for the transport of two 20 ft containers to the container terminal at the Japanese port of Yokohama. Herkules delivers on the basis of …?

2 Study the Incoterms 2010 on page 151 and 152 and find the English equivalents
M for the following German expressions.

1. Geschäftsräume des Verkäufers
2. Frachtführer
3. vom Käufer benannt
4. Gefahrenübergang
5. Beförderungskosten
6. Versicherung abschließen
7. entladebereit
8. Bestimmungsort
9. dem Käufer zur Verfügung stellen
10. Verschiffungshafen
11. sich an Bord befinden
12. Einfuhrzoll

Language and grammar
Complete these sentences with "some" or "any".

1. He says he has lived in the UK for … years.
2. Fortunately we did not have … trouble getting an import licence.
3. When we finally managed to go the cafeteria there was hardly … food left.
4. I don't think he will complete … of these tasks in time.
5. Could you lend me … of your knives and forks for the party?
6. I couldn't think of …thing else to buy.
7. Scarcely …body turned up for the meeting.
8. …body must help me with this update.
9. We doubt that …body could have solved that problem without help from the experts.
10. We will send you … samples by parcel post.
11. Has …body seen my car keys?
12. …body must have copied the data.
13. I wonder whether …body will bother to return the questionnaire.
14. There are scarcely … funds left for this project.

Language and grammar: some and any	
"Some" steht • in **bejahten Aussagen** und • in Fragen, auf die eine **positive Antwort** erwartet wird.	Examples: Here are **some** brochures for you. Can you give us **some** of these folders?
"Any" steht • in **verneinten Aussagen** und • in Fragen, auf die eine **negative Antwort** erwartet wird, • bei **"hardly"**, **"scarcely"** oder **"barely"** (deutsch: kaum), • in **Bedingungssätzen** und • nach Ausdrücken des **Zweifels**.	Examples: I am afraid there aren't **any** mint bars among the samples TOPSWEETS sent us. Are there **any** of those delicious ginger cookies left? There can hardly be **any** doubt about it. If you have **any** problems, let me know. I wonder whether **any** of the students will be satisfied with this reply.

Offers | Unit 10

Office expert

1 Office supplies fair

Lesen Sie den Auszug aus dem Internetauftritt der Office Expo und beantworten Sie die Fragen auf Deutsch.

officeexpo

home › exhibitors › events › search › contact

> **EVENT PROFILE**

Organized by Media Expos at New Delhi, India, the Office Expo in Mumbai is a pioneer show providing a platform for office equipment and supplies. It is an annual mega event offering enormous opportunities for exhibiting various products and trends in making office environments more efficient and effective.

> **VISITORS' PROFILE**
- architects and interior designers
- communication managers
- CEOs and presidents
- administrators
- secretaries
- purchasers from entertainment, healthcare, education and other industries
- importers and exporters of office equipment
- department stores

> **EXHIBITORS' PROFILE**

The exhibition is focused on the following segments of office improvement: office automation, equipment, office furniture, office security, office stationery, services, audio visual equipment and IT products.

Business timing:
10:00 am – 07:00 pm

Public timing:
12:00 am – 07:00 pm

---

1. Was ist die Office Expo?
2. Wie oft und wo findet die Office Expo statt?
3. Aus welchen Berufsgruppen stammen die Messebesucher?
4. Welche Produktarten werden auf der Messe ausgestellt?
5. Wie sind die Öffnungszeiten für
   a. Geschäftsleute?   b. die Öffentlichkeit?

Unit 10 | Offers

2 Comparing offers for office furniture

1 Answer the questions about three chairs of the British company Topchairs
R you saw at Office Expo.

STILLA ~~€295.00~~ €147.50

SIMPLEX €85.00

ARCO €549.00

1. **STILLA** Conference chair made in shiny welded aluminium with a fixed base. The seat is covered with fabric. This chair is a quality piece that combines aesthetics and functionality. It measures 55 cm (width), 100 cm (height) and 47 cm (depth).

2. **ARCO** Office chair made of aluminium with a leather seat. It has a reclining seat with a hydraulic control. The height and armrests are both adjustable thanks to its gas piston system allowing the chair to be perfectly adapted to the user's needs. It is 65 cm wide, 120 cm high and has a depth of 58 cm.

3. **SIMPLEX** This chair is manufactured in sturdy plastic and has a wheeled steel base. It is adjustable in height due to its gas piston system. Simplicity, practicality and design all in one. It is 60 cm wide, 110 cm high and has a depth of 60 cm.

1. Which is the most expensive/the cheapest chair?
2. Which chair is the lowest/highest/widest?
3. Which chair/s is/are made of more than one material?
4. Which chair is the best deal?

2 Fassen Sie die wesentliche Eigenschaften der drei Bürostühle in einer Tabelle auf
KMK Deutsch zusammen.

	Stilla	Arco	Simplex
1. Material			
2. Höhenverstellbarkeit			
3. Maße			
4. Preis			

✶ 3 Schreiben Sie per E-Mail eine Anfrage an die Firma Topchairs
KMK (info@topchairs.com) und berücksichtigen Sie dabei die folgenden Punkte:

- Erwähnen Sie wie Sie die Firma in Erfahrung gebracht haben.
- Bringen Sie Ihr Interesse an dem Bürostuhl Arco zum Ausdruck.
- Erkundigen Sie sich nach der Möglichkeit die Stühle mit der Farbe Ihrer Firma (Grasgrün) zu versehen.
- Fragen Sie nach möglichen Rabatten.
- Fragen Sie nach den Zahlungs- und Lieferbedingungen.
- Beenden Sie die E-Mail in angemessener Form.

Phrases: Offers

To say thank you for an enquiry

Many thanks for your enquiry **of** 2 October **about** our new range of …	Wir danken Ihnen vielmals für Ihre Anfrage vom 2. Oktober wegen unseres neuen Sortiments von …
We **were** pleased to hear that you are interested in our …	Wir freuen uns über Ihr Interesse an unseren …

To make an offer and to refer to prices and discounts

As requested, we are sending you enclosed our latest catalogue and price list.	Wie gewünscht, fügen wir unseren neuesten Katalog und unsere Preisliste bei.
We are pleased to quote as follows:	Wir freuen uns, Ihnen hiermit folgendes Angebot machen zu können:
We would now like to make the following quotation:	Wir möchten Ihnen nun folgendes Angebot unterbreiten:
… **at** a unit price of € …, including packing.	… zum Stückpreis von € … einschließlich Verpackung.
… less 30 % trade discount.	… abzüglich 30 % Händlerrabatt.
We can offer a 10 % quantity discount **on** orders **for** at least 500 units.	Für Aufträge über mindestens 500 Stück wird 10 % Mengenrabatt gewährt.
May we draw your attention **to** our special offer for …?	Dürfen wir Sie auf unser Sonderangebot für … aufmerksam machen?
We grant 2 % cash discount **for** payment within 10 days.	Für Barzahlung innerhalb von 10 Tagen gewähren wir 2 % Skonto.
We take pleasure **in** submitting the following cost estimate:	Wir freuen uns Ihnen folgenden Kostenvoranschlag zu unterbreiten:

To state your terms of delivery and payment

Our prices are quoted CIF Singapore.	Unsere Preise verstehen sich CIF Singapur.
Terms of delivery: EXW Neustadt	Lieferbedingungen: EXW (Ab Werk) Neustadt

Our usual terms of payment are:
 	
    cash **with** order
    cash **on** delivery
    30 days net, 10 days 2 %
    by irrevocable and confirmed letter of credit
	Normalerweise lauten unsere Zahlungsbedingungen:
	    Barzahlung bei Auftragserteilung
	    Barzahlung bei Lieferung
	    30 Tage netto, 10 Tage 2 % Skonto
	    durch unwiderrufliches und bestätigtes Akkreditiv

Unit 10 | Offers

Regular customers are granted open account terms.	Unseren Stammkunden gewähren wir offenes Zahlungsziel.
We would request payment **by** bank transfer **to** our account **with** ABC bank.	Wir bitten um Zahlung per Banküberweisung auf unser Konto bei der ABC Bank.

To refer to the delivery time

The delivery period is 6 weeks.	Die Lieferzeit beträgt 6 Wochen.
Delivery can be made ex stock.	Die Lieferung kann ab Lager erfolgen.

To inform the customer how long the offer is valid

The offer is
    firm **until** 31 March.
    without engagement.
    valid **as long as** stocks last.
	Das Angebot ist
	    fest bis 31. März.
	    unverbindlich.
	    gültig solange der Vorrat reicht.

The prices are **subject to** change without notice.	Preisänderungen bleiben vorbehalten.
The offer is **subject to** prior sale.	Zwischenverkauf vorbehalten.

To create goodwill

I hope this quotation will find your approval.	Ich hoffe, dieses Angebot sagt Ihnen zu.
We look forward to welcoming you as our customers.	Wir freuen uns darauf, Sie als Kunden begrüßen zu dürfen.
We assure you that your order **will be** dealt with promptly and carefully.	Wir sichern Ihnen eine rasche und sorgfältige Erledigung Ihres Auftrags zu.
Should you have any further queries, our staff **will be** pleased to assist you **at any** time.	Sollten Sie nun weitere Fragen haben, stehen Ihnen unsere Mitarbeiter jederzeit gerne zur Verfügung.

Unit 11
Orders

> **WORD BANK**
> initial order • trial order • standing order • repeat order • order on call • order form • quantity • description • item • article • sample • pattern • terms and conditions • unit price • total price • to choose • to order • to place an order • to process • to deliver

Orders are placed either in response to an offer or on the buyer's own initiative. A first order is also called an **initial order**. A **trial order** is placed for a small quanitity to test the merchandise or service. **Repeat orders** cover goods or services ordered before. **Standing orders** ensure that identical quantities are supplied at regular intervals. **Orders on call** are placed for large quantities, called for at irregular intervals. They play an important role within the concept of just-in-time delivery.

1 Read the text. Then cover it up and complete the sentences.

R/P
1. A first order is also called …
2. A trial order is placed for a small quantity to test …
3. Repeat orders cover goods or services …
4. Standing orders ensure that identical quantities are supplied at …
5. Orders on call are placed for large quantities, called for at …

2 Translate the text above.

M

Online-Link
808261-0011

Unit 11 | Orders

A Orders in writing

Sarah Brookfield has studied Herkules' offer for Turbostar running shoes and has read the attached test report. As she is favourably impressed by this report and by the results of the durability tests Sports Island conducted on the sample pairs, she decides to place a trial order.

1 Study Sarah Brookfield's order letter and the order form on the next page and choose the correct prepositions from the box.

by • for • from • of • to • with (2x)

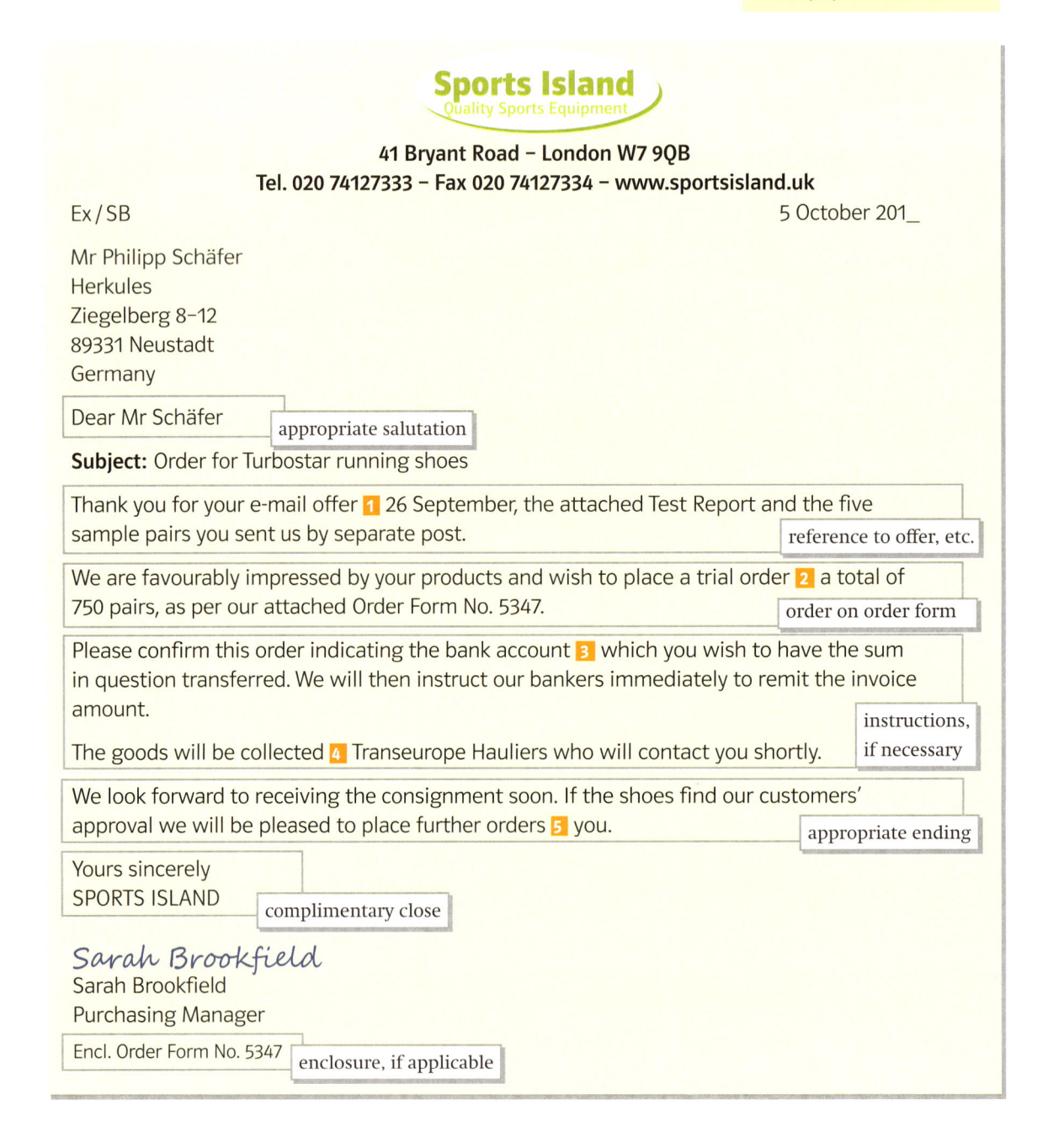

Sports Island
Quality Sports Equipment

41 Bryant Road – London W7 9QB
Tel. 020 74127333 – Fax 020 74127334 – www.sportsisland.uk

Ex / SB   5 October 201_

Mr Philipp Schäfer
Herkules
Ziegelberg 8–12
89331 Neustadt
Germany

Dear Mr Schäfer   *[appropriate salutation]*

Subject: Order for Turbostar running shoes

Thank you for your e-mail offer **1** 26 September, the attached Test Report and the five sample pairs you sent us by separate post.   *[reference to offer, etc.]*

We are favourably impressed by your products and wish to place a trial order **2** a total of 750 pairs, as per our attached Order Form No. 5347.   *[order on order form]*

Please confirm this order indicating the bank account **3** which you wish to have the sum in question transferred. We will then instruct our bankers immediately to remit the invoice amount.

The goods will be collected **4** Transeurope Hauliers who will contact you shortly.   *[instructions, if necessary]*

We look forward to receiving the consignment soon. If the shoes find our customers' approval we will be pleased to place further orders **5** you.   *[appropriate ending]*

Yours sincerely
SPORTS ISLAND   *[complimentary close]*

Sarah Brookfield
Sarah Brookfield
Purchasing Manager

Encl. Order Form No. 5347   *[enclosure, if applicable]*

Orders | Unit 11

Order form

Sports Island
Quality Sports Equipment

41 Bryant Road – London W7 9QB
Tel. 020 74127333 – Fax 020 74127334 – www.sportsisland.uk

ORDER NO. 5347   5 October 201_

Herkules
Ziegelberg 8–12
89331 Neustadt
Germany

order (on order form, if appropriate)
– quantity
– description (article No.)
– unit price, total price

Please supply

Quantity	Item	Sizes	Unit Price	Total Price
25 pairs each	Turbostar Running Shoes	5, 5 ½, 11, 12	€ 40.50	€ 4,050.00
50 pairs each		6, 6 ½, 7, 7 ½, 10	€ 40.50	€ 10,125.00
100 pairs each		8, 8 ½, 9, 9 ½	€ 40.50	€ 16,200.00

Terms of delivery: EXW Neustadt   *terms of delivery*

Terms of payment: Cash **6** order   *terms of payment*

Delivery: **7** stock   *delivery time*

Sarah Brookfield
Sarah Brookfield
for Sports Island

Unit 11 | Orders

2 Restore the correct order of these jumbled elements and rewrite the correspondence on a sheet of paper.

R/P

1. We have studied the enclosed spring catalogue and have chosen two models:

2. Dear Ms Martl

3. I would like to stress that this is a trial order. If we are satisfied with your shirts you may expect regular repeat orders.

4. Thank you very much for your letter of 11 November.

5.

Quantity	Article No.	Description	Colours	Sizes	Unit price
50 each	334 053 R	Sports Shirt	Canyon Red	L and XL	€17.50
50 each	334 062 T	Dress Shirt	White	L and XL	€21.70

6. We look forward to receiving the goods as soon as possible.

7. We would like to point out that this order qualifies for 3% early order discount, as mentioned in your letter.

8. Yours sincerely
Tony Shaw

Wilson & Thatcher Ltd.

9. This order is placed subject to the terms and conditions specified in your catalogue.
Payment will be made by bank transfer on receipt of your invoice.

10. Subject: Trial order for shirts

Orders | Unit 11

3 You work in the purchasing department of the German stationery shop,
P   Papier Gehrke, Bahnhofsallee 27, 19053 Schwerin, Tel. 0385 467095, e-mail m.gerke@papier-gehrke.de. Your boss, Martin Gehrke, has put this leaflet with his handwritten notes on your desk and has asked you to e-mail an order to Calendars 4 U.

Phrases

Calendars 4 U
proudly presents its multilingual animal calendar range

Kittens
You're certain to
be smitten
12" x 12" wall calendar

$11.99

gehen besonders gut!
30 Stück bestellen

Tigers !new!
Spectacular photos
12" x 12" wall calendar

$11.99

sehr interessant,
20 Stück bestellen

Puppies
Bright-eyed and
ready to romp
8" x 8" wall calendar

$9.99

fragen, ob auch in
"12 x 12" erhältlich,
wenn ja 20 Stück,
sonst nur 10 Stück

Horses
Superb photos
capture
their nobility
12" x 12" wall calendar
$11.99

nicht bestellen

We offer special rates for orders of 200+ items.
Please call us: 800/752-3326.

Calendars 4 U
100 Dolphin Way
San Sebastian, CA 94901
info@calendars4U.com
www.calendars4U.com

auf sofortige Lieferung per
Luftpost drängen
Zahlung, wie üblich, durch Überweisung bei Erhalt
der Rechnung
um kurze Auftragsbestätigung bitten
E-mail in meinem Namen an Cyrus B. Reid
senden: cb.reid@calendars4U.com

Unit 11 | Orders

4
KMK

Sie arbeiten bei Getränke König, Am Sprudelbach 17, 06122 Halle, Tel. 0345 785634, Fax 0345 785635 im Einkauf. Ihre Chefin, Nicole Sachse, hat von der irischen Glashütte Wexford Crystal plc, 1 Wexford Avenue, Sanditon, County Cork, Republic of Ireland, ein Angebot über farbige Kristallgläser für Long Drinks im Geschenkkarton erhalten. Die Gläser sollen guten Kunden zu Weihnachten geschenkt werden.

Sie bittet Sie, das Auftragsschreiben, das sie selbst unterschreiben wird, zu verfassen und dabei folgende Punkte zu berücksichtigen:

- Datum 10. September
- Ansprechpartner: Sean O'Sullivan
- Betreff
- Dank für Angebot vom 5. September
- Bestellung: je 1000 Sets bestehend aus je 2 Kristallgläsern für Long Drinks in den Farben rot, blau und grün, im Geschenkkarton
- Gesamtauftragsvolumen: 3000 Sets
- Preis: € 12,50 pro Set zu 2 Gläsern
- Mengenrabatt: 10 %
- Lieferungsbedingung: DAP Am Sprudelbach 17, 06122 Halle, Germany, Incoterms 2010
- Zahlung: bei Erhalt der Ware durch Banküberweisung auf das Konto bei der Cork County Bank.
- Bitte um strikte Einhaltung der versprochenen Lieferfrist von vier Wochen
- Bestellung wird auf Grund unserer beiliegenden allgemeinen Geschäftsbedingungen erteilt
- Anlage: Geschäftsbedingungen

5 Your boss wants "draper trestles" (Tischböcke) to furnish a factory outlet. Use the internet to find suppliers. Note down prices etc. in English and check that the supplier has an online ordering facility.

B Orders by phone

Kirsty Burnham from Global Catering in Manchester has received an order from an upmarket chain of delicatessens. She rings International Snacks in Düsseldorf and places an order with them.

1 Kopieren Sie das Bestellformular und füllen Sie es aus, während Sie das Telefonat zweimal hören.

KMK
A 1.24

Portionen	Code-Nr.	Artikel	Preis pro Portion
	PSF 135	Schwäbischer Wurstsalat	€ 0,55
	PSF 136	Schinkenröllchen mit Spargel	€ 0,45
	PSF 137	Salami-Aufschnitt auf Roggentaler	€ 0,60
	PSF 138	kleine Frankfurter Würstchen mit Senf	€ 0,45
	PSF 139	Mini-Frikadellen mit Kartoffelsalat und fettarmer Yoghurtsoße	€ 1,05
	PSG 234	Putencocktail in Melone	€ 0,85
	PSG 235	Geflügelsalat Hawaii	€ 0,75
	PSM 311	Räucherlachs auf Pumpernickel mit Meerrettich	€ 0,95
	PSM 312	Bismarckhering, gerollt mit Gürkchen	€ 0,35
	PSM 313	Matjesfilet mit Remoulade	€ 0,65
	PSM 314	Anchovisfilet, gerollt mit gefüllten Oliven	€ 0,85
	PSM 315	Eismeerkrabben-Cocktail	€ 1,15
	PSD 408	Früchtequark	€ 0,45
	PSD 409	Rote Grütze mit Vanillecreme	€ 0,45

Transportart:	Liefertag und -zeitpunkt:	Lieferort:	Rechnung an:

2 Schreiben Sie als Marcel Krenz die im Telefonat mit Kirsty Burnham angekündigte E-Mail als Auftragsbestätigung (siehe ausgefülltes Bestellformular) mit Versandanzeige.

KMK

Absender: marcel.krenz@internationalsnacks.de
Empfänger: burnham.globalcateringuk@aol.com
Sie haben inzwischen folgende Einzelheiten zum Versand geklärt:
- Versand per Luftfracht durch Spedition Fuhrmann & Söhne, Düsseldorf
- Flug-Nr. LH 3697, Abflug: Flughafen Düsseldorf, 13:05 Uhr deutsche Zeit
- Ankunft Manchester Airport, Freight Terminal, 13:25 Uhr britische Zeit

Unit 11 | Orders

3 Work with a partner. Sit back to back and act out the following telephone conversation. Then change roles.

Phrases

A

Sie sind Nico/Nicole Sachse und arbeiten bei Getränke König in Halle. Sie hatten ihren britischen Lieferanten BIG Beverages gestern in einem Fax gebeten, einen Auftrag über 500 Flaschen Fruchtsaft, Marke Tropicana, drei Tage früher auszuliefern.

Sie nehmen den Anruf entgegen. Reagieren Sie angemessen auf die Frage, wie es Ihnen geht.

Drücken Sie Ihre Enttäuschung aus und erklären Sie, dass Ihr Kunde den Fruchtsaft spätestens nächsten Freitag für einen großen Empfang benötigt.

Fragen Sie nach dem Preis dieses neuen Fruchtsafts.

Machen Sie Ihrem Gesprächspartner klar, dass Sie nicht in der Lage sind, so viel mehr zu bezahlen.

Zeigen Sie sich erfreut über dieses Entgegenkommen und fragen Sie, wann die 500 Flaschen abgeschickt werden können.

Danken Sie Ihrem Gesprächspartner für seine Bemühungen und beenden Sie das Gespräch.

B

You are Max/Maggy Lane from BIG Beverages in Chipping, UK. Yesterday you got a fax from a German customer, Getränke König from Halle requesting you to bring delivery of their order for 500 bottles of Tropicana fruit juice forward by three days. You ring them up. Begin the conversation with a few friendly personal remarks e.g. asking how the person taking the call is.

Refer to yesterday's fax and tell your partner that you regret that it is absolutely impossible to dispatch this particular fruit juice earlier.

Suggest that you send a substitute, your new fruit drink, called Tropical Sunset. The taste is very similar to that of Tropicana fruit juice.

Tell your partner that you are sorry to say that the price is 5 p higher per bottle as Tropical Sunset contains no artificial flavouring.

To accommodate the customer offer 2.5 % introductory discount on this particular order.

Reply that the consignment will be handed over to the forwarders tomorrow morning and will reach the customer the day after tomorrow.

Close with thanks for the order.

Orders | Unit 11

Language and grammar
Rewrite the following text, using capital letters where necessary.

the organisation of petroleum exporting countries (opec) was formed in 1960 with five founding members: iran, kuwait, saudi arabia and venezuela. by the end of 1971 six other nations had joined the group: qatar, indonesia, libya, united arab emirates, algeria and nigeria. since then opec has been trying to control crude oil prices by setting quotas for production. some major oil exporting countries such as russia, norway and mexico have remained outside opec. the british analyst jonathan baker writing in the june edition of the trade journal "global oil" says that oil prices are highly cyclical and are supported by high demand from south east asia, especially china and india.

Language and grammar: Use of capital letters

Geographische Eigennamen werden groß geschrieben. Im Gegensatz zum Deutschen werden im Englischen auch geographische Adjektive groß geschrieben.
> We have customers in **N**ew **S**outh **W**ales in **A**ustralia.
> Our **B**ritish and **I**talian subsidiaries are quite successful.

Wochentage, Monate und Feiertage werden groß geschrieben.
> The meeting will be held next **F**riday / in **S**eptember / before **C**hristmas.

Vorangestellte Titel, die Teil des Namens bilden, schreibt man groß. Nachgestellte Titel werden meist klein geschrieben.
> The report was presented by **V**ice-**P**resident Brian Laurel.
> John Hardy, chairman of Media Clusters, agreed to the proposal.

Die Namen von Ministerien, Behörden etc. werden groß geschrieben.
> The **F**ederal **C**ommunications **C**ommission ruled that the deal was illegal.
> The **D**epartment of **T**rade and **I**ndustry provides help for start-ups.

V5 Video lounge Manufacturing

BBC Motion Gallery

You are about to see a video about a company based on the Isle of Wight (small island off the south coast of England).
Watch the video, then answer the following questions:

1. What does the company manufacture?
2. What industry do orders for these products come from?
3. How are the products transported to customers?
4. What other industry on the Isle of Wight is mentioned?

167

Office expert

Comparing and ordering business cards

1 Ihr Vorgesetzter bittet Sie Angebote für neue Visitenkarten einzuholen.
KMK Vergleichen Sie die folgenden zwei Preisangebote im Internet, indem Sie die Fragen unten auf Deutsch beantworten.

BETTER BUSINESS CARDS

VALUE CARDS (digital print quality)
300g/sm card stock with high stiffness

Quantity	Single	Double
100	~~10.98€~~ 5.98€	~~17.34€~~ 9.98€

PREMIUM CARDS (offset print quality)
350g/sm card stock with EXTRA high stiffness

Quantity	Single	Double
100	~~17.34€~~ 9.98€	~~29.95€~~ 13.98€
250	~~23.95€~~ 15.98€	~~34.95€~~ 18.98€
500	~~31.95€~~ 20.98€	~~39.95€~~ 25.98€
1000	~~37.95€~~ 28.98€	~~47.95€~~ 36.98€

All prices include VAT and exclude shipping.

Discount Cards

	Single sided business cards						
	50	100	200	500	1000	2000	5000
Simple range	~~£8.95~~ £4.48	~~£12.95~~ £6.48	~~£18.95~~ £9.48	~~£33.95~~ £16.98	~~£53.60~~ £26.80	~~£77.95~~ £38.98	~~£167.95~~ £83.98
Premium range	~~£15.95~~ £7.98	~~£19.95~~ £9.98	~~£25.95~~ £12.98	~~£40.95~~ £20.48	~~£60.60~~ £30.30	~~£84.95~~ £42.48	~~£174.95~~ £87.48
Upload range	~~£15.95~~ £7.98	~~£19.95~~ £9.98	~~£25.95~~ £12.98	~~£40.95~~ £20.48	~~£60.60~~ £30.30	~~£84.95~~ £42.48	~~£174.95~~ £87.48

	Double business cards						
	50	100	200	500	1000	2000	5000
Simple range	~~£17.63~~ £8.81	~~£23.44~~ £11.72	~~£34.02~~ £17.01	~~£59.87~~ £29.93	~~£93.94~~ £46.97	~~£137.42~~ £68.71	~~£293.69~~ £146.85
Premium range	~~£25.85~~ £12.93	~~£31.67~~ £15.83	~~£42.24~~ £21.12	~~£68.09~~ £34.05	~~£102.17~~ £51.08	~~£145.64~~ £72.82	~~£301.92~~ £150.96
Upload range	~~£22.00~~ £11.00	~~£26.95~~ £13.48	~~£35.95~~ £17.98	~~£57.95~~ £28.98	~~£86.95~~ £43.48	~~£123.95~~ £61.98	~~£256.95~~ £128.48

1. Welche der beiden Firmen bietet ein breiteres Spektrum an Qualität an?
2. Was sind die Unterschiede zwischen den Value und den Premium Karten von Better Business Cards?
3. Welche Firma hat das bessere Angebot für 500 einseitig bedruckte Karten der gehobenen Klasse?
4. Was beinhalten die Preise bei Better Business Cards und was beinhalten sie nicht?
5. Bei welcher Firma ist der Preisunterschied zwischen einseitigem und beidseitigem Druck größer?

Orders | Unit 11

2 You have the task of preparing an online order for new business cards. Translate the specifics about the following managerial staff from German into English using an online dictionary.

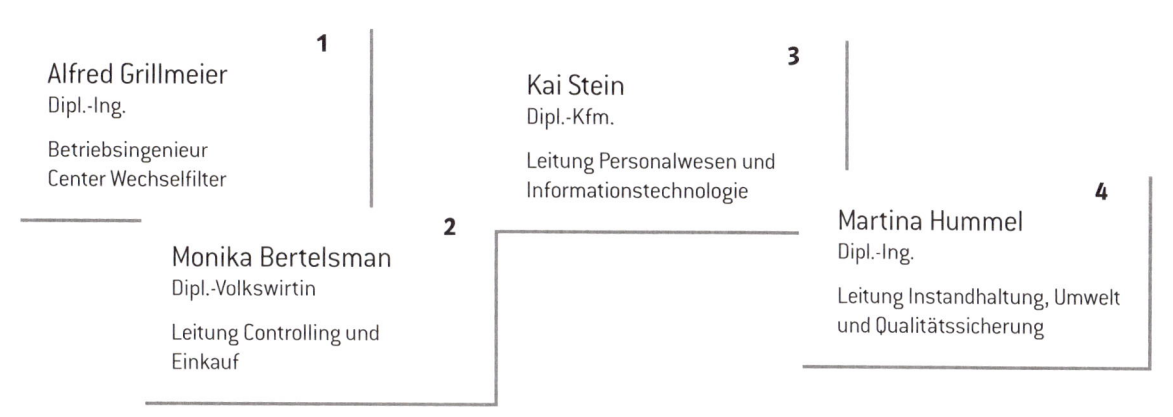

1
Alfred Grillmeier
Dipl.-Ing.

Betriebsingenieur
Center Wechselfilter

2
Monika Bertelsman
Dipl.-Volkswirtin

Leitung Controlling und Einkauf

3
Kai Stein
Dipl.-Kfm.

Leitung Personalwesen und Informationstechnologie

4
Martina Hummel
Dipl.-Ing.

Leitung Instandhaltung, Umwelt und Qualitätssicherung

3 Summarise in German the instructions for ordering cards on the internet.

Text editing and layout
Enter your text and select the font style in the boxes below and to the right. Press the "Update preview" button to preview your card. You can change the text layout by selecting one of the "Layout selector" thumbnails. You may place your own images on the card by clicking the "Add image" button. If you are satisfied with your layout click on "Approve" and you will go automatically to the next step in the order process.
The lines on the card are for reference only and will not appear on the finished card. The finished card will be trimmed at the trim-size (blue line) in the card preview. There is small tolerance in trimming, so the text must be kept inside the safe-zone (red line) to prevent it from being clipped. However, if you wish to have something continue to the edge of the card it must follow through to the bleed-line (green line).

4 Führen Sie in Partnerarbeit mithilfe der Rollenkarten einen Dialog.

Phrases

Role card: Partner A   **Role card partner B ⇨ page 254**

Sie besuchen die Messe Office Expo in Manchester und führen dort ein Gespräch mit einem/einer Vertreter/in von Better Business Cards.
- Stellen Sie sich vor und bekunden Sie Interesse am Kauf von Visitenkarten.
- Erkundigen Sie sich, ob die Karten mit der Farbe und dem Logo Ihrer Firma versehen werden können.
- Fragen Sie, ob die Karten zweisprachig (Deutsch/Englisch) bedruckt werden können.
- Fragen Sie, welche Papierqualitäten zur Auswahl stehen.
- Erkundigen Sie sich nach möglichen Rabatten.
- Fragen Sie nach den Zahlungs- und Lieferbedingungen.
- Bedanken Sie sich für das Gespräch und verabschieden Sie sich.

Unit 11 | Orders

Phrases: Orders

To refer to previous contacts and place an order

We have studied your quotation and enclose Purchase Order No. …	Wir haben Ihr Angebot genau durchgesehen und fügen unsere Bestellung Nr. … bei.
Please supply the following items **on** the terms stated below:	Bitte liefern Sie uns folgende Positionen zu den unten genannten Bedingungen:

To confirm prices and discounts

We would like to order model AC **at** the price of € … less 5 % introductory discount.	Wir möchten Modell AC zum Preis von € …, abzüglich 5 % Einführungsrabatt, bestellen.
We would like to confirm that the prices are taken **from** your price list **of** 1 September.	Wir möchten bestätigen, dass die Preise Ihrer Preisliste vom 1. September entnommen sind.

To confirm the method of payment and the terms of delivery and the delivery time

As agreed, we will effect payment **by** bank transfer 30 days **from** date of invoice.	Wie vereinbart werden wir die Zahlung 30 Tage nach Rechnungsdatum per Banküberweisung vornehmen lassen.
Payment will be made **by** irrevocable and confirmed letter of credit.	Die Zahlung erfolgt durch unwiderrufliches und bestätigtes Akkreditiv.
Your above-mentioned prices are quoted CIF Hamburg.	Ihre oben genannten Preise verstehen sich CIF Hamburg.
Delivery **is to** be made DAP Stuttgart.	Die Lieferung soll DAP Stuttgart erfolgen.
Complete delivery **by** … is a firm condition of this order.	Vollständige Lieferung bis … stellt eine feste Bedingung für diesen Auftrag dar.
Please note that the goods must reach us **by** 1 March at the latest.	Wir weisen darauf hin, dass die Ware bis spätestens 1. März hier eintreffen muss.

To give instructions and ask for confirmation

Please arrange for transportation **by** Eurotrans Ltd.	Bitte veranlassen Sie, dass der Transport von Eurotrans Ltd. durchgeführt wird.
Please make sure that the figurines are packed with the utmost care.	Bitte sorgen Sie dafür, dass die Figürchen äußerst sorgfältig verpackt werden.
Please acknowledge this order promptly.	Bitte bestätigen Sie diesen Auftrag umgehend.

To close the correspondence

We look forward to receiving the goods **in** time and to doing further business with you.	Wir sehen dem rechtzeitigen Eintreffen der Ware entgegen und freuen uns auf weitere Geschäfte mit Ihnen.

Unit 12
Transport and logistics

WORD BANK
transport • logistics • shipping • forwarding • cargo • freight • door-to-door delivery • modes of transport • types of packing • dispatch advice • waybill • consignment note • bill of lading • certificate of origin • packing list • insurance policy/certificate • to confirm • to acknowledge • to send • to ship • to transport • to pack • to wrap • to deliver

CONTAINER SHIPPING

World trade is forecast to continue growing strongly over the next decade. Today roughly 90% of non-bulk cargo is transported in containers stacked on transport ships. Cargo is also transported via roll on/roll off (ro-ro) ferries that offer easy loading and unloading. New cars, for instance, are simply driven on and off massive car carriers that hold thousands of vehicles. Ports such as Felixstowe in East Anglia are being deepened to accommodate the new generation of massive container ships.

The fact that the average consumer appears to have no idea how running shoes, washing machines, coffee or tonnes of toys arrive in the shops from all over the world is a constant source of irritation to the shipping world. "The global economy only exists thanks to shipping, in particular container shipping," says one industry analyst. The long-term downward trend in shipping costs has facilitated economic growth worldwide.

At the present time China clearly dominates world trade flows both in terms of exports of finished goods and imports of raw materials. However, shipping is a highly cyclical business reflecting growth and stagnation in the world economy. Carriers, ship-owners and terminal operators have constantly to invest in new ships and facilities. But they do not have a good record of getting the supply/demand ratio right and have often ended up either with inadequate or excess capacity.

Online-Link
808261-0012

Unit 12 | Transport and logistics

1 Beantworten Sie folgende Fragen zu vorstehendem Zeitungsartikel auf Deutsch.

R
1. Welches sind die größten und wichtigsten Transportmittel für den Welthandel?
2. Weswegen ist die Schifffahrtsbranche verärgert?
3. Wodurch wurde das rasche Wachstum des Welthandels erst ermöglicht?
4. Wie zeigt sich, dass die Schifffahrtsbranche von der Konjunktur abhängt?

✱ 2 Work in groups. Each group translates one paragraph from the text on page 171
M   in writing. Present your result to the class.

🌐 3 Use the internet to find out the percentages of goods transported by a. road and
b. rail in the EU.

A Modes of transport

Tobias Krabbe from the German company Form und Raum GmbH has been asked to collect first-hand information on the various modes of transport. He interviews Marie Boucher from the freight forwarding company FranceTransports which handles most of Form und Raum's international shipments.

1 Listen to the interview with Marie Boucher twice and complete the grid on a
KMK   separate sheet of paper. Then add whatever other advantages, disadvantages and
A 1.25   suitable cargoes you can think of. Compare your result with that of your neighbour.

	Road	Rail	Air	Sea / Inland Waterways
Advantages	door-to-door delivery, flexible timetables			
Disadvantages		unless a firm has its own private siding, goods must be transported to and collected from the station		slow; seaworthy packing required
Suitable cargoes			light, urgently required, perishable or valuable goods	

172

Transport and logistics | Unit 12

2 Work in groups. Choose one of the goods mentioned below and explain to your group which mode(s) of transport you would use, giving reasons for your choice. Use the expressions in the bubbles.

Example: "I'd send the wine by road from Spain to Poland because door-to-door delivery by lorry is probably faster than rail transport."

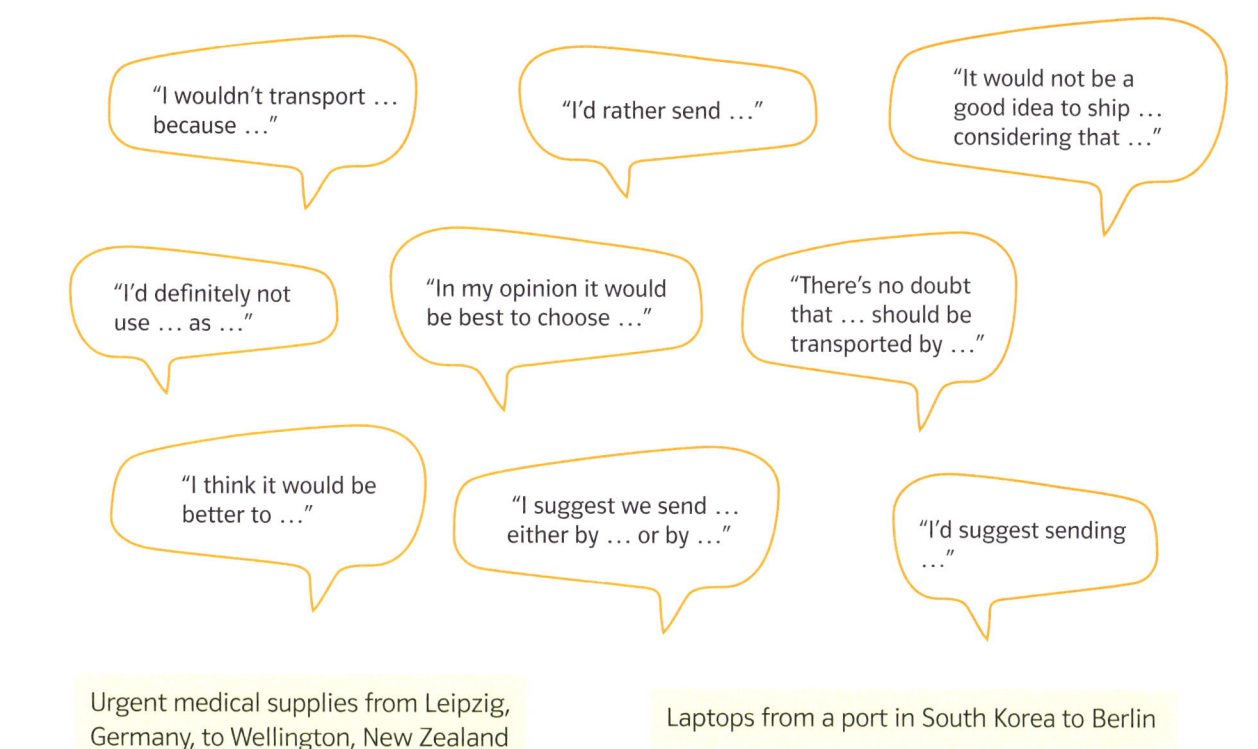

- "I wouldn't transport … because …"
- "I'd rather send …"
- "It would not be a good idea to ship … considering that …"
- "I'd definitely not use … as …"
- "In my opinion it would be best to choose …"
- "There's no doubt that … should be transported by …"
- "I think it would be better to …"
- "I suggest we send … either by … or by …"
- "I'd suggest sending …"

Urgent medical supplies from Leipzig, Germany, to Wellington, New Zealand

Laptops from a port in South Korea to Berlin

A large printing press from Mannheim in Germany to the port of Jeddah in Saudi Arabia

Tropical fruit from Brazil to Sweden

Designer shoes from Italy to Denmark

Furniture from a manufacturer in Westphalia to a hotel in Austria

Wine in bottles from Spain to Poland

50 cars from a plant in Munich to a car dealer in Lisbon, Portugal

Unit 12 | Transport and logistics

B Packing

Adequate packing is essential to ensure that goods arrive in perfect condition, regardless of the distance they have travelled.

1 Match the German terms (see photos above) with their English equivalents.

1. Eisenfass, Trommel
2. Holzkiste
3. Fass
4. folienumwickelter Karton
5. Rolle, Coil auf Europalette
6. Kunststoffbox mit Formeinlagen
7. Container
8. Ballen
9. Bündel mit Stahlbandumreifung
10. Lattenkiste, -verschlag
11. Einwegpalette
12. Sack

a. bale
b. bundle with steel strapping
c. coil on euro-pallet
d. container
e. crate
f. drum
g. foil-wrapped cardboard box
h. plastic box with mouldings
i. one-way pallet
j. sack
k. wooden case
l. barrel

2 The following sentences do not make much sense. Rearrange the words to form
R/P meaningful sentences.

1. The fruit will be packed in 15 bundles with steel strapping.
2. The pure new wool will be sent in a crate.
3. The steel rods will be shipped in bales.
4. The replacement Mp3 player will come on a reusable pallet.
5. The printing machine will be packed in a cardboard box.
6. The engine will be sent in a plastic gift box with mouldings.

174

Transport and logistics | Unit 12

C Dispatch advice

As soon as the goods are ready for dispatch it may be necessary to inform the customer that the goods can either be collected at the seller's premises or that they have been handed over to the carrier – depending on the Incoterms agreed upon in the sales contract. Remember that you are communicating with a customer and be as friendly and helpful as possible.

1 Dispatch advice in writing

Topelektronik has received an order for a total of 1,500 SomeThing Mp3 players from the British company Leigh & Co. Ltd. Cornelia Klinkenberg, head of sales at Topelektronik, informs James Leigh that the goods have now been shipped to the UK.

1 Complete Cornelia's e-mail using the verbs from the box.

accompanied • arrive • attached • delivered • given • packed • picked up • pleased • reach

From:	cornelia.klinkenberg@topelektronik.de
To:	james.leigh@leigh.co.uk
Cc:	
Sent:	201_-08-14 **Attachments:** Invoice No. 149 / 08 / 1_
Subject:	Your order dated 7 August for 1,500 SomeThing Mp3 Players

Dear Mr Leigh

We are **1** to inform you that the consignment has today been **2** by our forwarders, Transcontinental Logistik, to be **3** by road to your warehouse in Bristol.
The forwarders have **4** us the assurance that the goods will **5** you by Friday afternoon, at the latest.

The Mp3 players are **6** in 15 triple-walled cardboard boxes on one pallet.
The consignment is **7** by the required documents (consignment note, packing list and commercial invoice). A copy of the invoice is **8**.

Thank you once more for this order. We hope the goods will **9** safely and in good time. We look forward to serving you again.

Kind regards

Cornelia Klinkenberg
Topelektronik
Am Osthang 37
09114 Chemnitz
Tel. +49 371 460873
Fax. +49 371 460874

175

Unit 12 | Transport and logistics

2 Mr Kunal Mahajan, export manager at India Sports, has been processing an order
P for T-shirts from the German firm Herkules. He now sends them a dispatch advice.
Write his fax, using the following prompts:

- reference to their order of 20 Jan. and their letter of 1 Feb.
- consignment packed in one 20 ft container
- markings on the container: HKS, 3479, Antwerp
- yesterday loaded on board MV Maharani in the port of Mumbai
- expected time of arrival at Antwerp: on or about 12 March
- friendly closing phrase

India Sports

112 Delhi Road, Meerut-250 001
Uttar Pradesh, India
Fax +91 121 2512275
Tel. +91 121 2512270

Telefax

To:	Herkules Ziegelberg 8–12 89331 Neustadt, Germany	**Attention:**	Ms Laura Bayerle
		Fax:	+49 8358 88820
From:	Kunal Mahajan, Export Manager		
Date:	15 Feb 201_	**Pages (incl. this one):**	1
Subject:	Your order No. ABF/16 of 20 January and 1 February		

* 3 Sie (eigener Name) arbeiten bei der Münchner Firma Superdress GmbH,
KMK E-Mail: sales@superdress.munich.de. Ein britischer Kunde, Richard Knight,
Einkäufer bei der Warenhauskette Hamilton's, E-Mail: richard.knight@
hamiltons.co.uk, hatte bei Ihnen eine Sendung Herrenhemden bestellt, die
dringend für eine Modeschau benötigt werden.

Schreiben Sie eine E-Mail als Versandanzeige und berücksichtigen Sie dabei
Folgendes:

- Bezug auf Auftrag vom 18. August
- Sendung heute der Spedition Kleine zum Transport per Luftfracht übergeben
- British Airways Flug Nr. BA 777
- Abflug: Flughafen München, 22 August, 11:35 Uhr,
  Ankunft: Manchester Airport, 12:55 Uhr
- Erwartung, dass Hemden rechtzeitig für die Modeschau eintreffen
- nochmaliger Dank für den Auftrag

Transport and logistics | Unit 12

2 Order confirmation and inquiry concerning transport by phone

1 Thomas Krabbe from Form und Raum has received an order from a British customer. He confirms the order and the transport arrangements by phone. Listen to the dialogue and answer the following questions.

R
A 1.26

1. What is the name of Jennifer Ashley's firm?
2. Has Tobias spoken to Jennifer before?
3. When did Jennifer place the order?
4. How many Hermes standard lamps, Odin uplighters and Bauhaus coffee tables were ordered?
5. What are the first and the last order numbers, the second being O160u?
6. When is the consignment expected to arrive?

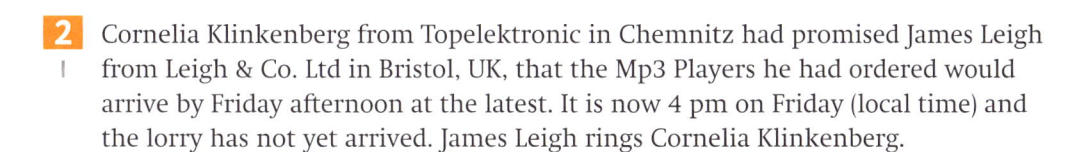

2 Cornelia Klinkenberg from Topelektronic in Chemnitz had promised James Leigh from Leigh & Co. Ltd in Bristol, UK, that the Mp3 Players he had ordered would arrive by Friday afternoon at the latest. It is now 4 pm on Friday (local time) and the lorry has not yet arrived. James Leigh rings Cornelia Klinkenberg.

I

Act out their dialogue with your neighbour using the prompts below.

Phrases

James Leigh	Cornelia Klinkenberg
	Topelektronik, Klinkenberg
James Leigh/Leigh & Co., Bristol/ Mp3 players/not yet arrived/ now 4 pm	
	Try to reach driver on his mobile phone/hold line?/ring back?
hold/urgent	
	spoken to driver/driver on motorway M4/ 20 miles away
here/next half hour?	
	driver confident/arrive before 5 pm/ reason for delay/held up in Channel Tunnel/ security check/false alarm/explosives in a van on the train/took almost 3 hours
glad to hear/arrive this afternoon/thanks	
	lucky still in office/5 pm in Germany
e-mail/as soon as goods have arrived/ nice weekend/Bye	
	too/Goodbye

Unit 12 | Transport and logistics

Language and grammar
Translate the statements into English.

1. Ich arbeite in einem Warenhaus und möchte Einzelhandelskaufmann werden.
2. Mein Chef ist leider ziemlich selbstbewusst und nicht sehr sympathisch.
3. Auf Seite 3 unseres Prospekts finden Sie Berichte unserer Kunden, die den Erfolg unserer Methode beweisen.
4. Ich bekomme ungefähr 50 E-Mails pro Tag.
5. Unsere Firma beobachtet die aktuellen Trends auf dem Markt sehr genau.
6. Diese Rechnungen müssen noch einmal geprüft werden.
7. Dieses System wird eventuell in unserem Büro eingeführt.

Language and grammar: False friends

Einige deutsche Wörter werden oft mit englischen Wörtern verwechselt, die etwas ganz anderes bedeuten

deutsches Wort	englische Bedeutung	nicht zu verwechseln mit	deutsche Bedeutung
aktuell	current(ly), topical	actual	tatsächlich, wirklich
bekommen	to get	to become	werden
Billion	trillion	billion	Milliarde
Chef*	boss	chef, chief	(Chef-)koch, Häuptling
eventuell	perhaps, possibly	eventual	schließlich
Fabrik	factory, works	fabric	Stoff
Gymnasium	grammar school	gym(nasium)	Sporthalle
Prospekt	brochure	prospect	Aussicht
Provision	commission	provision	Vorsorge
prüfen	to check, examine	to prove	beweisen
übersehen	to overlook	to oversee	überwachen
Warenhaus	department store	warehouse	Lagerhaus

*Ausnahme: Zusammengesetzte Begriffe wie chief accountant, chief executive officer

V6 Video lounge IT

BBC Motion Gallery

**This video illustrates important IT applications.
Look out for the answers to the following questions:**

1. What are the duties of the three staff members shown in the video?
2. Give a brief description of any one of them.
3. Why is it important to check everything carefully?
4. What possible problems do they have to watch out for?

Phrases: Transport and logistics

To give particulars about packing

The goods are packed in …	Die Ware ist verpackt in …
• polythene bags.	• Plastikbeutel.
• 20 bales weighing 50 kgs per bale.	• 20 Ballen zu je 50 kg.
• one 20 ft container.	• einem 20-Fuß-Container.
• fibreboard boxes with steel bands.	• Hartfaserkisten mit Stahlbändern.
The goods will be shipped …	Die Ware wird …
• **in** sturdy crates.	• in stabilen Lattenkisten
• **on** reusable pallets.	• auf Mehrwegpaletten
	versandt.

To say that the goods are ready for collection

We are pleased to inform you that the keyboards can now be collected **at** our plant in Leeds.	Wir freuen uns Ihnen mitteilen zu können, dass die Keyboards jetzt in unserem Werk in Leeds abgeholt werden können.

To give particulars about the transport

The consignment has today been handed over to the freight forwarders **for** transportation **to** Warsaw by lorry.	Die Sendung wurde heute der Spedition zur Beförderung nach Warschau per LKW übergeben.
Yesterday the machine was loaded **on board** MS Seagull in Bremerhaven.	Die Maschine wurde gestern in Bremerhaven auf die MS Seagull verladen.
The spare parts will be sent **by** air freight **on** Air Canada flight No. AC 442, arriving **at** Toronto airport at 11:55 **on** 25 September.	Die Ersatzteile werden per Luftfracht mit Air Canada, Flug Nr. AC 442 verschickt. Ankunft: Flughafen Toronto, 25. Sept., 11:55 Uhr.

To close on a friendly note

We hope the goods will arrive punctually and in good condition.	Wir hoffen, die Ware kommt pünktlich und in gutem Zustand bei Ihnen an.
We trust that the quality of our garments will meet your expectations.	Wir sind überzeugt, dass die Qualität unserer Bekleidungsartikel Ihren Erwartungen entspricht.
We feel sure that your customers will be pleased with our new range of …	Wir sind sicher, dass unser neues Sortiment von … Ihren Kunden gefallen wird.

Unit 13 | Payment and reminders

UNIT 13
Payment and reminders

WORD BANK

currency • commercial invoice • proforma invoice • IBAN • BIC • bank account • unit price • subtotal • total price • cash • credit card • debit card • cheque • bill of exchange • payment in advance • cash on delivery • open credit • open account • letter of credit • reminder • statement of account • amount due • settlement • to make out an invoice • to transfer • to delay • to collect • to take legal steps

CURRENCY QUIZ

Questions:
1. Which is the youngest of the currencies shown above?
2. Which is the oldest of these currencies?
3. Which of these currencies is the most widely used in international business transactions?
4. Which of these currencies do most individuals use for their daily purchases?

1. The Euro. Euro banknotes and coins replaced 12 former European currencies on 1 January 2002.
2. The Pound Sterling. It has been in use since the Middle Ages. The US Dollar was introduced in 1785, the Swiss Frank in 1798 and the Yen in 1871).
3. The US Dollar. On a global scale the US-Dollar is still the most widely used currency in business transactions.
4. The Euro. The number of inhabitants in the Euro zone (EU without Denmark, Sweden and the United Kingdom) is estimated at 325,7 million, approx. 306 million people live in the USA.

Payment and reminders | Unit 13

A The invoice

The **commercial invoice** (Handelsrechnung) is sent by the seller to the buyer and provides full details on the transaction, such as names, dates, numbers, descriptions, quantities, prices, discounts, terms, taxes (VAT) etc. When making out an export invoice you should make sure that it includes your company's IBAN and your bank's BIC.

A **proforma invoice** (Proformarechnung) contains all the details of the eventual commercial invoice. It may serve as a quotation or be required to apply for an import licence.

1 The above text contains three abbreviations. Study their German translations and
R   find the words that have been left out in the full English expressions.

VAT	Value-added **1**	= Mehrwert**steuer**
IBAN	International Bank **2** Number	= Internationale **Konto**nummer
BIC	Bank Identifier **3**	= Internationaler Bank-**Code**.

2 Philipp Schäfer is processing the trial order for Turbostar Running shoes which
R   his company, Herkules, has received from Sports Island, a major British chain of sports equipment retailers. (See Unit 11, A). The necessary arrangements for transportation having been made Philipp Schäfer now confirms the order by e-mail and sends the invoice as an attachment.

Study Philipp Schäfer's e-mail and decide which of the tenses in brackets is correct.

Dear Ms Brookfield

Thank you very much for your above-mentioned order.

We are pleased to inform you that the consignment **1 is picked up / will be picked up** by Transeurope Hauliers for transportation to the UK in two days' time, that is to say on Wednesday, 10 October. The forwarders **2 have given / had given** us the assurance that the running shoes **3 will be delivered / will have been delivered** to your premises in London on the following Friday, 12 October, between 9 and 11 a.m. your time.

Since this is a first order we **4 were sending / are sending** you our invoice No. GB113-14 as an attachment and would appreciate it if you **5 instructed / have instructed** your bankers at your earliest convenience to remit the sum of € 30,375.00 to our account with Bayernbank. For particulars see the attached invoice.

We **5 feel / felt** sure that your customers **6 will be pleased / are pleased** with the Turbostar running shoes as they are not merely comfortable, serviceable and durable but stylish as well. We look forward to receiving further orders from you in the near future.

Herkules
the global sports brand

Ziegelberg 8–12
89331 Neustadt
Tel. +49 8358 888-0
Fax +49 8358 88820
www.Herkules.com

USt. ID No. DE 812 039 979

INVOICE No. GB113-14

Sports Island
41 Bryant Road
London W7 9QB
UK

VAT No. 186 4405 32

Customer No. UK 22267

Date: 8 Oct 201_
Your Order No. 5347 of 5 Oct 201_

Person in charge: Mike Kappler
Tel.: +49 8358 888 317
Fax: +49 8358 888 300
E-Mail: accounts@herkules.com

Quantity	Item	Sizes	Unit Price	Subtotal
25 pairs each	Turbostar Running Shoes	5, 5 ½, 11, 12	€ 40.50	€ 4,050.00
50 pairs each		6, 6 ½, 7, 7 ½, 10	€ 40.50	€ 10,125.00
100 pairs each		8, 8 ½, 9, 9 ½	€ 40.50	€ 16,200.00

Total Price € 30,375.00

tax-exempt intra-Community delivery

Terms of delivery: EXW Neustadt
Terms of payment: Cash on receipt of invoice

Please instruct your bank to forward the payment order through

Bank: Bayernbank AG
BIC: BABADET TS08
In favour of: Herkules AG
Bank account number: 214365987
IBAN: DE49 2006 0460 0214 3659 87

Payment and reminders | Unit 13

3 Study the invoice and find words and expressions for the following German equivalents.

1. Gesamtpreis
2. Preis pro Einheit/Stückpreis
3. Zahlungsbedingungen
4. Artikel
5. Lieferbedingungen
6. Größen
7. Menge
8. Rechnung
9. Zwischensumme

4 Study the invoice again and draw up the invoice Cornelia Klinkenberg sent James Leigh on 14 August. Use your imagination for the missing details and refer back to:

1. the enquiry James Leigh sent Cornelia Klinkenberg (Unit 10, A)
2. the dispatch advice Cornelia Klinkenberg sent James Leigh (Unit 12, C)
3. James Leigh's reply to Cornelia Klinkenberg's reminder (Unit 13, C).

B Means and terms of payment

1 Means of payment in trade

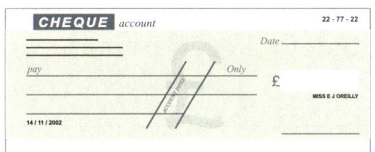

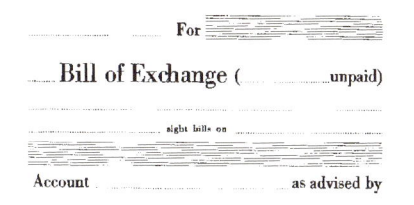

A **credit card** (Kreditkarte) issued by a major credit card company is widely accepted as a means of payment all over the world. The amount to be paid is advanced by the credit card company and debited to the cardholder's account at a later date.

A **debit (or bank) card** (Bankkarte) is issued by a bank. The account-holder may use it to pay for goods and services in shops without handling cash. It differs from credit cards in that the customer's account is immediately debited with the amount of the transaction. Bank cards can also be used to withdraw money from cash points (ATMs). The German EC card is a debit card.

A **cheque** (Scheck) is a written order to a bank to pay a sum of money to a named person or to the bearer (Überbringer) of the cheque. Crossed cheques (Verrechnungsschecks) require the sum to be paid into a bank account. In the UK cheques are still widely used in private and business transactions.

A **bill of exchange** (Wechsel) is a written order telling one person to pay a certain sum of money to a named person on demand or at a certain time in the future. Nowadays bills of exchange are used mainly in foreign trade. If the exporter wishes payment to be made immediately, he orders the importer to pay the invoice amount on demand, or "at sight", that means on presentation of the bill of exchange (B/E). Should the exporter be obliged to grant the importer credit, he will order him to pay the invoice amount at a certain time in the future, e.g. 60 days after the date of the B/E.

183

Unit 13 | Payment and reminders

1 Match the following expressions with their German equivalents.

1. to accept a credit card
2. to advance an amount
3. to debit an account
4. to grant credit
5. to issue a bank card
6. to withdraw money

a. Geld abheben
b. eine Kreditkarte annehmen
c. eine Bankkarte ausstellen
d. ein Konto belasten
e. Kredit gewähren
f. einen Betrag vorschießen

∗ 2 Study the text on the bill of exchange on page 183 and translate the following text.
M

Mittels eines Wechsels kann der Verkäufer den Käufer auffordern, eine bestimmte Summe zu einem bestimmten Zeitpunkt an eine bestimmte Person zu zahlen. Der Verkäufer könnte auf dem Wechsel auch vorschreiben, dass der Käufer den Betrag „auf Verlangen" zahlt. Die entsprechende Formulierung wäre dann „zahlbar bei Sicht", d. h. bei Vorlage des Wechsels.

∗ 3 Übersetzen Sie nachstehenden Text zum Einsatz von Kreditkarten in
KMK Großbritannien ins Deutsche. Im Internet haben Sie Übersetzungen für folgende Ausdrücke gefunden:

overindebted – überschuldet; to turn down an application – einen Antrag ablehnen; debit card – Bankkarte; cashback – Auszahlung von Bargeld; debt levels – Ausmaß der Verschuldung; check-out – Ladenkasse

Payment by plastic cards

In the UK payment by plastic cards overtook cash payments several years ago as consumers use credit or debit cards more frequently. The vast majority of retail outlets accept these cards as a matter of course and supermarkets offer cashback*. Adults now have an average of 4 cards each and this is expected to rise to 5 cards by 2013. Last year the number of credit cards issued rose by 13 per cent and the number of debit cards rose by 6 per cent. Well over half of all debit card holders use their cards on a regular basis when shopping.

Recently banks and other credit card providers have come in for criticism because of fears that consumers are becoming over-indebted. A spokesman for the banks said that between 40 and 50 per cent of all credit card applications were turned down. Debt levels were a problem only for 4 per cent of households.

Plastic cards are essential for e-commerce. Four out of five adults who have access use the internet for online shopping. A third of all online purchases are made from work and top sites include major supermarkets and a well-known young people's fashion chain.

* If the customer wishes, they provide a sum in cash at the check-out, as stipulated by the customer.

4 Use the internet to find statistics on the preferred payment methods – cash, credit card, debit card, cheque, bank transfer – in Germany and the UK.

2 Terms of payment in foreign trade

The terms of payment chosen in an international transaction will depend on the size of the order, the creditworthiness of the customer and the banking system and political situation in the customer's country.

Payment in advance (Vorauszahlung) provides maximum security for the seller, e.g. when the goods have to be manufactured to the buyer's specifications. Payment in advance may also be part of staggered payment, e.g. ⅓ with order, ⅓ on delivery, ⅓ 30 days after delivery.

If **Cash on delivery (COD)** (Zahlung durch Nachnahme) has been agreed upon, the carrier (e.g. the postman) will hand over the goods to the buyer against payment or against written proof by the bank that payment has been effected.

Open credit (Zahlung gegen einfache Rechnung) terms are terms like "30 days net, 10 days 2%", which means that the buyer has to remit the invoice amount within 30 days. If he pays the amount within 10 days he will be entitled to deduct 2% cash discount from the invoice amount. Open credit terms provide little security for the seller but are widely used in transactions involving comparatively small sums and/or trusted customers.

In long-standing business relations it is customary to trade on **open account** terms (offenes Zahlungsziel). This means that the buyer does not pay individual invoices, but waits for the monthly statement of account.

A **letter of credit (L/C)** (Akkreditiv) is a promise made by the importer's bank to pay a certain sum to the exporter on presentation of specified documents, the most important of which is a clean bill of lading (see Unit 12). Nowadays L/Cs are irrevocable (unwiderruflich) that means they cannot be revoked without the consent of all parties concerned. As the L/C offers maximum security for both buyer and seller it has become one of the most widely used methods of payment in foreign trade. The exporter can be sure to receive payment as he can rely on the promise made by the importer's bank (the opening bank) – and in the case of a confirmed (bestätigtes) L/C – also on the promise of a bank in his own country (the confirming bank). The importer can be sure to receive the goods as the bank(s) will only advance the money against presentation of the shipping documents which prove that shipment has been effected.

Unit 13 | Payment and reminders

1 Study the paragraph on the Letter of Credit on page 185. Choose the correct prepositions from the box for the following text. Then translate the text into German.

R/M

at • by • in • until

In a major export transaction the terms of payment may read as follows: **Terms of payment:** Payment **1** irrevocable and confirmed letter of credit, to be opened **2** our favour, payable **3** a German bank and valid **4** 31 July.

2 Complete the following business transactions by matching the terms of payment from the box with the numbers.

R

cash on delivery • letter of credit • open account terms • open credit • payment in advance

Wilson & Thatcher Ltd, a British retailer, also sells its high-quality shirts and blouses via the Internet. As a means of payment the firm accepts all major credit cards. For customers who refuse to disclose their credit card details on the internet, the retailer's terms of payment are **1** which means that the postman will collect the amount due.

International Snacks GmbH, a German food processing company, gets a phone call from its long-standing customer, Global Catering in Manchester, asking for another 500 tins of mini smoked sausages. These two business partners most likely trade on **2** .

Powertools plc from Cardiff has received an enquiry from a new German customer who wishes to have 10,000 drill heads (Bohrköpfe) manufactured to the German firm's specifications. As Powertools would be unable to sell these drill heads to another customer if the deal broke down, Powertools will insist on **3** .

Norland Industries made an offer for colour printers to De Boer Office Equipment in Durban, South Africa. The terms of payment stipulated were: net cash within 30 days from receipt of invoice. Such terms of payment are referred to as **4** .

At Herkules, a German manufacturer of sports shoes and bags, the managers in charge of exports are discussing the terms of payment for a substantial order for sports bags from a firm in Bolivia they do not know. They decide to demand payment by **5** .

C Reminders

There are times when bills go unpaid and steps must be taken to collect the invoice amount. One or several reminders may have to be sent, with the requests for payment becoming increasingly insistent. At first a copy of the invoice or statement of account is sent suggesting that the invoice may have been overlooked. If further reminders by telephone, e-mail, fax, or letter have failed to produce the desired reaction, the seller will threaten to charge interest on arrears and to take legal steps unless payment is received by a certain deadline.

1 Reminders in writing

On 18 August the British department stores Hamilton's placed an urgent order for men's shirts with Superdress GmbH. Payment was to be effected 30 days after date of invoice. The goods were shipped by air and must have arrived at Manchester Airport on 22 August. It is now 10 October and no communication from Hamilton's has been received. Bastian Schneider, who is in charge of accounts at Superdress GmbH, decides to send a first polite reminder by fax.

1 Complete Bastian Schneider's fax using the words from the box.

above • aware • dated • due • grateful • immediate

Superdress GmbH

Fritz-Walter-Str. 28, 80469 München
Tel. +49 89 4677524, Fax +49 89 4677625
www.superdress.munich.de

Telefax Message

Date: 10 Oct 201_   **Sender:** Bastian Schneider, Accounts

To: Hamilton's Department Stores   **Attention:** Richard Knight
Hamilton House
Beaumont Rd   **Fax:** +44 161 234 57799
Bolton
BL3 4TA   **Pages:** 1 (including this)

Re: Our invoice no. OHGB / 42778 **1** 21 August *(reference to invoice)*

Dear Mr. Knight

According to our records the **2** invoice, which was **3** on 21 September, has not been settled.

I wonder whether the invoice has been overlooked or if there has been a problem with this order of which we are not **4** ? *(request for explanation)*

We should be **5** for an **6** settlement and look forward to serving you again. *(request for settlement)*

Yours sincerely
Superdress GmbH

Unit 13 | Payment and reminders

2 You are Richard Knight, purchasing manager at Hamilton's Department Stores,
P   e-mail: richard.knight@hamiltons.co.uk. You have just received the fax on
    page 187 from Superdress GmbH.

Send Mr Schneider, whose e-mail address is b.schneider@superdress.munich.de, an e-mail:

- thanks for fax
- apologize for the delay in payment
- reason: new software in accounts department faulty
- operations now running smoothly at last
- bank instructed to remit invoice amount
- further orders probably next month

3 **Restore the correct order of these jumbled elements of a final request for**
R   **payment.**

1. I still hope that you will make this action unnecessary by remitting the amount in full within the next seven days.

2. Dear Mr Clarke

3. This account has now remained unpaid for eight weeks and I cannot allow this state of affairs to continue. I regret that I will have to take legal steps unless payment is received in the course of one week.

4. Yours sincerely

   Barbara Bruno
   Legal Department

5. I am surprised to have received no reply to our previous e-mails and faxes asking for immediate settlement of the attached statement of account.

6. Re: Our statement of account number NZ/7034 of 9 December 201_

Payment and reminders | Unit 13

4 Sie arbeiten bei Topelektronik in der Exportabteilung. Ihre Chefin hat gestern
KMK nachstehende E-Mail eines britischen Kunden erhalten.

Bitte beantworten Sie die E-Mail und berücksichtigen Sie dabei die handschriftlichen Anweisungen Ihrer Chefin.

From:	james.leigh@leigh.co.uk	
To:	cornelia.klinkenberg@topelektronik.de	
Cc:		
Sent:	201_-09-27	Attachments:
Subject:	Your invoice No. 149 / 08 / 14	

Dear Ms Klinkenberg

We have received your fax of 15 September concerning the above invoice and would like to apologize for the delay in payment.

Today we have instructed our bank to transfer € 30,000 to your account. Much to our regret we have to ask you to grant us a respite of eight weeks for the rest of the invoice amount.

Dank für Überweisung

You may have heard of the severe gale that devastated the South of England two weeks ago. Unfortunately our warehouse was severely hit by the storm, parts of the roof were taken off and much of our stock was soaked by the rain. As the insurance company will take some time to assess the damage and compensate us, we are having to advance considerable sums for the repairs to our warehouse and for the replacement of the damaged stock. This is why we must ask you for the extension.

Bedauern über Sturmschäden, im Fernsehen Bilder gesehen

We hope you will understand our difficulties and grant us this concession.

Mit Aufschub grundsätzlich einverstanden

We are very sorry for the inconvenience caused and look forward to your comments.

Dennoch Bitte um Überweisung des Restbetrags sobald Leigh dazu in der Lage

Yours sincerely

*Grußformel: Best wishes
(Setzen Sie meinen Namen darunter)*

James Leigh
Leigh & Co. Ltd.
17 Camden Place   *Klinkenberg*
Bristol
BS6 6HR
Tel. 0117 4430030

Unit 13 | Payment and reminders

✱ 5 Sie (eigener Name) arbeiten im Rechnungswesen des Reisebüros Ferne
KMK Horizonte, Erfurt, Fax. +49 361 476903, Tel. +49 361 476900. Für den britischen
Reiseveranstalter Sunshine Flights Ltd., Fax +44 1233 443006, hatten Sie für eine
Gruppe eine Mountainbike-Tour im Thüringer Wald organisiert. Die Rechnung
hierfür ist seit 6 Wochen überfällig. Eine erste Erinnerung war ohne Reaktion
geblieben.

Schreiben Sie eine Mahnung unter Berücksichtigung folgender Punkte:

- Datum: 28. November
- Ansprechpartner: Margaret Allen
- Bezug auf Rechnung Nr. 009575 vom 04. Oktober
- Verweis auf Ihr Schreiben vom 14. November
- Rechnung inzwischen 6 Wochen überfällig
- Frage nach möglichen Gründen für Zahlungsverzug, da früher pünktlich gezahlt
- Bitte um sofortige Überweisung des Rechnungsbetrags, sonst Rücknahme der günstigen Zahlungsbedingungen
- Erwartung einer umgehenden Reaktion

2 Reminders and replies to reminders by telephone

1 Angela Schirmer from Digitaldruck GmbH in Wiesbaden rings
R   their Spanish customer Imago S.A.
A 1.27

Listen to the dialogue and mark on your own sheet of paper whether the following statements are TRUE or FALSE.

1. Carmen Gonzales is the best person to talk to.
2. Olivia Rubio works in accounts.
3. The reference number is Z2P 7900.
4. Olivia Rubio transferred the amount of € 13,723 five weeks ago.
5. This is the first time this year that there has been a delay in payment.
6. Olivia Rubio is going to transfer the amount immediately.

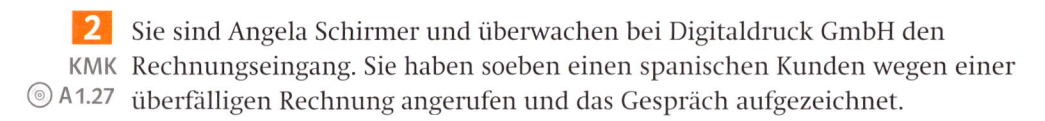

2 Sie sind Angela Schirmer und überwachen bei Digitaldruck GmbH den
KMK Rechnungseingang. Sie haben soeben einen spanischen Kunden wegen einer
A 1.27 überfälligen Rechnung angerufen und das Gespräch aufgezeichnet.

Hören Sie sich das Gespräch noch einmal an und verfassen Sie darüber eine Aktennotiz für den Abteilungsleiter Dr. Klaus Werner.

```
MEMO

Für:

Verfasser/in:                           Datum:

Gesprächspartner/in:

Betreff:
```

Payment and reminders | Unit 13

✱ 3 Work with a partner. Sit back to back and act out the telephone conversation using the prompts on the role cards on pages 254 and 255. Then change roles.

Language and grammar
Translate the following sentences.

1. Wir machen Sie darauf aufmerksam, dass die Zahlung per Kreditkarte erfolgen soll.
2. Das Unternehmen soll in 5 selbstständige Geschäftseinheiten aufgeteilt werden.
3. Sollen wir Ihnen die Preisliste per E-Mail zukommen lassen?
4. Soll die Rechnung Nr. ABC/1234 storniert werden?
5. Die neue Geschäftsleitung soll weiteren Stellenabbau planen.
6. Die neue Autobahn soll von einem privaten Unternehmen betrieben werden.
7. Der neue Exportleiter soll sehr tüchtig sein.

Language and grammar:
How to translate the German word "sollen"

Wendungen mit **sollen** werden von Deutschen häufig ungeschickt wiedergegeben.

Die direkte Entsprechung **shall** passt nur bei • Fragen • und juristischen Texten	Shall I help you? The parties to this contract shall notify the administrator within 24 hours.
should bedeutet **sollte (eigentlich)**:	You should put more emphasis on this point.
sollen kann im Geschäftskontext in Fragen mit **do you want me / us to …?** übersetzt werden: Sollen wir diese Teile zurückschicken?	Do you want us to return these components?
to be to … ist eine passende Übersetzung für **sollen** im Sinne einer Anordnung oder einer Absicht bzw. eines festen Planes: Die Bauarbeiter sollen sofort anfangen. Das Problem soll durch weitere Verhandlungen gelöst werden.	The builders are to start work immediately. The problem is to be solved by further negotiations.
Im Falle einer Absicht / eines Plans kann **to be to …** durch **to be intended to / planned to …** präzisiert werden: Die Erhöhung der Mehrwertsteuer soll den Haushalt ausgleichen. Die Ausstellung soll Anfang nächsten Jahres stattfinden.	The increase in VAT is intended to balance the budget. The exhibition is planned to take place early next year.
to be said to … bedeutet **sollen** im Sinne von **es heißt, man sagt**: Die Firma soll sich in Schwierigkeiten befinden.	The company is said to be in trouble.

Unit 13 | Payment and reminders

Office expert

1 Handling money

1 There are many different words for payment, depending on who pays, who gets the money and what for. Match the following forms of payment (1.–10.) to their definitions (a.–j.).

1. bonus
2. commission
3. dividend
4. fee
5. grant
6. interest
7. pension
8. rent
9. salary
10. subsidy
11. taxes
12. welfare

a. amount of money paid for a job or service
b. aid given for a special purpose (e.g. student education)
c. a share in a company's profits paid to its shareholders
d. money earned from savings or owed to a bank
e. money given in addition to a salary, e.g. at Christmas
f. money paid by a company or the government to retirees
g. money paid by the government to help poor people
h. money paid for the use of something (e.g. a flat)
i. money paid on a regular basis to an employee
j. money paid to help support firms
k. money paid to the government
l. payment to someone who sells goods which is related to how many goods are sold

2 Use an online dictionary and find the German equivalents for these English phrases. Do not translate the sentences literally.

1. If we play our cards right, we should be able to land the deal with the Chinese suppliers.
2. Her boss thought she was worth her weight in gold and gave her a blank cheque to refurnish her office.
3. You might think the project is a money-spinner, but for my money we're going to end up paying through the nose.
4. I thing you should put your money where your mouth is – the ball is in your court now.
5. The penny finally dropped when she realised that the company was just a nickel and dime operation.
6. Investing anything more in the project would simply be money down the drain – I think we should cash in our chips while we are ahead of the game.
7. I'd bet my bottom dollar that he was paid hush money from their slush fund – he seems to be rolling in money.

Payment and reminders | Unit 13

3 Put the following instructions (A.–L.) for using an ATM into the correct order.

R

A. Select a language.
B. Or if you want to deposit money, enter the amount, confirm and then insert the envelope/deposit slip into the slot when the machine opens it.
C. Enter your PIN (Personal Identification Number), then press Enter.
D. Wait while the system processes your transaction.
E. Once you arrive at the bank, insert your ATM card into the machine.
F. If you want to withdraw money, enter the amount, confirm and then put the cash directly into your wallet.
G. First of all, always be alert, especially at night or in an unfamiliar area.
H. Remember to take an envelope and prepare deposits ahead of time.
I. Choose whether you want a receipt by selecting Yes or No.
J. Select a transaction.
K. Use the receipt to record the transaction in your passbook.
L. Choose whether to do an additional transaction.

2 Writing a reminder

A reminder can be written not only to notify customers of unpaid invoices *(Mahnbrief)* but also to remind customers of services or goods on offer *(Erinnerungsbrief)*.

KMK Sie arbeiten für die Reinigungsfirma Blitzblank und sollen einen Ihrer Stammkunden kontaktieren (Firma Interteam, Prins Hendrikkade 87, Amsterdam-Centrum, 1011 AK Amsterdam, Niederlande; Ansprechperson: Frau Stiekema).

Phrases

Schreiben Sie einen Erinnerungsbrief an die Firma Interteam und berücksichtigen dabei folgende Punkte:

- Nehmen Sie Bezug auf den vermutlich vollen Terminkalender Ihres Ansprechpartners.
- Weisen Sie darauf hin, dass der Dienstleistungsvertrag mit Ihrer Firma bald auslaufen wird.
- Geben Sie der Hoffnung Ausdruck, dass die Firma bis dato mit Ihren Dienstleistungen zufrieden war.
- Verweisen Sie auf das beigefügte Vertragsformular, um die Abwicklung der Vertragsverlängerung zu erleichtern.
- Weisen Sie darauf hin, dass Sie für etwaige Fragen oder weitere Informationen zur Verfügung stehen.
- Äußern Sie die Erwartung weiterer Zusammenarbeit und sichern Sie weiterhin erstklassige Reinigungsleistungen zu.

Phrases: Invoices and reminders

To refer to the invoice or statement of account

We are sending you our invoice No. 43-298 **amounting to** €304.75 as an attachment.	Als Anhang senden wir Ihnen unsere Rechnung Nr. 43-298 in Höhe von €304,75.
The enclosed statement of account shows a balance of €5,402.90 **in** our favour.	Der beiliegende Kontoauszug weist einen Saldo von €5.402,90 zu unseren Gunsten auf.
The invoice was due **on** 31 July.	Die Rechnung war am 31. Juli fällig.
The invoice amount is now four weeks overdue.	Der Rechnungsbetrag ist nun vier Wochen überfällig.

To suggest an oversight or demand an explanation

I wonder whether the invoice has been overlooked.	Ich frage mich, ob die Rechnung übersehen wurde.
You have not given us any explanation for the delay **in** payment.	Sie haben uns keinerlei Erklärung für den Zahlungsverzug gegeben.

To demand payment and to point out consequences of non-payment

Please remit the amount due immediately.	Bitte überweisen Sie den fälligen Betrag umgehend.
We should be grateful for an early settlement of our statement of account.	Für baldigen Ausgleich unseres Kontoauszugs wären wir dankbar.
We would ask you to clear the balance without further delay.	Wir möchten Sie bitten, den Saldo unverzüglich auszugleichen.
We must insist that you make payment **by** 5 May at the latest.	Wir müssen darauf bestehen, dass Sie die Zahlung bis spätestens 5. Mai vornehmen.
Should you fail to meet this deadline we shall have no option **but** to change our terms of payment.	Sollten Sie diese Frist nicht einhalten, bleibt uns keine andere Wahl als unsere Zahlungsbedingungen zu ändern.
If we do not receive payment **by** the end of the week, we will have to stop further deliveries.	Wenn Ihre Zahlung nicht bis Ende der Woche hier eingeht, müssen wir die Belieferung einstellen.
I will have to take legal steps if you do not settle the account within 7 days.	Ich werde juristische Schritte einleiten müssen, falls Sie die Rechnung nicht innerhalb von 7 Tagen begleichen.
Unless you remit the amount **in** time, we will hand the matter over to a collection agency.	Wenn Sie den Betrag nicht rechtzeitig überweisen, übergeben wir die Angelegenheit einem Inkassounternehmen.

To close the reminder

If payment has already been effected in the meantime, please disregard this letter.	Sollte die Zahlung inzwischen erfolgt sein, betrachten Sie diesen Brief bitte als gegenstandslos.
We should be sorry to lose a long-standing customer and would ask you to contact us immediately.	Wir würden einen langjährigen Kunden nur ungern verlieren, setzen Sie sich deshalb bitte sofort mit uns in Verbindung.
We are looking forward to an early settlement.	Wir erwarten Ihre baldige Zahlung.

To reply to a reminder

We have instructed our bank to transfer the sum of €7,455 **to** your account **with** Sachsenbank.	Wir haben unsere Bank angewiesen, den Betrag von €7.455 auf Ihr Konto bei der Sachsenbank zu überweisen.
We have received your letter **of** 2 July and thank you for your patience.	Wir haben Ihr Schreiben vom 2. Juli erhalten und danken Ihnen für Ihre Geduld.
We assure you that payment will be effected in full as soon as our computers are operational again.	Wir versichern Ihnen, dass die Zahlung in voller Höhe erfolgt, sobald unsere Rechner wieder funktionieren.
We are deeply sorry that the invoice has become overdue.	Es tut uns sehr leid, dass die Rechnung überfällig wurde.
We apologize for the delay **in** payment.	Wir entschuldigen uns für den Zahlungsverzug.
The delay was due to • an oversight. • a breakdown of our computer system. • an error **by** our bank.	Der Grund für den Zahlungsverzug war • ein Versehen. • eine Störung unserer EDV-Anlage. • ein Irrtum unserer Bank.
We are afraid we must ask you **for** an extension of 4 weeks.	Wir müssen Sie leider um einen Aufschub von 4 Wochen bitten.
We suggest that we pay **in** 3 instalments **of** $30,330.	Wir schlagen vor, dass wir in 3 Raten von $30.330 zahlen.
We are prepared to pay 7% interest on arrears.	Wir erklären uns bereit, Verzugszinsen in Höhe von 7% zu entrichten.
We hope you will understand our difficult situation and grant us this concession.	Wir hoffen, Sie haben Verständnis für unsere schwierige Lage und machen uns dieses Zugeständnis.

UNIT 14
Complaints and adjustments

WORD BANK
complaint • inconvenience • transaction • explanation • adjustment • solution • replacement • substitute • discount • compromise • faulty • damaged • too late • defective • wrong • justified • unjustified • to complain • to insist on • to cancel • to return • to apologize • to grant • to repair • to replace • to take back

A Making complaints

Even though in business transactions not "everything that can go wrong, will" – as the saying goes – it will sometimes be necessary to make a complaint. Goods or services may have been supplied too late, goods may be faulty or damaged, services may prove unsatisfactory, the wrong goods or the wrong quantities may have been delivered etc. In such cases the customer must promptly notify the seller of the problem in writing, especially if a complaint by telephone has not brought the desired result. A complaint should not be written to express anger, but to get results. It should be calm and polite but also firm. In your written complaint you should
- give all the necessary details of the transaction (order No., date of delivery, etc.)
- describe the problem clearly (327 mugs broken, hotel noisy, etc.)
- stress the inconvenience caused
- suggest a solution (replacement, discount, etc.)
- ask for immediate action

Complaints and adjustments | Unit 14

* 1 Übertragen Sie den Text auf Seite 196 ins Deutsche.
KMK

2 Match the causes for complaint on the left with the suggested solutions on the right. Sometimes several solutions may be appropriate.

1. delay in delivery
2. faulty goods
3. goods damaged
4. services unsatisfactory
5. the wrong goods
6. wrong quantity

a. grant a price reduction
b. improve the service rendered
c. repair the goods
d. replace the goods
e. send the goods by air freight
f. send the missing quantity
g. take back the goods
h. take back the surplus goods
i. send a credit note

3 Describe to your class a recent experience when you had reason to complain or
P actually made a complaint. If you can't think of any, use the prompts below.

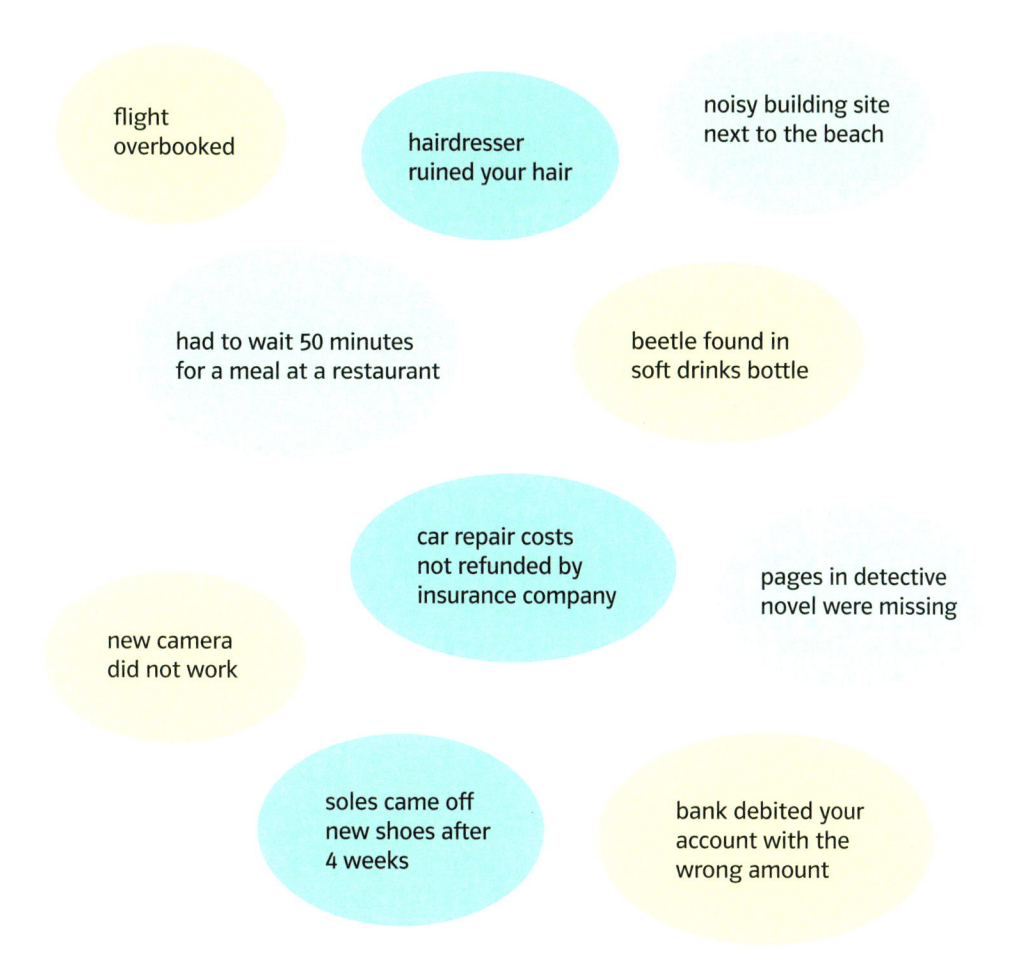

- flight overbooked
- hairdresser ruined your hair
- noisy building site next to the beach
- had to wait 50 minutes for a meal at a restaurant
- beetle found in soft drinks bottle
- new camera did not work
- car repair costs not refunded by insurance company
- pages in detective novel were missing
- soles came off new shoes after 4 weeks
- bank debited your account with the wrong amount

Unit 14 | Complaints and adjustments

1 Complaints in writing

The British chain of sports equipment, SPORTS ISLAND, has just received a consignment of polo shirts from a new supplier in India. Unfortunately their Incoming Goods Control has found that most of the polo shirts are not correctly labelled. Sarah Brookfield, the purchasing manager, decides to complain by e-mail.

From:	sarah.brookfield@sportsisland.co.uk
To:	mahajan@indiasports.id
Cc:	
Sent:	201_-01-31 **Attachments:**
Subject:	Polo shirts, our purchase order No. PH/346/06 of 18 Dec 201_

detailed reference to order

Dear Mr Mahajan

The consignment of 5,000 polo shirts under our above-mentioned purchase order arrived yesterday in due course.

However, when our Incoming Goods Control checked the merchandise we were dismayed to find that most of the polo shirts are not labelled correctly. The sizes printed on the inside tags sewn onto the shirts do not correspond to the actual sizes of the garments. Needless to say, the polo shirts cannot be sold with these incorrect tags.

description of problem

As it would be rather time-consuming to return the goods to you at your expense and wait for a replacement delivery, I would like to suggest that we commission a local firm to remove the tags and replace them with the right ones. You would, of course, have to bear the costs for the reworking and send us the required number of tags by air as soon as possible.

solution suggested

We are disappointed at the way you have handled our first order and look forward to receiving your comments on this matter in the very near future.

request for prompt adjustment

Best regards

Sarah Brookfield
Purchasing Manager

SPORTS ISLAND
41 Bryant Road
London W7 9QB
Tel. 020 74127333
Fax 020 74127334

Complaints and adjustments | Unit 14

1 Read Sarah Brookfield's e-mail several times. Then cover it up and complete these
R   sentences on your own sheet of paper.

1. The consignment of polo shirts arrived yesterday **1**.
2. We were dismayed to find that most of the polo shirts **2**.
3. **3** the polo shirts cannot be sold with these incorrect tags.
4. As it would be **4** to return the goods to you at your expense …
5. You would, of course, **5** for the reworking …
6. We are disappointed **6** our first order …

2 Restore the correct order of these jumbled elements of a complaint about a delay
R   in delivery.

| 1 | This matter is causing us great inconvenience and we hope you will do your utmost to deliver the tool kits without any further delay. |

| 2 | On 31 July we placed the above mentioned order with you which you confirmed the next day assuring us of delivery within 3 weeks. |

| 3 | Subject: Delay in delivery of our order No. W-549 / 07 for 1000 household tool kits |

| 4 | We hope to receive your comments by return. |

| 5 | Dear Mr Vernon |

| 6 | Since then 5 weeks have passed and we have neither received the tool kits nor heard anything from you. |

| 7 | Yours sincerely
Hammer Werkzeughandel |

| 8 | Tanja Kirchner
Purchasing Department |

| 9 | As our own customers are getting impatient we must insist on immediate delivery. Should you fail to deliver by the end of next week we are afraid that we shall have no option but to cancel the order and seek another supplier. |

Unit 14 | Complaints and adjustments

3
P
You (Markus Reber) work in the personnel department of Otto Greiling GmbH (e-mail: personnel@ottogreiling.aol.com), a major supplier to the car industry. For several years your firm has been sending junior executives to a language school in Brighton, UK, for intensive coaching in business English. This year's two participants were, however, not completely satisfied with the language school's services when they attended the course from October 14 to 20.

Send the principal an e-mail. (E-mail: pam.robinson@businessspeak.co.uk)

- Point out the following shortcomings:
  – accommodation at private hotel inadequate – central heating system out of order
  – participants' needs (the language of export procedures) not properly taken into account
  – one morning teacher did not turn up, took school three hours to organise replacement
  – golf course closed for refurbishment.
- Ask for refund of part of the course fees.
- Ask the school to take up the matter with the hotel.
- Close on a friendly note considering your long business relationship.

✱ 4
KMK
Sie sind Christiane Sauer und sind bei Ihrer Firma, Zuckermann & Sacher, Farinweg 19, 73979 Suessen, für den Einkauf von Büromaterial zuständig. Seit 4 Jahren beziehen Sie jedes Quartal Drucker- und Kopierpapier sowie Umschläge aller Art von der britischen Firma East Anglia Stationery Ltd., 6 Malvern Business Park, Ely, CB6 4JR, UK. In der letzten Zeit hat Ihnen dieser Lieferant wiederholt Anlass zur Unzufriedenheit gegeben.

Schreiben Sie einen förmlichen Beschwerdebrief an den Geschäftsführer, Charles Bingley, und führen Sie dabei Folgendes an:

- Datum: 30 Juli
- In den ersten Jahren keine Beanstandungen
- Seit letztem Jahr allmähliche Verschlechterung des Service:
  – Ware häufig nicht vorrätig
  – Lieferzeiten immer länger
  – keine prompte Reaktion auf E-Mails und Faxe
  – stets wechselnde Ansprechpartner am Telefon
  – dieses Jahr schon einmal zu viel und einmal zu wenig geliefert
- Mängel bei der heutigen Lieferung:
  – 150 000 Umschläge DIN A3 nicht selbstklebend (self-adhesive), (Auftrag Nr. 200-5437 vom 23. Juni)
  – Muster der beanstandeten Umschläge beigefügt
  – Bitte um Abholung der beanstandeten Umschläge bei nächster Gelegenheit
  – sofortiger Ersatz erforderlich
- Drei Monate Frist für Verbesserung des Service
- Andernfalls keine Verlängerung des Liefervertrags
- Anlage

Complaints and adjustments | Unit 14

2 Complaints by telephone

1 Maria Sanchez from Papier Gehrke in Schwerin has placed an order for
R multilingual wall calendars with the US firm Calendars 4 U. Two weeks after the date the calendars should have arrived in Germany she rings Joan Reid at Calendars 4 U, whom she knows very well from numerous previous transactions.

Restore the order of their jumbled dialogue. Match the numbers with the letters.

Joan

1. Calendars 4U. Joan speaking. How can I help you?
2. Hi Maria. Can you give me the order number and date?
3. Here it is on my monitor. Is there a problem?
4. I see that they should arrive in Germany any day now. We dispatched them a week ago by air-mail.
5. I am very sorry about this. I was going to call you but whenever I got around to it, it seemed to be the wrong time of day in Europe.
6. That's true. I am so sorry. I promise it won't happen again.
7. Thank you very much for your patience.
8. Bye Maria.

Maria

a. Certainly. It is 4900/312 dated 18 July.
b. You're welcome. Good bye Joan.
c. Yes, there certainly is. The calendars have not arrived yet. They ought to have been here two weeks ago.
d. You could have mailed me.
e. Hello Joan, this is Maria Sanchez from Papier Gehrke in Schwerin, Germany. I'm calling about our order for calendars.
f. Well, as long as the calendars arrive in the next few days, no harm will be done.
g. Why didn't you let us know that delivery would be made two weeks later?

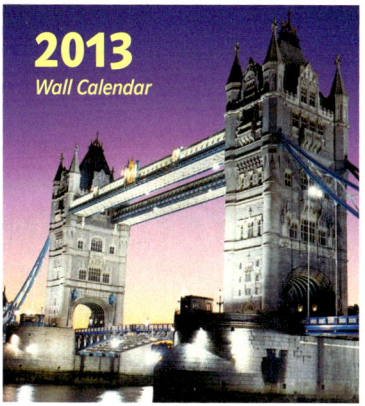

2013 *English French German*

2013 *Wall Calendar*

2 Work with a partner. Draw up a similar dialogue about a delay in delivery.
I Then act it out with your partner.

Phrases

201

Unit 14 | Complaints and adjustments

3
R
◎ A 1.28

Kirsty Burnham of Global Catering in Manchester asks Kevin Sears to ring an Italian firm about their consignment of Italian speciality convenience foods.

Listen to the dialogue and answer the following questions.

1. Which firm does Kevin Sears work for?
2. What is Chiara Durini's position at Buongusto Italiano?
3. What is the problem with the sell-by date of the Parma ham and the mortadella antipasti?
4. Would it help if Chiara Durini gave Global Catering a discount?
5. By which means of transport is Chiara Durini going to send the replacement delivery?

4
R/P
◎ A 1.28

You are Kevin Sears. First copy the form below. Then listen to the conversation again and write a memo in English for your boss, Kirsty Burnham.

```
TELEPHONE MEMO

For:

From:

Date:

Caller:

Subject:
```

202

Complaints and adjustments | Unit 14

5 Nicole Sachse from Getränke König in Halle, Germany, had ordered 3000 sets of long drink glasses from Wexford Crystal in Sanditon, County Cork, Ireland. The consignment arrived punctually, but inspection has revealed that some glasses are broken und some are smaller than the others. Nicole rings Sean O'Sullivan at Wexford Crystal.

Act out their dialogue with your neighbour using the prompts below.

Nicole Sachse	Sean O'Sullivan
	Wexford Crystal/Exports/ Sean O'Sullivan
Nicole Sachse/Getränke König/Halle, Germany/ order of 10 September/3000 sets of long drink glasses	
	on monitor/colours red, blue and green/arrived?
arrived punctually/ inspection/disappointed/ one box damaged/50 sets of green glasses broken	
	sorry to hear/all sets checked before dispatch/ must have happened in transit/contact forwarders immediately
terms of delivery DAP Halle/Wexford Crystal deal with forwarder and/or insurance company/need replacements urgently	
	send replacements/by air/ this afternoon
transport free of charge/ confirmation by fax	
	certainly/once more apologies
afraid/must mention/ roughly ⅓ of the glasses/ slight differences in height/ about 1mm shorter	
	easy to explain/glasses pipe-blown by hand/differences inevitable/sign of hand-made glass/much more valuable/machine-made glasses always identical
sounds plausible/customers may not notice	
	pleased with the sets?
yes/colours brilliant/crystal glass clear/remind of replacements/good-bye	
	promise immediate dispatch/ again sorry thanks for call/bye

203

Unit 14 | Complaints and adjustments

✱ 6 Work with a partner. Sit back to back and act out the telephone conversation
I   using the prompts on the role cards. Then change roles.

> **Role card: Partner A (buyer)**   **Role card partner B ⇨ page 255**
>
> Sie haben über das Internet ein überaus preiswertes Skateboard gekauft und mit Kreditkarte bezahlt. In der Beschreibung des Skateboards auf der Webseite des Verkäufers war als zulässiges Höchstgewicht für den Benutzer 70 kg angegeben. Als das Skateboard wie versprochen nach 3 Tagen ankommt, müssen Sie feststellen, dass auf dem englisch beschrifteten Karton ein zulässiges Höchstgewicht von (nur) 90 lbs (= 40,8 kg) aufgedruckt ist. Sie rufen die Firma an und verlangen Rücknahme des Skateboards.

7   **Communicating across cultures**
M   Drücken Sie folgende Aussagen in (möglichst höflichem) Englisch aus:

1. Wir teilen Ihnen hiermit mit, dass wir mit Ihrem Kundendienst sehr unzufrieden sind.
2. Die Farbe entspricht nicht dem Muster.
3. Wir bestehen darauf, dass Sie uns den vollen Kaufpreis erstatten.

> **Communicating across cultures:**
> **Complaining about products or services**
>
> In Germany correspondence in connection with complaints tends to be direct, stating the facts bluntly and requiring adjustment in no uncertain tones. This is the accepted usage here and nobody takes offence at the curt and no-nonsense style of German complaints. In the English-speaking world, on the other hand, complaints are formulated in a different way. The style is much more indirect, polite and conciliatory as nothing would be gained by antagonizing the other party; he/she would simply be less cooperative. So remember to express your complaint in a friendly and understanding manner.
>
> | **Do not say:** | **Say instead:** |
> |---|---|
> | I want to complain about … | I'm afraid I have to raise the matter of … |
> | The glasses are broken. | Unfortunately, the glasses are broken. |
> | You have made a mistake. | There must have been an error on your part / There seems to have been a mix-up somewhere. |
> | You are wrong. | I'm afraid I cannot quite agree. |
> | We expect you to send replacements. | We would be grateful if you would send replacements. |
> | Therefore, we request a discount of 20%. | We think a discount of 20% would be appropriate. |

🌐 8 Use the Internet to find other examples of cultural differences or problems of intercultural communication. Make notes and compare your findings with the group.

B Adjusting complaints

It is much easier to hold on to existing customers than to find new ones, so it is essential to manage customer complaints well. Remember, disgruntled customers are twice as likely as satisfied customers to tell others about their experience with your firm. When dealing with customer complaints you should

- thank the customer for making you aware of the problem
- treat the customer with courtesy and patience and tell him that you are sorry
- respond to the complaint quickly, telling the customer what will happen next
- if possible, give an explanation for what has happened
- involve the customer in the process of finding a solution
- suggest a compromise that meets the customer halfway if the complaint is not wholly justified
- ensure that all action promised is executed promptly
- explain the reasons before saying no, if the complaint is unjustified.

1 Study the text above and translate the following recommendations taken from a textbook.

21

Die Erledigung von Reklamationen muss mit großer Sorgfalt geschehen, um den Kunden nicht zu verlieren. Zunächst sollten Sie dem Kunden dafür danken, dass er Sie auf ein Problem aufmerksam
5   gemacht hat, und ihn dann in die Suche nach einer Lösung einbeziehen.
Beschwerden müssen umgehend beantwortet und der Kunde über den Fortgang der Erledigung auf dem Laufenden gehalten werden. Wenn möglich,
10 sollten Sie dem Kunden erklären, wie es zu der für ihn unbefriedigenden Situation kommen konnte. Zudem müssen Sie den Kunden davon überzeugen, dass Sie Maßnahmen treffen werden oder schon eingeleitet haben, die sicherstellen, dass sich
15 solche Vorfälle nicht wiederholen.
Falls die Reklamation nur teilweise begründet ist, sollten Sie versuchen, sich mit dem Kunden auf einen Kompromiss zu einigen. Sind Sie gezwungen, die Reklamation als völlig unbegründet
20 zurückzuweisen, empfiehlt es sich zuerst die Gründe zu erläutern, bevor die Absage erteilt wird.

Unit 14 | Complaints and adjustments

2 Match the complaints on the left with the appropriate explanations on the right.

1. Although you promised delivery within a week, our order no. 7040 has not yet arrived. Could you please look into this matter?

2. On 18 January we ordered 700 jars of tomato relish by phone but you sent us only 400 jars. Would you please arrange for the missing 300 to be shipped to us immediately?

3. When we signed the contract for the building of the conservatory you promised that the work would be completed in four weeks. That was 2 months ago and the work is still only half finished.

4. The packaging of the DVDs appeared to be in perfect condition. On unpacking the DVDs, however, we discovered a number of scratches. A list of the damaged DVDs is enclosed.

a. 300 jars of tomato relish have already been handed over to our forwarders for transportation to Germany. We are very sorry for this oversight. It seems that the person processing your order must have mistaken the handwritten 7 on the telephone memo for a 4.

b. We are at a loss to understand how this could have happened. Nevertheless we will be sending you replacements for the damaged goods first thing tomorrow morning. A thorough investigation into our quality control procedures has already been initiated.

c. Please accept our apologies for the delay. Your order was dispatched the day before yesterday and should reach you in the next few days. We apologize once more for the delay that was due to the introduction of new software in our dispatch department.

d. I would like to apologize for the delay for which we are, however, not entirely to blame. When work was in progress you asked for a number of alterations that held up work. For example, there was an additional delivery time for the Italian tiles you insisted on instead of the British ones provided for in our offer.

Complaints and adjustments | Unit 14

3 Kunal Mahajan from India Sports replies to Sarah Brookfield's e-mail concerning the faulty labelling of the polo shirts SPORTS ISLAND had ordered from India Sports.

Complete Kunal's e-mail using the expressions from the box.

> prepared to • promise to improve • the inconvenience caused • the trouble you have had • to our attention

From:	mahajan@indiasports.id
To:	sarah.brookfield@sportsisland.co.uk
Cc:	
Sent:	201_-02-01 Attachments:
Subject:	Polo shirts, your purchase order No. PH / 346 / 06 of 18 Dec 201_

Dear Ms Brookfield

Thank you for your e-mail drawing a serious problem **1** . *[thanks for information]*

We are very sorry for **2** by the incorrect labelling of the polo shirts and thank you for suggesting a solution. We perfectly agree with you that it would be best to ask a firm in Britain to replace the tags. An ample quantity of new tags have already been dispatched to your address by air. *[apologies and suggestion for adjustment]*

It goes without saying that we are **3** bear the costs for the re-labelling of the polo shirts.

Meanwhile we have started investigations into how this faulty labelling could have happened and **4** our quality control procedures. *[promise of improvement]*

To make up for **5** , we would like to offer you a price reduction of 10% on your next order. *[goodwill ending]*

We look forward to hearing from you again.

Best regards

Kunal Mahajan
Export Manager
India Sports
112 Delhi Road, Meerut-250 001
Uttar Pradesh, India
Tel. +91 121 2512270
Fax +91 121 2512275

Unit 14 | Complaints and adjustments

4 Restore the correct order of these jumbled elements of a reply to a complaint about a delay in delivery.

R

1 We are, therefore, prepared to release you from the contract.

2 Dear Ms Kirchner

3 We have not contacted you before because we were hoping to locate another manufacturer willing to supply similar tool kits at short notice. So far, however, we have not met with success.

4 Yours sincerely
James Vernon
Export Manager

5 Please accept our sincere apologies. We hope to be of service to you at another time in the future.

6 Re: Your order no. W-549 / 07

7 I'm afraid we are after all unable to execute your order for 1000 household tool kits for the time being as our own supplier, our parent company, has become insolvent.

8 Thank you for your e-mail.

Complaints and adjustments | Unit 14

5 You are Pam Robinson, principal of BUSINESS SPEAK, the language school
P   in Brighton which 2 junior executives from Otto Greiling GmbH, Germany, attended for a week's intensive coaching in business English. Markus Reber from their human resources department has sent you an e-mail complaining about some shortcomings concerning the course from October 14 to 20:

- accommodation at private hotel inadequate – central heating system out of order
- participants' needs (the language of export procedures) not properly taken into account
- one morning teacher did not turn up, took school three hours to organise replacement
- golf course closed for refurbishment

Reply by e-mail, bearing in mind that Markus Reber has been sending staff to your courses for several years.

- spoken with hotel manager, hotel prepared to reduce price by ⅓, cheque under way by post
- export procedures dealt with as always, never any complaint about this before
- apologies for teacher not turning up one morning, had a fall in the bathroom, had to be taken to hospital, you did your best to organise replacement
- participants informed in advance that the golf course would be out of use
- very sorry that participants should be dissatisfied
- sent them each a copy of "Doing Business in the UK" in compensation
- hope that cordial relations will not be affected

✱ 6 Sie sind Henry Crawford, der neue Geschäftsführer von East Anglia Stationery
KMK Ltd., 6 Malvern Business Park, Ely CB6 4JR, UK. Die deutsche Firma Zuckermann & Sacher, Farinweg 19, 73979 Suessen, bezieht von Ihnen seit Jahren Drucker- und Kopierpapier sowie Umschläge. Christiane Sauer, zuständig für den Einkauf von Büromaterial, ist inzwischen mit Ihrem Service unzufrieden und hat sich bei Ihnen in einem förmlichen Schreiben beschwert (siehe S. 200).

Beantworten Sie ihren Brief in Englisch unter Berücksichtigung folgender Punkte:

- Datum: 5. August
- Vorstellung Ihrer Person
- Ihr Vorgänger, Charles Bingley, nach längerer Krankheit im Ruhestand
- Beanstandete Unzulänglichkeiten verursacht durch Mr. Bingley's Abwesenheit
- Radikale Maßnahmen eingeleitet
- Service in Kürze wieder einwandfrei
- Entschuldigung
- Ersatzlieferung Umschläge bereits unterwegs
- 20 % Rabatt auf diesen Auftrag
- Beanstandete Umschläge werden kommenden Mittwoch abgeholt
- Hoffnung auf weitere gute Beziehungen

Unit 14 | Complaints and adjustments

Language and grammar
Find the correct form of the verbs in brackets.

1. We will grant you 10% quantity discount if you (order) at least 500 units.
2. We would place a substantial order if you (can promise) delivery within one week.
3. We would not have dispatched the goods if they (not be) in perfect condition.
4. We (be glad) if you looked into the matter without delay.
5. Unless you instruct us to the contrary, shipment (be effected) on receipt of new supplies.
6. It (be) most helpful if the sets could reach us before the end of the month.
7. You would be taking a great risk if you (invest) your money in that project.
8. Should you be uncertain about any aspect of it, please (not hesitate) to give me a call.
9. If we (accept) their order we would have to recruit three additional workers.
10. If she had worked harder she (not fail) the exam.

Language and grammar: Conditional clauses

Bedingungssätze (conditional clauses) werden im Englischen nach einem relativ festen Schema gestaltet. Es gibt drei Grundtypen von Bedingungssätzen:

Hauptsatz	Nebensatz der Bedingung
We will take the goods back (FUTURE) (wir **werden** …)	if you return them at your expense. (PRESENT TENSE)
We would grant you a discount (CONDITIONAL) (wir **würden** …)	if you increased your order. (SIMPLE PAST)
He would have taken part in the meeting (CONDITIONAL PERFECT) (er **hätte** …)	if he had not been away on a business trip. (PAST PERFECT)

Das Schema gilt auch dann, wenn der Nebensatz der Bedingung vor dem Hauptsatz steht:

If it is fine on Friday	we will have the office party in the park.
If you applied	you would get the job.
If you had applied	you would have got the job.

Ferner gilt das Schema, wenn der Nebensatz durch eine andere Konjunktion eingeleitet wird: wie z.B. unless (wenn nicht, außer wenn), provided (that) (vorausgesetzt, dass), on condition (that) (unter der Bedingung, dass):

They will not place any further orders	unless you offer a satisfactory solution.
Employees may smoke	provided they go out into the courtyard.

Eine besondere Form stellt der Bedingungssatz ohne Konjunktion dar:

Should you have any further questions	please do not hesitate to ask.
But for John helping out (If John had not helped out …)	we would never have coped with the sudden demand.

Eine Ausnahme von diesem Schema bildet die höfliche Bitte in der Geschäftskorrespondenz:

We would be grateful	if you would grant us a respite of 4 weeks.

Office expert

1 Key account management

1 KMK Sie arbeiten in der Marketing Abteilung eines internationalen Unternehmens als Assistent/in einer neu angestellten Großkundenberaterin. Sie wollen sich genauer über Ihr neues Arbeitsfeld informieren und finden im Internet folgenden Text. Lesen Sie den Text und beantworten Sie die Fragen dazu auf Deutsch.

A key account manager deals with the customers that are most important to a company. These key accounts are usually the customers with whom the company has the largest volume of business or who produce the most profit for a company. Developing customer relations to such key accounts and making sure they remain loyal customers is the job of the key account manager. They need to determine the needs of these customers and to take measures to make sure they receive the best customer service. On a day to day basis, sales proposals need to be prepared and the market situation analysed.

A key account manager's job is similar to that of a sales manager but they usually only have a limited number of accounts to look after. This means they can get to know their customers and their businesses well to be able to better meet their needs. A good understanding of the customer's business as well as factors such as prices, delivery times and forms of payment is important. The job calls for a high degree of negotiation and communication skills.

The assistant of a key account manager is responsible for administrative tasks such as filing sales reports, answering the phone, coordinating appointments and dealing with customer correspondence. An accounts assistant should be familiar with standard software programmes and have business-related training. Above all, he or she should have a friendly, outgoing manner in dealing with customers.

1. Was ist mit *key accounts* gemeint?
2. Worin besteht die Aufgabe eines Großkundenberaters im Allgemeinen?
3. Welche Aufgaben fallen einem Großkundenberater konkret zu?
4. Was unterscheidet einen Verkaufsberater von einem Großkundenberater?
5. Welche Kenntnisse und Fähigkeiten sollte ein Großkundenberater haben?
6. Welche Aufgaben hat der/die Assistent/in eines Großkundenberaters?
7. Welche Qualifikationen sollte der/die Assistent/in mitbringen?

2 Coping with the copy machine

KMK
A 2.17

Matthew, ein neuer Mitarbeiter aus den USA, bittet seine Kollegin Karin um Hilfe mit dem Kopierer. Hören Sie sich das Gespräch zweimal an und beantworten Sie die folgenden Fragen auf Deutsch.

1. Wobei benötigt Matthew Hilfe?
2. Wo befindet sich das Kartuschenfach und wie lässt es sich öffnen?
3. Womit sollte man Tonerflecken auf Kleidung auf keinen Fall entfernen?
4. Wo befindet sich die Anweisung zum Kartuschenwechsel?
5. Beschreiben Sie die Schritte zum Einsatz der neuen Kartusche.
6. Was geschieht mit der alten Kartusche?

3 Licence agreements

R

You would like to buy a library of templates from Boxed Business. Before you can download the software you have to agree to an End User Licence Agreement (EULA). Read the extract from the EULA and choose the right options below.

Grant of licence The library is licensed as follows: (1) Installation and use. Boxed Business grants you the right to install and use copies of the library on your computer. (2) Backup copies. You may also make copies of the library as may be necessary for backup and archival purposes.

Termination Boxed Business may terminate this EULA if you fail to comply with its terms and conditions. In such event, you must destroy all copies of the library in your possession.

Limitation of liability In no event shall Boxed Business be liable for any damages (including, without limitation, lost profits, business interruption or lost information) arising out of the use of the library, even if Boxed Business has been advised of the possibility of such damages.

1. The EULA gives you permission to do the following with the library:
   a. install and use it; b. install it and make backup copies; c. install and resell it.
2. Boxed Business can cancel the EULA if you
   a. destroy your copies; b. violate the contract; c. misuse the library.
3. Boxed Business is not responsible for damages
   a. without limitation; b. of lost profits or data; c. if they warn you.
4. May you cancel the EULA with Boxed Business?
   a. Yes, if you suffer damages. b. Yes, if you lose money or business.
   c. No reasons are given.

Phrases: Complaints and adjustments

To start a complaint

We are writing **with** reference to our order no …	Wir nehmen Bezug auf unseren Auftrag Nr. …
We regret to report that we have not yet received the goods ordered **on** 18 May.	Wir bedauern, Ihnen mitteilen zu müssen, dass wir die am 18. Mai bestellten Waren noch nicht erhalten haben.

To give reasons for your complaint

On unpacking the cases our Incoming Goods Control discovered that 15 items are missing.	Beim Auspacken der Kisten stellte unsere Warenannahme fest, dass 15 Positionen fehlen.
We are afraid that several units are – seriously damaged/defective. – broken/badly scratched/stained.	Leider sind mehrere Teile – schwer beschädigt/schadhaft. – zerbrochen/stark zerkratzt/verschmutzt.
The goods should have arrived a week **ago**.	Die Waren hätten schon vor einer Woche eintreffen sollen.
We are sorry to point out that the repair work has been poorly executed.	Wir müssen leider darauf hinweisen, dass die Reparatur schlecht ausgeführt wurde.

To mention likely reasons for the problem

We believe that the damage may be due to rough handling **in** transit.	Wir glauben, dass der Schaden auf unsachgemäße Behandlung beim Transport zurückzuführen ist.
Apparently, our order was **mixed up** with another customer's order.	Unser Auftrag wurde anscheinend mit einem anderen verwechselt.

To inform the seller what you expect him to do and what steps you are taking

Please arrange **for** the immediate dispatch of the missing items.	Bitte sorgen Sie dafür, dass die fehlenden Artikel sofort abgeschickt werden.
We would ask you to – replace the faulty goods **at** your expense. – have the defective articles collected **at** our warehouse. – grant us a price reduction **of** 20 %. – cut the price **to** € 780.	Wir möchten Sie bitten, – die mangelhafte Ware auf Ihre Kosten zu ersetzen. – die schadhaften Artikel von unserem Lager abholen zu lassen. – uns einen Preisnachlass von 20 % zu gewähren. – den Preis auf € 780 zu senken.

To demand prompt adjustment

We expect that you will settle this matter speedily and **to** our entire satisfaction.	Wir erwarten, dass Sie die Sache rasch und zu unserer vollen Zufriedenheit regeln.

Unit 14 | Complaints and adjustments

To refer to a complaint received

Thank you for your e-mail drawing a serious problem **to** our attention.	Danke für Ihre E-Mail, mit der Sie uns auf ein ernstes Problem aufmerksam gemacht haben.

To apologize

We wish to apologize for this mistake.	Wir bitten für diesen Fehler um Entschuldigung.
We are extremely sorry **for** the poor service you have received.	Es tut uns außerordentlich leid, dass Sie so schlecht bedient wurden.

To explain the problem or promise to investigate it

The damage was caused **by** a software failure.	Der Schaden wurde durch fehlerhafte Software verursacht.
We will investigate the matter thoroughly and inform you of the steps taken.	Wir werden die Angelegenheit gründlich untersuchen und Sie über die Schritte informieren, die wir unternommen haben.

To suggest a solution and inform the buyer what you expect him to do

We are pleased to say that replacements are now **on** their way to you.	Wir freuen uns, Ihnen mitteilen zu können, dass Ersatz bereits unterwegs ist.
Please return the faulty items **at** our expense.	Bitte senden Sie die mangelhaften Artikel auf unsere Kosten zurück.
We are prepared to reduce the price **by** 15% if you decide to keep the goods.	Wir sind bereit, den Preis um 15% zu senken, wenn Sie sich entschließen, die Ware zu behalten.

To reject an unfounded claim

After careful examination of the case we must say that the order was carried out in accordance with the contract.	Nach gründlicher Untersuchung des Falles müssen wir festhalten, dass der Auftrag vertragsgemäß ausgeführt wurde.
As we are **in no way** to blame we have no alternative but to reject your claim.	Da uns keinerlei Schuld trifft, bleibt uns nichts anderes übrig, als Ihre Reklamation zurückzuweisen.

To close on a note designed to promote goodwill

We hope that this proposal will find your approval.	Wir hoffen, dieser Vorschlag findet Ihre Zustimmung.
We trust that the solution suggested will help to settle the matter **to** the satisfaction of all parties concerned.	Wir hoffen, dass die vorgeschlagene Lösung dazu beiträgt, die Angelegenheit zur Zufriedenheit aller Beteiligten zu erledigen.

Unit 15
Marketing products and services

WORD BANK

marketing • marketing mix • life cycle • market research • target group • interview • distribution • manufacturer • wholesaler • warehouse • retailer • retail outlets • agent • commission • E-commerce • advertising • slogans • consumer goods • media • mail shots • advertisements • commercials • posters • trade journals • internet advertising • trade fairs • public relations • sponsoring • to conduct research • to aim at • to break bulk • to represent • to advertise • to promote

Marketing includes a wide range of activities. Even when a product or service is still at the idea or design stage, companies set about finding out what sort of a market exists – for instance, what age group they should aim at and how likely people in this age group are to buy this product or service. When a company is planning a new product they need to decide on the "marketing mix" or 4Ps (product, price, place, promotion) – i.e. what kind of product to develop, what price to charge and what channels to sell it through – cheap chain or exclusive boutique, for instance. Finally, they will have to decide how and where to advertise.

1 Life cycle of a product

Products may be thought of as having a life cycle with five phases – introduction, growth, maturity, decline and phasing out. The focus of marketing changes, depending on the phase.

Online-Link
808261-0015

Unit 15 | Marketing products and services

Product life cycle

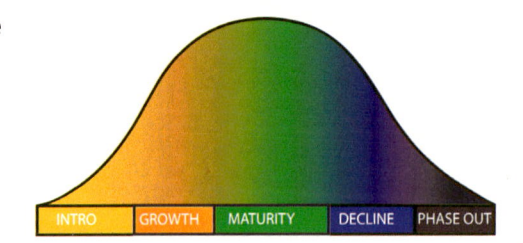

INTRO | GROWTH | MATURITY | DECLINE | PHASE OUT

1 Study the text on page 215 and the illustration above and decide whether the following statements are TRUE or FALSE.

1. Marketing is the same as advertising.
2. Marketing includes advertising.
3. Companies first design and produce a product and then see whether there's a market for it or not.
4. It is important for a company to have a clear idea of what group it is targeting.
5. Marketing is the same as selling.
6. It is always best to sell as cheaply as possible.
7. A product has a life cycle of six phases.
8. Sales reach a peak in the last phase.

2 Use the internet to select what you consider to be the five leading brands in the UK. Make a few notes on what is associated with the brands and discuss your results with the group.

2 Market research

Companies conduct market research to find out what people think about them and their products. They also try to establish what needs or desires a particular target group may have and how able or willing they will be to pay for a particular product or service. This may involve "desk" research (e.g. statistics) or "field research". The following is an example of field research.

Listen to the interview. The interviewer is ringing a random sample of people taken from the local telephone book. Complete the following sentences.

A 1.29

1. Could you possibly spare a few minutes **1**?
2. I am actually in a bit **2**.
3. We are doing a market survey **3**.
4. I tend to book flights and holidays **4**.
5. We are particularly interested in **5**.
6. Do you buy these articles regularly and how much do you **6**?
7. I can do my shopping when I **7**.
8. Prices are often more **8**.
9. I often give up in **9**.
10. Would you visit the website more often if it were **10**?

216

Marketing products and services | Unit 15

A Distribution channels

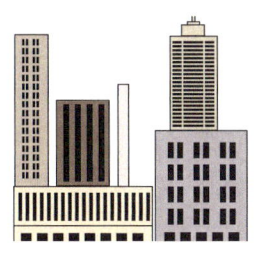

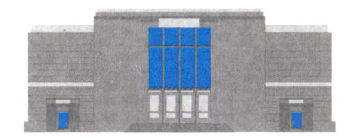

Manufacturer   Wholesaler   Retailer

Retailer

Retailer

Distribution is also a part of marketing. Traditionally, wholesalers are the link between manufacturers and retailers. Manufacturers generally sell goods in large quantities to wholesalers who sell them on in smaller quantities to retailers (= "breaking bulk"). Retailers sell them to end users.

1 Retailers, wholesalers and agents

Retailers

Retailers ensure a supply of goods to the general public. There is a wide variety of retail outlets, starting with small specialist shops such as independent chemists, beauty consultants, opticians and exclusive fashion boutiques. Most High Street stores are, however, major chains with branches in a large number of towns and often in several countries. Supermarkets generally belong to one of a small number of major chains. Department stores sell many different kinds of goods under one roof. Large retailers, who buy in bulk, may order directly from manufacturers without involving a wholesaler.

Recently, online retailing has become the fastest growing segment.

217

Unit 15 | Marketing products and services

Wholesalers
Wholesalers provide a range of services from which both manufacturers and retailers benefit. They may have a sales force to keep contact to their customers, they have warehousing facilities, offer a range of products from a number of manufacturers, and may offer credit facilities to their customers. Finally, they provide advisory services. However, wholesalers charge for their services and are, therefore, also a cost factor (putting up the price).

Agents
In foreign trade manufacturers often appoint an agent in the foreign country. This has a number of advantages. The agent speaks the language, he is familiar with the foreign market and will have the necessary contacts. He has an office and possibly warehousing facilities. He is usually paid on a commission basis which means he receives a percentage (say 3%) on sales. He is thus only paid when he succeeds in selling something. His principal has therefore few overheads.

1 Übertragen Sie folgende Sätze ins Deutsche.

KMK
1. Wholesalers are the link between manufacturers and retailers.
2. They may offer credit facilities to their customers.
3. Supermarkets belong to a small number of major chains.
4. Wholesalers charge for their services and are therefore a cost factor.
5. Wholesalers generally have warehousing facilities.

2 Answer the following questions.

1. In what way do wholesalers make life easier for manufacturers?
2. Why does a small retailer (e.g. a 24-hour mini-market or a small fashion boutique) need wholesalers?
3. Why may large retailers try to cut out the wholesaler?
4. Give examples of independent retailers (not part of chains).
5. What is the characteristic feature of a department store?

✱ 3 Übertragen Sie den obigen Text über „Agents" ins Deutsche.

KMK

218

4 Decide whether the following statements are TRUE or FALSE.
R

1. Agents are paid a commission whether they sell anything or not.
2. Wholesalers generally have warehousing facilities.
3. Retailers sell to end users.
4. Retailers buy in bulk and sell to wholesalers.
5. Wholesalers perform a useful service both for manufacturers and retailers.

5 Describe briefly the activities of retailers, wholesalers and agents.
P

6 Listen to the following statements in which young people taking part in a training seminar describe their place of employment. Take notes.
R
A 1.30

7 Now listen to the statements again, use your notes and answer the following questions in writing.
R / P
A 1.30

1. Does speaker 1 work for a wholesaler?
2. Does speaker 2 work for a retailer?
3. What does speaker 3 mean by "retail customers"?
4. Does speaker 4 work for a retailer or a wholesaler?
5. What sort of a company does speaker 5 work for?
6. What kind of customers help the shop of speaker 6 to survive?
7. Who does the company of speaker 7 sell its products through?
8. What kind of an organisation does speaker 8 work for?

2 E-commerce

1 Complete the following text using words from the box.
R

> outlets • major • credit cards • retail • via • online • charges • customers • facilities • wholesalers

An important development at the present time is the rapid growth of e-commerce. This is revolutionising some **1** sectors. Internet retailing operations are growing faster than traditional retail **2** . Shopping and booking flights, hotels and holidays **3** the internet is becoming more and more popular. Some **4** supermarkets have large internet operations. You can do your shopping **5** and have the goods delivered.

Airlines offer online booking **6** , which makes it easy to compare prices and avoid paying travel agents' **7** .

Wholesalers may also offer their **8** internet facilities (Business to Business – B2B – services) to enable them to do their ordering at any time of the day or night. However, internet exchanges are making **9** superfluous in some fields.

E-commerce is at present the fastest growing retail segment paralleled by a rapid increase in the number of **10** .

Unit 15 | Marketing products and services

2 Beantworten Sie die Fragen zum folgenden Zeitungstext schriftlich in deutscher Sprache.
KMK

1. Warum mussten Online-Einzelhändler ihren Service stark verbessern?
2. Welche Vorteile bietet das Internet beim Preisvergleich?
3. Welche Möglichkeiten gibt es im Internet, sich über Produkte zu informieren?
4. Warum mussten Firmen neue Strategien in der Werbung und im Marketing entwickeln?
5. Welche Altersgruppe soll besonders durch die Internet-Werbung angesprochen werden?

E-Commerce takes off

Consumers love to shop on the internet. After initial problems leading websites now offer an excellent service. Competition on the web is fierce and many sites have had little choice but to raise service levels, often far above those of offline retailers. Price transparency is the great advantage for the consumer. It is possible to check the price offered by hundreds of merchants with a couple of mouse clicks. Consumers also have access to an unprecedented amount of information, not just from manufacturers' websites but also from online reviews written by other customers.

To reach online customers companies have had to look at new and different advertising and marketing strategies. This is why firms pay for sponsored links to appear on search sites like *Google* and *Yahoo!*. It has become one of the most effective marketing tools, especially for people who spend as much time on the internet as watching television, such as teenagers.

Video lounge Retailing

BBC Motion Gallery

You are about to see a video on retail marketing.
Watch it carefully and then answer the following questions:

1. Describe the marketing expert.
2. The video speaks of "sales consultants" and "professional friends". How is this different from the traditional sales assistant?
3. What method is used to show them how NOT to approach the customer?
4. What is meant by "linked selling"?
5. What are the rewards of successful customer care for the "consultants"?
6. Would you like to be served by this kind of assistant?

B Advertising

There are many different ways of promoting sales and attracting potential clients or customers depending on the product and target group.

1 Advertising consumer goods

Mail shots: One form of advertising we are all confronted with is mail shots. Since a large proportion go straight into the wastepaper basket, companies will try to obtain up to date and selective lists of people who are likely to be really interested. This may be the cheapest and most effective way for local companies to make potential clients aware of their goods and services.

TV advertising is suitable for consumer goods with a very wide appeal. Like **cinema** advertising it can suggest a whole lifestyle associated with the product. TV advertising is very expensive.

Consumer goods can also be advertised on the **radio**, in **newspapers** and **magazines**. In the case of magazines, the manufacturer will be able to appeal to a specific target group (affluent men between the ages of 20 and 30, keen gardeners with sufficient money to buy a glossy magazine, health-conscious young women, retired people with money and time on their hands (grey power!)).

Posters, hoardings/billboards are an effective means of out of home advertising as they reach a large number of people who cannot help noticing them as they pass or drive through the streets.

Unit 15 | Marketing products and services

Internet advertising is also a rapidly growing segment. A website itself is an important part of the way in which a company presents itself. How well-designed and efficient is the website? Does it allow you to do what you want to do with a minimum of complication? We have all experienced frustrating websites which provide a lot of information that one is not interested in, or that do not seem to have a "BACK" button.

1 Match the expressions on the left with the translations on the right.

1. affluent
2. appeal
3. glossy
4. hoardings
5. mail shots
6. retired
7. selective
8. target group

a. Anziehungskraft
b. ausgewählt
c. hier: auf Hochglanzpapier gedruckt
d. im Ruhestand/in Rente
e. Plakatwände
f. Postwurfsendungen
g. wohlhabend
h. Zielgruppe

2 Work in groups. Discuss recent advertisements on TV, in magazines, in the cinema and on posters. Tell your group what you liked or disliked about them. What kind of advertisements are you most influenced by? The following expressions may help to start you off.

- I think it's effective because …
- I don't like this kind of advertisement because …
- It doesn't really appeal to …
- Have you seen the most recent ad for … ?
- In my opinion the message is …
- I'm afraid I don't agree with you because …
- I think it is …
- I think this commercial is very convincing as …

Internet advertising boom helps Ad.Slot.com to double sales

Ad.Slot.com, one of Europe's biggest independent media buying agencies, says that it will double turnover from placing advertisements on the internet this year as its clients continue to seek alternatives to traditional media.

5 The company said yesterday that it expects to achieve total sales of more than $450 million this year, up from about $350 million last year. The proportion of sales contributed by the new media rose rapidly to 17 per cent.

In the first few months of
10 the year more money was spent on advertising on the internet and mobile phones and less on advertising in conventional media, like the
15 radio, TV and print media.

A spokesman for the company said that the trend towards advertising in the new media was the result
20 of changing technology and habits. People still watch television and read newspapers, but they use the internet and their mobile
25 phones to socialise and search for information. They have DVD recorders that allow them to skip TV commercials.

3 Beantworten Sie folgende Fragen zu diesem Zeitungsartikel auf Deutsch.

KMK
1. Wodurch erwartet Ad.Slot.com dieses Jahr seinen Umsatz zu verdoppeln?
2. Welchen Beitrag werden die neuen Medien dabei leisten?
3. Welche Veränderung hat sich in den ersten Monaten dieses Jahres ergeben?
4. Warum nimmt das Interesse an den alternativen Medien zu?
5. In welchen Medien sucht man zunehmend nach Informationen?
6. Warum wird TV-Werbung häufig nicht wahrgenommen?

2 Advertising industrial goods

Where do you advertise if your product is not a consumer good but, say, a specialised machine or precision instrument?

A company can place an advertisement in a trade journal, a specialist periodical devoted to a particular sector.

For these companies the relevant **trade fairs** at which companies in the given sector present their latest products are important. They are attended by many people from the trade, some of them buyers who intend to place orders and competitors who use the trade fair as a means of seeing what the competition is up to. Trade fairs are, therefore, a way of advertising industrial goods.

Companies may write directly to potential customers (direct mail) informing them of their range of products and enclosing sales literature.

Übertragen Sie den obigen Text ins Deutsche.

3 Public relations (PR)

This is usually distinguished from advertising as the focus is the company rather than specific products. Some companies sponsor sports events, others donate money to universities, schools and cultural events. It may be important for a company to emphasise the amount of money it invests in research, its respect for the environment or multi-ethnic society. They may emphasise their commitment to the local community and try to get positive coverage in the local press. Large companies have PR departments, while in smaller companies there is at least one person responsible for PR. Companies large and small take outside advice from specialist agencies.

Study the above text and say whether the following statements are TRUE or FALSE.

1. PR is the same as advertising.
2. Companies sponsor sports events to project a particular image.
3. Small companies are less interested in PR than large companies.
4. All companies use the services of specialist agencies.
5. Some companies are more interested in donating money to universities and schools than sponsoring sports events.

Marketing products and services | Unit 15

Language and grammar
Choose the correct form of the adjective or adverb in brackets.

1. Our elegant sofas are the (good) value ever.
2. We are the market leaders because we have reacted (swiftly) to changing markets.
3. This company has expanded (dramatic) than its competitors over the past year.
4. Last year the winter was (severe) than this year.
5. These are the (late) designer furnishings from Milan.
6. This is the (expensive) holiday I have booked so far.

**Language and grammar:
Comparatives and superlatives**

Adjektive, meist in Form von Komparativen oder Superlativen, spielen in der Werbung eine große Rolle.

Einsilbig gesprochene Adjektive bilden Komparativ und Superlativ durch Anhängen von *-er*, *-est* an das Adjektiv.

bright – brighter – brightest
This car has **smoother** handling than any other car in its class.

Drei- oder mehrsilbige Adjektive bilden Komparativ und Superlativ durch Voranstellen von *more* und *most* vor das Adjektiv.

interesting – more interesting – most interesting
This is the **most sophisticated** MP3 player available today.

Zweisilbige Adjektive werden entweder wie einsilbige oder wie mehrsilbige gesteigert: Adjektive, die auf *-er*, *-ow*, *-y* oder *-le* enden, hängen *-er*, *-est* an. Vor Adjektive, die auf *-ful* oder *-re* enden, wird *more* oder *most* gesetzt.

clever – cleverer – cleverest	narrow – narrower – narrowest
pretty – prettier – prettiest	noble – nobler – noblest
careful – more careful – most careful	obscure – more obscure – most obscure

This is a **most restful** way of spending a weekend abroad.

Einige englische Adjektive besitzen die Wirkung von Superlativen.
Cutting-edge* technology goes into this stereo system.
Get this **state of the art** handset at all authorised dealers.
Get the coolest, **up to the minute**, **must-have** accessories at all our boutiques.
This car has **superb** handling.

Auch Adverbien können gesteigert werden. Komparativ und Superlativ von Adverbien wird durch Voranstellen von *more* und *most* gebildet.
quickly – more quickly – most quickly
They dealt with our order **more efficiently** than we had expected.
Technology is changing **more and more rapidly** (= immer schneller).

---

* Diese Wendungen können sowohl mit als auch ohne Bindestriche geschrieben werden.

Office expert

1 Purchasing incentives

1 Match the buying incentives (1.–8.) to their German equivalents (a.–h.).

1. cash discount
2. contest
3. coupon
4. discount
5. freebie
6. gift
7. rebate
8. sample

a. Geschenk
b. Gutschein
c. Preisausschreiben, Wettbewerb
d. Preisnachlass
e. Rückzahlung
f. Skonto
g. Warenprobe
h. Werbegeschenk

2 Work in groups and answer the following questions.

1. Which purchasing incentives do you find most motivating? Say why.
2. Do you take part in contests? Have you ever won?
3. How often do you send away for free samples or receive freebies?
4. Do you often/sometimes/never ask for a discount or cash discount?
5. Which purchasing incentives are used in your company? Give examples.

2 Ergonomics in the office

1 Choose the best definition of the concept of ergonomics.

1. Term used to describe adjustable furniture.
2. Finding the cause of an injury for insurance purposes.
3. Study of working conditions in order to increase efficiency.
4. Study and development of automation.

✱ 2 You work for an office supplier which would like to determine how satisfied customers are with their current equipment. Your boss has made some notes and asks you to rewrite them as survey questions. Then use the questions to interview your classmates or colleagues at work. Report back your findings in class.

Example: Which features of your office chair should be adjustable?
        a. seat height b. armrests c. backrests d. seat inclination

- adjustable chair features: seat height / armrests / backrests / seat inclination
- desk: keyboard tray / height adjustable / standing / extra writing space
- keyboard: built-in palm rest / wireless / zoom function / 4-way scrolling
- mouse: wireless / joystick design / programmable buttons / palm rest
- monitor: wide-screen / tilt function / flat screen / high-quality resolution

3 Complete the text about the office of the future with the words from the box.

available • collect • displays • freedom • happier • in tandem • lower • phrases • productivity • sensors • technology

Visions of the office of the future are being developed at research labs of **1** and office-equipment companies. Ideas include **2** that detect when you get to the office to inform colleagues that you're **3** to talk. There are also micro-electro-mechanical systems that produce super-sharp images on **4** the size of a wall. They work **5** with tablet computers that network to a shared-team display. Business software can help users find and **6** information by learning relationships among the words and **7** people use. Some companies are experimenting with doing away with dedicated desks and offices to give employees the **8** to choose where, when and how they work. Results indicate a **9** workforce, improved staff retention rates, increased **10** and **11** building costs.

3 Costs and calculations

1 You work as the team assistant for the marketing department of your company and need to prepare material for an upcoming meeting. Read the description of the annual sales development and draw the equivalent line graph.

In January sales stood at just around $3.5 million. In February they rose slightly to just over $4.5 million and then remained constant through March. From March to April there was a sharp increase to over $9 million. After that, sales fell steadily, starting off with a slight dip between April and May, and then dropping constantly till bottoming out in August at just under $5 million. There was another healthy increase in September to almost $8 million, but then they declined steadily again between September and November to reach just around $4 million. In December they shot up again to peak at almost $10 million at year's end.

2 Study this graph of advertising expenses and write a text describing it.

▶ Phrases

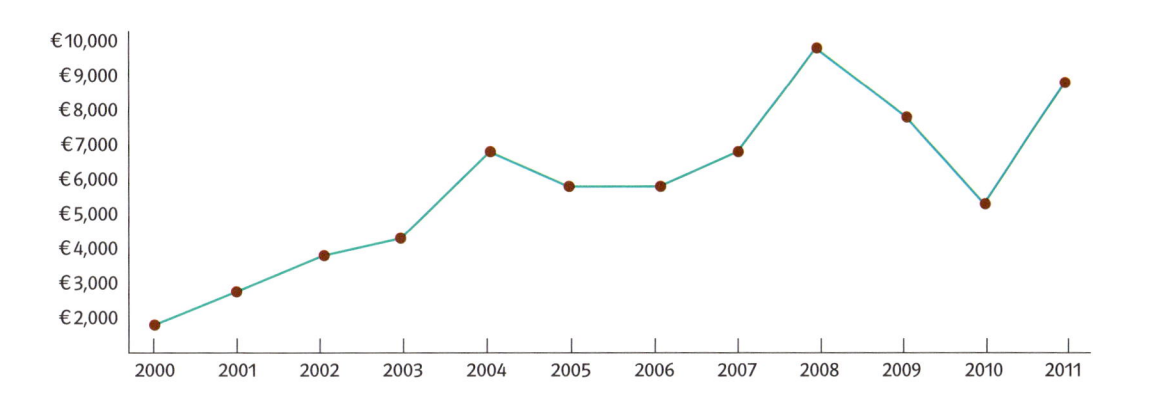

Unit 15 | Marketing products and services

Phrases: Advertising

This state-of-the-art mobile phone is easy to operate with its simple slide-out keyboard.	Dieses Handy, das auf dem neuesten technischen Stand ist, hat eine leicht zu bedienende ausziehbare Tastatur.
It has an easy to use touch screen.	Es hat einen leicht zu bedienenden Touch-Screen.
This must-have versatile gizmo includes all the latest features.	Dieses vielseitige Hi-Tech-Spielzeug, das man unbedingt haben muss, hat all die neuesten Funktionen.
You'll love its slim compact shape.	Die schlanke, kompakte Form wird Sie begeistern.
You'll be bewitched by the dazzling designs of our new collection.	Lassen Sie sich verführen von den bestechenden Designs unserer neuen Kollektion.
The ultimate **in** costume jewellery.	Der ultimative Modeschmuck.
We use a minimum of packaging to minimise the environmental impact.	Wir verwenden ein Minimum an Verpackung, um die Auswirkungen auf die Umwelt so gering wie möglich zu halten.
Your finger-nails will look flawless and perfectly cared **for**.	Ihre Fingernägel sehen makellos und perfekt gepflegt aus.
… subdued autumnal colours …	… dezente Herbstfarben …
This is a portable stereo-system **of** truly diminutive dimensions.	Es handelt sich um eine tragbare Super-Mini-Stereoanlage.
This hand-crafted leather bag combines perfect chic with amazing capacity.	Diese handgearbeitete Ledertasche ist superschick und dabei unglaublich geräumig.
We rely **on** tried and tested craftsmanship.	Wir verlassen uns auf unser erprobtes handwerkliches Können.
Weekends feel simply wonderful in our silky soft-touch tops.	Erleben Sie romantische Wochenenden mit unseren flauschig-kuscheligen Tops.
This downy soft luxury scarf will go with all your winter garments.	Dieser daunenweiche Luxusschal passt zu Ihrer gesamten Wintergarderobe.
… ideal for sensitive skins …	… ideal für die empfindliche Haut …

UNIT 16
Job applications in Germany and the EU

WORD BANK

job application • vacancy • opening • job exchange • job centre • research facilities • recruitment agencies • letter of application • CV • education • training • experience • skills • hobbies • interview • strengths • references • to advertise • to recruit • to apply • to paraphrase • to invite • to shortlist • to employ • European Union • free movement • member countries • European Commission • president • commissioners • Council of Ministers • European Parliament

The first thing is to find a vacancy. Companies advertise openings in newspapers on certain days which differ from place to place and country to country and also from sector to sector. Job exchanges on the Internet have become an important source of information. Often, it is possible to type in your job specification and receive notification by e-mail when anything suitable turns up. Job centres may be able to assist in the search for a suitable position and provide research facilities such as directories and internet access. Finally, there are private sector recruitment agencies which specialise in a particular sector. People often send unsolicited applications to major organisations on the off-chance that they are looking to recruit people.

1 Tell the class how you found your job / apprenticeship. Discuss which of the above are the most effective ways of looking for a job. Give reasons to support your answers.

Online-Link
808261-0016

229

Unit 16 | Job applications in Germany and the EU

THE CARING COMPANY
NATURAL BEAUTY
first-rate natural products for hair and skin care

We are seeking young persons from the Continent to
assist our Birmingham-based sales team
REF.: NB 605

We offer employment in a challenging, fast-paced environment where enthusiasm is the norm.

Successful applicants will have
- sales experience
- good English language skills
- native speaker competence in Italian, French or German

Successful applicants will be
- PC literate, including Excel
- able to meet deadlines
- self-motivated and hard-working

We offer an attractive salary and will help you with finding accommodation.

If you are interested please send your CV with a covering letter to

Catherine Bennet • Recruitment Officer • NATURAL BEAUTY • 17 Laura Place • Birmingham • B12 1AC

Automotive Services Ltd
Wholesaler and Importer of Automotive Parts

REF.: JR 673

In view of our rapidly growing business with Continental Europe
we are looking to recruit bilingual assistants (German-English or French-English)
to work in our import department.

Applicants should be fluent in German or French and have a good command of English. Office skills and familiarity with import procedures are essential. Must enjoy working in a team.

Send application enclosing CV and certificates in English to:

Jennifer O'Rourke (Mrs) | Automotive Services Ltd | 103 Selsdown Drive | London E14 9LA

Small Tour Operator

Requires well-organised full-time travel consultant with admin and accounts background and fluent German and/or French. Hotel or travel experience desirable, but not essential. Must be team worker and have MS Office and typing skills.

Send CV and letter of application by e-mail to
jobs@dreamworldholidays.com or by post to:

Dreamworld Holidays
28 Percival St
London
W1T 1DW

Quote ref.: DH 15 Pw

2 Read the advertisement on page 230 (Natural Beauty) and formulate the
R questions to which the following statements are the answers. The elements
   suggesting the question word are in bold type.

Example:
Answer: 1. Natural Beauty is based **in Birmingham**.
Question: 1. **Where** is Natural Beauty based?

Answers

1. Natural Beauty is based **in Birmingham**.
2. Natural Beauty is seeking **young persons**.
3. Successful applicants will have **good English language skills**.
4. Successful applicants' mother tongue will be **Italian, French or German**.
5. **The following qualifications** are essential: PC-literacy, ability to work hard and meet deadlines.
6. **Natural Beauty** will help you with finding accommodation.
7. Your CV should be sent **to Catherine Bennet**.

3 Discuss with a partner what German qualifications would equip you for the jobs
I advertised in the three advertisements on page 230.

4 Describe your (future) qualifications (school leaving certificate, e.g. Abitur,
P apprenticeship, traineeship etc, language certificates) and state briefly what kind
   of job you would like. For job titles refer back to UNIT 1.

Example:
"I have just completed my training as a publisher's assistant and would like to work in a publishing house in or around Cologne. I spent a year in the United States and attended High School there, so I'd welcome the opportunity to use my English in my job."

5 Stellen Sie einem Freund / einer Freundin die Stellenanzeigen auf der Seite 230
KMK auf Deutsch vor. Beachten Sie dabei folgende Punkte:

- Firma bzw. Branche
- Anforderungen an Bewerber
- Gehalt
- Sonstige Leistungen der Firma
- Standort des Arbeitsplatzes
- Gewünschte Art der Kontaktaufnahme

Unit 16 | Job applications in Germany and the EU

A Letter of application

Your letter of application should be set out clearly and include the points below:

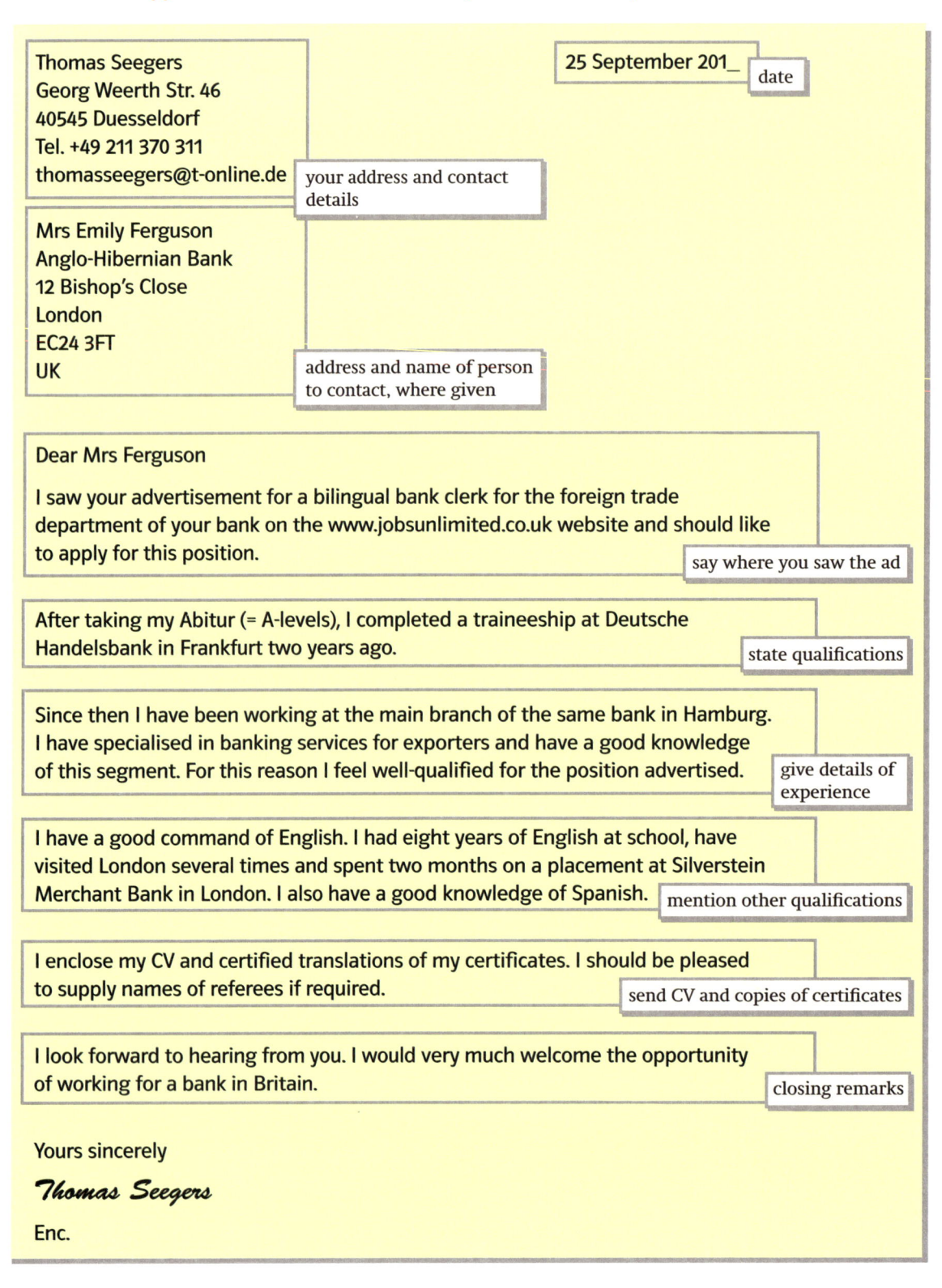

Thomas Seegers
Georg Weerth Str. 46
40545 Duesseldorf
Tel. +49 211 370 311
thomasseegers@t-online.de *(your address and contact details)*

25 September 201_ *(date)*

Mrs Emily Ferguson
Anglo-Hibernian Bank
12 Bishop's Close
London
EC24 3FT
UK *(address and name of person to contact, where given)*

Dear Mrs Ferguson

I saw your advertisement for a bilingual bank clerk for the foreign trade department of your bank on the www.jobsunlimited.co.uk website and should like to apply for this position. *(say where you saw the ad)*

After taking my Abitur (= A-levels), I completed a traineeship at Deutsche Handelsbank in Frankfurt two years ago. *(state qualifications)*

Since then I have been working at the main branch of the same bank in Hamburg. I have specialised in banking services for exporters and have a good knowledge of this segment. For this reason I feel well-qualified for the position advertised. *(give details of experience)*

I have a good command of English. I had eight years of English at school, have visited London several times and spent two months on a placement at Silverstein Merchant Bank in London. I also have a good knowledge of Spanish. *(mention other qualifications)*

I enclose my CV and certified translations of my certificates. I should be pleased to supply names of referees if required. *(send CV and copies of certificates)*

I look forward to hearing from you. I would very much welcome the opportunity of working for a bank in Britain. *(closing remarks)*

Yours sincerely

Thomas Seegers

Enc.

Job applications in Germany and the EU | Unit 16

1 Übertragen Sie die folgenden Sätze ins Deutsche.
KMK
1. I have decided to apply on the off-chance.
2. I am interested in applying for this vacancy.
3. I know you are recruiting staff at present.
4. I feel I am suitably qualified for this position.
5. I have completed a traineeship as an export clerk.

2 Complete the following letter of application as the applicant using one of the
P advertisements on page 230.

(Your address etc)

(Company address)

Reference no. (given in advertisement)

Dear Sir/Madam

I saw your **1** in the **2** yesterday and am interested in **3** this position.
I have now completed a **4** as an export clerk. My experience is limited to the **5** of my present firm.
I have a good **6** of English and Spanish and am keen **7** these languages.
I **8** my curriculum vitae and copies of certificates. Please let me know if you **9** the names and addresses of referees.

I look forward to **10** you soon.

With best regards*
(Your name and signature)

Enclosures: CV, certificates

* "Yours sincerely" is also possible. "Yours faithfully" is very formal and is hardly used nowadays.

233

Unit 16 | Job applications in Germany and the EU

B Curriculum Vitae (CV)

A neatly arranged CV is an essential part of any application. The following are two German CVs with paraphrases in English. As indicated in UNIT 1 German job titles often have no direct equivalent in English. It is important that you paraphrase your job title (e.g. Industriekaufmann, Hotelfachfrau etc.) in such a way that a potential employer has a clear and realistic impression of your training and experience. When applying for a job in English – and there is an increasing number of companies in continental Europe whose company language is English – it is important to be aware of differences. In an English CV do not give details of your parents' profession, your religious denomination, or the number of your brothers and sisters. International CVs do not include a photograph. Modern CVs often reverse the chronological order and start with the most recent developments in your career.

1 Study the following CVs of Fatma Gülsuyu and Daniel Paulat with a suggested paraphrase in English.

German CV I

Tabellarischer Lebenslauf

Persönliche Angaben

Name	Fatma Gülsuyu
Adresse	Dülkener Str. 5, 40235 Düsseldorf
	Tel.: 0211 571364, E-Mail: fatmaguelsuyu@t-online.de
Staatsangehörigkeit	türkisch
Geburtstag	23.01.89
Geburtsort	Düsseldorf
Familienstand	ledig

Schulbildung

1995–1999	Grundschule Niederkassel
1999–2007	Schiller-Gymnasium, Düsseldorf
2007	Abitur (Leistungskurse: Englisch, Mathematik, Grundkurse: Sozialwissenschaften, Türkisch, Gesamtnote: 2,2)

Tätigkeiten

August 2005–Juli 2006	Hausaufgabenhilfe im „Lernzentrum", Düsseldorf
August 2006–Juni 2007	Aushilfstätigkeit im Reisebüro „Evren", Düsseldorf
seit September 2007	Ausbildung als Kauffrau für Bürokommunikation im Reisebüro „Evren"

Sprachkenntnisse	Deutsch: wie Muttersprache
	Türkisch: Muttersprache
	Englisch: gut in Wort und Schrift
	Italienisch: Grundkenntnisse
PC-Kenntnisse	Windows, Excel, Powerpoint
Interessen	Musik (Saz spielen, im Chor singen), Volleyball

English paraphrase CV I

Curriculum Vitae

Personal details

Name and address	Fatma Gülsuyu Dülkener Str 5 40235 Düsseldorf, Germany Tel. + 49 (0)211 571364 E-mail: fatmaguelsuyu@t-online.de
Nationality	Turkish
Date of birth	23 January, 1989
Place of birth	Düsseldorf, Germany
Marital status	single

Education

1995–1999	Primary School Niederkassel
1999–2007	Schiller Gymnasium Düsseldorf (grammar school)
2007	Abitur (= A-Levels) Major subjects: English, Mathematics Basic courses: Social Sciences, Turkish Overall grade: 2.2 (= good = B)

Job experience and other activities

August 2005 to July 2006	Assisting pupils with homework at the Lernzentrum (Learning Centre) in Düsseldorf
August 2006–June 2007	Temporary employment at the "Evren" travel agency in Düsseldorf
from September 2007	Traineeship as office communications clerk/office management assistant at the "Evren" travel agency

Languages

German: native command
Turkish: mother tongue
English: good command of both spoken and written English
Italian: basic knowledge

Computer skills

Windows, Excel, Powerpoint

Hobbies

Music (playing saz, singing in a choir), volleyball

German CV II

Tabellarischer Lebenslauf

Persönliche Angaben

Name	Daniel Paulat
Adresse	44369 Dortmund
	Servatiusstr. 37
	Tel. 0231 4669834
	E-Mail: danielpaulat@aol.com
Staatsangehörigkeit	deutsch
Geburtstag	17.1.1990
Geburtsort	Hagen
Familienstand	ledig

Schulbildung

1996–2000	Grundschule Haspe, Hagen
2000–2004	Albert-Einstein-Realschule, Hagen
2004–2006	Gesamtschule am Teich, Dortmund
	Abschluss: Fachoberschulreife
2006–2008	Höhere Handelsschule, Kaufmännische Schule II, Dortmund
	Abschluss: Fachhochschulreife

Ausbildung

2009–2012	Ausbildung zum Industriekaufmann bei Kabel AG, Leverkusen
	Schwerpunkte: Rechnungswesen, Einkauf
2011	Zertifikatsprüfung Englisch für kaufmännische und verwaltende Berufe, Niveau I
voraussichtlich Mai 2012	Abschlussprüfung

Tätigkeiten

2006–2008	Aushilfstätigkeit als Fahrradkurier
2008–2009	Zivildienst in einer Behindertenwerkstatt

Sonstige Kenntnisse

MS Office, Linux
Englisch fließend, Spanisch ausbaufähig

Interessen

Fitness, Fußball, Fantasy-Literatur

English paraphrase CV II

Curriculum Vitae

Personal details

Name	Daniel Paulat
Address	44369 Dortmund, Germany
	Servatiusstr. 37
	Tel.: +49 (0)231 4669834
	E-mail: danielpaulat@aol.com
Nationality	German
Date of birth	17 January, 1990
Place of birth	Hagen (North Rhine-Westphalia)
Marital status	single

Education/Training

1996–2000	Primary school Haspe, Hagen
2000–2004	Albert Einstein Realschule (= higher secondary school), Hagen
2004–2006	Gesamtschule am Teich (comprehensive), Dortmund School-leaving certificate: Fachoberschulreife (= certificate enabling student to continue education at higher vocational school)
2006–2008	Höhere Handelsschule, Kaufmännische Schule II (higher commercial college), Dortmund Final examination: Fachhochschulreife (examination enabling student to enrol at a polytechnic university)
2009–2012	Traineeship as an industrial clerk/industrial business management assistant at Kabel AG, Leverkusen
2011	Special subjects: accounting, purchasing Zertifikatsprüfung (state examination)
probably May, 2012	English for clerical and administrative professions, Level I Final examination traineeship

Job activities

2006–2008	Temporary employment as cycle courier
2008–2009	Social service (in lieu of military service) in a workshop for handicapped people

Other skills

MS Office, Linux/Fluent English, basic Spanish

Personal interests

Working out, football, fantasy literature

Unit 16 | Job applications in Germany and the EU

✱ 2 Now write your own CV in English using the examples above and referring back to
P UNIT 1 for job titles. Use a dictionary if necessary.

Phrases

3 You have applied for a job with GlaxoSmithKline (UK). You feel you have a good chance of being invited to an interview. Research the company and its products and make brief notes in English.

4 Daniela Zeischegg sent off an application three weeks ago to the British company
I Tolaron plc in reply to an advertisement in which the company was looking for a German mother-tongue export clerk. Since she has not received a reply she decides to ring the company. Roleplay the dialogue below.

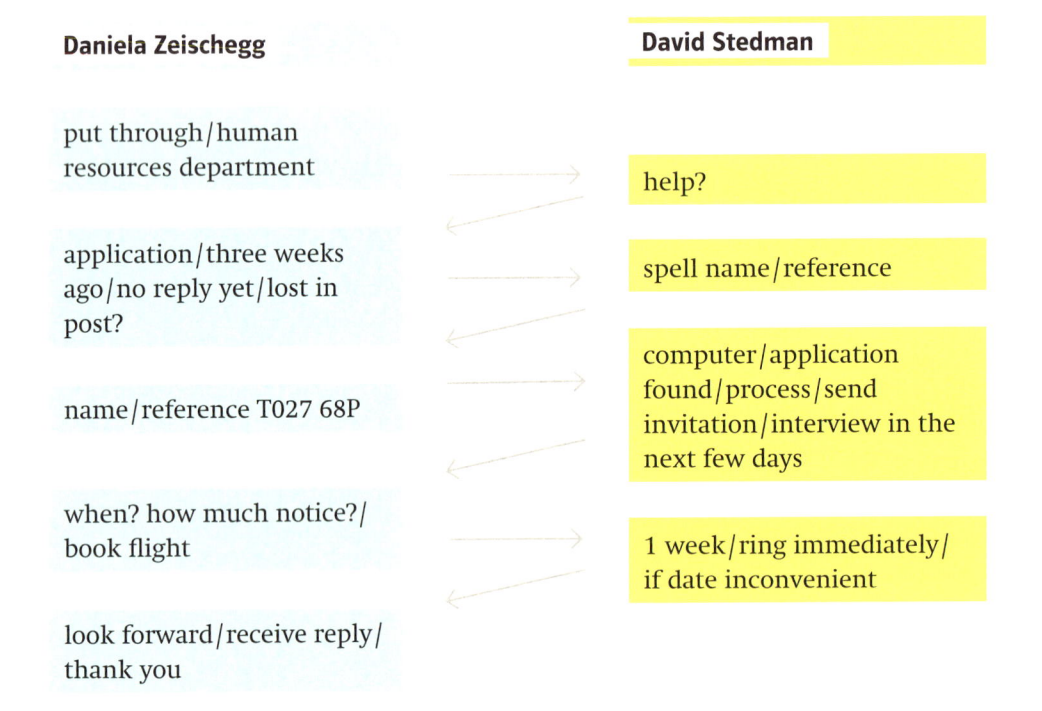

Daniela Zeischegg	**David Stedman**
put through/human resources department	
	help?
application/three weeks ago/no reply yet/lost in post?	
	spell name/reference
name/reference T027 68P	
	computer/application found/process/send invitation/interview in the next few days
when? how much notice?/ book flight	
	1 week/ring immediately/ if date inconvenient
look forward/receive reply/ thank you	

Video lounge Travel and Tourism

BBC Motion Gallery

You are about to see a video on the travel and tourist industry. Read through the questions below and listen for the answers as you watch the video:

1. What kind of tour operator does the young man work for?
2. Try and list as many of the qualifications and characteristics that are mentioned as desirable in a tour leader.
3. What kind of person is likely to apply for a job as a tour leader?
4. How did he prepare for his job in Egypt?
5. What sort of disadvantages does life as a tour leader have?

C Interviews

If your application meets with the approval of the company or its personnel department, your name will be put on a shortlist and you will be invited to an interview.

How can you prepare for the interview?

It is important to find out as much as you can about the company, its products and the image it projects so that you make an informed impression and demonstrate that you are interested in the company.

Think beforehand of any questions you would like to ask if they are not covered by the interviewer, e.g. location, type of work, starting salary, opportunities for further training, opportunities to use your language skills, catering arrangements, company pension scheme, how big is the office you will be working in? Will you have contact with customers or is it a back office?

What are your other interests? Think carefully about this. If you say "cinema" expect to be asked about the last film you saw. If you mention an interest in your CV, e.g. working out at a gym, you should think in advance what you would say if asked about it.

Finally, do not underestimate the importance of so-called "soft skills" – a neat, clean appearance, shirt tucked neatly into trousers, polished shoes with laces tied, hair neatly cut and combed, etc. Women should go for a suit or skirt or trousers and jacket. Don't risk wearing jeans and a T-shirt.

1 Answer the following questions on the text above.

1. What may happen if the company has a lot of applications and you are one of the fortunate ones?
2. Why is it a good idea to know something about the company?
3. What questions might you want to ask if the interviewer doesn't cover them?
4. What interests or hobbies would you mention?
5. What is meant by the term "soft skills"?

Unit 16 | Job applications in Germany and the EU

2 Choose what you regard as appropriate from this list of do's and don'ts.
R
1. Your first question should be about annual holidays.
2. You should dress smartly.
3. You should take some gum with you to chew to help you relax.
4. The interviewer can't expect you to know much about the firm before you even work there.
5. You should feel free to tell the interviewer that you are bored with your present job.
6. You should be prepared (and able) to talk about any interests you mention.
7. You should make eye contact with the interviewer, smile and nod to express agreement or ethusiasm.
8. You should tell the interviewer straight away that you are applying for other jobs at the moment.
9. You should refuse to describe your strengths and weaknesses.

3 Send an encouraging e-mail to an anxious friend who has an interview in a couple
P   of days. Make sentences by matching the bubbles with suitable parts from the list below.

- Make sure you …
- Wear …
- Don't forget to …
- Remember to …
- Be …
- Don't wear …
- Don't just …
- Be sure to …
- Remember…
- You mustn't …

… go to bed early the night before.
… go to the hairdresser's beforehand.
… put on a clean set of clothes.
… a sweatshirt or fleece (boy)/see-through top or mini-skirt (girl).
… a smart costume (girl)/jacket (boy).
… wear sneakers.
… have a look at the firm's website before the interview.
… get there on time.
… yourself and act naturally.
… answer "yes" or "no". Take the initiative and volunteer information.
… that there are other fish in the sea.

4 Daniela Zeischegg has been invited to an interview at Tolaron plc's head office
R   in Croydon, South London. She takes an early flight from Cologne-Bonn airport
A1.31 to London Gatwick. She takes the train from Gatwick to South Croydon and presents herself at Tolaron at 11 am. She wears a neatly tailored suit in navy blue and a white blouse.

Listen to the interview and write down the job details mentioned.

240

Job applications in Germany and the EU | Unit 16

5 Listen to the interview again and translate the following sentences into English.

R/M
A1.31
1. Sie haben eine Ausbildung bei einem großen Kölner Unternehmen der verarbeitenden Industrie gemacht.
2. Wir benötigen jemanden, der Deutsch spricht, weil wir eine große Anzahl von Kunden in Deutschland und Österreich haben.
3. Leider können wir Ihnen bei der Suche nach einer Unterkunft nicht behilflich sein.
4. Müsste ich am 1. August anfangen, wie in der Anzeige angegeben?
5. Ich habe mich gefreut, Sie kennen zu lernen. Sie werden von mir hören.

6 Match these 10 questions with the answers given below.

R
1. Why do you wish to leave your present position?
2. What would you say are your strengths and weaknesses?
3. Why would you like to work for this company?
4. Which animal do you most readily identify with?
5. What are your professional aims?
6. What are your expectations as far as salary is concerned?
7. What would you say was your advantage compared with other applicants?
8. What did you find most satisfying in your previous jobs?
9. What three positive things would your previous boss say about you?
10. What reasons would you give why we should employ you?

A. I particularly like lions/monkeys/elephants.
B. I don't know the other applicants. All I know is that I am highly motivated and keen to do this job.
C. Eventually I would like to be an export manager/head of department/set up in business on my own.
D. I am very enthusiastic and have all the necessary qualifications plus good references.
E. I have always enjoyed dealing with people. I liked being in the front office. I had a good rapport with customers.
F. I like my present job and the people I work with but it doesn't give me any opportunity to use my languages/I have no contact with clients.
G. My previous boss would probably say I had a good sense of humour, was good at working to deadlines and that I had a good manner with customers.
H. My strengths are that I'm good at working with clients, deadlines don't faze me. My weaknesses – I need praise and to feel that I'm needed. My motivation level drops if I feel unloved or unappreciated.
I. The company has a very good reputation for well-designed products and a positive approach to the environment. I also know that you have a good reputation as an equal opportunities employer.
J. From advertisements for similar positions I know that the usual starting salary is about Euro 2000. I would be happy with this salary but would hope that the career structure makes promotion possible.

Unit 16 | Job applications in Germany and the EU

✱ 7 Work with a partner. Prepare and act out the following interview as a role play in English using the prompts on the role cards.

> Phrases

Role card: Partner A (interviewer)   Role card partner B ⇨ page 256

Sie sind Jennifer O'Rourke von Automotive Services Ltd., London, oder deren Kollege John Middleton. Mittels einer Stellenanzeige haben Sie eine/n zweisprachige/n Mitarbeiter/in für die Importabteilung gesucht. Ein/e Bewerber/in kommt zum Vorstellungsgespräch.

Beginnen Sie das Gespräch mit allgemeinen Fragen z. B. nach:
- Flug
- Heimatstadt des Bewerbers
- Wetter

Fassen Sie die Anforderungen kurz zusammen:
- zweisprachig
- teamfähig
- vertraut mit Einfuhrformalitäten

Fragen Sie nach Berufserfahrung:
- Dauer
- Arbeitsgebiete
- Software-Kenntnisse

Erkundigen Sie sich nach den Gründen für den Wunsch in GB zu arbeiten.

Fragen Sie nach den Gehaltsvorstellungen.

Gehen Sie auf das im CV genannte Interesse an Tennis ein:
- Sie spielen selbst.
- Ihre Firma besorgt für die Mitarbeiter Karten für Wimbledon.

Versprechen Sie in einer Woche Bescheid zu geben.

Verabschieden Sie den Bewerber freundlich.

D Employment in the EU

One of the central principles of the EU is the free movement of labour. This means that in principle any EU citizen can look for a job in any EU member country without having to apply for permits etc. An EU citizen also has the right to take up residence in any EU country.

1 Jonathan Oxfurt, a 23-year-old German from Quedlinburg who has recently completed an apprenticeship as an export clerk, is thinking of looking for a job in another European country. He is talking on the telephone to an English friend, Daniel Peterson, whom he met while on a work placement in England and who is working in Bracknell at the logistics and warehousing operation of a major supermarket.

R
A1.32

Listen to the conversation and decide whether the following statements are TRUE or FALSE.

1. Jonathan has sent off lots of applications.
2. He would need a green card to work in Britain.
3. A lot of companies have their head offices in Bracknell.
4. Jonathan's certificates do not need to be translated into English.
5. Jonathan could stay for a while with Daniel.
6. Daniel suggests he should apply to the export department.

2 Marcel Krenz has seen that Global Catering are looking for an assistant to the export manager who speaks French and German. Kirsty Burnham has been promoted and the new export manager is Zoe Lovegrove. Marcel is excited about the job and would love to work in Manchester. He decides to ring Kirsty Burnham.

R
A1.33

Listen to the dialogue and complete the following sentences.

Would you **1** for a moment, please?
As you know, **2** are now the big thing.
I have seen that your company is advertising for **3** who can speak German.
Of course, it will have to go through **4**.
Tell Herr Diepholz this is **5** for you.
I'll get **6** off right away.

Unit 16 | Job applications in Germany and the EU

3 Listen to the dialogue again and translate the following sentences into German.

R/M
A1.33

1. Kirsty Burnham has been promoted.
2. Global Catering are looking for an assistant to the export manager.
3. We are in the process of acquiring a US chain of organic snack outlets.
4. I would be able to involve you in the US projects.
5. I am dreading telling Herr Diepholz.
6. Keep your fingers crossed!

> **Communicating across cultures: Job applications**
>
> You should NOT include references from previous employers in your application when applying in Britain. You will usually be asked to give the names and addresses of possible referees so that the company can approach them direct. In your covering letter you may indicate that you are prepared to provide names of referees on request.
>
> It is obviously a good idea to ask possible referees beforehand whether they are happy to provide a reference.
>
> You should NOT include a photo in your application when applying in the USA or Britain nor make any reference to your religion or race, unless specifically asked to do so.

> **Info: EU-Facts and figures**
>
> **EU member countries** (27 at present):
>
> Austria, Belgium, Bulgaria, Cyprus, Czech Republic, Denmark, Estonia, Finland, France, Germany, Greece, Hungary, Ireland, Italy, Latvia, Lithuania, Luxemburg, Malta, The Netherlands, Poland, Portugal, Romania, Slovakia, Slovenia, Spain, Sweden, United Kingdom
>
> **Total area**: 4,324,782 sq. km.
>
> **Total population**: c. 501.26 million
>
> **Total GDP**: between $14 and $16 trillion
>
> **Languages**: There are over 20 official languages. English is spoken by 34% of European citizens – the most widely spoken foreign language.

Job applications in Germany and the EU | Unit 16

Office expert

1 Internship training abroad

1 Read the following two texts and decide if the statements below are
R a. TRUE of both texts, b. TRUE of text 1 only, c. TRUE of text 2 only.

1

INTERNATIONAL PARTICIPATION
We are seeking international organizations able to provide us with a source of qualified, enthusiastic trainees. Internship4America provides domestic and international internships for students and young professionals from around the world. Our USA internships, summer internships, hospitality internships and international internships provide housing, transportation and a stipend for qualified trainees. We develop corporate internship programs. Our programs are designed to meet the US State Department Exchange Visitors Program criteria. Submit your résumé and application to be considered for our program.

2

Willing to work in a multicultural office environment?
Take a big step forward with our internship program! At Studios Limited we offer you the chance to gain hands-on office work experience to give you an advantage over future competitors in the job market. Our interns come from different companies, cultures and countries, from all over Europe. Our program runs all through the year, lasting from two weeks up to a year, so you can choose your start and end dates yourself.
Join our team of young and motivated people. The program includes the practical application of all aspects of office work, as well as the opportunity to advance your communication and foreign language skills. Experience learning to live and work within a multicultural office setting.

1. The programme is targeted towards college students/graduates.
2. The programme gives young people the chance to work abroad.
3. It would be possible to do an internship during holiday break.
4. Applicants are invited to send in their curriculum vitae.
5. The programme arranges for a place to live and a small salary.
6. The programme is in keeping with government regulations.
7. People from all over the world participate in the programme.
8. The programme promises to improve your career opportunities.

2 Find synonyms for the following words in the texts above.
R

1. opportunity
2. get
3. practical
4. rival
5. improve
6. offer
7. company
8. send in
9. search

245

Unit 16 | Job applications in Germany and the EU

✱ 3 Translate the following collocations into German. Are the German translations also collocations?
M

1. willing to work
2. a big step forward
3. join our team
4. language skills
5. young professionals
6. domestic and international
7. from around the world
8. submit your résumé

2 Office job fairs

1 Match the sentence parts to formulate tips for attending a job fair.
R

1. Allow enough time
2. Ask questions
3. Be polite
4. Dress appropriately
5. Follow up
6. Orientate yourself
7. Prepare yourself
8. Request cards
9. Take notes
10. Update your CV

a. by reviewing employers and jobs prior to the fair.
b. because this demonstrates your interest.
c. and bring many copies to the fair.
d. because first impressions are important.
e. and come as early as possible.
f. when asking about the next steps (e.g. hiring dates).
g. because complete contact information can be helpful.
h. by studying the layout of the venue.
i. and keep your questions brief if others are waiting.
j. and submit applications promptly.

2 Find synonyms for the following words in Exercise 1.
R

1. in advance
2. shows
3. suitably
4. résumé
5. locality
6. write down
7. full
8. short
9. ask for

3 Eine Praktikantin in Ihrem Unternehmen hat Ihnen den folgenden Text zu einer Berufseinsteigermesse in Madison, USA, geschickt und bittet Sie, die wesentlichen Informationen für sie auf Deutsch zusammenzufassen.
KMK

Announcing the Second Annual Madison Business Job Fair

A growing number of businesses in the Madison area are in dramatic need of new office personnel. Skilled office workers of all sorts are required: team and personal assistants, general clerical staff and administrative specialists. The open positions include full- and part-time jobs, for recent and past graduates at all qualification levels.
Refreshments will be served and there will be drawings for give-aways!

Students: Be sure to bring copies of your up-to-date résumé and transcript!
Date: Thursday, March 15th, 201_   Time: 2:30 pm to 5:30 pm
Location: Union South

For more information, or if your company would like to participate in this job fair, please contact Prof. Barton Miller, http://www.cs.wisc.edu/~bart/.

3 Europass

Ein Kollege hat Ihnen folgenden Text über den Europass gegeben.
Lesen Sie den Text und beantworten Sie die Fragen dazu auf Deutsch.

> The Europass is designed to encourage mobility and lifelong learning in an expanding Europe. It aims to help over 830 million citizens make their skills and qualifications transparent and easy to understand throughout Europe.
>
> Brought together into a single framework, the Europass provides a standardised overview of an individual's education and occupational qualifications: language competences, work experience, education and training qualifications and other skills, and competences gained outside formal training schemes. By making diplomas, certificates and qualifications more transparent it enables citizens to better communicate and present their know-how and skills throughout Europe. The Europass promotes both occupational mobility and educational mobility between countries as well as across sectors.
>
> It is available in 13 languages and is frequently used across Europe. Anyone who wants to use the Europass can start by completing the Europass CV. Other documents can be attached to the CV.

1. Weshalb wurde der Europass entwickelt? Was sind die Ziele?
2. Worüber bietet der Europass einen Überblick?
3. Was ermöglicht der Europass den Bürgern Europas?
4. Umfasst der Europass lediglich formale Qualifikationen?
5. In wie vielen Sprachen und welchen Regionen wird der Europass verwendet?
6. Was müssen Sie tun, um den Europass zu verwenden?

4 Starting your own business

1 You'd like to start your own business offering a variety of office services such as message taking, bookkeeping, accounts, copying, mailings and writing services. Put the following business start-up checklist into logical order.

> ✔ Choose a location for the business or make space in the house for it
> ✔ Check into business insurance needs
> ✔ Choose a business based on your skills and interests
> ✔ Research the business idea
> ✔ Choose a business name
> ✔ Have business phone or extra residential phone lines installed
> ✔ Get any required business licences or permits
> ✔ Register the business name
> ✔ See if the business name is available (check it out on the internet)
> ✔ Write a business plan and marketing plan

Unit 16 | Job applications in Germany and the EU

✱ 2 Match the ten essential rules for succeeding in your own business (1.–10.) with the suitable explanations (a.–j.).

1. Be true to customers!
2. Be true to yourself!
3. Budget realistic costs and double them!
4. Choose profitable products or services!
5. Don't expect wonders!
6. Find a need and fill it!
7. Learn marketing!
8. Remember: One is the loneliest number!
9. Treat suppliers and vendors with respect!
10. Use the internet!

a. Many businesses forget about extra costs or underestimate them.
b. One product, one service, one main customer is a recipe for failure.
c. Enjoy, be proud of your business or let it be.
d. It is easier to sell what people really need.
e. To get and keep customers you need to market effectively and continuously.
f. If customers can't find you in their online queries, they are likely to choose a competitor.
g. The difference between your costs and selling price (profit margin) shouldn't be too low.
h. Don't lie or promise what you can't deliver.
i. They are an important part of your team.
j. Building up a business requires time and effort.

🌐 3 Complete the list of key office items you will need with the words in the box. Use a dictionary if necessary.

> costly • decreased • DSL • features • light • limited • multi-functional • present • price • promotion

- **Phone:** It should be a system that meets both your **1** and future needs. This means buying one that can grow as your business does.
- **Computer:** When buying office computers, it's essential that you know your needs so you can weigh the costs against the **2** that each offers.
- **Printers:** Monochrome laser printers offer speed at a good **3**, though more expensive colour ones are now within the budget of many small businesses. If your office has **4** printing needs, you can buy a **5** printer/copier/scanner.
- **Copier:** For limited use and **6** workloads, small offices can avoid buying one by scanning documents and printing multiple copies, or by using a three-in-one.
- **Security system:** It doesn't need to be elaborate, but if you have **7** equipment and/or valuable data in your office, some type of security system is a must.
- **Internet connectivity:** For limited use you can do with a 56k modem or **8**, but as your needs grow you'll want either a cable modem or a dedicated T-1 line.
- **Fax machine:** The need for fax machines has **9** with the use of e-mail, but, it is still best to have an inexpensive one on-hand should the need arise.
- **Digital camera:** Many businesses find buying a simple point-and-shoot model beneficial for product marketing, **10** and other business needs.

Phrases: Applications

To refer to the source of address

I saw your advertisement **in** …	Ich habe Ihre Anzeige in … gesehen.
I saw this vacancy advertised **on** the … website.	Ich habe diese Stellenanzeige auf der … Webseite gefunden.
I should like to apply for the position advertised in the …	Ich möchte mich für den in der … ausgeschriebenen Posten bewerben.
I have been given your address **by** … who told me that you have a vacancy **for** …	Ich habe Ihre Anschrift von … bekommen, der mich darauf aufmerksam machte, dass bei Ihnen die Stelle eines … frei geworden ist.
I am applying on the off-chance that you may have a vacancy.	Ich erlaube mir, Ihnen eine Initiativbewerbung zu schicken, für den Fall, dass bei Ihnen eine Stelle frei ist.

To give reasons for applying

I am particularly attracted **to** this position as …	Ich bin an dieser Stelle besonders interessiert, weil …
I have just completed a traineeship **at** …	Ich habe gerade meine Ausbildung bei … abgeschlossen.
I completed an apprenticeship two years ago.	Vor zwei Jahren haben ich meine Ausbildung abgeschlossen.
I have some experience in the export trade.	Ich habe Erfahrungen im Außenhandel.
I am familiar **with** this kind of work.	Mit dieser Tätigkeit bin ich vertraut.
I am used to working with people.	Ich bin es gewohnt mit Menschen zu arbeiten.
I enjoy working with people.	Ich arbeite gern mit anderen Menschen zusammen.
I enjoy working in a team.	Ich arbeite gern im Team.
I would welcome the opportunity to …	Ich würde mich über die Möglichkeit freuen …
I am keen to use my knowledge **of** English and French.	Ich möchte sehr gerne meine Englisch- und Französischkenntnisse anwenden.

To refer to your German school career

From … to … I attended … comparable **to** • primary (UK)/elementary (USA) school • grammar school (UK) • higher secondary school • secondary modern school	Von … bis … besuchte ich • die Grundschule • das Gymnasium • die Realschule • die Hauptschule

Unit 16 | Job applications in Germany and the EU

• comprehensive (school) • high school (USA) • vocational school • commercial school • business college • polytechnic university, university of applied sciences	• Gesamtschule (Einheitsschule für die Sekundarstufe) • die Berufsschule • die Höhere Handelsschule • das Berufskolleg • die Fachhochschule
In … I obtained the • certificate enabling a student to continue education at higher vocational school • German higher education entrance qualification • German university entrance qualification	Im Jahre … erwarb ich das Zeugnis der • Fachoberschulreife • Fachhochschulreife • allgemeine Hochschulreife (Abitur)

In … I passed the
• state examination in English for clerical and administrative professions
 	
• Chamber of Commerce examination
  – "Certified Foreign Language Correspondent"
  – "English for Commercial Trainees"
	Im Jahre … legte ich die …
	• Zertifikatsprüfung Englisch für kaufmännische und verwaltende Berufe (KMK-Zertifikat)
	• IHK-Prüfung
	  – „Geprüfte/r Fremdsprachen-korrespondent/in"
	  – „Zusatzqualifikation Englisch für kaufmännische Auszubildende"
	ab.

To refer to qualifications

I **took** my Abitur two years ago.	Vor zwei Jahren machte ich das Abitur.
My main subjects included English and Maths.	Meine Leistungskurse waren Englisch und Mathematik.
I have trained **as a** …	Ich bin gelernte/r …
I have completed an apprenticeship **in** …	Ich habe eine Ausbildung als … abgeschlossen.
I did my apprenticeship **with** the … company.	Ich habe eine Ausbildung bei der Firma … gemacht.
I spent two months in St. Albans **on** a placement.	Ich war zwei Monate zu einem Praktikum in St. Albans.
I have done a practical **with** a small travel operator.	Ich habe ein Praktikum bei einem kleinen Reiseveranstalter gemacht.
I have good admin and bookkeeping skills.	Ich verfüge über gute Kenntnisse und Fertigkeiten, was Organisation und Buchhaltung angeht.

To refer to certificates and references

I enclose certified copies of my certificates.	Als Anlage übersende ich Ihnen beglaubigte Zeugniskopien.
I enclose certified translations of …	Ich füge beglaubigte Übersetzungen von … bei.
I should be happy to provide the names of referees.	Ich würde Ihnen gerne Referenzen angeben.

To refer to starting date and relocation

I would be able to start **at** short notice.	Ich kann kurzfristig anfangen.
I would have to give the usual notice **at** my present firm.	Ich müsste die übliche Kündigungsfrist einhalten.
I could start **on** 1 August.	Ich könnte am 1. August anfangen.
I would be prepared to move **to** …	Ich wäre bereit nach … umzuziehen.

To close the letter

I look forward to hearing from you.	Ich sehe Ihrer Antwort mit Interesse entgegen.
I should be grateful if you would consider my application.	Ich würde mich freuen, wenn Sie meine Bewerbung berücksichtigen.
I hope that you will consider my application suitable and give me the opportunity to present myself **at** an interview.	Ich hoffe, dass Sie meine Bewerbung in Betracht ziehen und mir die Möglichkeit geben, mich Ihnen persönlich vorzustellen.

Role cards Partner B

Unit 5 C 5

Role card: Partner B **Role card partner A ⇨ page 71**

1. 0033 (0) 4 92 04 89 20
2. 12 Gansevoort Street New York, NY 10014 USA Tel.: 001-212-2422455 info@usatech.com,
3. www.visitengland.com
4. e-mail: info@shanghai-cd.com, phone: 86-21-5365-8941
5. address: 12J-1 Golden Bell Plaza 18 Huaihai Zhong Lu Shanghai 200021 China

Unit 5 C 8

Role card: Partner A / B

Persons for whom the message is intended:	Possible contents of message:
Mr. Collins	Mr. Campbell ill with the flu / can't take part in the conference
Sales Manager	Meeting on Wednesday scheduled from 1:00 pm to 3:30 pm / 15 participants
Miss Otway in Purchasing	Proposal accepted / further details tomorrow
Dr. Temme	New deadline for application 16 October, must be kept whatever happens
Frau Sabine Johänntges	Flight delayed by one hour / arrival now at 10:15 London Heathrow

Unit 6 A 8

Role card: Partner B **Role card partner A ⇨ page 88**

Sie sind James Critchley von der Firma SmartMart Ltd. und wollen für eine Geschäftsreise in den USA ein Auto mieten. Jennifer Ainsworth von Saskatchewan Airlines hat Ihnen die Mietwagenfirma Excelsior Limos Inc. in Chicago empfohlen. **Rufen Sie dort an.**
- Auto vom 25. bis 30. Juni benötigt
- Abholung und Rückgabe am Flughafen O'Hare in Chicago
- Kleinwagen genügt / Preis für fünf Tage? / Versicherung inbegriffen?
- Zusatzversicherung für Selbstbeteiligung (excess coverage) erwünscht?
- Rabatt für Kunden der Saskatchewan Airlines?
- Gesamtpreis für eine Woche?
- Zahlung per Kreditkarte?
- Visa Nr. 4731 5026 7100 5314, gültig bis 07/14
- Adresse: Brunswick Avenue, Brighton BN3 1NA, UK

Unit 6 B1 1

Role card: Partner B **Role card partner A ⇨ page 89**

Kirsty Burnham's appointment diary

Monday 13 June
9–11 am: meeting to discuss Madrid; 1 pm working lunch with John Markham from PolisMedia; 2.30 pm meeting at office with Barbara Lonsdale from Cosmopolitan Gourmet

Tuesday 14 June

Wednesday 15 June
From 10 am: visiting suppliers in Birmingham

Thursday 16 June
5 pm: work-out at Royal Gym with Laurie

Friday 17 June
10 am: Leeds / Amanda Rees from Snack Attack / introduction of trial range
4 pm: hairdresser

Unit 9 B 4

Role card: Partner B **Role card partner A ⇨ page 137**

Jane/James Vernon from Powertools plc, Cardiff, gets a call.
He/she offers to send brochures, price lists and detailed technical descriptions by e-mail and asks for Hammer Werkzeughandel's e-mail address.
Details about delivery times, quantity discounts etc. are dealt with in the brochure.
Jane/James thanks the caller for his/her interest in Powertool's products.

Unit 11 Office expert 4

Role card: Partner B **Role card partner A ⇨ page 169**

Sie vertreten die Firma Better Business Cards auf der Messe Office Expo in Manchester. Dort führen Sie ein Gespräch mit einem potentiellen Kunden.
- Begrüßen Sie den Kunden und heben Sie zwei Vorzüge von Business Cards hervor.
- Beantworten Sie die Frage zur Auswahl einer bestimmten Farbe und dem Abdruck des Firmenlogos positiv.
- Visitenkarten können problemlos zweisprachig gedruckt werden.
- Sie bieten Visitenkarten in zwei Qualitäten an: 1. Value Cards (Digitaldruck, hohe Festigkeit); 2. Premium Cards (Offsetdruck, extrem hohe Festigkeit).
- Sie bieten ein Skonto von 2 % sowie 5 % Mengenrabatt ab 20 Stück.
- Bei einer Erstbestellung ist Vorkasse und Lieferung ab Werk üblich, danach Lieferung auf Rechnung.
- Bedanken Sie sich für das Gespräch und verabschieden Sie sich.

Unit 13 C2 3

Role card: Student A (seller) **Role card partner B ⇨ page 255**

You are the chief-accountant Jane/John Thorpe at Topsweets Ltd. in Edinburgh. At the end of last month but one (use the appropriate month) you supplied 1,500 kgs mint bars to Zuckermann & Sacher in Suessen, Germany, a regular customer of yours.
Ring Zuckermann & Sacher and remind them of your invoice
- invoice No. 34500-2
- invoice amount: € 20,450.50
- due date: 14 days ago

Up to now punctual settlements
- invoice overlooked?
- reason for complaint?

Be helpful and polite but insist on payment by the end of next week.
Impossible to grant 3 months' respite for the entire sum.
Insist on down payment of at least half the sum.
Accept one of the solutions offered and close on a friendly note.

Unit 13 C2 3

Role card: Student B (buyer) **Role card partner A ⇨ page 254**

Sie (eigener Name) bearbeiten die Rechnungen der Firma Zuckermann & Sacher in Suessen. Ende vorletzten Monats hatten Sie von der Firma Topsweets Ltd aus Edinburgh, Schottland, 1500 kg Pfefferminzriegel bezogen. Die Rechnung war vor 14 Tagen fällig. Nun ruft Sie Jane/John Thorpe deswegen an.

Fragen Sie nach Rechnungsnummer, -datum und -betrag.
Kein Versehen, kein Grund zur Beanstandung
Entschuldigung für Zahlungsverzug
Grund: Insolvenz eines wichtigen Kunden, einer Kette von Süßwarengeschäften
Bitte um 3 Monate Zahlungsaufschub
Falls abgelehnt: Ihr Verhandlungsspielraum für Anzahlung: € 7,000 – 10,000
Ihr Verhandlungsspielraum für Restzahlung:
- in 3 Raten im Abstand von 6 Wochen oder
- gesamter Rest in 10 Wochen.

Bei Entgegenkommen weitere Aufträge

Unit 14 A2 6

Role card: Partner B (seller) **Role card partner A ⇨ page 204**

You receive a call from a customer who had expected to be supplied with a skateboard for a maximum weight of 70 kg. On checking the package the customer has found that the maximum admissible weight is only 90 lbs. The price the customer paid is the price for this smaller model. However, on your website you had quoted this lower price for the bigger model by mistake. Apologize. Try to persuade the customer to keep the smaller skateboard – as a present for a kid? – and promise to let him have the bigger one half price. Should the customer refuse this generous offer you will have to agree to take back the small skateboard at your expense and refund the purchase price.

Anhang | Role cards

Unit 16 C 7

Role card: Partner B (interviewee)   **Role card partner A ⇨ page 242**

Sie (eigener Name) haben sich bei Automotive Services Ltd., London, als zweisprachige/r Importsachbearbeiter/in beworben und sind zu einem Vorstellungsgespräch eingeladen worden. Sie sind 23 Jahre alt und haben vor einem Jahr ihre Ausbildung als Kaufmann/-frau im Groß- und Außenhandel beendet.

Beantworten Sie die allgemeinen Fragen zu Beginn ganz nach Wunsch
- Flug angenehm/unruhig
- Wetter heiter/wolkig
- einige Sätze zu ihrer Heimatstadt

Sie kennen die Anforderungen und glauben sie vollständig zu erfüllen
- Deutsch Muttersprache, Englisch gut: Insgesamt 9 Jahre in der Schule, 1 Jahr in USA
- arbeiten gern im Team
- mit allen Export- und Importverfahren vertraut

Berufserfahrung
- Ausbildung in verschiedenen Abteilungen eines Stuttgarter Automobilherstellers (Verkauf, Einkauf, Lagerhaltung, Rechnungs- und Personalwesen)
- nach Abschluss der Lehre ein volles Jahr bis jetzt in einer Importabteilung für elektronische Bauelemente
- vertraut mit SAP Office

Begründen Sie Ihre Absicht in GB zu arbeiten ganz nach Ihrer Wahl
Gehaltsvorstellung noch nicht konkret, in Deutschland ca. €2000 pro Monat

Tennis
- Sie spielen für Ihren Klub in der Regionalliga
- Sie versuchen immer möglichst viel von Wimbledon im Fernsehen zu sehen

Bitten Sie um baldige Nachricht, weil Sie rechtzeitig kündigen müssen.

Alphabetical word list | Anhang

Videotraining: Englische Aussprache

Perfekte englische Aussprache leicht gemacht: Mit dem Lernprogramm zur englischen Lautschrift können Sie alle Laute einüben. Wählen Sie einfach in der Navigation rechts den entsprechenden Reiter (*Vowels* oder *Consonants*) aus und dann klicken Sie auf das gewünschte phonetische Symbol. Sprechen Sie die Wörter laut nach.
Unter www.klett.de geben Sie einfach den Online-Link 808201-1000 ein. Von dort aus können Sie die Webanwendung online starten.

Hinweis: Unitbegleitendes Vokabular zum Herunterladen über Online-Link 808261-0000!

(AE) = American English
(BE) = British English

A

abbreviation [əˌbriːvɪˈeɪʃn] Abkürzung 115
ability [əˈbɪləti] Fähigkeit 100
able to work in a team [ˌeɪbl tʊ ˌwɜːk ɪn ə ˈtiːm] teamfähig 242
abroad [əˈbrɔːd] im/ins/aus dem Ausland 41
to absorb [əbˈzɔːb] aufnehmen 101
access [ˈækses] Zugang 31
accident [ˈæksɪdənt] Unfall 88
to accommodate [əˈkɒmədeɪt] aufnehmen, unterbringen, entgegenkommen 171
accomodation [əˌkɒməˈdeɪʃn] Unterkunft, Wohnung 31
to accompany [əˈkʌmpəni] begleiten 175
according to [əˈkɔːdɪŋ tʊ] entsprechend, gemäß 101
account [əˈkaʊnt] Konto 14
accountant [əˈkaʊntənt] Bilanzprüfer/in, Buchprüfer/in, Buchhalter/in 56
to account for [əˈkaʊnt fɔː] ausmachen 108
account-holder [əˈkaʊntˌhəʊldə] Kontoinhaber/in 183
accounting [əˈkaʊntɪŋ] Buchhaltung, Rechnungswesen 14
accounts [əˈkaʊnts] Rechnungsabteilung 65
accurate(ly) [ˈækjərət(li)] genau, präzise, akkurat 69
to ache [eɪk] schmerzen, wehtun 65
to achieve [əˈtʃiːv] erreichen 109
a couple of [ə ˈkʌpl əv] ein paar 220
to acquire [əˈkwaɪə] sich aneignen 100
actually [ˈæktʃʊəli] eigentlich 216

additions [əˈdɪʃnz] Hinzufügungen 90
additional [əˈdɪʃənl] zusätzlich 74
additional / supplementary insurance [əˌdɪʃənl / ˌsʌplɪməntəri ɪnˈʃɔːrəns] Zusatzversicherung 88
addressee [ˌædresˈiː] Adressat, Empfänger 116
to adjust [əˈdʒʌst] anpassen, sich anpassen 148
adjustable [əˈdʒʌstəbl] verstellbar 156
adjustment [əˈdʒʌstmənt] Ausgleich, Bereinigung, Erledigung 196
admin and accounts [ˌædmɪn ən əˈkaʊnts] Verwaltung und Rechnungswesen 230
administration [ədˌmɪnɪˈstreɪʃn] Verwaltung 56
administrator [ədˈmɪnɪstreɪtə] Vergleichs-/Vermögensverwalter 191
admirable [ˈædmərəbl] bewundernswert, ausgezeichnet 150
adult [ˈædʌlt] Erwachsene/r 184
to advance [ədˈvɑːns] vorschießen, auslegen 183
advantage [ədˈvɑːntɪdʒ] Vorteil 220
advent [ˈædvent] Ankunft 63
advertisement [ədˈvɜːtɪsmənt, ˈædvətaɪzmənt] Anzeige 134
advertising [ˈædvətaɪzɪŋ] Werbung 165
advertising agency [ˈædvətaɪzɪŋ ˌeɪdʒənsi] Werbeagentur 8
advertising assistant [ˈædvətaɪzɪŋ əˌsɪstənt] Kaufmann/-frau für Marketingkommunikation 8
advertising campaign [ˈædvətaɪzɪŋ kæmˌpeɪn] Werbekampagne, -feldzug 132
to advise [ədˈvaɪz] (be)raten; benachrichtigen 118
advisory services [ədˈvaɪzəri ˌsɜːvɪsɪz] Beratungsdienst 218
to affect [əˈfekt] betreffen, beeinflussen 202
affluent [ˈæflʊənt] wohlhabend 221

age group [ˈeɪdʒ ˌgruːp] Altersgruppe 215
agenda [əˈdʒendə] Tagesordnung; Termine 85
agent [ˈeɪdʒənt] (Handels-)Vertreter/in 132
a good command of English [ə ˌgʊd kəˌmɑːnd əv ˈɪŋglɪʃ] gute Englischkenntnisse 230
ahead of time [əˌhed əv ˈtaɪm] im Voraus 193
aid [eɪd] Hilfe, Unterstützung 192
air-conditioning [ˈeəkənˌdɪʃənɪŋ] Klimaanlage 26
air freight [ˈeəfreɪt] Luftfracht 126
airline [ˈeəlaɪn] Fluggesellschaft 219
airy [ˈeəri] luftig 26
aisle [aɪl] Gang *(Flugzeug/Kirche/Supermarkt)* 87
alert [əˈlɜːt] wachsam 193
alteration [ˌɒltəˈreɪʃn, ˌɔːltəˈreɪʃn] Änderung 206
amateur chef [ˌæmətjʊə ˈʃef] Hobbykoch 29
amazing [əˈmeɪzɪŋ] erstaunlich 41
ambitious [æmˈbɪʃəs] ehrgeizig, anspruchsvoll 104
amenities [əˈmiːnətiz] Freizeiteinrichtungen, Zusatzleistungen 33
among [əˈmʌŋ] unter 20
amount [əˈmaʊnt] Betrag, Summe 177
ample [ˈæmpl] reichlich, üppig 207
ancient [ˈeɪnʃnt] (ur)alt 25
anger [ˈæŋgə] Zorn 196
annual holidays [ˌænjʊəl ˈhɒlɪdeɪz] Jahresurlaub 240
answering machine *(BE)*, **voice mail** *(AE)* [ˈɑːnsərɪŋ məˌʃiːn, ˌvɔɪs meɪl] Anrufbeantworter 64
to antagonize [ænˈtægənaɪz] vor den Kopf stoßen 204
apart from [əˈpɑːt frəm] abgesehen von 40
apology [əˈpɒlədʒi] Entschuldigung 92

257

Anhang | Alphabetical word list

appeal [ə'piːl] Anziehung(skraft) 221
to appeal to [ə'piːl tʊ]] ansprechen, gefallen; appellieren 123
appetising ['æpətaɪzɪŋ] schmackhaft 55
apple juice ['æpl ˌdʒuːs] Apfelsaft 21
appliances [ə'plaɪənsɪz] Geräte 64
applicant ['æplɪkənt] Bewerber/in 230
application [ˌæplɪ'keɪʃn] Bewerbung 229
applications [ˌæplɪ'keɪʃnz] Anwendungen, Funktionen 64
to apply to [ə'plaɪ tʊ] betreffen, zutreffen 14
to appoint [ə'pɔɪnt] ernennen, bestellen 218
appointment [ə'pɔɪntmənt] Verabredung, Treffen, Termin 14
approach [ə'prəʊtʃ] Haltung, Herangehensweise, Ansatz 241
to approach [ə'prəʊtʃ] sich nähern, herangehen an, ansprechen 220
appropriate [ə'prəʊpriət] geeignet, passend, angebracht 116
approval [ə'pruːvl] Billigung, Zustimmung, Beifall 160
to approve [ə'pruːv] annehmen, zustimmen, billigen 169
approx(imately) [ə'prɒks(ɪmətli)] ungefähr, ca. 107
to arouse [ə'raʊz] wecken (Interesse, Gefühle) 101
artificial [ˌɑːtɪ'fɪʃl] künstlich 166
as a result of [əz ə rɪ'zʌlt əv] auf Grund 20
as a rule [əz ə 'ruːl] in der Regel 89
as a whole [əz ə 'həʊl] insgesamt 100
a set break [ə ˌset 'breɪk] eine Pause zu festgesetzter Zeit 55
as long as stocks last [əz ˌlɒŋ əz ˌstɒks 'lɑːst] solange Vorrat reicht 142
asparagus [ə'spærəgəs] Spargel 28
to assess [ə'ses] (hier:) bewerten, einschätzen 104
to assign [ə'saɪn] zuordnen, benennen 14
to assist [ə'sɪst] helfen 229
assistance [ə'sɪstəns] Hilfe 91
to associate with [ə'səʊʃieɪt wɪð] in Verbindung bringen mit 221
association [əˌsəʊʃi'eɪʃn] Vereinigung, Verband 144
assortment [ə'sɔːtmənt] Sortiment, Auswahl 19
to assume [ə'sjuːm] annehmen, von etwas ausgehen 117
assurance [ə'ʃɔːrəns] Zusicherung, Versicherung 175
athlete ['æθliːt] Sportler/in, Athlet/in 39
athletics [æθ'letɪks] (Leicht-)Athletik 43

ATM (automated teller machine) [ˌeɪtiː'em, ˌɔːtəmeɪtɪd 'telə məˌʃiːn] Geldautomat 183
at short notice [ət ˌʃɔːt 'nəʊtɪs] kurzfristig, ohne Voranmeldung 67
at sight [ət 'saɪt] bei Sicht/Vorlage 183
to attach [ə'tætʃ] anhängen (Datei), befestigen, anbringen 115
attached [ə'tætʃt] angeschlossen 55
attachment [ə'tætʃmənt] (hier:) Anhang (E-Mail) 94
to attempt [ə'tempt] versuchen, sich bemühen 38
to attend [ə'tend] besuchen, teilnehmen 33
to attend a course [əˌtend ə 'kɔːs] an einem Kurs teilnehmen 200
to attend a fair [əˌtend ə 'feə] an einer Messe teilnehmen 85
attention [ə'tenʃn] Aufmerksamkeit 15
at the bottom [ət ðə 'bɒtm] unten 107
at the latest (nachgestellt) [ət ðə 'leɪtɪst] spätestens 166
at the top [ət ðə 'tɒp] oben, an der Spitze 107
at your disposal [ət jɔː dɪ'spəʊzl] zu Ihrer Verfügung 101
at your earliest convenience [ət jɔːr ˌɜːliəst kən'viːniəns] so bald wie möglich 181
audience ['ɔːdiəns] Publikum 100
author ['ɔːθə] (hier:) Urheber/in; Verfasser/in, Autor/in 76
automobile sales management assistant [ˌɔːtəməʊbiːl ˌseɪlz 'mænɪdʒmənt əˌsɪstənt] Automobilkaufmann/-frau 11
available [ə'veɪləbl] erhältlich, zur Verfügung stehend 163
average ['ævrɪdʒ] Durchschnitt 184
average consumer [ˌævrɪdʒ kən'sjuːmə] Durchschnittsverbraucher/in 171
average price [ˌævrɪdʒ 'praɪs] Durchschnittspreis 106
to avoid [ə'vɔɪd] vermeiden 77
to award points [əˌwɔːd 'pɔɪnts] Punkte vergeben (z.B. Wettbewerb) 104
aware [ə'weə] bewusst 234
awareness [ə'weənəs] Bewusstsein 15
awful ['ɔːfl] scheußlich 21

B

background ['bækgraʊnd] (hier:) Ausbildung, Erfahrung 230
backlit ['bæklɪt] von hinten/innen beleuchtet 146
back office [ˌbæk 'ɒfɪs] Büro ohne Publikumsverkehr 51
to bake [beɪk] backen, im Ofen braten 28
balance ['bæləns] Rest, Saldo; Gleichgewicht 150

to balance ['bæləns] ausgleichen, ins Gleichgewicht bringen 191
balanced ['bælənst] ausgewogen 26
balancing ['bælənsɪŋ] Bilanzierung 14
bale [beɪl] Ballen 174
ballet ['bæleɪ] (klassisches) Ballett 8
bank business management assistant [ˌbæŋk ˌbɪznɪs 'mænɪdʒmənt əˌsɪstənt] Bankkaufmann/-frau 9
bank clerk ['bæŋk ˌklɑːk] Bankkaufmann/-frau 8
banknote ['bæŋknəʊt] Geldschein 180
bank transfer ['bæŋk ˌtrænsfɜː] Banküberweisung 162
banquet ['bæŋkwɪt] Festessen, Bankett 31
bar chart ['bɑː ˌtʃɑːt] Balkendiagramm 105
barman / barmaid ['bɑːmən / 'bɑːmeɪd] Bedienung hinter der Theke 89
barrier ['bæriə] Absperrung, Schranke 96
based in ['beɪst ɪn] mit Sitz in 231
basically ['beɪsɪkli] im Grunde 165
battery ['bætəri] Batterie 146
Bavarian cuisine [bəˌveəriən kwɪz'iːn] bayerische Küche 85
to be able [bi 'eɪbl] in der Lage sein 216
bean [biːn] Bohne 28
bearer ['beərə] (hier:) Überbringer/in 183
to bear with someone, bore, born [beə 'wɪð ˌsʌmwʌn, bɔː, bɔːn] (hier:) etwas Geduld haben, so lange warten (am Telefon) 65
beauty consultant ['bjuːti kənˌsʌltənt] Kosmetiker/in 217
to be aware of a problem [bɪ əˌweər əv ə 'prɒbləm] sich eines Problems bewusst sein 187
to become aware [bɪˌkʌm ə'weə] bewusst werden 103
to be cooperative [bɪ kəʊ'ɒprətɪv] zur Zusammenarbeit bereit sein 204
beef broth [ˌbiːf 'brɒθ] Fleischbrühe 28
to be entitled [bɪ ɪn'taɪtld] berechtigt sein, Anspruch haben 185
beetle ['biːtl] Käfer 197
beforehand [bɪ'fɔːhænd] vorher 239
to be in a hurry [bɪ ˌɪn ə 'hʌri] es eilig haben 216
to be inclined [bɪ ɪn'klaɪnd] dazu neigen, geneigt sein 127
to be in demand [bɪ ɪn dɪ'mɑːnd] gefragt sein, nachgefragt werden 165
to be in keeping with [bɪ ɪn 'kiːpɪŋ wɪð] in Einklang/Übereinstimmung mit etwas sein 245
to be in line with [bɪ ɪn 'laɪn wɪð] übereinstimmen, im Einklang stehen mit 122

to be in progress [bɪ ɪn 'prəʊgres] im Gang sein, in Bearbeitung sein 206
to be likely [bɪ 'laɪklɪ] wahrscheinlich sein, wahrscheinlich geschehen 113
bend [bend] Kurve 24
to benefit ['benəfɪt] profitieren 218
to be on a familiar footing [bɪ ˌɒn ə fəˌmɪlɪə 'fʊtɪŋ] auf vertrautem Fuße stehen 117
to be on hand [bɪ ˌɒn 'hænd] zugegen sein, da sein 91
to be put on a shortlist [bɪ ˌpʊt ɒn ə 'ʃɔːtlɪst] in die engere Auswahl kommen 239
berry ['berɪ] Beere 29
to be subject to [bɪ 'sʌbdʒɪkt ˌtuː] unterliegen, abhängen von, unterworfen sein 142
to bet [bet] wetten 192
to be to blame [bɪ tʊ 'bleɪm] schuld sein 206
to be up to [bɪ 'ʌp tuː] im Schilde führen, anstellen, in der Lage sein 224
beverage wholesaler [ˌbevərɪdʒ 'həʊlˌseɪlə] Getränkegroßhandlung 135
to be worth one's weight in gold [ˌwɜːθ wʌnz ˌweɪt ɪn 'gəʊld] Gold wert sein 192
BIC (bank identifier code) [ˌbiːaɪˈsiː (ˌbæŋk aɪˈdentɪfaɪə ˌkəʊd)] internationaler Bank-Code 181
bilingual [baɪˈlɪŋgwəl] zweisprachig 230
bill [bɪl] Rechnung 90
billboards (AE) ['bɪlbɔːdz] Plakatwände 221
bill of exchange [ˌbɪl əv ɪksˈtʃeɪndʒ] Wechsel 183
biro ['baɪrəʊ] Kugelschreiber 52
blank [blæŋk] unbeschrieben, leer 115
blank cheque [ˌblæŋk 'tʃek] Blankoscheck 192
blasting area ['blɑːstɪŋ ˌeərɪə] Sprenggebiet 78
blogging ['blɒgɪŋ] Bloggen *(Internet-Tagebücher schreiben)* 59
blunt(ly) [blʌnt(lɪ)] *(hier:)* unverblümt 204
boarding ['bɔːdɪŋ] *(Flugzeug/Zug)* besteigen 96
board meeting ['bɔːd ˌmiːtɪŋ] Vorstandssitzung 102
bodily injury [ˌbɒdɪlɪ 'ɪndʒərɪ] körperliche Verletzung 78
body language ['bɒdɪ ˌlæŋgwɪdʒ] Körpersprache 103
to boil [bɔɪl] kochen, sieden 28
bold type [ˌbəʊld 'taɪp] Fettdruck 122
booking charge ['bʊkɪŋ ˌtʃɑːdʒ] Buchungsgebühr 73
booking reference ['bʊkɪŋ ˌrefrəns] Buchungsnummer 87

to bore [bɔː] langweilen 102
bored [bɔːd] gelangweilt 240
both … and … [bəʊθ … ənd …] sowohl … als auch … 119
to bottom out [ˌbɒtəm 'aʊt] Tiefstand erreichen 227
brackets ['brækɪts] Klammern 115
branch [brɑːntʃ] Filiale 19
brand [brænd] Marke, Markenartikel 219
breadcrumbs ['bredkrʌmz] Brotkrümel, Paniermehl 27
to break bulk [ˌbreɪk 'bʌlk] große Gebinde aufbrechen 217
brewery ['bruːərɪ] Brauerei 25
brief(ly) [briːf(lɪ)] kurz 7
briefcase ['briːfkeɪs] Aktentasche 102
bright [braɪt] hell, glänzend; klug 163
bright yellow [ˌbraɪt 'jeləʊ] leuchtend gelb 25
to bring forward [brɪŋ 'fɔːwəd] vorziehen, vorverlegen 119
brochure ['brəʊʃə] Broschüre, Prospekt 39
Brussels sprouts [ˌbrʌslz 'spraʊts] Rosenkohl 28
bubble ['bʌbl] Blase, Bläschen 19
budget ['bʌdʒɪt] (Staats-)Haushalt, Etat 191
building materials ['bɪldɪŋ məˌtɪərɪəlz] Baustoffe, -material 12
building site ['bɪldɪŋ ˌsaɪt] Baustelle 197
bulk goods [ˌbʌlk 'gʊdz] Massen-, Schüttgüter 172
bulk mail [ˌbʌlk 'meɪl] Massensendungen *(per E-Mail)* 129
bulky ['bʌlkɪ] sperrig, unhandlich, übergroß 172
bullet point ['bʊlɪt ˌpɔɪnt] Auflistungspunkt 110
bumpy ['bʌmpɪ] unruhig, holprig 20
bundle with steel strapping [ˌbʌndl wɪð ˌstiːl 'stræpɪŋ] Bündel mit Stahlbandumreifung 174
business relations ['bɪznɪs rɪˌleɪʃnz] Geschäftsbeziehungen 144
business section ['bɪznɪs ˌsekʃn] Gewerbeteil 64
business terms ['bɪznɪs ˌtɜːmz] Geschäftsbedingungen 132
business unit, division ['bɪznɪs ˌjuːnɪt, dɪˈvɪʒn] Geschäftseinheit, Unternehmensbereich 191
business venture ['bɪznɪs ˌventʃə] geschäftliches Unternehmen 27
buyer ['baɪə] Einkäufer/in 224
by means of [ˌbaɪ 'miːnz əv] mittels 184
by return [ˌbaɪ rɪˈtɜːn] umgehend 118

C

cabbage ['kæbɪdʒ] Kohl 27
calculator ['kælkjəleɪtə] Taschenrechner 52

calm [kɑːm] ruhig, gelassen 196
calorie count ['kælərɪ ˌkaʊnt] Kalorienangabe 55
canapé ['kænəpeɪ] Cocktailhappen 31
to cancel an invoice [ˌkænsl ən 'ɪnvɔɪs] Rechnung stornieren 191
to cancel an order [ˌkænsl ən 'ɔːdə] einen Auftrag annullieren 199
canteen [kænˈtiːn] Kantine 23
capable of ['keɪpəbl ˌəv] in der Lage, fähig, tüchtig 41
capitalization [ˌkæpɪtəlaɪˈzeɪʃn] Großschreibung 110
to capitalize ['kæpɪtəlaɪz] in Großbuchstaben schreiben 117
to capture ['kæptʃə] (ein)fangen; erfassen *(Daten)* 163
carbon paper ['kɑːbn ˌpeɪpə] Kohlepapier 115
car carrier ['kɑː ˌkærɪə] Autotransporter, -transportschiff 171
cardholder ['kɑːdˌhəʊldə] Karteninhaber/in 183
card stock ['kɑːd ˌstɒk] Karton 168
care [keə] Sorgfalt 205
cargo ['kɑːgəʊ] (See-)Fracht, Ladung 171
car hire/rental company ['kɑːˌhaɪə/ˌrentl ˌkʌmpənɪ] Mietwagenfirma 88
carnivorous [kɑːˈnɪvərəs] fleischfressend 27
carriage ['kærɪdʒ] Transport(kosten), Fracht(kosten) 152
carriage by sea [ˌkærɪdʒ baɪ 'siː] Seetransport 172
carrier ['kærɪə] Frachtführer 171
carrots ['kærəts] Möhren, Karotten 28
to carry out work [ˌkærɪ ˌaʊt 'wɜːk] Arbeit ausführen 143
cartridge ['kɑːtrɪdʒ] (Tinten-)Patrone 212
cash discount [ˌkæʃ 'dɪskaʊnt] Skonto, Barzahlungsrabatt 185
cash on delivery [ˌkæʃ ɒn dɪˈlɪvərɪ] Zahlung durch Nachnahme/bei Lieferung 185
cash payment [ˌkæʃ 'peɪmənt] Barzahlung 184
cash point ['kæʃpɔɪnt] Geldautomat 183
cash with order [ˌkæʃ wɪð 'ɔːdə] Bezahlung bei Auftragserteilung, Vorkasse 144
casual ['kæʒʊəl] zwanglos, leger 6
to catch, caught, caught [kætʃ, kɔːt, kɔːt] *(hier:)* mitbekommen 67
to cater for ['keɪtə fɔː] *(hier:)* etwas bieten für 85
cauliflower ['kɒlɪˌflaʊə] Blumenkohl 28
celebrated ['seləbreɪtɪd] gefeiert 149
cell [sel] Zelle 60

certified [ˈsɜːtɪfaɪd] beglaubigt; zertifiziert 232
chair, chairperson [tʃeə, ˈtʃeəˌpɜːsn] Vorsitzende/r 92
chairman of the board [ˌtʃeəmən əv ðə ˈbɔːd] Vorstandsvorsitzender 56
challenging [ˈtʃælɪndʒɪŋ] herausfordernd 230
champagne reception [ˌʃæmpeɪn rɪˈsepʃn] Sektempfang 32
change(s) [tʃeɪndʒ, ˈtʃeɪndʒɪz] Veränderung(en) 223
change [tʃeɪndʒ] Wechselgeld 90
changeable [ˈtʃeɪndʒəbl] wechselhaft 21
channel [ˈtʃænl] (hier:) Vertriebsweg 215
characteristic feature [ˌkærəktərɪstɪk ˈfiːtʃə] typisches Merkmal 218
characters [ˈkærɪktəz] (hier:) Buchstaben, Zeichen 15
charge [tʃɑːdʒ] Belastung, Gebühr 149
to charge [tʃɑːdʒ] (hier:) berechnen 215
to charge for [ˈtʃɑːdʒ fɔː] bezahlen lassen 218
cheap chain [ˈtʃiːp ˌtʃeɪn] Billigladenkette 215
to check [tʃek] (über)prüfen 220
check-out [ˈtʃekaʊt] (Supermarkt-)Kasse 184
chemist [ˈkemɪst] Apotheker/in 217
cheque (BE), check (AE) [tʃek] Scheck 183
chicken [ˈtʃɪkɪn] Hähnchen, Hühnerfleisch 28
chief accountant [ˌtʃiːf əˈkaʊntənt] Leiter/in des Rechnungswesens 23
chief executive officer (CEO) [ˌtʃiːf ɪɡˌzekjətɪv ˈɒfɪsə] Firmenchef/in, Vorstandsvorsitzende/r 56
chilled [tʃɪld] eisgekühlt 27
to choose, chose, chosen [tʃuːz, tʃəʊz, ˈtʃəʊzn] wählen 87
to chop [tʃɒp] klein schneiden, hacken 28
clean bill of lading [ˈkliːn ˌbɪl əv ˈleɪdɪŋ] reines Konnossement 185
clerical staff [ˈklerɪkl ˌstɑːf] Büropersonal, Sachbearbeiter 84
to clip [klɪp] abschneiden, verkürzen 169
closely followed by [ˌkləʊsli ˈfɒləʊd ˌbaɪ] (hier:) dicht gefolgt von 107
club [klʌb] Disko; Verein 20
coaching [ˈkəʊtʃɪŋ] Training 200
coffee break [ˈkɒfi ˌbreɪk] Kaffeepause 55
coffee table [ˈkɒfi ˌteɪbl] Couchtisch 177
coil on euro-pallet [ˌkɔɪl ɒn ˈjuːrəʊˌpælɪt] Rolle, Coil auf Europalette 174
coin [kɔɪn] Münze, Geldstück 180
to collect [kəˈlekt] abholen, (ein)sammeln 160
collection [kəˈlekʃn] Sammlung 59
to collect the invoice amount [kəˌlekt ðɪ ˈɪnvɔɪs əˌmaʊnt] den Rechnungsbetrag eintreiben 187
colour printer [ˈkʌləˌprɪntə] Farbdrucker 148
column [ˈkɒləm] (Text-)Spalte 59
to comb [kəʊm] kämmen 239
to come across [ˌkʌm əˈkrɒs] (hier:) wirken 73
comeback [ˈkʌmbæk] (hier:) Reaktion 65
comfort [ˈkʌmfət] Behaglichkeit, Komfort; Trost 144
comfortable [ˈkʌmftəbl] bequem 181
command [kəˈmɑːnd] Beherrschung; Befehl, Anweisung 15
commencement [kəˈmensmənt] Anfang, Beginn 150
commercial invoice [kəˌmɜːʃl ˈɪnvɔɪs] Handelsrechnung 175
to commission [kəˈmɪʃn] beauftragen 198
commission [kəˈmɪʃn] Provision 41
commitment to [kəˈmɪtmənt ˌtuː] Engagement für 224
common sense [ˌkɒmən ˈsens] gesunder Menschenverstand 77
communication [kəˌmjuːnɪˈkeɪʃn] Nachricht, Mitteilung, Information 187
community [kəˈmjuːnəti] Gemeinschaft 224
comparative(ly) [kəmˈpærətɪv(li)] verhältnismäßig 185
to compare [kəmˈpeə] vergleichen 219
comparing prices [kəmˌpeərɪŋ ˈpraɪsɪz] Preisvergleich 220
to compensate [ˈkɒmpənseɪt] entschädigen 189
to compete [kəmˈpiːt] an einem Wettkampf teilnehmen, konkurrieren 39
competition [ˌkɒmpəˈtɪʃn] Konkurrenz, Wettbewerb 148
competitive prices [kəmˌpetətɪv ˈpraɪsɪz] günstige, konkurrenzfähige Preise 216
competitor [kəmˈpetɪtə] Mitbewerber/in, Wettbewerber/in 94
complaint [kəmˈpleɪnt] Beschwerde, Beanstandung, Reklamation, Mängelrüge 196
to complete [kəmˈpliːt] abschließen 231
complimentary [ˌkɒmplɪˈmentri] im Preis inbegriffen, gratis 34
complimentary close [ˌkɒmplɪmentəri ˈkləʊz] Grußformel 114
to comply with [kəmˈplaɪ wɪð] einhalten, befolgen 212
to comply with regulations [kəmˌplaɪ wɪð ˌreɡjəˈleɪʃnz] Vorschriften einhalten 202
components [kəmˈpəʊnənts] Bestandteile 114
comprehensive [ˌkɒmprɪˈhensɪv] umfangreich 128
to comprise [kəmˈpraɪz] umfassen 134
computer projector [kəmˌpjuːtə prəˈdʒektə] Beamer 103
concept [ˈkɒnsept] Konzept, Begriff, Auffassung 159
concerning [kənˈsɜːnɪŋ] bezüglich 14
concerns [kənˈsɜːnz] (hier:) Sorgen, Fragen 90
concession [kənˈseʃn] Zugeständnis 125
conciliatory [kənˈsɪliətri] versöhnlich 204
concise [kənˈsaɪs] kurz und bündig 75
conclusion [kənˈkluːʒn] Schluss 101
to conduct [ˈkɒndʌkt] (durch)führen, leiten 14
to conduct a test [kənˌdʌkt ə ˈtest] einen Test durchführen 160
confectionery [kənˈfekʃənri] Süßwaren 34
confident [ˈkɒnfɪdənt] selbstbewusst 103
confidential [ˌkɒnfɪˈdenʃl] vertraulich 15
to confirm [kənˈfɜːm] bestätigen 181
confirmation [ˌkɒnfəˈmeɪʃn] Bestätigung 87
connectivity [ˌkɒnekˈtɪvəti] Netzwerkfähigkeit 248
consent [kənˈsent] Zustimmung, Einwilligung 185
conservatory [kənˈsɜːvətri] Wintergarten 206
to consider [kənˈsɪdə] erwägen, überlegen; ansehen als 127
consideration [kənˌsɪdəˈreɪʃn] Erwägung, Überlegung 26
consignment [kənˈsaɪnmənt] (Waren-)Sendung, Lieferung 172
consignment note [kənˈsaɪnmənt ˌnəʊt] Frachtbrief 175
consistency [kənˈsɪstənsi] Beständigkeit 110
conspicuous [kənˈspɪkjuəs] auffällig 25
construction work [kənˈstrʌkʃn ˌwɜːk] Bauarbeiten 104
consumer [kənˈsjuːmə] Verbraucher/in 220
consumer goods [kənˈsjuːmə ˌɡʊdz] Konsumgüter 221
contact person [ˈkɒntækt ˌpɜːsn] Ansprechpartner/in 200
to contain [kənˈteɪn] enthalten 166
content [ˈkɒntent] Inhalt 49
contest [ˈkɒntest] Wettbewerb 226
context [ˈkɒntekst] Zusammenhang, Kontext 113

contract ['kɒntrækt] Vertrag 113
to contribute [kən'trɪbju:t] beitragen 223
contribution [,kɒntrɪ'bju:ʃn] Beitrag 223
convenience food [kən'vi:nɪəns ,fu:d] Fertiggerichte 55
convenient [kən'vi:nɪənt] bequem, praktisch 132
conventional [kən'venʃənl] herkömmlich, traditionell 216
converted [kən'vɜ:tɪd] umgebaut 51
to convince [kən'vɪns] überzeugen 145
convincing [kən'vɪnsɪŋ] überzeugend 44
cooking ['kʊkɪŋ] Art zu kochen, Küche 7
co-operation [kəʊ,ɒpə'reɪʃn] (hier:) Hilfe; Mit-, Zusammenarbeit 119
to cope with something ['kəʊp wɪð ,sʌmθɪŋ] fertig werden mit etwas, etwas schaffen 210
copper ['kɒpə] Kupfer 104
cordial ['kɔ:dɪəl] herzlich, freundlich 209
corner stand ['kɔ:nə ,stænd] Eckstand 93
corn starch ['kɔ:n ,stɑ:tʃ] Stärkemehl 29
corporate ['kɔ:pərət] Firmen- 31
corporate (e.g. culture) ['kɔ:pərət] Unternehmens- (z. B. -kultur), bezogen auf Firmen/Unternehmen 102
corresponding to [,kɒrɪ'spɒndɪŋ tu:] entsprechend, passend zu 14
corridor ['kɒrɪdɔ:] Gang 18
cost estimate ['kɒst ,estɪmət] Kostenvoranschlag 142
cost price ['kɒst ,praɪs] Selbstkostenpreis 26
cottage ['kɒtɪdʒ] (hier:) Ferienhäuschen 73
Could you tell me the way to …? [kʊd jʊ ,tel mɪ ðə 'weɪ tʊ …] Können Sie mir sagen, wie ich zu/nach … komme? 24
countryside ['kʌntrɪsaɪd] Landschaft, Gegend; ländliche Gegend 26
court [kɔ:t] Gericht(shof), Hof 113
courtesy ['kɜ:təsɪ] Höflichkeit 205
courtyard ['kɔ:tjɑ:d] Hof 210
to cover ['kʌvə] decken, abdecken 101
covering letter ['kʌvərɪŋ ,letə] Begleitschreiben 230
covering page ['kʌvərɪŋ ,peɪdʒ] Deckblatt 118
crash course ['kræʃ ,kɔ:s] Kompaktkurs 137
crate [kreɪt] Lattenkiste 174
to create [krɪ'eɪt] (er)schaffen, erzeugen, erstellen 38
credit note ['kredɪt ,nəʊt] Gutschrift 197
creditworthiness ['kredɪt,wɜ:ðɪnəs] Kreditwürdigkeit 185

crossed cheque [,krɒst 'tʃek] Verrechnungsscheck 183
crowded ['kraʊdɪd] überfüllt 89
crude oil [,kru:d 'ɔɪl] Rohöl 172
crystal glass [,krɪstl 'glɑ:s] Kristallglas 135
cucumber ['kju:kʌmbə] Gurke 28
cues [kju:z] Stichworte 101
currency ['kʌrənsɪ] Währung 180
current ['kʌrənt] laufend, gegenwärtig, derzeitig, aktuell, gültig 57
curt [kɜ:t] knapp, schroff 204
customary ['kʌstəmərɪ] üblich 185
customer base ['kʌstəmə ,beɪs] Kundenstamm 107
customer relations [,kʌstəmə rɪ'leɪʃnz] Kundendienst; Kundenbeziehungen 65
customer service [,kʌstəmə 'sɜ:vɪs] Kundendienst 56
to customise ['kʌstəmaɪz] anpassen 77
customs formalities ['kʌstəmz fɔ:,mælətɪz] Zollformalitäten 152
to cut off [kʌt 'ɒf] (hier:) unterbrechen 67
to cut out [kʌt 'aʊt] (hier:) umgehen; ausschneiden 218
cutting-edge [,kʌtɪŋ 'edʒ] auf dem neuesten Stand 225
CV (curriculum vitae) [,si:'vi: (kə,rɪkjələm 'vi:taɪ)] tabellarischer Lebenslauf 230
cycling ['saɪklɪŋ] Radfahren 9

D

database ['deɪtəbeɪs] Datenbank 14
data processing, EDP ['deɪtə ,prəʊsesɪŋ, ,i:di:'pi:] Datenverarbeitung, EDV 23
deadline ['dedlaɪn] letzte Frist, letzter Termin 139
deal [dɪəl] (hier:) Angebot 156
to deal with, dealt, dealt [dɪəl wɪð, delt, delt] sich befassen mit 14
debit card ['debɪt ,kɑ:d] Bankkarte 183
to debit to an account [,debɪt tʊ ən ə'kaʊnt] von einem Konto abbuchen 183
to debit to someone's account [,debɪt tʊ ,sʌmwʌnz ə'kaʊnt] das Konto von jemandem belasten 177
debt level ['det ,levl] Schuldenstand 184
decade ['dekeɪd] Jahrzehnt 171
decline [dɪ'klaɪn] Rückgang 106
to decline [dɪ'klaɪn] sinken, zurückgehen 106
dedicated ['dedɪkeɪtɪd] (hier:) fest zugeordnet 227
to deduct [dɪ'dʌkt] abziehen 185
to deepen ['di:pn] vertiefen, tiefer machen 171
deer [dɪə] Rotwild 27

defective [dɪ'fektɪv] schadhaft, beschädigt, unzulänglich 202
definitely ['defɪnətlɪ] auf jeden Fall 20
degree [dɪ'gri:] Grad, Ausmaß; akademischer Grad 112
delay [dɪ'leɪ] Verzögerung 126
delay in payment [dɪ,leɪ ɪn 'peɪmənt] Zahlungsverzug 190
to delete [dɪ'li:t] löschen 59
delicatessens [,delɪkə'tesənz] Feinkostgeschäfte 165
delighted [dɪ'laɪtɪd] entzückt, begeistert 145
delivery [dɪ'lɪvərɪ] Lieferung, Auslieferung 116
delivery [dɪ'lɪvərɪ] (hier:) das Halten (eines Vortrags) 100
denomination [dɪ,nɒmɪ'neɪʃn] Konfession (Religion) 234
department store [dɪ'pɑ:tmənt ,stɔ:] Warenhaus, Kaufhaus 217
departure time [dɪ'pɑ:tʃə ,taɪm] Abfahrtszeit 96
to depend on [dɪ'pend ɒn] abhängen von, sich verlassen auf 145
to deposit [dɪ'pɒzɪt] (hier:) einzahlen 193
deposit slip [dɪ'pɒzɪt ,slɪp] Einzahlungsbeleg 193
description [dɪ'skrɪpʃn] Beschreibung 161
to design [dɪ'zaɪn] entwerfen, erstellen 7
desirable [dɪ'zaɪərəbl] wünschenswert 230
desires [dɪ'zaɪəz] Wünsche 216
desk [desk] Schreibtisch 52
desk lamp ['desk ,læmp] Schreibtischlampe 52
desk research ['desk ,rɪ'sɜ:tʃ] (Markt-) Forschung am Schreibtisch; Sekundärforschung 216
desk tidy ['desk ,taɪdɪ] Stifteköcher 52
despair [dɪ'speə] Verzweiflung 65
to despatch, dispatch [dɪ'spætʃ] (ab/ver)senden, (ab/ver)schicken 144
dessert [dɪ'zɜ:t] Nachspeise 27
destination [,destɪ'neɪʃn] Ziel, Bestimmung(sort) 24
to destroy [dɪ'strɔɪ] vernichten, zerstören 202
details ['di:teɪlz] Einzelheiten 232
detailed ['di:teɪld] ausführlich 126
to detect [dɪ'tekt] entdecken, feststellen 227
detective novel [dɪ'tektɪv ,nɒvl] Kriminalroman 197
to devastate ['devəsteɪt] verwüsten 189
to develop [dɪ'veləp] entwickeln 220
development [dɪ'veləpmənt] Entwicklung 219
devoted [dɪ'vəʊtɪd] gewidmet 224

Anhang | Alphabetical word list

dialling tone ['daɪəlɪŋ ˌtəʊn] Freizeichen 64
diary ['daɪərɪ] Terminkalender, Tagebuch 14
to differ ['dɪfə] unterschiedlich sein 229
dip [dɪp] Sinken 227
directory [daɪ'rektərɪ, dɪ'rektərɪ] Nachschlagewerk, Verzeichnis 229
directory enquiries [daɪˌrektərɪ ɪn'kwaɪərɪz, dɪˌrektərɪ ɪn'kwaɪərɪz] Telefonauskunft 64
to direct someone [daɪ'rekt ˌsʌmwʌn, dɪ'rekt ˌsʌmwʌn] jemandem den Weg sagen/zeigen 23
discerning [dɪ'sɜːnɪŋ] anspruchsvoll, guten Geschmack besitzend 145
disclaimer [dɪ'skleɪmə] Haftungsausschluss, Widerruf 43
to disclose [dɪ'skləʊz] offenlegen, preisgeben 186
discount ['dɪskaʊnt] (Preis-)Nachlass, Rabatt 34
disgruntled [dɪs'ɡrʌntld] verärgert, verstimmt 205
disgusting [dɪs'ɡʌstɪŋ] abscheulich 27
dish [dɪʃ] (hier:) Speise, Gericht 102
to dislike [dɪ'slaɪk] nicht mögen 222
dismayed [dɪ'smeɪd] entsetzt 198
dispatch advice [dɪ'spætʃ ədˌvaɪs] Versandanzeige 175
distribution [ˌdɪstrɪ'bjuːʃn] Vertrieb 48
distribution channels [dɪstrɪ'bjuːʃn ˌtʃænlz] Vertriebskanäle 217
to divide up [dɪˌvaɪd 'ʌp] einteilen, aufteilen 101
diving ['daɪvɪŋ] Tauchen, Tauchsport 8
to do a traineeship / an apprenticeship [duː ə ˌtreɪ'niːʃɪp / ˌən ə'prentɪʃɪp] eine Ausbildung machen 7
dock [dɒk] Dock, Kai, Hafenbecken 153
domestic market [dəˌmestɪk 'mɑːkɪt] Inlandsmarkt 103
dominant ['dɒmɪnənt] beherrschend, dominierend 40
dominated ['dɒmɪneɪtɪd] beherrscht, dominiert 25
to donate [dəʊ'neɪt] spenden 224
to double ['dʌbl] (hier:) eine doppelte Funktion erfüllen 101
down the drain [ˌdaʊn ðə 'dreɪn] unwiederbringlich verloren sein 192
draft [drɑːft] Entwurf 90
drawing ['drɔːɪŋ] Verlosung, Tombola 246
to draw up, drew, drawn [drɔː ˌʌp, druː, drɔːn] zusammenstellen, verfassen 151
dreadful ['dredfəl] schrecklich 65
to dread something [dred ˌsʌmθɪŋ] Angst vor etwas haben 244
dressing ['dresɪŋ] Salatsoße 29

drill head [drɪl ˌhed] Bohrkopf 186
drizzle ['drɪzl] Nieselregen 21
to drop [drɒp] fallen 106
drop-down menu [ˌdrɒpdaʊn 'menjuː] Pull-down Menü 48
drum [drʌm] Fass, Barrel 174
to dry [draɪ] abtrocknen 30
due [djuː] fällig 186
dumpling ['dʌmplɪŋ] Kloß, Knödel 27
durability [ˌdjʊərə'bɪlətɪ] Haltbarkeit 160
durable ['djʊərəbl] haltbar 181
duties ['djuːtɪz] (hier:) Aufgaben 56
duty ['djuːtɪ] (hier:) Zoll(gebühr) 152

E

early order discount [ˌɜːlɪ ˌɔːdə 'dɪskaʊnt] Frühbuchungsrabatt 123
to earn one's living [ˌɜːn wʌnz 'lɪvɪŋ] seinen Lebensunterhalt verdienen 42
e-commerce ['iːˌkɒmɜːs] Internethandel 184
economic growth [ˌiːkənɒmɪk 'ɡrəʊθ] Wirtschaftswachstum 171
edition [ɪ'dɪʃn] Ausgabe 59
effective [ɪ'fektɪv] wirksam 220
efficient [ɪ'fɪʃnt] leistungsfähig, wirksam, tüchtig 41
effort ['efət] Anstrengung, Bemühung 43
elderly person [ˌeldəlɪ 'pɜːsn] ältere Person 56
electrical equipment [ɪˌlektrɪkl ɪ'kwɪpmənt] Elektrogeräte 53
electrical goods industry [ɪˌlektrɪkl 'ɡʊdz ˌɪndəstrɪ] Elektroartikelbranche 10
electricity cut [elɪk'trɪsətɪ ˌkʌt] Stromsperre 125
electronic components [elekˌtrɒnɪk kəm'pəʊnənts] elektronische Bauelemente 240
embarrassed [ɪm'bærəst] peinlich, verlegen 90
embarrassment [ɪm'bærəsmənt] Verlegenheit 65
embassy ['embəsɪ] Botschaft(sgebäude) 134
emphasis ['emfəsɪs] Nachdruck 191
to emphasise ['emfəsaɪz] betonen, hervorheben 38
to employ [ɪm'plɔɪ] beschäftigen, einstellen 39
employment [ɪm'plɔɪmənt] Beschäftigung 230
empty ['emptɪ] leer 202
to enable [ɪ'neɪbl] ermöglichen 48
to enclose [ɪn'kləʊz] beifügen 230
enclosure [ɪn'kləʊʒə] Anlage (Brief) 113
to encourage [ɪn'kʌrɪdʒ] ermutigen 247
to end up [end ˌʌp] (hier:) landen 25

end user ['end ˌjuːzə] Endverbraucher/in 217
energy content [ˌenədʒɪ ˌkɒntent] Brennwert (Energiegehalt) 55
engaged [ɪn'ɡeɪdʒd] besetzt 64
engine ['endʒɪn] Motor 174
enquiry (BE), inquiry (AE) [ɪn'kwaɪərɪ] Anfrage, Nachfrage 14
to enrol [ɪn'rəʊl] sich einschreiben 237
ensuite bathroom [ˌɒnswiːt 'bɑːθruːm] eigenes Bad (Hotelzimmer) 86
to ensure [ɪn'ʃɔː] sichern, gewährleisten 217
to enter ['entə] eintreten, eintragen, eingeben 115
enterprise ['entəpraɪz] Unternehmen 63
to entertain [ˌentə'teɪn] sich um jemanden kümmern, unterhalten 18
enthusiasm [ɪn'θjuːzɪæzm] Begeisterung 230
entire(ly) [ɪn'taɪə(lɪ)] ganz, gänzlich 125
to entrust [ɪn'trʌst] anvertrauen 126
entry ['entrɪ] Eintrag 15
envelope ['envələʊp] (Brief-)Umschlag 200
environment [ɪn'vaɪərənmənt] Umwelt, Umfeld 172
environmentally friendly [ɪnˌvaɪərənˌmentəlɪ 'frendlɪ] umweltfreundlich 103
equal opportunities employer [ˌiːkwəl ɒpə'tjuːnətɪz ɪmˌplɔɪə] Firma, der Chancengleichheit ein Anliegen ist 241
to equip [ɪ'kwɪp] (hier:) befähigen; ausstatten, ausrüsten 231
equipment [ɪ'kwɪpmənt] Geräte 52
equipped [ɪ'kwɪpt] ausgestattet 33
equivalent [ɪ'kwɪvələnt] Entsprechung 234
ergonomics [ˌɜːɡə'nɒmɪks] Ergonomie (Erforschung der Leistungsmöglichkeiten und optimalen Arbeitsbedingungen des Menschen) 226
error ['erə] Irrtum, Fehler 204
essential [ɪ'senʃl] wichtig, wesentlich 231
to establish [ɪ'stæblɪʃ] (hier:) feststellen 216
established [ɪ'stæblɪʃt] eingeführt, feststehend 118
to estimate ['estɪmeɪt] schätzen 129
evaluation scheme [ɪˌvæljʊ'eɪʃn ˌskiːm] Bewertungsschema 104
even though [ˌiːvn 'ðəʊ] obgleich 196
event management assistant [ɪˌvent 'mænɪdʒmənt əˌsɪstənt] Veranstaltungskaufmann/-frau 10
eventual(ly) [ɪ'ventʃʊəl(ɪ)] letztendlich, letztlich, schließlich 181

evidence ['evɪdəns] Beweis, Nachweis 113
to exceed [ɪk'siːd] übersteigen, überschreiten 144
exception [ɪk'sepʃn] Ausnahme 110
excitement [ɪk'saɪtmənt] *(hier:)* Interesse 104
exclamation mark [,eksklə'meɪʃn ,mɑːk] Ausrufezeichen 117
to execute ['eksɪkjuːt] aus-, durchführen 139
execution [,eksɪ'kjuːʃn] Aus-, Durchführung 125
executives [ɪg'zekjətɪvz] leitende Angestellte 85
exhibition [,eksɪ'bɪʃn] Ausstellung 132
exhibition grounds [,eksɪ'bɪʃn ,graʊndz] Ausstellungsgelände 86
expectation [,ekspek'teɪʃn] Erwartung 109
expenditure [ɪk'spendɪtʃə] Ausgaben, Auslagen 41
expense [ɪk'spens] Ausgabe 60
experience [ɪk'spɪərɪəns] Erfahrung 230
to experience [ɪk'spɪərɪəns] erleben 222
expiry date [ɪk'spaɪərɪ ,deɪt] Verfallsdatum *(bei Kreditkarten)* 88
exploration [,eksplə'reɪʃn] Erkundung neuer Lagerstätten, Probegrabungen/-bohrungen 104
export clerk ['ekspɔːt ,klɑːk] Exportkaufmann/-frau 7
exposure [ɪk'spəʊʒə] Aussetzung, Belastung 78
to express [ɪk'spres] ausdrücken 65
expressly [ɪk'spreslɪ] ausdrücklich 142
extension [ɪk'stenʃn] Durchwahl, Nebenstelle 65
extract ['ekstrækt] Auszug 212

F

fabric ['fæbrɪk] Stoff 156
fabulous ['fæbjələs] fabelhaft, sagenhaft, toll 123
to face [feɪs] sich gegenübersehen, konfrontiert sein mit 148
to facilitate [fə'sɪlɪteɪt] ermöglichen, erleichtern 171
facilities [fə'sɪlətɪz] Einrichtungen, Anlagen 171
factual ['fæktʃʊəl] sachlich, den Tatsachen entsprechend 127
fair [feə] Messe 41
familiarity [fə,mɪlɪ'ærətɪ] Vertrautheit 230
familiar with [fə'mɪlɪə wɪð] vertraut mit 218
fare [feə] Fahrpreis 96
fashion ['fæʃn] Mode 43
fashion chain ['fæʃn ,tʃeɪn] Kette von Modegeschäften 184
fast-paced [,fɑːst'peɪst] tempogeladen, hektisch 230

faultless, perfect, unobjectionable ['fɒltləs / 'fɔːltləs, 'pɜːfɪkt, ,ʌnəb'dʒekʃənəbl] einwandfrei 209
faulty ['fɒltɪ, 'fɔːltɪ] fehlerhaft, mangelhaft 196
favourite (dish) [,feɪvərɪt 'dɪʃ] Lieblings(gericht) 29
to faze [feɪz] aus der Fassung bringen 241
feasibility study [,fiːzə'bɪlətɪ ,stʌdɪ] Machbarkeitsstudie 41
feature ['fiːtʃə] Merkmal 48
to feature ['fiːtʃə] eine Rolle spielen, sich auszeichnen, kennzeichnen 39
fee [fiː] Honorarkosten, Gebühr 60
feedback ['fiːdbæk] Rückmeldungen, Feedback 103
fermented white cabbage [fə,mentɪd ,waɪt 'kæbɪdʒ] Sauerkraut 29
ferry ['ferɪ] Fähre 171
field (of work) [fiːld (əv ,wɜːk)] Arbeitsgebiet 242
field research ['fiːld ,rɪsɜːtʃ] Feldforschung, Primärforschung 216
fierce [fɪəs] *(hier:)* scharf 220
figures ['fɪgəz] Zahlen(material) 59
file [faɪl] Akte, Datei 115
filing ['faɪlɪŋ] Ablage 14
filing cabinet ['faɪlɪŋ ,kæbɪnət] Aktenschrank, Ablage 52
filled rolls [,fɪld 'rəʊlz] belegte Brötchen 55
to finalise ['faɪnəlaɪz] zum Abschluss bringen 48
first floor [,fɜːst 'flɔː] erste Etage *(BE)*, Erdgeschoss *(AE)* 23
first name [,fɜːst 'neɪm] Vorname 7
first-rate [,fɜːst'reɪt] erstklassig 230
to fit in with [,fɪt 'ɪn wɪð] sich richten nach, übereinstimmen mit 88
fixed line set [,fɪkstlaɪn 'set] Festnetzanlage 64
to flash [flæʃ] (auf)blinken 77
flat [flæt] flach 106
flavouring ['fleɪvərɪŋ] Geschmackszusatz, Aroma 166
flooding ['flʌdɪŋ] Überschwemmung 125
floor plan ['flɔː ,plæn] Grundriss 23
flowchart ['fləʊtʃɑːt] Flussdiagramm 101
to fluctuate ['flʌktʃʊeɪt] schwanken 106
fluent ['fluːənt] fließend 230
focus ['fəʊkəs] Schwerpunkt 215
to focus ['fəʊkəs] (sich) konzentrieren, in den Mittelpunkt stellen 117
fog [fɒg] Nebel 22
foil-wrapped cardboard box [,fɔɪlræpt ,kɑːdbɔːd 'bɒks] folienumwickelter Karton 174
folder ['fəʊldə] Ordner 33

follow-up order [,fɒləʊ ,ʌp 'ɔːdə] Folgeauftrag 165
font [fɒnt] Schriftart 110
food processing ['fuːd ,prəʊsesɪŋ] Verarbeitung von Lebensmitteln 120
food processing company ['fuːd ,prəʊsesɪŋ ,kʌmpənɪ] Lebensmittel verarbeitendes Unternehmen 19
for approval [fər ə'pruːvl] zur Genehmigung 92
to forecast ['fɔːkɑːst] vorhersagen 171
foreign language correspondent / secretary with modern languages [,fɒrən 'læŋgwɪdʒ ,kɒrɪ,spɒndənt / ,sekrətrɪ wɪð ,fɒrən 'læŋgwɪdʒɪz] Fremdsprachenkorrespondent/in 10
foreign trade [,fɒrən 'treɪd] Außenhandel 218
for instance [fər 'ɪnstəns] zum Beispiel 6
form [fɔːm] Formular; Form 69
formal ['fɔːml] förmlich, formell 112
formal park [,fɔːml 'pɑːk] Parkanlage 25
for my money [fə 'maɪ ,mʌnɪ] wenn es nach mir geht 192
for the time being [fə ðə ,taɪm 'biːɪŋ] zurzeit, vorläufig 208
to forward ['fɔːwəd] weiterleiten, befördern, transportieren 115
forwarder ['fɔːwədə] Spedition 203
fossils ['fɒsəlz] Fossilien, Versteinerungen 149
to found [faʊnd] gründen 40
framework ['freɪmwɜːk] Rahmen 247
freebie ['friːbɪ] Werbegeschenk 226
free movement of labour [,friː ,muːvmənt əv 'leɪbə] Freizügigkeit der Arbeitnehmer, freie Wahl des Arbeitsplatzes 243
free of charge [,friː əv 'tʃɑːdʒ] kostenlos, unentgeltlich 149
freight forwarding and logistics services clerk [,freɪt 'fɔːwədɪŋ ənd lə,dʒɪstɪks 'sɜːvɪsɪz ,klɑːk] Kaufmann/-frau für Spedition und Logistikdienstleistung 9
freight forwarding company [,freɪt 'fɔːwədɪŋ ,kʌmpənɪ] Spedition, Transportunternehmen 172
French fries [,frentʃ 'fraɪz] Pommes frites 28
frequent(ly) ['friːkwənt(lɪ)] häufig, oft 43
fridge [frɪdʒ] Kühlschrank 55
fried potatoes [,fraɪd pə'teɪtəʊz] Bratkartoffeln 28
front desk [,frʌnt 'desk] Rezeption, Empfang 34
front office [,frʌnt 'ɒfɪs] Büro mit Publikumsverkehr 51
full board [,fʊl 'bɔːd] Vollpension 149
funeral ['fjuːnərəl] Beerdigung 77

Anhang | Alphabetical word list

furnishings [ˈfɜːnɪʃɪŋz] Einrichtungsgegenstände 225
further training [ˌfɜːðə ˈtreɪnɪŋ] Weiterbildung 239
to fuse [fjuːz] verschmelzen 43

G

gale [ɡeɪl] Orkan, Sturm 189
gale-force winds [ˌɡeɪlfɔːs ˈwɪndz] stürmische Winde 22
game [ɡeɪm] Wild 28
garlic [ˈɡɑːlɪk] Knoblauch 27
garment [ˈɡɑːmənt] Kleidungsstück 198
gas piston [ˈɡæs ˌpɪstən] Gaskolben 156
gathering [ˈɡæðərɪŋ] Versammlung 106
generally [ˈdʒenrəli] im Allgemeinen 217
general manager [ˌdʒenərəl ˈmænɪdʒə] Hauptgeschäftsführer/in 57
general terms and conditions [ˌdʒenərəl ˌtɜːmz ənd kənˈdɪʃnz] allgemeine Geschäftsbedingungen 164
generous [ˈdʒenərəs] großzügig 148
Gents / Ladies [dʒents/ˈleɪdɪz] Herren-/Damen-WC 23
germ [dʒɜːm] Bazillus, Keim 116
gestures [ˈdʒestʃəz] Gesten, Gestik 65
get [ɡet] (hier:) mitbekommen, hören 67
to get around to it [ɡet əˈraʊnd tʊ ɪt] dazu kommen, Zeit dazu haben 201
to get on well [ɡet ˌɒn ˈwel] gut miteinander auskommen 54
to get something over [ɡet ˌsʌmθɪŋ ˈəʊvə] etwas hinter sich bringen 103
ghastly [ˈɡɑːstli] entsetzlich 21
gift box [ˈɡɪft ˌbɒks] Geschenkkarton 164
gig [ɡɪɡ] Musikevent 20
ginger cookies [ˌdʒɪndʒə ˈkʊkɪz] Ingwerkekse 154
to give a refusal, to refuse a request [ˌɡɪv ə rɪˈfjuːzl, rɪˌfjuːz ə rɪˈkwest] Absage erteilen 205
to give notice [ˌɡɪv ˈnəʊtɪs] (hier:) im Voraus Bescheid sagen 238
to give someone a lift [ɡɪv ˌsʌmwʌn ə ˈlɪft] jemanden mitnehmen (im Wagen) 30
to give someone a ring [ɡɪv ˌsʌmwʌn ə ˈrɪŋ] jemanden anrufen 30
global economy [ˌɡləʊbl ɪˈkɒnəmi] Weltwirtschaft 171
glossy [ˈɡlɒsi] Hochglanz- 221
goal [ɡəʊl] Ziel 109
to go clubbing [ɡəʊ ˈklʌbɪŋ] in die Disko gehen 9
to go for [ˈɡəʊ fə] wählen 239
good value [ˌɡʊd ˈvæljuː] preisgünstig 225

to go public [ɡəʊ ˈpʌblɪk] sich in eine Aktiengesellschaft umwandeln, an die Börse gehen 41
to go through the usual channels [ˌɡəʊ θruː ðə ˌjuːʒəl ˈtʃænlz] die üblichen Instanzen durchlaufen 244
to go window-shopping [ɡəʊ ˈwɪndəʊ ˌʃɒpɪŋ] einen Schaufensterbummel machen 8
to go without saying [ɡəʊ wɪðˌaʊt ˈseɪɪŋ] selbstverständlich sein 207
gradual(ly) [ˈɡrædʒʊəl(i)] allmählich 106
graduate [ˈɡrædʒʊət] Absolvent/in 245
grant [ɡrɑːnt] Stipendium 192
to grant [ɡrɑːnt] gewähren 137
to grant a concession [ˌɡrɑːnt ə kənˈseʃn] ein Zugeständnis machen 189
to grant a discount [ˌɡrɑːnt ə ˈdɪskaʊnt] Rabatt einräumen 146
to grant a respite [ˌɡrɑːnt ə ˈrespaɪt] einen Zahlungsaufschub gewähren 189
to grant credit [ˌɡrɑːnt ˈkredɪt] Kredit gewähren 183
graph [ɡrɑːf] Grafik 101
green card [ˌɡriːn ˈkɑːd] Arbeitserlaubnis für die USA 243
grid [ɡrɪd] Raster 112
ground [ɡraʊnd] gemahlen 28
ground beef [ˌɡraʊnd ˈbiːf] Rindergehacktes 28
ground floor [ˌɡraʊnd ˈflɔː] Parterre, Erdgeschoss 23
growth [ɡrəʊθ] Wachstum 215
to guarantee [ˌɡærənˈtiː] garantieren 26
guideline [ˈɡaɪdlaɪn] Richtlinie 78
gym [dʒɪm] Turnhalle, Fitnessraum 7

H

habits [ˈhæbɪts] Gewohnheiten 223
haddock [ˈhædək] Schellfisch 28
half board [ˌhɑːf ˈbɔːd] Halbpension 150
ham [hæm] Schinken 202
handicapped [ˈhændɪkæpt] behindert 237
to handle [ˈhændl] handhaben, erledigen, bearbeiten 172
handling [ˈhændlɪŋ] (hier:) Fahreigenschaften 225
hands-free device [ˌhændzfriː dɪˈvaɪs] Freisprechanlage 77
hard copy [ˌhɑːd ˈkɒpi] Computerausdruck 128
harmful [ˈhɑːmfəl] schädlich 172
to have access to [hæv ˈækses tuː] Zugang haben zu 220
to have little choice but [hæv ˌlɪtl ˈtʃɔɪs bət] keine andere Wahl haben als 220

to have the goods delivered [ˌhæv ðə ˌɡʊdz dɪˈlɪvəd] sich die Ware liefern lassen 219
heading [ˈhedɪŋ] Rubrik 104
head of department [ˌhed əv dɪˈpɑːtmənt] Abteilungsleiter/in 56
headquarters [ˌhedˈkwɔːtəz] Hauptverwaltung 85
health [helθ] Gesundheit 90
health-conscious [ˌhelθˈkɒnʃəs] gesundheitsbewusst 221
height [haɪt] Höhe 203
helpful [ˈhelpfəl] hilfsbereit 18
high-end [ˌhaɪˈend] Luxus-, Nobel- 31
to highlight [ˈhaɪlaɪt] (hier:) markieren 128
high street bank [ˌhaɪstriːt ˈbæŋk] Bank mit zahlreichen Zweigstellen 10
high street stores [ˌhaɪstriːt ˈstɔːz] Geschäfte in der Innenstadt 217
highway robbery [ˌhaɪweɪ ˈrɒbəri] Raubüberfälle auf Fernstraßen 172
hint [hɪnt] Hinweis, Andeutung 8
hire option [ˈhaɪər ˌɒpʃn] Mietmöglichkeit 32
hiring date [ˈhaɪərɪŋ ˌdeɪt] Einstellungsdatum 246
hit [hɪt] (hier:) Zugriff; Schlag, Stoß, Treffer 41
hoardings (BE) [ˈhɔːdɪŋz] Plakatwände 221
to hold, held, held [həʊld, held, held] (hier:) warten 65
horseradish [ˈhɔːsˌrædɪʃ] Meerrettich 165
hospitality [ˌhɒspɪˈtæləti] Gastfreundschaft, Bewirtung 31
host family [ˈhəʊst ˌfæməli] Gastfamilie 149
hot [hɒt] heiß, scharf 28
to house [haʊz] beherbergen 25
household tool kit [ˌhaʊshəʊld ˈtuːl ˌkɪt] Haushaltswerkzeugsatz 137
however [haʊˈevə] jedoch 112
how you come across [ˌhaʊ jʊ ˌkʌm əˈkrɒs] welchen Eindruck man macht 103
human resources department [ˌhjuːmən ˈriːsɔːsɪz dɪˌpɑːtmənt] Personalabteilung 209
humorous [ˈhjuːmərəs] humorvoll 104
hush money [ˈhʌʃ ˌmʌni] Schweigegeld 192
hyperlink [ˈhaɪpəlɪŋk] Hyperlink 48
hyphenation [ˌhaɪfənˈeɪʃn] Worttrennung 128

I

IBAN (international bank account number) [ˈaɪbæn, ˌaɪbiːeɪˈen (ˌɪntənæʃənl ˈbæŋk əˌkaʊnt ˌnʌmbə)] internationale Kontonummer 181
illegible [ɪˈledʒəbl] unleserlich 202

I'm afraid ... [aɪm əˈfreɪd] Leider ... 73
image [ˈɪmɪdʒ] Bild, Vorstellung 38
imagination [ɪˌmædʒɪˈneɪʃn] Phantasie, Vorstellungskraft 134
imaginative [ɪˈmædʒɪnətɪv] phantasievoll 102
immediate [ɪˈmiːdɪət] sofortig 65
I'm on a diet [aɪm ˌɒn ə ˈdaɪət] ich mache eine Diät 21
to impair [ɪmˈpeə] beeinträchtigen 78
impatient [ɪmˈpeɪʃnt] ungeduldig 199
to imply [ɪmˈplaɪ] beinhalten, besagen, stillschweigend voraussetzen 125
impolite [ˌɪmpəˈlaɪt] unhöflich 73
import licence [ˈɪmpɔːt ˌlaɪsəns] Importlizenz, Einfuhrgenehmigung 76
to impress [ɪmˈpres] beeindrucken 160
impression [ɪmˈpreʃn] Eindruck 18
imprint [ˈɪmprɪnt] Impressum 43
to improve [ɪmˈpruːv] verbessern 220
inadequate [ɪˈnædɪkwət] unzureichend 171
in advance [ɪn ədˈvɑːns] im Voraus 239
in bulk [ɪn ˈbʌlk] in großen Mengen 217
incentive [ɪnˈsentɪv] Anreiz 114
in charge of [ɪn ˈtʃɑːdʒ əv] verantwortlich für 19
incident [ˈɪnsɪdənt] Zwischenfall, Ereignis 126
inclination [ˌɪnklɪˈneɪʃn] Neigung 226
to include [ɪnˈkluːd] einschließen, beinhalten, umfassen 6
included in the price [ɪnˌkluːdɪd ɪn ðə ˈpraɪs] im Preis enthalten 88
incoming goods control [ˌɪnkʌmɪŋ ˈɡʊdz kənˌtrəʊl] Wareneingangskontrolle 198
in conclusion [ɪn kənˈkluːʒn] zum Abschluss, abschließend 133
in confidence [ɪn ˈkɒnfɪdəns] vertraulich 139
inconvenience [ˌɪnkənˈviːnɪəns] Unannehmlichkeiten 126
inconvenient [ˌɪnkənˈviːnɪənt] ungünstig 238
to increase [ɪnˈkriːs] zunehmen, steigern 106
increasing(ly) [ɪnˈkriːsɪŋ(li)] zunehmend 112
independent [ˌɪndɪˈpendənt] unabhängig 76
to indicate [ˈɪndɪkeɪt] anzeigen, andeuten 77
indicator [ˈɪndɪkeɪtə] Anzeiger, Anzeigetafel 89
in due course [ɪn ˌdjuː ˈkɔːs] fristgemäß 198
industrial business management assistant [ɪnˌdʌstrɪəl ˌbɪznɪs ˈmænɪdʒmənt əˌsɪstənt] Industriekaufmann/-frau 7

industrial clerk [ɪnˈdʌstrɪəl ˌklɑːk] Industriekaufmann/-frau 7
industrial goods [ɪnˌdʌstrɪəl ˈɡʊdz] Industrieerzeugnisse 224
industry analyst [ˈɪndəstrɪ ˌænəlɪst] Branchenexperte/-expertin 171
I need to freshen up a bit [aɪ ˌniːd tə ˌfreʃn ˈʌp ə ˌbɪt] ich muss mich ein bisschen frisch machen 24
to influence [ˈɪnfluəns] beeinflussen 222
in fourth place [ɪn ˌfɔːθ ˈpleɪs] an vierter Stelle 107
in full [ɪn ˈfʊl] in voller Höhe 188
inhabitant [ɪnˈhæbɪtənt] Einwohner/in 180
initials [ɪˈnɪʃlz] Initialen, Anfangsbuchstaben des Namens 121
initial [ɪˈnɪʃl] anfänglich 220
initial order [ɪˌnɪʃl ˈɔːdə] Erstauftrag 159
to initiate [ɪˈnɪʃɪeɪt] in die Wege leiten, einleiten 206
to initiate measures [ɪˌnɪʃɪeɪt ˈmeʒəz] Maßnahmen einleiten 209
in law [ɪn ˈlɔː] rechtlich, vor Gericht 92
in lieu of [ɪn ˈljuː əv] an Stelle von 237
in line with [ɪn ˈlaɪn wɪð] in Übereinstimmung mit, parallel zu 41
in our favour [ɪn ˌaʊə ˈfeɪvə] zu unseren Gunsten 186
in principle [ɪn ˈprɪnsɪpl] im Prinzip 90
to insert [ɪnˈsɜːt] einfügen, einlegen 12
to insist on [ɪnˈsɪst ɒn] bestehen auf 186
insistent [ɪnˈsɪstənt] nachdrücklich 187
insolvent [ɪnˈsɒlvənt] zahlungsunfähig 208
in stock [ɪn ˈstɒk] vorrätig, auf Lager 72
to instruct [ɪnˈstrʌkt] anweisen, unterweisen 181
to instruct to the contrary [ɪnˌstrʌkt tə ðə ˈkɒntrəri] gegenteilige Anweisungen erteilen 210
insurance [ɪnˈʃɔːrəns] Versicherung 152
insurance business management assistant [ɪnˌʃɔːrəns ˌbɪznɪs ˈmænɪdʒmənt əˌsɪstənt] Versicherungskaufmann/-frau, Kaufmann/-frau für Versicherungen und Finanzen 9
insurance clerk [ɪnˈʃɔːrəns ˌklɑːk] Versicherungskaufmann/-frau, Kaufmann/-frau für Versicherungen und Finanzen 9
integration [ˌɪntɪˈɡreɪʃn] Eingliederung, Integration 88
to intend [ɪnˈtend] beabsichtigen 224
interest [ˈɪntrəst] (hier:) Zinsen 60
interest in [ˈɪntrəst ɪn] Interesse an 223
interest on arrears [ˌɪntrəst ɒn əˈrɪəz] Verzugszinsen 187

in terms of [ɪn ˈtɜːmz əv] in Bezug auf, was ... betrifft 171
internet exchanges [ˈɪntənet ɪksˌtʃeɪndʒɪz] Online-Börsen 219
internship [ˈɪntɜːnʃɪp] Praktikum 245
to interpret [ɪnˈtɜːprɪt] dolmetschen 91
interpreter [ɪnˈtɜːprɪtə] Dolmetscher/in 93
to interrupt [ˌɪntəˈrʌpt] unterbrechen 77
interval [ˈɪntəvl] Abstand 159
interview [ˈɪntəvjuː] Vorstellungsgespräch, Interview 39
in the course of [ɪn ðə ˈkɔːs əv] im Laufe von 72
in the foreseeable future [ɪn ðə fɔːˌsiːəbl ˈfjuːtʃə] in absehbarer Zukunft 104
in transit [ɪn ˈtrænzɪt] beim Transport 203
introduction [ˌɪntrəˈdʌkʃn] Einführung, Vorstellung 215
introductory discount [ˌɪntrədʌktəri ˈdɪskaʊnt] Einführungsrabatt 137
investigation [ɪnˌvestɪˈɡeɪʃn] Untersuchung 207
investment portfolio [ɪnˈvestmənt pɔːtˌfəʊlɪəʊ] Bestand an Wertpapieren 104
invoice [ˈɪnvɔɪs] Rechnung 160
to involve [ɪnˈvɒlv] (hier:) beinhalten 216
in working order [ɪn ˌwɜːkɪŋ ˈɔːdə] funktionstüchtig 91
iron ore [ˈaɪən ˌɔː] Eisenerz 172
irrevocable [ˌɪrɪˈvəʊkəbl] unwiderruflich 185
irritation [ˌɪrɪˈteɪʃn] Verärgerung 171
is paralleled by [ɪz ˈpærəleld ˌbaɪ] geht einher mit 219
issue [ˈɪʃuː] (hier:) Ausgabe, Heft 134
to issue [ˈɪʃuː] ausstellen, (her)ausgeben 183
it doesn't appeal to me [ɪt ˌdʌznt əˌpiːl tʊ ˈmiː] es gefällt mir nicht 222
item [ˈaɪtəm] Punkt, Artikel 48
IT specialist [ˌaɪˈtiː ˌspeʃəlɪst] Fachinformatiker/in 9
it tastes like ... [ɪt ˌteɪsts laɪk ˈ...] es schmeckt wie ... 28

J

jar [dʒɑː] Glas (z.B. Marmelade), Topf (z.B. Senf) 206
jelly [ˈdʒeli] Götterspeise, Gelee, Aspik 29
job exchanges [ˈdʒɒb ɪksˌtʃeɪndʒɪz] Job-, Stellenbörsen 229
job specification [ˌdʒɒb ˌspesɪfɪˈkeɪʃn] Stellenbeschreibung 229
to join [dʒɔɪn] (hier:) sich jemandem anschließen, mitkommen 27
joint [dʒɔɪnt] gemeinsam 27

Anhang | Alphabetical word list

joint venture [ˌdʒɔɪnt ˈventʃə] Joint Venture *(Gemeinschaftsunternehmen)* 71
to jumble [ˈdʒʌmbl] durcheinander werfen/bringen 116
jumbled [ˈdʒʌmbld] durcheinander geworfen 21
to jump [dʒʌmp] springen, sprunghaft ansteigen 104
to jump by … from … to … [ˈdʒʌmp baɪ … frəm … tʊ …] sprunghaft ansteigen um … von … auf … 106
junction [ˈdʒʌŋkʃn] Kreuzung 24
junior executive [ˌdʒuːnɪər ɪɡˈzekjətɪv] Nachwuchsführungskraft 200
justification [ˌdʒʌstɪfɪˈkeɪʃn] Bündigkeit 128
justified [ˈdʒʌstɪfaɪd] gerechtfertigt, berechtigt 205
justified complaint [ˌdʒʌstɪfaɪd kəmˈpleɪnt] begründete Reklamation 205

K

keen [kiːn] sehr interessiert, eifrig 221
to keep an eye on [ˌkiːp ən ˈaɪ ɒn] aufpassen auf 30
to keep a record [ˌkiːp ə ˈrekɔːd] aufzeichnen 84
to keep informed [ˌkiːp ɪnˈfɔːmd] auf dem Laufenden halten 205
to keep one's fingers crossed [ˌkiːp wʌnz ˈfɪŋɡəz ˌkrɒst] den Daumen halten 244
key [kiː] Schlüssel 100
key account management [ˌkiː əˈkaʊnt ˌmænɪdʒmənt] Key Account Management, Großkundenberatung 211
keyboard [ˈkiːbɔːd] Tastatur 52
kitchenette [ˌkɪtʃɪˈnet] Kochgelegenheit; Teeküche 93
kitchen facilities [ˈkɪtʃɪn fəˌsɪlətɪz] Küchenanlagen 26
kitten [ˈkɪtn] Kätzchen 163

L

label [ˈleɪbl] Etikett 15
to label, to provide with an inscription [ˈleɪbl, prəˌvaɪd wɪð ən ɪnˈskrɪpʃn] beschriften 198
laces [ˈleɪsɪz] Schnürsenkel 239
ladies' room *(AE)* [ˈleɪdɪz ˌruːm] Damentoilette 23
lamb [læm] Lamm 28
landlady [ˈlændˌleɪdɪ] Vermieterin 243
landline [ˈlændlaɪn] Festnetz(leitung) 64
largely [ˈlɑːdʒlɪ] weitgehend 92
lately [ˈleɪtlɪ] in letzter Zeit 20
to launch [lɔːntʃ] einführen, starten, in die Wege leiten 138
layout [ˈleɪaʊt] Anordnung, Gestaltung 114

lbs (pounds) [paʊndz] *(englisches Gewichts-)*Pfund *(453,59 g)* 204
leading [ˈliːdɪŋ] führend 135
to leave much to be desired [liːv ˌmʌtʃ tʊ bɪ dɪˈzaɪəd] viel zu wünschen übrig lassen 91
leeks [liːks] Lauch 27
legal [ˈliːɡl] rechtlich, gesetzlich, legal, juristisch 56
legal information [ˌliːɡl ɪnfəˈmeɪʃn] rechtliche Angaben 48
legal steps [ˌliːɡl ˈsteps] juristische Schritte 187
leisure [ˈleʒə] Freizeit 102
lentils [ˈlentəlz] Linsen 29
less [les] abzüglich 147
to let someone know [let ˌsʌmwʌn ˈnəʊ] jemandem Bescheid sagen 30
letterhead [ˈletəhed] Briefkopf 121
letter of credit [ˌletər əv ˈkredɪt] Akkreditiv 185
letting agent [ˈletɪŋ ˌeɪdʒənt] Makler für Mietimmobilien, -wohnungen 240
lettuce [ˈletɪs] Kopfsalat 29
to level off [ˌlevl ˈɒf] sich einpendeln 110
licence agreement [ˈlaɪsəns əˌɡriːmənt] Lizenzvereinbarung 212
life [laɪf] Lebensdauer 146
likewise [ˈlaɪkwaɪz] ebenfalls 88
limit [ˈlɪmɪt] Beschränkung 88
limitation of liability [lɪmɪˌteɪʃn əv ˌlaɪəˈbɪlətɪ] Haftungsbeschränkung 212
line [laɪn] Verbindung 67
line graph [ˈlaɪn ˌɡrɑːf] Liniendiagramm 105
lingua franca [ˌlɪŋɡwə ˈfræŋkə] Verkehrssprache 18
link [lɪŋk] Verbindung, Bindeglied 217
to link [lɪŋk] verbinden, verknüpfen 220
linking words [ˈlɪŋkɪŋ ˌwɜːdz] verbindende Wörter 125
lipstick [ˈlɪpstɪk] Lippenstift 108
to load [ləʊd] beladen, einladen 171
local [ˈləʊkl] örtlich, ortsansässig, hiesig 39
to locate [ləʊˈkeɪt] ausfindig machen, lokalisieren 132
location [ləʊˈkeɪʃn] Standort 103
logistics and warehousing operation [ləˌdʒɪstɪks ənd ˈweəhaʊzɪŋ ˌɒpəˌreɪʃn] Logistik- und Lagerungsunternehmen 243
long-distance running [ˌlɒŋdɪstəns ˈrʌnɪŋ] Langstreckenlauf 8
to lose one's way, lost, lost [ˌluːz wʌnz ˈweɪ, lɒst, lɒst] sich verirren, sich verlaufen 23
low [ləʊ] Tief(punkt) 106

M

machinery [məˈʃiːnərɪ] Maschinen 39
madness [ˈmædnəs] Wahnsinn, Wahn- 77
magnificent [mæɡˈnɪfɪsənt] großartig, prächtig 25
mail merge [ˈmeɪlˌmɜːdʒ] Serienbrief 59
mail shots [ˈmeɪl ˌʃɒts] Postwurfsendungen 221
main branch [ˌmeɪn ˈbrɑːntʃ] Hauptfiliale 232
main course [ˌmeɪn ˈkɔːs] Hauptgericht, -gang 27
main entrance [ˌmeɪn ˈentrəns] Haupteingang 23
main road [ˌmeɪn ˈrəʊd] Hauptstraße 24
to maintain [meɪnˈteɪn] *(hier:)* pflegen 14
major [ˈmeɪdʒə] groß, wichtig, Haupt- 51
to make an offer [ˌmeɪk ən ˈɒfə] ein Angebot abgeben 143
to make computations [ˈprəʊses] Berechnungen durchführen 14
to make someone aware of [ˌmeɪk ˌsʌmwʌn əˈweər əv] jemanden aufmerksam machen auf 221
to make someone feel welcome [ˌmeɪk ˌsʌmwʌn fiːl ˈwelkəm] dafür sorgen, dass sich jemand wohl fühlt 18
to make sure [meɪk ˈʃɔː] sich vergewissern 103
to make up [meɪk ˈʌp] *(hier:)* erfinden 69
to manage complaints [ˌmænɪdʒ kəmˈpleɪnts] Beschwerden bearbeiten 205
management [ˈmænɪdʒmənt] Geschäftsleitung 126
management assistant for tourism and leisure [ˈmænɪdʒmənt əˌsɪstənt fə ˌtʊərɪzm ən ˈleʒə] Kaufmann/-frau für Tourismus und Freizeit 11
management assistant in advertising [ˈmænɪdʒmənt əˌsɪstənt ɪn ˈædvətaɪzɪŋ] Werbekaufmann/-frau 11
management assistant in event organisation [ˈmænɪdʒmənt əˌsɪstənt ɪn ɪˌvent ˌɔːɡənaɪˈzeɪʃn] Veranstaltungskaufmann/-frau 11
management assistant in freight forwarding [ˈmænɪdʒmənt əˌsɪstənt ɪn ˌfreɪt ˈfɔːwədɪŋ] Speditionskaufmann/-frau 9
management assistant in informatics [ˈmænɪdʒmənt əˌsɪstənt ɪn ˌɪnfəˈmætɪks] Informatikkaufmann/-frau 11

management assistant in office communication ['mænɪdʒmənt əˌsɪstənt ɪn ˌɒfɪs kəˌmjuːnɪ'keɪʃn] Kaufmann/-frau für Bürokommunikation 11
management assistant in publishing ['mænɪdʒmənt əˌsɪstənt ɪn 'pʌblɪʃɪŋ] Verlagskaufmann/-frau 9
management assistant in retail business ['mænɪdʒmənt əˌsɪstənt ɪn ˌriːteɪl 'bɪznɪs] Kaufmann/-frau im Einzelhandel 9
management assistant in wholesale and foreign trade ['mænɪdʒmənt əˌsɪstənt ɪn ˌhəʊseɪl ənd ˌfɒrən 'treɪd] Kaufmann/-frau im Groß- und Außenhandel 9
managing director [ˌmænɪdʒɪŋ daɪ'rektə] Geschäftsführer/in 56
manner ['mænə] Umgangsstil 241
manufacturer [ˌmænjə'fæktʃərə] Hersteller/in, Produzent/in 217
to manufacture to specification [ˌmænjə'fæktʃə tʊ ˌspesɪfɪ'keɪʃn] als Sonderanfertigung herstellen 185
manufacturing [ˌmænjə'fæktʃərɪŋ] Fertigung, Fabrikation 39
manufacturing (industry) [ˌmænjə'fæktʃərɪŋ (ˌɪndəstri)] verarbeitende Industrie 241
margin ['mɑːdʒɪn] Rand 110
to marinate ['mærɪneɪt] marinieren, einlegen 27
marital status [ˌmærɪtl 'steɪtəs] Familienstand 121
marketing tools ['mɑːkɪtɪŋ ˌtuːlz] Marketinginstrumente 220
market leader [ˌmɑːkɪt 'liːdə] Marktführer 39
market research [ˌmɑːkɪt 'riːsɜːtʃ] Marktforschung 216
market share [ˌmɑːkɪt 'ʃeə] Marktanteil 172
market survey [ˌmɑːkɪt 'sɜːveɪ] Marktstudie, -untersuchung 216
markings ['mɑːkɪŋz] Markierung 176
mart [mɑːt] Markt 41
mashed potatoes [ˌmæʃt pə'teɪtəʊz] Kartoffelpüree 28
maturity [mə'tjʊərəti] Reife 215
maximum admissible weight [ˌmæksɪməm ədˌmɪsəbl 'weɪt] zulässiges Höchstgewicht 204
means of payment [ˌmiːnz əv 'peɪmənt] Zahlungsmittel 183
meat [miːt] Fleisch 28
meatball ['miːtbɔːl] Frikadelle 28
medical supplies [ˌmedɪkl sə'plaɪz] Artikel zur medizinischen Versorgung 173
Mediterranean countries [medɪtərˌeɪnɪən 'kʌntrɪz] Länder am Mittelmeer 8

to meet deadlines [miːt 'dedlaɪnz] Termine/Fristen einhalten 230
to meet halfway [miːt ˌhɑːf'weɪ] auf halbem Weg entgegenkommen 205
to meet someone [miːt 'sʌmwʌn] jemanden kennenlernen, treffen 18
to meet with approval [ˌmiːt wɪð ə'pruːvl] auf Zustimmung stoßen 239
member ['membə] Mitglied 167
memo ['meməʊ] Aktennotiz 26
memory stick ['memrɪ ˌstɪk] USB-Speicher 52
menu ['menjuː] Speisekarte; Menü *(Computer)* 29
merchandise ['mɜːtʃəndaɪs] Ware, Gut, Handelsartikel 159
merchant ['mɜːtʃənt] Händler 220
message ['mesɪdʒ] Nachricht, Botschaft 115
Middle Ages [ˌmɪdl 'eɪdʒɪz] Mittelalter 180
mince(d) meat ['mɪns(t) ˌmiːt] Gehacktes 28
minor ['maɪnə] gering(fügig) 139
mint bar ['mɪnt ˌbɑː] Pfefferminzriegel 145
minute [maɪ'njuːt] peinlich genau; winzig 43
minutes ['mɪnɪts] Protokoll, Niederschrift 59
misunderstanding [ˌmɪsʌndə'stændɪŋ] Missverständnis 112
mixed [mɪkst] gemischt 29
mix-up ['mɪksʌp] Verwechslung 204
mode of transport [ˌməʊd əv 'trænspɔːt] Transportart 172
moderate(ly) ['mɒdərət(li)] mäßig, maßvoll 106
modification [ˌmɒdɪfɪ'keɪʃn] Änderung 85
to modify ['mɒdɪfaɪ] ab-, verändern 26
to modulate ['mɒdjəleɪt] *(hier:)* dämpfen, abschwächen 77
money-spinner ['mʌnɪˌspɪnə] Goldgrube 192
monitor ['mɒnɪtə] PC-Bildschirm 87
monotonous(ly) [mə'nɒtənəs(li)] eintönig 103
moreover [mɔː'rəʊvə] überdies, außerdem 125
mother tongue [ˌmʌðə 'tʌŋ] Muttersprache 231
motor-car mechanic [ˌməʊtəkɑː mə'kænɪk] Kfz-Mechaniker/in 56
move [muːv] *(hier:)* Umzug 30
mug [mʌg] Becher 196
multilingual [ˌmʌltɪ'lɪŋgwəl] mehr-, vielsprachig 201
mushrooms ['mʌʃruːmz] Champignons, Pilze 27
mustard ['mʌstəd] Senf 165

N

nail varnish ['neɪl ˌvɑːnɪʃ] Nagellack 108
named [neɪmd] namentlich genannt 183
native ['neɪtɪv] einheimisch, inländisch, Landes- 149
navy (blue) ['neɪvɪ('bluː)] marineblau, dunkelblau 118
neat(ly) [niːt(li)] ordentlich, adrett 234
needs [niːdz] Bedarf, Bedürfnisse 216
to need, to require [niːd, rɪ'kwaɪə] benötigen 241
negotiation [nɪˌgəʊʃɪ'eɪʃn] Verhandlung 211
neighbouring ['neɪbərɪŋ] benachbart 39
net [net] netto 145
newsagent ['njuːzˌeɪdʒənt] Zeitungshändler/in 21
nickel and dime [ˌnɪkl ənd 'daɪm] Billig- 192
nobility [nəʊ'bɪləti] Adel, Vornehmheit 163
noisy ['nɔɪzɪ] laut 22
non-attendance [ˌnɒnə'tendəns] Fehlen, Abwesenheit 92
non-bulk cargo [ˌnɒnbʌlk 'kɑːgəʊ] Stückgutfracht 171
note pad ['nəʊtpæd] Notizblock 52
notification [ˌnəʊtɪfɪ'keɪʃn] Benachrichtigung 229
to notify ['nəʊtɪfaɪ] benachrichtigen 191
novel ['nɒvl] Roman 9
novelist ['nɒvəlɪst] Romanschriftsteller/in 149
nowadays ['naʊədeɪz] heutzutage 183
nutritionally conscious [njuːˌtrɪʃənlɪ 'kɒnʃəs] ernährungsbewusst 26
nutritional science [njuːˌtrɪʃənl 'saɪəns] Ernährungswissenschaft 26

O

obesity [əʊ'biːsəti] Fettleibigkeit, klinisches Übergewicht 90
to obey [ə'beɪ] gehorchen 78
objective [əb'dʒektɪv] Ziel 101
obligation [ˌɒblɪ'geɪʃn] Verpflichtung, Verbindlichkeit 151
obscure [əb'skjʊə] unbekannt 225
to observe [əb'zɜːv] beachten 77
to observe the delivery period [əbˌzɜːv ðə dɪ'lɪvərɪ ˌpɪərɪəd] Lieferfrist einhalten 164
to obtain [əb'teɪn] erhalten 221
obvious(ly) ['ɒbvɪəs(li)] offensichtlich 165
occasion [ə'keɪʒn] Anlass, Gelegenheit 120
occupational [ˌɒkjə'peɪʃənl] beruflich 247
to occur, to result [ə'kɜː, rɪ'zʌlt] sich ergeben 223

Anhang | Alphabetical word list

offer [ˈɒfə] Angebot 142
to offer credit facilities [ˌɒfə ˈkredɪt fəˌsɪlətɪz] Kredite anbieten 218
office administration clerk [ˌɒfɪs ədˌmɪnɪˈstreɪʃn ˌklɑːk] Bürokaufmann/-frau 7
office management assistant [ˌɒfɪs ˈmænɪdʒmənt əˌsɪstənt] Bürokaufmann/-frau 9
office suite [ˈɒfɪs ˌswiːt] Office-/Büro-Paket 59
old-established [ˌəʊldɪˈstæblɪʃt] alteingesessen 38
old-fashioned [ˌəʊldˈfæʃnd] altmodisch 64
to omit [əʊˈmɪt] aus-, weglassen 121
on a large scale [ɒn ə ˌlɑːdʒ ˈskeɪl] in großem Stil/Umfang 40
on behalf of [ɒn bɪˈhɑːf ˌəv] im Auftrag von/für 84
on delivery [ɒn dɪˈlɪvəri] bei Lieferung 185
on demand [ɒn dɪˈmɑːnd] auf Verlangen/Abruf 183
one-off [ˌwʌnˈɒf] Einmal- 148
onion [ˈʌnjən] Zwiebel 27
on presentation [ɒn ˌprezənˈteɪʃn] bei Vorlage 183
on request [ɒn rɪˈkwest] *(hier:)* wenn gewünscht; auf Anfrage 244
on the left/left-hand side [ɒn ðə ˈleft / ˌlefthænd ˈsaɪd] links 23
on the off-chance [ɒn ði ˌɒftʃɑːns] auf Verdacht 229
on/to the right [ɒn/tʊ ðə ˈraɪt] rechts 23
open account terms [ˌəʊpn əˌkaʊnt ˈtɜːmz] offenes Zahlungsziel 144
open credit [ˌəʊpn ˈkredɪt] Zahlung gegen einfache Rechnung 185
openings [ˈəʊpnɪŋz] offene Stellen 229
opening bank [ˌəʊpnɪŋ ˈbæŋk] ausstellende Bank 185
open-plan office [ˌəʊpnplæn ˈɒfɪs] Großraumbüro 23
to operate [ˈɒpəreɪt] bedienen 103
operation [ˌɒpəˈreɪʃn] Betrieb 78
operations [ˌɒpəˈreɪʃnz] Betriebskosten, Arbeitsprozess 60
opportunity [ˌɒpəˈtjuːnəti] Gelegenheit 12
opposite [ˈɒpəzɪt] gegenüber 24
opposite number [ˌɒpəzɪt ˈnʌmbə] Gegenüber, Kollege/Kollegin 85
optician [ɒpˈtɪʃn] Optiker/in 217
oral [ˈɔːrəl] mündlich 100
order [ˈɔːdə] Auftrag, Bestellung 159
to order [ˈɔːdə] bestellen; anordnen 39
order confirmation [ˈɔːdə kɒnfəˌmeɪʃn] Auftragsbestätigung 163
order on call [ˌɔːdər ɒn ˈkɔːl] Abrufauftrag 159
or else [ˌɔːrˈels] andernfalls, sonst 115

organic [ɔːˈgænɪk] biologisch, Bio- 26
organic foods [ɔːˈgænɪk ˌfuːdz] Bio-Lebensmittel 90
organisation [ˌɔːgənaɪˈzeɪʃn] Firma, Unternehmen, Organisation 219
original(ly) [əˈrɪdʒənl(i)] ursprünglich 7
other business [ˌʌðə ˈbɪznɪs] Verschiedenes 90
outcome [ˈaʊtkʌm] Ergebnis 126
outgoing [ˈaʊtgəʊɪŋ] aufgeschlossen 211
to outlaw [ˈaʊtlɔː] verbieten, für ungesetzlich erklären 77
outlet [ˈaʊtlet] Verkaufsstelle, Vertriebsmöglichkeit 133
out of order [ˌaʊt əv ˈɔːdə] kaputt, außer Betrieb 200
outside advice [ˌaʊtsaɪd ədˈvaɪs] Beratung von außen 224
outward journey [ˌaʊtwədˌˈdʒɜːni] Hinfahrt 96
overcast [ˈəʊvəkɑːst] bedeckt, bezogen *(Himmel)* 20
overdue [ˌəʊvəˈdjuː] überfällig 190
overheads [ˈəʊvəhedz] fixe Kosten 218
overindebted [ˌəʊvərɪnˈdetɪd] überschuldet 184
to overlook [ˌəʊvəˈlʊk] übersehen 187
overseas [ˌəʊvəˈsiːz] aus dem/ins Ausland, ausländisch 148
to oversee, oversaw, overseen [ˌəʊvəˈsiː, ˌəʊvəˈsɔː, ˌəʊvəˈsiːn] beaufsichtigen, leiten 85
oversight [ˈəʊvəsaɪt] Versehen 126
to overtake, overtook, overtaken [ˌəʊvəˈteɪk, ˌəʊvəˈtʊk, ˌəʊvəˈteɪkn] überholen 184
overview [ˈəʊvəvjuː] Überblick 101
overwhelmed [ˌəʊvəˈwelmd] überwältigt 41
to owe [əʊ] schulden 192
owner [ˈəʊnə] Eigentümer/in 56

P

pace [peɪs] Geschwindigkeit 109
package [ˈpækɪdʒ] Paket(angebot) 31
package tour [ˈpækɪdʒ ˌtʊə] Pauschalreise 114
packaging material [ˈpækɪdʒɪŋ məˌtɪəriəl] Verpackungsmaterial 73
packing list [ˈpækɪŋ ˌlɪst] Packliste 175
pair of scissors [ˌpeər əv ˈsɪzəz] Schere 52
pallet [ˈpælɪt] Palette 174
palm rest [ˈpɑːm ˌrest] Handballenauflage 226
paper [ˈpeɪpə] *(hier:)* Vortrag 71
paragraph [ˈpærəgrɑːf] Absatz 124
paramount [ˈpærəmaʊnt] vorrangig 26
to paraphrase [ˈpærəfreɪz] umschreiben 13
parcel post [ˈpɑːsl ˌpəʊst] Paketpost 154

parent company [ˌpeərənt ˈkʌmpəni] Muttergesellschaft 208
parsley [ˈpɑːsli] Petersilie 29
participant [pɑːˈtɪsɪpənt] Teilnehmer/in 33
to participate [pɑːˈtɪsɪpeɪt] teilnehmen 245
particular [pəˈtɪkjələ] besonders, speziell 38
partnership [ˈpɑːtnəʃɪp] Personengesellschaft 121
to pass a message on [ˌpɑːs ə ˈmesɪdʒ ˌɒn] eine Nachricht weitergeben 30
passbook [ˈpɑːsbʊk] Sparbuch 193
passing of risk [ˌpɑːsɪŋ əv ˈrɪsk] Gefahrenübergang 152
to pass on [ˌpɑːs ˈɒn] weiterreichen, -geben 116
patience [ˈpeɪʃəns] Geduld 67
patron saint [ˌpeɪtrən ˈseɪnt] Schutzheilige/r 25
to pause [pɔːz] eine Pause einlegen 75
payable at [ˈpeɪəbl ət] zahlbar bei 186
payable to [ˈpeɪəbl tuː] zahlbar an 73
to pay into a bank account [peɪˌɪntʊˌə ˈbæŋk əˌkaʊnt] auf ein Konto einzahlen 183
payment in advance [ˌpeɪmənt ɪn ədˈvɑːns] Vorauszahlung 185
payment, money transfer, remittance [ˈpeɪmənt, ˈmʌni ˌtrænsfɜː, rɪˈmɪtəns] Überweisung 94
payroll [ˈpeɪrəʊl] Gehaltsliste, Löhne 60
to pay through the nose [ˌpeɪ θruː ðə ˈnəʊz] blechen müssen 192
PC-literacy [ˌpiːsiːˈlɪtrəsi] PC-Kenntnisse 231
PC literate [ˌpiːsiːˈlɪtrət] PC-erfahren 230
peak [piːk] Gipfel, Höchststand 106
peak season [ˌpiːk ˈsiːzn] Hochsaison 73
pearl [pɜːl] Perle 149
pea soup [ˌpiːˈsuːp] Erbsensuppe 28
peppers [ˈpepəz] Paprikaschoten 28
percentage [pəˈsentɪdʒ] Prozentsatz 218
to perform [pəˈfɔːm] ausführen 14
periodical [ˌpɪəriˈɒdɪkl] Zeitschrift 224
perishable [ˈperɪʃəbl] (leicht) verderblich 172
permission [pəˈmɪʃn] Erlaubnis 212
permit [ˈpɜːmɪt] Genehmigung, Erlaubnis 243
personal assistant [ˌpɜːsnl əˈsɪstənt] Sekretär/in 56
personnel [ˌpɜːsənˈel] Personal 56
personnel department [ˌpɜːsənˈel dɪˌpɑːtmənt] Personalabteilung 200
person to contact [ˌpɜːsn tə ˈkɒntækt] Kontaktperson 232
to persuade [pəˈsweɪd] überreden 58

Alphabetical word list | Anhang

to phase out [feɪz 'aʊt] allmählich vom Markt zurückziehen 215
to pick someone up [pɪk ˌsʌmwʌn 'ʌp] jemanden abholen 30
to pick up [pɪk 'ʌp] abholen 181
picnic hamper ['pɪknɪk ˌhæmpə] Picknickkorb 116
pie chart ['paɪ ˌtʃɑːt] Tortendiagramm 104
pipe-blown by hand [ˌpaɪpbləʊn baɪ 'hænd] mundgeblasen 203
to place [pleɪs] (hier:) aufgeben 14
to place an order [ˌpleɪs ən 'ɔːdə] einen Auftrag erteilen 133
placement ['pleɪsmənt] Praktikum 232
place of destination [ˌpleɪs əv ˌdestɪ'neɪʃn] Bestimmungsort 152
place of employment [ˌpleɪs əv ɪm'plɔɪmənt] Arbeitsstätte 219
place of worship [ˌpleɪs əv 'wɜːʃɪp] Gotteshaus 77
plaice [pleɪs] Scholle 28
plain [pleɪn] (hier:) ungemustert, einfarbig; schlicht, unscheinbar 118
plant [plɑːnt] Werk, Anlage; Pflanze 153
plant tour ['plɑːnt ˌtʊə] Firmenbesichtigung 14
plastic box with mouldings [ˌplæstɪk 'bɒks wɪð 'məʊldɪŋz] Kunststoffbox mit Formeinlagen 174
platter ['plætə] Servierplatte, (Holz-)Teller 165
plausible ['plɔːzɪbl] plausibel, einleuchtend, glaubhaft 203
to point out [pɔɪnt 'aʊt] hinweisen auf 162
polished ['pɒlɪʃt] mit Schuhcreme geputzt, poliert 239
polite [pə'laɪt] höflich 73
pollution [pə'luːʃn] (Umwelt-)Verschmutzung 172
to pop into [ˌpɒp 'ɪntʊ] eben schnell hineintun 102
pork escalope [ˌpɔːk 'eskəlɒp] Schweineschnitzel 29
port [pɔːt] Hafen 171
port of destination [ˌpɔːt əv ˌdestɪ'neɪʃn] Bestimmungshafen 152
port of shipment [ˌpɔːt əv 'ʃɪpmənt] Verschiffungshafen 152
to portray [pɔː'treɪ] darstellen 109
possession [pə'zeʃn] Besitz 212
to post [pəʊst] (per Post) verschicken 14
postcode (BE), **postal code** (BE), **zip code** (AE) ['pəʊstkəʊd, 'pəʊstl ˌkəʊd, 'zɪpkəʊd] Postleitzahl 69
posted ['pəʊstɪd] beschildert 78
poster ['pəʊstə] Plakat 221
to postpone [pəs'pəʊn] verschieben 71
potential customer [pəˌtenʃl 'kʌstəmə] Interessent/in 143

pot plant ['pɒt ˌplɑːnt] Topfpflanze 52
poultry ['pəʊltrɪ] Geflügel 28
praise [preɪz] Lob 241
to precede [prɪ'siːd] vor(an)gehen, davor stehen 122
precisely [prɪ'saɪslɪ] (hier:) genau, exakt, präzise 69
precisely then [prɪˌsaɪslɪ 'ðen] gerade dann 67
precision instruments [prɪˌsɪʒn 'ɪnstrəmənts] Präzisionsinstrumente 224
preferably ['prefrəblɪ] vorzugsweise 103
preliminary [prɪ'lɪmɪnərɪ] vorläufig 114
premises ['premɪsɪz] Geschäftsräume, Firmengebäude, -gelände 145
prerequisite [ˌpriː'rekwɪzɪt] Voraussetzung, Bedingung 103
to present [prɪ'zent] vorstellen 222
press coverage ['pres ˌkʌvərɪdʒ] Berichterstattung in der Presse 224
prestigious [pres'tɪdʒəs] repräsentativ 51
pretzel ['pretsl] Brezel 25
to prevent [prɪ'vent] hindern, verhindern, vermeiden 115
preview ['priːvjuː] Voransicht 169
previous ['priːvɪəs] früher, vorhergehend 241
price reduction ['praɪs rɪˌdʌkʃn] Preisnachlass 197
prices are subject to change without notice ['praɪsɪz ə ˌsʌbdʒɪkt tʊ ˌtʃeɪndʒ wɪðˌaʊt 'nəʊtɪs] Preisänderungen vorbehalten 142
principal ['prɪnsɪpl] (hier:) Schulleiter/in; Auftraggeber/in 200
printing press ['prɪntɪŋ ˌpres] Druckerpresse 173
print quality ['prɪnt ˌkwɒlətɪ] Druckqualität 168
privacy ['praɪvəsɪ] private Atmosphäre 54
privacy policy [ˌpraɪvət 'pɒləsɪ] (hier:) Datenschutz(bestimmungen) 48
private individual [ˌpraɪvət ˌɪndɪ'vɪdʒʊəl] Privatperson 41
procedure [prə'siːdʒə] Verfahren 15
proceedings [prə'siːdɪŋz] (hier:) Ablauf der Konferenz 84
to process ['prəʊses] bearbeiten, verarbeiten 143
produce ['prɒdjuːs] (landwirtschaftliche) Erzeugnisse 26
production site [prə'dʌkʃn ˌsaɪt] Fertigungsstätte, Produktionsbetrieb 39
product range ['prɒdʌkt ˌreɪndʒ] Produktpalette 88
professional [prə'feʃnl] beruflich, professionell 6

profit margin ['prɒfɪt ˌmɑːdʒɪn] Gewinnspanne/marge 248
proforma invoice [prəʊˌfɔːmər 'ɪnvɔɪs] Proformarechnung 181
progress ['prəʊgres] Fortgang 205
to project an image [prəˌdʒekt ən 'ɪmɪdʒ] ein Image pflegen 224
prolonged [prəʊ'lɒŋd] langanhaltend 125
to promote [prə'məʊt] befördern 243
to promote sales [prəˌməʊt 'seɪlz] den Absatz fördern 221
promotion [prə'məʊʃn] Aufstieg, Beförderung 12
prompt [prɒmpt] Hinweis, Stichwort 22
prompt cards ['prɒmpt ˌkɑːdz] Stichwortkarten 101
to pronounce [prə'naʊns] aussprechen 75
pronounced [prə'naʊnst] ausgeprägt 58
proof [pruːf] Beweis, Nachweis 185
to proofread ['pruːfriːd] Korrektur lesen 110
proportion [prə'pɔːʃn] Anteil 221
proposal [prə'pəʊzl] Angebot 211
to propose [prə'pəʊz] vorschlagen 95
prospects ['prɒspekts] Aussichten 12
prospective [prəs'pektɪv] zukünftig, voraussichtlich, potentiell 143
to prosper ['prɒspə] gedeihen, florieren 39
protective cap [prəˌtektɪv 'kæp] Schutzkappe 212
protective software [prəˌtektɪv 'sɒftweə] Software zum Schutz 113
proud(ly) [praʊd(lɪ)] stolz 163
to prove [pruːv] beweisen, nachweisen 185
to provide [prə'vaɪd] zur Verfügung stellen 218
provider [prə'vaɪdə] Versorger, Anbieter, Lieferant 184
proximity [prɒk'sɪmɪtɪ] Nähe 77
public ['pʌblɪk] Öffentlichkeit 63
publicity [pʌb'lɪsətɪ] Werbung, Öffentlichkeitsarbeit 60
public relations [ˌpʌblɪk rɪ'leɪʃnz] Werbe-/Öffentlichkeitsabteilung, Öffentlichkeitsarbeit 31
publisher's assistant ['pʌblɪʃəz əˌsɪstənt] Verlagskaufmann/-frau 231
publishing house ['pʌblɪʃɪŋ ˌhaʊs] Verlag 231
punch [pʌntʃ] Locher 52
punctual ['pʌŋktʃʊəl] pünktlich 21
puppy ['pʌpɪ] Hündchen, Welpe 163
purchase ['pɜːtʃɪs] Kauf 31
purchase order ['pɜːtʃɪs ˌɔːdə] Bestellung, Lieferungsauftrag 198
purchasing (department) ['pɜːtʃəsɪŋ (dɪˌpɑːtmənt)] Einkauf(sabteilung) 56

269

purchasing manager [ˈpɜːtʃəsɪŋ ˌmænɪdʒə] Einkaufsleiter/in 133
pure new wool [ˌpjʊə njuː ˈwʊl] reine Schurwolle 174
purpose-built [ˌpɜːpəsˈbɪlt] für bestimmten Zweck gebaut 51
to put someone through [pʊt ˌsʌmwʌn ˈθruː] durchstellen, verbinden 65

Q

to qualify for [ˈkwɒlɪfaɪ fɔː] Voraussetzungen erfüllen für, Anspruch haben auf 162
quantity discount [ˌkwɒntətɪ ˈdɪskaʊnt] Mengenrabatt 144
quarter finals [ˌkwɔːtə ˈfaɪnlz] Viertelfinale 20
quarterly [ˈkwɔːtəlɪ] vierteljährlich 144
quay [kiː] Kai, Dock, Anlegestelle 151
query [ˈkwɪərɪ] (Rück-)Frage 248
quota [ˈkwəʊtə] Quote, Rate, Kontingent, Anteil 167
quotation [kwəʊˈteɪʃn] Angebot mit Preisangabe 132
to quote [kwəʊt] Preis angeben; zitieren 144

R

rabbit [ˈræbɪt] Kaninchen 28
radio frequency [ˈreɪdɪəʊ ˌfriːkwənsɪ] Funkfrequenz 78
rail siding [ˈreɪl ˌsaɪdɪŋ] Gleisanschluss 172
rail transport [ˈreɪl ˌtrænspɔːt] Schienentransport 172
to raise [reɪz] erhöhen 220
to raise a matter [reɪz ə ˈmætə] eine Sache ansprechen 204
to ramble [ˈræmbl] abschweifen 109
random sample [ˌrændəm ˈsɑːmpl] Zufallsprobe 216
range [reɪndʒ] Sortiment, Kollektion, Auswahl 163
to range from … to [ˈreɪndʒ frəm … tʊ] reichen von … bis 100
range of products [ˌreɪndʒ əv ˈprɒdʌkts] Produktpalette 39
rapid [ˈræpɪd] schnell 104
rapport [ræˈpɔː, rəˈpɔː] Verhältnis 241
raw materials [ˌrɔː məˈtɪərɪəlz] Rohstoffe 171
re [riː] bezüglich, wegen 208
rebate [ˈriːbeɪt] Rückzahlung 226
receipt [rɪˈsiːt] Beleg, Quittung 193
receipt of order [rɪˌsiːt əv ˈɔːdə] Auftragseingang 145
to receive [rɪˈsiːv] erhalten, empfangen 64
receiver [rɪˈsiːvə] Hörer 64
recent [ˈriːsənt] nicht lange zurückliegend, vor kurzem geschehen 112
reception [rɪˈsepʃn] Empfang 134

receptionist [rɪˈsepʃənɪst] Rezeptionist/in, Mitarbeiter/in am Empfang 23
recipient [rɪˈsɪpɪənt] Empfänger 115
reclining seat [rɪˌklaɪnɪŋ ˈsiːt] (verstellbarer) Lehnstuhl; Liegesitz 156
to recognize [ˈrekəgnaɪz] erkennen, anerkennen 113
to recommend [ˌrekəˈmend] empfehlen 93
recommendation [ˌrekəmenˈdeɪʃn] Empfehlung 15
record [ˈrekɔːd] (hier:) Datensatz 59
records [ˈrekɔːdz] Unterlagen, Verzeichnisse 187
to record [rɪˈkɔːd] aufzeichnen, eintragen 119
to recruit [rɪˈkruːt] einstellen 229
recruitment agencies [rɪˈkruːtmənt ˌeɪdʒənsɪz] Stellenvermittlungsagenturen 229
to redesign [ˌriːdɪˈzaɪn] neu-, umgestalten 26
to redirect [ˌriːdaɪˈrekt, ˌriːdɪˈrekt] umleiten 65
referee [ˌrefəˈriː] (hier:) jemand, der eine Empfehlung/ein Zeugnis schreibt 232
reference [ˈrefrəns] Bezug 147
to refer to [rɪˈfɜː tuː] sich beziehen auf 76
refreshments [rɪˈfreʃmənts] Erfrischung(en) 19
refund [ˈriːfʌnd] Rückerstattung 14
to refund [ˌriːˈfʌnd] erstatten 197
refurbishment [ˌriːˈfɜːbɪʃmənt] Renovierung 200
to refurnish [ˌriːˈfɜːnɪʃ] neu einrichten 192
regardless of [rɪˈgɑːdləs əv] ungeachtet, trotz 174
to register [ˈredʒɪstə] eintragen, registrieren 138
regularly [ˈregjələlɪ] regelmäßig 216
regulations [ˌregjəˈleɪʃnz] Vorschriften, Verordnungen 120
to rehearse [rɪˈhɜːs] proben, einüben 103
to reinforce [ˌriːɪnˈfɔːs] verstärken 101
to reject [rɪˈdʒekt] zurückweisen 205
to release from a contract [rɪˌliːs frəm ə ˈkɒntrækt] von einem Vertrag entbinden 208
relevant [ˈrelәvənt] wichtig, sachdienlich 69
reliable [rɪˈlaɪəbl] zuverlässig 38
relieved [rɪˈliːvd] erleichtert 71
remainder, balance [rɪˈmeɪndə, ˈbæləns] Restbetrag 59
to remain unchanged [rɪˌmeɪn ʌnˈtʃeɪndʒd] unverändert bleiben 106
to remind [rɪˈmaɪnd] erinnern 103

reminder [rɪˈmaɪndə] (Zahlungs-)Erinnerung, Mahnung 180
to remit [rɪˈmɪt] überweisen 181
remittance [rɪˈmɪtəns] Überweisung 189
to remove [rɪˈmuːv] entfernen 198
to render a service [ˌrendər ə ˈsɜːvɪs] einen Dienst leisten, eine Dienstleistung erbringen 197
to renew a contract [rɪˌnjuː ə ˈkɒntrækt] einen Vertrag verlängern 200
rent [rent] Miete 73
to rent [rent] mieten 39
repairs [rɪˈpeəz] Reparatur 43
repeat order [rɪˌpiːt ˈɔːdə] Folgeauftrag 159
repetitive [rɪˈpetətɪv] sich wiederholend 15
to replace [rɪˈpleɪs] auflegen; ersetzen 64
replacement [rɪˈpleɪsmənt] Ersatz(lieferung) 174
replacement Mp3 player [rɪˌpleɪsmənt ˌempiːˈθriː ˌpleɪə] Ersatz-MP3-Spieler 174
to replicate [ˈreplɪkeɪt] nachbilden, reproduzieren 15
to report to [rɪˈpɔːt tuː] unterstehen 56
representative [ˌreprɪˈzentətɪv] Vertreter/in 139
reputation [ˌrepjəˈteɪʃn] Ruf 241
request [rɪˈkwest] Bitte 73
to request [rɪˈkwest] bitten um 90
to require [rɪˈkwaɪə] (hier:) verlangen, auffordern 100
requirement [rɪˈkwaɪəmənt] Anforderung, Erfordernis 14
research [ˈriːsɜːtʃ] Forschung 23
residence permit [ˈrezɪdəns ˌpɜːmɪt] Aufenthaltsgenehmigung 243
residential [ˌrezɪˈdentʃl] Wohn- 247
resolution [ˌrezəˈluːʃn] (Bildschirm-)Auflösung 226
resort [rɪˈzɔːt] Urlaubs-, Badeort 149
8000 and 6000 customers, respectively [ˈeɪt ˌθaʊsənd ənd ˌsɪks ˌθaʊsənd ˌkʌstəməz rɪˈspektɪvlɪ] 8000 bzw. 6000 Kunden 107
respite [ˈrespaɪt] Zahlungsaufschub 210
to respond [rɪˈspɒnd] antworten, reagieren 205
responsible for [rɪˈspɒnsəbl fɔː] verantwortlich für 57
to restore [rɪˈstɔː] wiederherstellen, restaurieren 116
restricted [rɪˈstrɪktɪd] beschränkt 92
restroom (AE) [ˈrestˌruːm] Toilette 23
résumé (AE) [ˈrezjuːmeɪ] Lebenslauf 245
retail customer [ˌriːteɪl ˈkʌstəmə] Privatkunde (bei einer Bank) 219
retailer [ˈriːteɪlə] Einzelhändler/in 133

retailing operations [ˈriːteɪlɪŋ ˌɒpəˌreɪʃnz] Einzelhandelsgeschäftstätigkeit 219
retail outlet [ˌriːteɪl ˈaʊtlet] Einzelhandelsverkaufsstelle 184
retail sales [ˌriːteɪl ˈseɪlz] Umsatz im Einzelhandel 125
retail trade [ˈriːteɪl ˌtreɪd] Einzelhandel 165
to retain [rɪˈteɪn] halten, beibehalten 137
retired [rɪˈtaɪəd] im Ruhestand, pensioniert 221
retiree [rɪˌtaɪəˈriː] Rentner/in, Pensionär/in 192
retirement [rɪˈtaɪəmənt] Ruhestand 209
to retrieve [rɪˈtriːv] abrufen 59
return [rɪˈtɜːn] *(hier:)* Rückfahrkarte 96
to return [rɪˈtɜːn] *(hier:)* zurückschicken 93
to reveal [rɪˈviːl] enthüllen, aufzeigen 203
revenue [ˈrevənjuː] Erlös, Einnahmen 60
to reverse [rɪˈvɜːs] umkehren 234
reviews [rɪˈvjuːz] Berichte, Besprechungen 220
to review [rɪˈvjuː] überprüfen 246
to revoke [rɪˈvəʊk] widerrufen, annullieren, stornieren 185
reworking [ˌriːˈwɜːkɪŋ] Um-, Nacharbeitung 198
rice [raɪs] Reis 28
right away [ˌraɪtəˈweɪ] sofort 243
ring tone [ˈrɪŋtəʊn] Klingelton 77
to rise, rose, risen [raɪz, rəʊz, rɪzn] steigen 106
rising demand for [ˌraɪzɪŋ dɪˈmɑːnd fə] steigende Nachfrage nach 104
roast pork [ˌrəʊst ˈpɔːk] Schweinebraten 28
to roll over to [ˌrəʊl ˈəʊvə tuː] umschalten auf 77
to romp [rɒmp] herumtollen 163
roof [ruːf] Dach 217
roughly one third [ˌrʌflɪ ˌwʌn ˈθɜːd] rund/etwa ein Drittel 203
roundabout [ˈraʊndəbaʊt] Kreisverkehr 24
to round up [raʊnd ˈʌp] aufrunden 90
to route [ruːt] weiterleiten 14
rubber *(BE)*, eraser *(AE)* [ˈrʌbə, ɪˈreɪzə] Radiergummi 52
rude [ruːd] grob, ungehobelt, unverschämt 127
to rule [ruːl] entscheiden, verfügen, anordnen 167
rules [ruːlz] Regeln, Vorschriften 120
ruler [ˈruːlə] Lineal 52
to run out of something [ˌrʌn ˈaʊt əv ˌsʌmθɪŋ] ausgehen, zur Neige gehen 148
rush [rʌʃ] Ansturm 86

S

salary [ˈsælərɪ] Gehalt 230
sales (department) [ˈseɪlz (dɪˌpɑːtmənt)] Verkauf(sabteilung) 56
sales assistant [ˈseɪlz əˌsɪstənt] Verkäufer/in 220
sales consultant [ˈseɪlz kənˌsʌltənt] Verkaufsberater/in 220
sales force [ˈseɪlz ˌfɔːs] Vertreterstab 218
sales literature [ˈseɪlz ˌlɪtrətʃə] Prospektmaterial 38
sales representative [ˈseɪlz reprɪˌzentətɪv] Handelsvertreter/in, Außendienstmitarbeiter/in 114
salmon [ˈsæmən] Lachs 28
salutation [ˌsæljəˈteɪʃn] *(hier:)* Anrede; Begrüßung 114
sample [ˈsɑːmpl] Muster, Probestück 133
satisfaction [ˌsætɪsˈfækʃn] Zufriedenheit 202
to satisfy [ˈsætɪsfaɪ] zufrieden stellen 200
sausage [ˈsɒsɪdʒ] Wurst 28
savoury [ˈseɪvərɪ] herzhaft, pikant 28
scale [skeɪl] Maß, Maßstab 180
scarce(ly) [ˈskeəs(lɪ)] knapp; kaum 154
scared [skeəd] ängstlich 100
schedule [ˈʃedjuːl, ˈskedjuːl] (Termin-/Fahr-)Plan; Schema, Aufstellung 14
school-leaving certificate [ˌskuːl ˈliːvɪŋ səˈtɪfɪkət] Schulabschlusszeugnis 231
Sci-Fi film [ˈsaɪfaɪ ˌfɪlm] Science-Fiction-Film 9
scope [skəʊp] Umfang, Bereich 56
scotch tape [ˌskɒtʃ ˈteɪp] Klebeband 52
scratch [skrætʃ] Kratzer 206
to screen [skriːn] überprüfen, aussondern 14
to scroll [skrəʊl] scrollen, blättern 77
search engine [ˈsɜːtʃ ˌendʒɪn] Suchmaschine 132
seaworthy packing [ˌsiːwɜːðɪ ˈpækɪŋ] seetaugliche Verpackung 172
second floor [ˌsekənd ˈflɔː] zweite Etage *(BE)*, erste Etage *(AE)* 23
sector [ˈsektə] Branche 219
secure [sɪˈkjʊə, sɪˈkjɔː] sicher 41
to seek, sought, sought [siːk, sɔːt, sɔːt] suchen 230
segment [ˈsegmənt] Marktsegment 217
selection [səˈlekʃn] Auswahl 103
selective [səˈlektɪv] ausgewählt 221
sell-by date [ˈselbaɪˌdeɪt] Verfallsdatum *(Lebensmittel)* 202
to sell on [sel ˈɒn] weiterverkaufen 217
to sell well [ˌsel ˈwel] sich gut verkaufen, gut gehen 163
senior [ˈsiːnjə] höherrangig 26
series [ˈsɪəriːz] Reihe 110
serious [ˈsɪərɪəs] ernst, schwerwiegend 207

service [ˈsɜːvɪs] Dienstleistung, Service 48
serviceable [ˈsɜːvɪsəbl] zweckdienlich, praktisch, strapazierfähig 181
service centre / center [ˈsɜːvɪs ˌsentə] Kundendienst(zentrum) 204
to set [set] festsetzen, ansetzen, einrichten 167
to set about [set əˈbaʊt] sich daran machen 215
setting [ˈsetɪŋ] Einstellung 77
to settle an invoice [ˌsetl ən ˈɪnvɔɪs] eine Rechnung begleichen 187
settlement [ˈsetlmənt] Abrechnung, Bezahlung, Ausgleich, Erledigung 144
to settle the matter [ˌsetl ðə ˈmætə] die Angelegenheit erledigen 202
to set up [set ˈʌp] einrichten 48
to set up in business on one's own [set ˌʌp ɪn ˈbɪznɪs ɒn wʌnz ˌəʊn] eine eigene Firma gründen 241
severe(ly) [səˈvɪə(lɪ)] schwer, ernstlich, streng, hart 125
to sew, sewed, sewn [səʊ, səʊd, səʊn] nähen 198
shade [ʃeɪd] *(hier:)* Schattierung 110
shareholder [ˈʃeəˌhəʊldə] Aktieninhaber/in 192
to share the costs [ˌʃeə ðə ˈkɒsts] sich die Kosten teilen 165
sharp [ʃɑːp] scharf 24
to shield [ʃiːld] abschirmen 78
to ship [ʃɪp] versenden, verschiffen 72
shipping [ˈʃɪpɪŋ] Seetransport, Verschiffung, Versand 171
shoemaker [ˈʃuːˌmeɪkə] Schuhmacher/in, Schuster/in 39
shopping cart [ˈʃɒpɪŋˌkɑːt] Einkaufswagen 43
shortcomings [ˈʃɔːtˌkʌmɪŋz] Unzulänglichkeiten 200
shortcut [ˈʃɔːtkʌt] Abkürzung; Tastenkombination 15
shortly [ˈʃɔːtlɪ] in Kürze, bald 160
shuttle service [ˈʃʌtl ˌsɜːvɪs] Pendelbus 86
sights [saɪts] Sehenswürdigkeiten 24
signatory [ˈsɪgnətərɪ] Unterzeichner/in 121
signature [ˈsɪgnətʃə] Unterschrift 113
signature footer [ˈsɪgnətʃə ˌfʊtə] Unterschriftsfußzeilen 114
significant(ly) [sɪgˈnɪfɪkənt(lɪ)] bedeutend 106
to signpost [ˈsaɪnpəʊst] kennzeichnen, darlegen 109
to simplify [ˈsɪmplɪfaɪ] vereinfachen 216
single [ˈsɪŋgl] *(hier:)* Einzelfahrkarte 96
single [ˈsɪŋgl] ledig 235
single room [ˌsɪŋgl ˈruːm] Einzelzimmer 85

Anhang | **Alphabetical word list**

single sided [ˌsɪŋgl'saɪdɪd] einseitig 168
sister-in-law ['sɪstərɪnlɔː] Schwägerin 56
site [saɪt] Standort, Abbaustelle 104
size [saɪz] Größe 74
skill [skɪl] Fertigkeit 100
skin care ['skɪn ˌkeə] Hautpflege 230
to skip [skɪp] überspringen 223
to sleep [sliːp] (hier:) Schlafmöglichkeit bieten 73
slice [slaɪs] Scheibe, Anteil 104
slide [slaɪd] Folie 101
slight(ly) [slaɪt(lɪ)] leicht, gering(fügig) 106
slight drizzle [ˌslaɪt ˌdrɪzl] leichter Nieselregen 22
slot [slɒt] Geldeinwurf, Schlitz 193
to slump [slʌmp] stark fallen 106
slush [slʌʃ] Schmiergeld 192
smart [smɑːt] ordentlich, gepflegt, schick 240
smitten ['smɪtn] hingerissen 163
smoked [sməʊkt] geräuchert 28
smoked salmon [ˌsməʊkt 'sæmən] Räucherlachs 138
smooth(ly) [smuːð(lɪ)] glatt, reibungslos 125
smudged [smʌdʒd] verwischt, verschmiert 202
to soak [səʊk] durchnässen, einweichen 189
to soar [sɔː] sprunghaft steigen, in die Höhe schnellen 148
sociable ['səʊʃəbl] gesellig, umgänglich 26
social service [ˌsəʊʃl 'sɜːvɪs] Ersatzdienst 237
soft drinks [ˌsɒft 'drɪŋks] alkoholfreie Getränke 91
sole [səʊl] Sohle 197
solicited offer [səˌlɪsɪtɪd 'ɒfə] verlangtes Angebot 142
to some extent [tə ˌsʌm ɪk'stent] in gewissem Maße 65
sophisticated [sə'fɪstɪkeɪtɪd] hoch entwickelt, technisch ausgefeilt 225
sour [saʊə] sauer 28
source [sɔːs] Quelle 229
spacing ['speɪsɪŋ] Abstände, Abstandseinteilung 119
spacious ['speɪʃəs] geräumig 51
to spare [speə] übrig haben 216
spare parts [ˌspeə 'pɑːts] Ersatzteile 172
sparing(ly) ['speərɪŋ(lɪ)] sparsam, mäßig 110
spark [spɑːk] Funke 78
sparkling mineral water [ˌspɑːklɪŋ 'mɪnərəl ˌwɔːtə] Mineralwasser mit Kohlensäure 91
special features [ˌspeʃl 'fiːtʃəz] besondere Eigenschaften 86
specialist agency [ˌspeʃəlɪst 'eɪdʒənsɪ] Fachagentur 224

specialist shops [ˌspeʃəlɪst 'ʃɒps] Fachgeschäfte 217
special treat [ˌspeʃl 'triːt] besonderes Vergnügen, spezielles Extra 149
to spend, spent, spent [spend, spent, spent] ausgeben 216
spicy ['spaɪsɪ] würzig 27
spirits ['spɪrɪts] Spirituosen 219
to split [splɪt] trennen, spalten 128
spokesman ['spəʊksmən] Sprecher 223
spouse [spaʊs] Ehegatte, Ehegattin 31
spreadsheet ['spredʃiːt] Tabellenkalkulation 59
square [skweə] Platz 25
to stack [stæk] aufstapeln, aufschichten 171
staff [stɑːf] Belegschaft, Personal 39
staff member ['stɑːf ˌmembə] Mitarbeiter/in 178
staff retention [ˌstɑːf rɪ'tenʃn] Personalerhaltung 227
stage [steɪdʒ] (hier:) Stadium 215
to stage [steɪdʒ] veranstalten 165
staggered payment [ˌstægəd 'peɪmənt] gestaffelte Zahlungsweise 185
to stagnate [stæg'neɪt] stagnieren 125
stagnation [stæg'neɪʃn] Stillstand 171
standard lamp ['stændəd ˌlæmp] Stehlampe 177
to stand in for someone [stænd 'ɪn fə ˌsʌmwʌn] jemanden vertreten 30
standing order [ˌstændɪŋ 'ɔːdə] Dauerauftrag 159
stapling machine / stapler ['steɪplɪŋ məˌʃiːn / 'steɪplə] Tacker 52
starter ['stɑːtə] Vorspeise 27
start-up (business) ['stɑːtʌp (ˌbɪznɪs)] Neugründung, junges Unternehmen 41
statement ['steɪtmənt] Aussage, Äußerung 8
statement of account [ˌsteɪtmənt əv ə'kaʊnt] Kontoauszug 185
state of affairs [ˌsteɪt əv ə'feəz] Zustand, Stand der Dinge 188
state-of-the-art [ˌsteɪtəvðɪ'ɑːt] auf dem neuesten Stand (der Technik) 38
state rooms ['steɪt ˌruːmz] Empfangssäle 25
stationery ['steɪʃənrɪ] Büromaterial 200
steady, steadily ['stedɪ(lɪ)] stetig 106
steel [stiːl] Stahl 148
steel rods [ˌstiːl 'rɒdz] Stahlstäbe 174
stew, soup [stjuː, suːp] Eintopf 29
to stew [stjuː] kochen, dünsten, schmoren 28
to stick to ['stɪk tuː] (hier:) festhalten an 110
stiffness ['stɪfnəs] Festigkeit, Steifheit 168
to stipulate, to specify ['stɪpjəleɪt, 'spesɪfaɪ] vorschreiben 184
stock [stɒk] Vorrat, Lager(bestand) 142

to stock up on [stɒk 'ʌp ɒn] Lager(bestand) auffüllen 148
storage ['stɔːrɪdʒ] Speicher(n) 15
straight [streɪt] (hier:) geradewegs, direkt 221
straight away [ˌstreɪtə'weɪ] sofort, unverzüglich 165
straightforward [ˌstreɪt'fɔːwəd] einfach, unkompliziert 20
streamlining ['striːmlaɪnɪŋ] Rationalisierung(smaßnahme) 15
strengths [streŋkθs] Stärken 240
to stress [stres] betonen 162
striking ['straɪkɪŋ] auffallend 25
study group ['stʌdɪ ˌgruːp] Arbeitsgruppe 76
stuffed [stʌft] gefüllt 28
sturdy ['stɜːdɪ] robust, solide 156
stylish ['staɪlɪʃ] schick, modisch 181
sub-category [ˌsʌb'kætəgərɪ] Unterkategorie/begriff 48
subject ['sʌbdʒɪkt] (hier:) Betreff; Gegenstand 114
subject matter ['sʌbdʒɪkt ˌmætə] Gegenstand, Thema 115
to submit [səb'mɪt] einreichen, vorlegen 245
subsidiary [səb'sɪdɪərɪ] Tochtergesellschaft 167
subsidy ['sʌbsədɪ] Zuschuss, Subvention 192
substantial [səb'stænʃl] erheblich, beträchtlich 186
substitute ['sʌbstɪtjuːt] Ersatz (durch Ähnliches) 146
suburb ['sʌbɜːb] Vorort, Stadtteil im Außenbezirk 71
to succeed in [sək'siːd ɪn] gelingen 218
sufficient(ly) [sə'fɪʃənt(lɪ)] genug, genügend, ausreichend 41
to suggest [sə'dʒest] (hier:) hinweisen auf, suggerieren 221
suggestion [sə'dʒestʃn] Vorschlag 165
suit [suːt] Kostüm (Damen), Anzug 239
suitable ['suːtəbl] geeignet 229
to summarise ['sʌməraɪz] (kurz) zusammenfassen 109
sunset ['sʌnset] Sonnenuntergang 166
superb [suː'pɜːb] hervorragend 21
superfluous [suː'pɜːfluəs] überflüssig 219
superior [suː'pɪərɪə] Vorgesetzte/r 56
to supervise ['suːpəvaɪz] beaufsichtigen 91
supervised ['suːpəvaɪzd] überwacht, beaufsichtigt 34
supplementary charge [ˌsʌplɪmentərɪ 'tʃɑːdʒ] Zuschlag 89
supplier [sə'plaɪə] Lieferant, Anbieter 132
supply [sə'plaɪ] Angebot 217

supply / demand ratio [sə‚plaɪ dɪˈmɑːnd ‚reɪʃɪəʊ] Verhältnis zwischen Angebot und Nachfrage 171
to support [səˈpɔːt] unterstützen, helfen 7
to suppose [səˈpəʊz] vermuten 216
surname [ˈsɜːneɪm] Familienname 8
surplus [ˈsɜːpləs] überschüssig 197
surprisingly [səˈpraɪzɪŋli] überraschenderweise 20
to surround [səˈraʊnd] umgeben 26
survey [ˈsɜːveɪ] Umfrage 129
to survive [səˈvaɪv] überleben 219
suspicious [səˈspɪʃəs] verdächtig 116
sweets [swiːts] Süßwaren, Süßigkeiten 134
swift(ly) [ˈswɪft(li)] schnell 225
swivel chair [‚swɪvl ˈtʃeə] Drehstuhl 52

T

table [ˈteɪbl] (hier:) Tabelle 14
tag [tæg] Etikett, Anhängeschildchen 198
tailback [ˈteɪlbæk] Stau 22
tailored suit [‚teɪləd ˈsuːt] Kostüm 240
tailor-made [‚teɪləˈmeɪd] maßgeschneidert 149
to take [teɪk] (hier:) in Anspruch nehmen, dauern 20
to take a call [‚teɪk ə ˈkɔːl] einen Anruf entgegennehmen 88
to take advantage of [‚teɪk ədˈvɑːntɪdʒ ɒv] sich zunutze machen, ausnutzen 38
to take a message [‚teɪk ə ˈmesɪdʒ] eine Nachricht entgegennehmen 69
to take down [‚teɪk ˈdaʊn] notieren 69
to take into account [‚teɪk ‚ɪntə əˈkaʊnt] berücksichtigen 200
to take measures [‚teɪk ˈmeʒəz] Maßnahmen ergreifen 211
to take offence at something [‚teɪk əˈfens ət ‚sʌmθɪŋ] etwas übel nehmen 204
to take off the roof [‚teɪk ɒf ðə ˈruːf] das Dach abdecken 189
to take over [‚teɪk ˈəʊvə] (eine Firma) übernehmen 39
to take part in [‚teɪk ˈpɑːt ɪn] teilnehmen an 219
to take the minutes [‚teɪk ðə ˈmɪnɪts] Protokoll führen 92
to take up [‚teɪk ˈʌp] aufnehmen, sich verlegen auf; hochheben 39
to take up residence [‚teɪk ʌp ˈrezɪdəns] wohnhaft werden 243
to target [ˈtɑːgɪt] ansprechen, anpeilen 216
tart [tɑːt] herb, säuerlich 28
to taste [teɪst] schmecken 28
tattoo [tætˈuː] (hier:) Musikparade 32
tax [tæks] Steuer 181

tax-exempt intra-Community delivery [‚tæksɪgˈzemt ‚ɪntrəkəˈmjuːnəti dɪˈlɪvəri] steuerfreie Innergemeinschaftslieferung (innerhalb der EU) 182
tedious [ˈtiːdiəs] langweilig, lästig 22
telephone directory [ˈteləfəʊn daɪ‚rektəri, ˈteləfəʊn dɪ‚rektəri] Telefonbuch 64
telephony [təˈlefəni] Telefonverkehr 63
template [ˈtempleɪt] Dokumentvorlage 15
temporary [ˈtempərəri] vorübergehend, befristet 235
to tempt [tempt] in Versuchung führen 27
to tend to be [ˈtend tʊ biː] dazu neigen 127
tennis court [ˈtenɪs ‚kɔːt] Tennisplatz 34
terminal operator [ˈtɜːmɪnl ‚ɒpəreɪtə] Betreiber eines Terminals 171
termination [‚tɜːmɪˈneɪʃn] Beendigung, Aufhebung 212
terms of payment and delivery [‚tɜːmz əv ‚peɪmənt ənd dɪˈlɪvəri] Zahlungs- und Lieferbedingungen 133
terms of use [‚tɜːms əv ˈjuːs] Nutzungsbedingungen 48
terrible [ˈterɪbl] furchtbar 21
text-building block [ˈtekstbɪldɪŋ ‚blɒk] Textbaustein 125
textured [ˈtekstʃəd] strukturiert 110
theft [θeft] Diebstahl 172
the penny dropped [ðə ‚peni ˈdrɒpt] der Groschen ist gefallen 192
thesaurus [θɪˈsɔːrəs] Synonymwörterbuch 128
to thicken [ˈθɪkn] eindicken 29
those involved [‚ðəʊz ɪnˈvɒlvd] die Beteiligten 92
those present [‚ðəʊz ˈpreznt] die Anwesenden 92
to threaten [ˈθretn] drohen 187
thumbnail [ˈθʌmneɪl] (hier:) Miniaturansicht 169
thus [ðʌs] daher 218
ticket office [ˈtɪkɪt ‚ɒfɪs] Fahrkartenschalter 96
to tie [taɪ] binden 239
tiles [taɪlz] Fliesen, Kacheln 206
tilt function [ˈtɪlt ‚fʌŋkʃn] Kippfunktion 226
time-consuming [ˈtaɪmkən‚sjuːmɪŋ] zeitraubend 41
to have time on their hands [hæv ‚taɪm ɒn ðeə ˈhændz] Zeit (übrig) haben 221
timetable [ˈtaɪm‚teɪbl] Fahrplan 89
tip [tɪp] (hier:) Trinkgeld 90
toner hatch [ˈtəʊnə ‚hætʃ] Tonerkartusche 212

tool [tuːl] Werkzeug 63
tool kit [ˈtuːl ‚kɪt] Werkzeugsatz 199
topics [ˈtɒpɪks] (hier:) Punkte, Themen 92
topic of conversation [‚tɒpɪk əv ‚kɒnvəˈseɪʃn] Gesprächsthema 21
tournament [ˈtɔːnəmənt] Turnier 22
tour operator [ˈtʊər ‚ɒpəreɪtə] Reiseveranstalter 230
towering [ˈtaʊərɪŋ] turmhoch, überragend 25
town hall [‚taʊn ˈhɔːl] Rathaus 24
to track [træk] verfolgen 43
trade association [ˈtreɪd əsəʊsɪ‚eɪʃn] Branchenverband 132
trade discount [‚treɪd ˈdɪskaʊnt] Wiederverkaufsrabatt, Händlerrabatt 137
trade fair [ˈtreɪd ‚feə] (Fach-)Messe 132
trade flows [ˈtreɪd ‚fləʊz] Handelsströme 171
trade journal [ˈtreɪd ‚dʒɜːnl] Fachzeitschrift 224
trainee [‚treɪˈniː] Auszubildende/r 10
training course [ˈtreɪnɪŋ ‚kɔːs] Ausbildungslehrgang 12
train ride [ˈtreɪn ‚raɪd] Zugfahrt 21
transcript (AE) [ˈtrænskrɪpt] (hier:) Zeugnis 246
to transfer [trænsˈfɜː] überweisen, übertragen 160
transmitter [‚trænzˈmɪtə] Sendegerät 78
transparencies [trænˈspærənsiz] Folien 101
travel agency / agent [ˈtrævl ‚eɪdʒənsɪ / ‚eɪdʒənt] Reisebüro 8
travel consultant [ˈtrævl kənˌsʌltənt] Reiseverkehrskaufmann/-frau 8
tray [treɪ] Ablagekorb 52
trial order [‚traɪəl ˈɔːdə] Probeauftrag 159
to trim [trɪm] (ab)schneiden 169
triple-walled cardboard box [‚trɪplwɔːld ‚kɑːdbɔːd ˈbɒks] 3-wandiger Karton 175
trousers [ˈtraʊzəz] Hose 239
trout [traʊt] Forelle 28
to trust [trʌst] vertrauen 185
to tuck into [‚tʌk ˈɪntuː] hineinstecken in 239
tuition [tjʊˈɪʃn] Unterricht, Unterweisung 149
turkey [ˈtɜːki] Pute, Truthahn 28
to turn down [‚tɜːn ˈdaʊn] ablehnen 184
turnover, sales [ˈtɜːn‚əʊvə, seɪlz] Umsatz 223
turn-taking [ˈtɜːn‚teɪkɪŋ] sich anstellen, warten bis man dran ist 89
to turn up [‚tɜːn ˈʌp] auftauchen 229

Anhang | Alphabetical word list

TV advertising, TV commercials [ˌtiːviː ˈædvətaɪzɪŋ, ˌtiːviː kəˈmɜːʃlz] TV-Werbung 221
typo [ˈtaɪpəʊ] Tippfehler 128

U

unappreciated [ˌʌnəˈpriːʃieɪtɪd] nicht genügend geschätzt 241
unauthorised [ʌnˈɔːθəraɪzd] unbefugt 113
unavoidable [ˌʌnəˈvɔɪdəbl] unvermeidlich 65
to undercut [ˌʌndəˈkʌt] unterbieten 94
to underestimate [ˌʌndərˈestɪmeɪt] unterschätzen 102
understanding [ˌʌndəˈstændɪŋ] verständnisvoll 204
unemployment [ˌʌnɪmˈplɔɪmənt] Arbeitslosigkeit 243
unique [juːˈniːk] einzigartig 15
to unload [ʌnˈləʊd] entladen, löschen 171
unprecedented [ʌnˈpresɪdəntɪd] noch nie dagewesen 220
unreliable [ˌʌnrɪˈlaɪəbl] unzuverlässig 113
unsatisfactory [ˌʌnˌsætɪsˈfæktəri] unbefriedigend, ungenügend, unzureichend 113
unsolicited offer [ˌʌnsəlɪsɪtɪd ˈɒfə] unverlangtes Angebot 142
to update [ʌpˈdeɪt] aktualisieren 14
uplighter [ˈʌplaɪtə] Deckenfluter 177
upmarket [ˌʌpˈmɑːkɪt] im oberen Marktsegment 55
upper and lower case letters [ˌʌpər ən ˌləʊə keɪs ˈletəz] Groß- und Kleinbuchstaben 101
up the hill [ˌʌp ðə ˈhɪl] den Berg hinauf 24
up to date [ˌʌptəˈdeɪt] aktuell 221
urgent [ˈɜːdʒənt] dringend, eilig 165
usage [ˈjuːsɪdʒ] Gepflogenheit, übliche Praxis 121

V

vacancy [ˈveɪkənsi] offene Stelle 229
valid [ˈvælɪd] gültig, bindend, rechtskräftig 96
valuable [ˈvæljʊbl] wertvoll 203
value [ˈvæljuː] Wert 59
van [væn] Kleintransporter 172
variety [vəˈraɪəti] Vielfalt 217
VAT (value-added tax) [ˌviːeɪˈtiː (ˌvæljuː ˌædɪd ˈtæks)] Mehrwertsteuer 181
veal [viːl] Kalbfleisch 28
vegan [ˈviːgən] Veganer/in 27
vegetable(s) [ˈvedʒtəbl(z)] Gemüse 28
veggieburger [ˈvedʒɪˌbɜːgə] Gemüsebratling 27
vehicle [ˈviːɪkl] Fahrzeug 78
vendor [ˈvendə] Verkäufer/in 248
venison [ˈvenɪsən] Hirsch, Rotwild (als Fleisch) 27
venue [ˈvenjuː] Veranstaltungsort 33
via [vaɪə, ˈviːə] über 102
vibrant [ˈvaɪbrənt] lebendig 20
vicinity [vɪˈsɪnɪti] Nachbarschaft, Nähe 34
view [vjuː] (hier:) Ausblick 54
vinegar [ˈvɪnɪgə] Essig 29
to violate [ˈvaɪəleɪt] gegen etwas verstoßen 212
virtually [ˈvɜːtʃʊəli] nahezu, so gut wie, praktisch 172
visible [ˈvɪzəbl] sichtbar 89
visual aids [ˌvɪʒʊəl ˈeɪdz] visuelle Hilfsmittel 101
vocational college [vəʊˈkeɪʃənl ˌkɒlɪdʒ] Berufskolleg, Berufsfachschule 10
vocational school [vəʊˈkeɪʃənl ˌskuːl] Berufsschule 7
volume order [ˌvɒljuːm ˈɔːdə] Großauftrag 136

W

waiter service [ˌweɪtə ˈsɜːvɪs] Bedienung 89
to wait one's turn [ˌweɪt wʌnz ˈtɜːn] warten bis man an die Reihe kommt 27
wall calendar [ˈwɔːl ˌkæləndə] Wandkalender 201
warehouse [ˈweəhaʊs] Lager 218
wastepaper bin/basket [weɪstˈpeɪpə ˌbɪn/ˌbɑːskɪt] Papierkorb 52
to watch [wɒtʃ] aufpassen auf 55
to wave your arms around [ˌweɪv jɔːr ˈɑːmz əˌraʊnd] mit den Armen herumfuchteln 103
weather forecast [ˈweðə ˌfɔːkɑːst] Wettervorhersage 21
welfare [ˈwelfeə] Sozialhilfe 192
well-substantiated [ˌwelsʌbˈstænʃieɪtɪd] gut belegt 104
we've already met [wiːv ˌɔːlredi ˈmet] wir kennen uns schon 19
whatever the price [wɒtˌevə ðə ˈpraɪs] ganz unabhängig vom Preis 202
What is the weather like …? [ˌwɒt ɪz ðə ˌweðə ˌlaɪk] Wie ist das Wetter …? 21
wheeled [wiːld] rollend, Roll-, auf Rädern 156
whenever [wenˈevə] immer dann, wenn 113
whereas [weəˈræz] wohingegen, dagegen 121
wholesale and export clerk [ˌhəʊlseɪl ənd ˈekspɔːt ˌklɑːk] Kaufmann/-frau im Groß- und Außenhandel 8
wholesaler [ˈhəʊlˌseɪlə] Großhändler 217
wide range [ˌwaɪd ˈreɪndʒ] breite Palette 215
willing [ˈwɪlɪŋ] bereit 216
wireless [ˈwaɪələs] drahtlos 34
with order [wɪð ˈɔːdə] bei Auftragserteilung 185
to withdraw money from an account, withdrew, withdrawn [wɪðˈdrɔː ˌmʌni frəm ən əˈkaʊnt, wɪðˈdruː, wɪðˈdrɔːn] Geld von einem Konto abheben 183
without engagement [wɪˌðaʊt ɪnˈgeɪdʒmənt] freibleibend 142
to wonder [ˈwʌndə] sich fragen 65
wooden case [ˌwʊdn ˈkeɪs] Holzkiste 174
wording [ˈwɜːdɪŋ] Formulierung 184
word processor [ˈwɜːd ˌprəʊsesə] Textverarbeitungssystem/programm 59
word wrap [ˈwɜːd ˌræp] automatischer Zeilenumbruch 128
workforce [ˈwɜːkfɔːs] Belegschaft, Gesamtheit der Mitarbeiter 39
to work on one's own [ˌwɜːk ɒn wʌnz ˈəʊn] selbständig arbeiten 12
work-out [ˈwɜːkaʊt] Fitnesstraining 8
to work out [ˌwɜːk ˈaʊt] sich körperlich fit halten, trainieren 7
work placement [ˈwɜːk ˌpleɪsmənt] Praktikum 243
world championship [ˌwɜːld ˈtʃæmpiənʃɪp] Weltmeisterschaft 39
written order [ˌrɪtn ˈɔːdə] schriftliche Anweisung 183

Glossary | Anhang

Communication
Written communication
Spoken communication
Collocations relating to communication
On the phone
Information and communcations technology

Company organisation
Types of company and company structures
Departments and functions
Jobs and responsibilities
Places at work

Products, brands and marketing
Describing products
Marketing and promotion

Sales and distribution
Distribution channels
Terms of payment and delivery
Transport and shipping
Packing and labelling

Business travel
Preparation and booking
Flying and the airline industry
Hiring a car
Staying in a hotel
Rail travel
Conferences, trade fairs and exhibitions

Human resources
Hiring and firing
Wages and salaries
Training and assessment

Quality
Standards
Measures and approaches

Business and the economy
Business sectors
Cycles and trends
Government policy
Credit control and banking
International issues and policy

Hinweis: Glossar zum Herunterladen über Online-Link 808261-0000!

Communication

Written communication
agenda Tagesordnung
application Bewerbung, Antrag
attach, to anhängen
attachment Anhang *(E-Mail)*
brochure Broschüre, Prospekt
catalogue *(BE)*, catalog *(AE)* Katalog
contract Vertrag
documents Unterlagen
draft Entwurf
enclosure Anlage *(Brief)*
enquiry *(BE)*, inquiry *(AE)* Anfrage
leaflet Flugblatt, Infoblatt, Prospekt
letter Brief
message Nachricht
minutes Protokoll
notice Aushang
offer Angebot
order Auftrag, Bestellung
paperwork Verwaltungsarbeit, Schreibarbeit
post-it note Haftnotiz, Klebezettel
reminder (Zahlungs-)Erinnerung, Mahnung
report Bericht
schedule (≈ **itinerary, timetable**) Zeitplan, Fahrplan, Stundenplan
subject *(in a letter / e-mail)* Betreff
memo *(short for:* **memorandum***)* interne Notiz, Vermerk
paragraph Absatz, Paragraph

Spoken communication
advise, to beraten
advice Rat, Ratschlag
announce, to ankündigen, bekannt geben, ansagen
announcement (to make an announcement) Ankündigung, Bekanntgabe, Durchsage
apologise for something, to sich für etwas entschuldigen
apology Entschuldigung
available erhältlich, erreichbar, verfügbar
chat, to plaudern, schwätzen
controversy Kontroverse, Auseinandersetzung
debriefing Nachbesprechung
demonstration (to give / do a demonstration) Vorführung, Demonstration
dispute Streit
gossip, to schwätzen, plaudern
interview (to hold / give an interview) Interview, Vorstellungsgespräch
lecture (to hold / give a lecture) Vortrag, Vorlesung
negotiate, to verhandeln
negotiation Verhandlung
phone call (= **telephone conversation**) Telefongespräch

Anhang | Glossary

presentation (to give / do a presentation) Präsentation, Vortrag, Referat
speech (to hold / give a speech) Rede
thank somebody for something sich bei jemandem für etwas bedanken

Collocations relating to communication

circulate the agenda, to die Tagesordnung verteilen
clarify a matter, to eine Angelegenheit klären
co-ordinate an event, to eine Veranstaltung koordinieren/organisieren
confirm an agreement, to eine Vereinbarung bestätigen
have an objection to something, to (= to object to something) Einwand gegen etwas erheben, etwas beanstanden
liaise with colleagues / business partners, to zusammenarbeiten mit, in Verbindung stehen mit
make a complaint about something, to (= to complain) etwas reklamieren, sich über etwas beschweren
make an appointment, to einen Termin vereinbaren
make an enquiry, to (= to enquire about something) eine Anfrage machen
make an offer, to ein Angebot machen
make arrangements, to Vorkehrungen treffen
notify somebody of something, to jemanden über etwas informieren, jemandem Bescheid geben
place an order, to (with a firm / for a product) einen Auftrag erteilen
postpone an appointment, to einen Termin verschieben
solve a problem, to ein Problem lösen
take the minutes, to das Protokoll führen
update information, to Daten/Informationen aktualisieren
write up the minutes, to das Protokoll schreiben

On the phone

"I'll put you through." „Ich stelle Sie durch."
"Speaking." „Am Apparat."
"The line is busy."/"The line is engaged." „Die Leitung ist besetzt."
answerphone (BE), answering machine (BE), voice mail (AE) Anrufbeantworter
bad line schlechte Verbindung
dial the wrong number, to sich verwählen
dial, to wählen
extension Durchwahl
hang up, to auflegen
hold the line, to am Apparat bleiben
landline phone Festnetztelefon
leave a message, to eine Nachricht hinterlassen
mobile phone (BE), cell(ular) phone (AE) Mobiltelefon, Handy
put through, to durchstellen, verbinden
receiver Hörer
return a call, to zurückrufen

Information and communications technology (ICT)

cursor Cursor, Positionsmarke
click on something, to etwas anklicken
digital / computer projector Beamer
keyboard Tastatur
screen Bildschirm
text message SMS

Company organisation

Types of company and company structures

affiliate Schwestergesellschaft, Schwesterfirma
agency Agentur, Vertretung
board of directors Geschäftsleitung, Vorstand und Aufsichtsrat
branch Filiale, Niederlassung, Zweigstelle
company Firma, Gesellschaft
conglomerate Firmengruppe
consultancy Beratungsfirma
cooperative Genossenschaft
core business Hauptgeschäft, Kerngeschäft
cost centre Kostenstelle
executive board Vorstand
firm Firma
franchise Franchise
go public, to an die Börse gehen
group Konzern
headquarters Hauptsitz, Firmenzentrale, Hauptgeschäftsstelle
Inc. (= incorporated) *Abkürzung für amerikanische Kapitalgesellschaft*
joint stock company (BE), stock corporation (AE) Kapitalgesellschaft
limited liability beschränkte Haftung
limited partnership Kommanditgesellschaft
Ltd. (= limited company) *(etwa:)* GmbH
mail order business Versandhandel
multinational company (MNC) multinationales Unternehmen
offshoring das Auslagern ganzer Geschäftsprozesse ins Ausland
outsourcing Produktionsverlagerung *(z. B. ins Ausland)*
parent company Muttergesellschaft
partnership Personengesellschaft, *(etwa:)* OHG
PLC (= public limited company) (BE) britische Aktiengesellschaft
private limited company britische Gesellschaft mit beschränkter Haftung
retail outlet Verkaufsstelle
retailer Einzelhändler
self-employed selbständig
service provider Dienstleister
sole trader (BE), sole proprietorship (AE) Einzelunternehmer/in
stakeholder Interessenvertreter, Mitglied einer Interessengruppe
subcontractor Sub-Unternehmer
subsidiary Tochtergesellschaft, Tochterfirma
supervisory board Aufsichtsrat
supplier Lieferant, Zulieferer
wholesaler Großhändler

Departments and functions

accounts, accountancy Finanzbuchhaltung, Finanzabteilung
advertising Werbung
after-sales service Kundendienst
board of directors Direktion, Geschäftsleitung
customer service Kundendienst, Kundenbetreuung
department (dept.) Abteilung
distribution Vertrieb

executive board Vorstand
finance Finanz-
human resources (HR) / personnel Personal
legal department Rechtsabteilung
logistics Logistik
maintenance Wartung
marketing Marketing
organisation chart Organigramm
payroll Lohn- und Gehaltsabrechnung
PR (= public relations) Öffentlichkeitsarbeit
production Produktion
purchasing (≈ procurement) Einkauf, Beschaffung
quality assurance Qualitätssicherung
recruitment Personalbeschaffung
research and development (R&D) Forschung und Entwicklung
sales Verkauf
security Sicherheit
supervisory board Aufsichtsrat

Jobs and responsibilities

accountant Bilanzbuchhalter/in
administration Verwaltung
agent Vertreter/in *(auf Provisionsbasis)*
apprentice Lehrling, Auszubildende/r, Praktikant/in
automated teller machine (ATM) Geldautomat
back office Büro ohne Publikumsverkehr
blue-collar worker Arbeiter/in *(in der Produktion)*
board (of directors) Geschäftsleitung, Vorstand
boss Chef/in
caretaker *(BE)*, janitor *(AE)* Hausmeister/in
Chief Executive Officer (CEO) Vorstandsvorsitzende/r, Hauptgeschäftsführer/in
Chief Financial Officer Leiter/in der Finanzabteilung
clerical staff (= clerk) Büroangestellte
co-worker *(AE)* Mitarbeiter/in
colleague Kollege/Kollegin
consultant Berater/in
department head Abteilungsleiter/in
director Mitglied des Vorstands/Aufsichtsrats
employee Arbeitnehmer/in, Mitarbeiter/in
employer Arbeitgeber/in
executive leitende/r Angestellte/r
executive board Vorstand
founder Gründer/in
freelancer Freiberufler/in, freie/r Mitarbeiter/in
head of department / department, head Abteilungsleiter/in
internee Praktikant/in
management Geschäftsleitung
management assistant in office communication Kaufmann/-frau für Bürokommunikation
management assistant (industrial business) *(etwa:)* Industriekaufmann/-frau
managing director (MD) Geschäftsführer/in
office management assistant, office administration clerk Bürokaufmann/-frau
owner Eigentümer/in, Besitzer/in
PA (= personal assistant) *(etwa:)* Chefsektretär/in
person responsible Verantwortliche/r
predecessor Vorgänger/in
project manager Projektleiter/in, Projektmanager/in
sales representative Außendienstmitarbeiter/in, Vertriebsmitarbeiter/in

staff (= personnel) Personal
successor Nachfolger/in
supervisor Vorgesetzte/r, Betreuer/in, Aufseher/in, Kontrolleur/in
supervisory board Aufsichtsrat
team leader Teamleiter/in
technical support Technischer Dienst
temp (= temporary staff) Aushilfe, Zeitarbeiter/in
trainee Praktikant/in
trainer Ausbilder/in, Trainer/in
white-collar staff Büroangestellte
workforce Arbeiterschaft, Belegschaft

Places at work

canteen (= cafeteria) Kantine, Mensa
conference room Konferenzraum, Sitzungszimmer
conference venue Konferenzort, Tagungsort
desk Schreibtisch
environment Umwelt
factory Fabrik
infrastructure Infrastruktur
lift *(BE)*, elevator *(AE)* Aufzug
located, to be (≈ situated) sich befinden
location Ort
on the outskirts am Rande von (einer Stadt)
open-plan office Großraumbüro
plant Anlage
premises Räumlichkeiten, Firmengelände, Geschäftsräume
reception Empfang
relocation Standortwechsel, Umzug
shop floor (= production area) Produktionsbereich, Fertigungsbereich
stockroom Lager, Lagerraum
venue Veranstaltungsort
warehouse Lager, Lagerhalle
work station Arbeitsplatz, Arbeitsstation
workshop Werkstatt

Products, brands and marketing

Describing products

additives Zusatzstoffe
affordable bezahlbar, erschwinglich
approximately (approx.) ungefähr, zirca (ca.)
brand image Markenimage
brand loyalty Markentreue
brand name Markenname
commodity Handelsware, Handelsgut, Gebrauchsgut
convenient praktisch, gelegen, bequem
convert (conversion), to umrechnen, konvertieren (Umrechnung)
device Gerät, Mittel
economical sparsam, effizient, wirtschaftlich
environmentally-friendly umweltfreundlich
equipment Gerät, Ausrüstung, Ausstattung
fabric Stoff
faulty defekt, fehlerhaft
feature Eigenschaft, Merkmal
fuel capacity Benzinverbrauch
handy praktisch, nützlich

have a good reputation for something, to einen guten Ruf in Bezug auf etwas haben
high (height) hoch (Höhe)
industrial goods Industriegüter, Investitionsgüter, Produktionsgüter
ingredient Zutat
label Label, Marke
long (length) lang (Länge)
manufacturer's brand Herstellermarke
measure (measurement), to messen (Maß)
merchandise Ware, Handelsware, Handelsgüter
on average im Durchschnitt
option (Auswahl-)Möglichkeit
practical (practicality) praktisch (Nutzbarkeit)
product line Produktlinie
product range Produkpalette, Produktsortiment
prototype Prototyp
range Sortiment, Auswahl
reliability Zuverlässigkeit
sell well, to sich gut verkaufen (lassen)
speed Geschwindigkeit
standard version Standardausführung
state-of-the-art auf dem neuesten Stand der Technik
sturdy robust
stylish (to have style) stilvoll (Stil haben)
synthetic künstlich, aus Kunststoff
tool Werkzeug
trademark Markenzeichen, Schutzmarke, Warenzeichen
unreliable (unreliability) unzuverlässig (Unzuverlässigkeit)
up-to-date modern, aktuell
user-friendly benutzerfreundlich, anwenderfreundlich
weigh (weight), to wiegen (Gewicht)
well-designed gut gestaltet, gut konzipiert
wide (width) breit, weit (Breite)

Marketing and promotion

account manager (≠ accounts manager) Kundenbetreuer/in (≠ Finanzmanager/in)
advertise, to werben
advertisement Werbung, Annonce, Reklame
advertising Werbung *(als Tätigkeit)*
advertising strategy Werbestrategie
after-sales Kundendienst
appeal Anziehungskraft, Reiz
associate something with something, to eine Sache mit etwas in Verbindung bringen
attract, to anziehen
benefit Nutzen, Vorteil
claim (to make a claim) Anspruch, Behauptung, Werbeversprechen
commercial Werbespot
compete with, to konkurrieren mit
competition Konkurrenz, Wettbewerb, Preisausschreiben
competitive konkurrenzfähig, wettbewerbsfähig
competitor Konkurrent/in
consumer Verbraucher/in, Konsument/in
consumption Verbrauch
demand (for) Nachfrage (nach)
demonstrate, to vorführen
end user Endverbraucher/in
enter a market, to einen neuen Markt erschließen
event Veranstaltung
feature (≈ characteristic) Eigenschaft, Merkmal

field research Feldforschung, Primärforschung
giveaway (= freebie) Werbegeschenk
launch a product on(to) the market, to ein Produkt auf den Markt bringen/einführen
margin Gewinnmarge, Handelsspanne
market research Marktforschung
market share Marktanteil
marketing campaign Marketingkampagne
market penetration Marktdurchdringung
marketing mix Marketing-Mix
mass-market Massenmarkt
media Medien
niche market Marktniche, Nischenmarkt
offer, to (offer) anbieten (Angebot)
packaging Verkaufsverpackung
persuade, to (persuasion, persuasive) überzeugen, überreden
phase out a product, to ein Produkt (langsam) auslaufen lassen
press release Pressemitteilung
product development Produktentwicklung
promotional item Werbegeschenk
prospective customer (prospect) Kaufinteressent/in
public relations Öffentlichkeitsarbeit
purchasing power Kaukraft
questionnaire Fragebogen
quote / quotation Preisangebot, Zitat
sales Absatz, Verkauf, Schlussverkauf
sample Muster, Probe, Kostprobe
segment (≠ sector) Segment
slogan Werbespruch
special offer Sonderangebot
subject to availability (= while stocks last) solange der Vorrat reicht
survey (to carry out / conduct a survey) Umfrage
target market / group Zielmarkt, angestrebter Markt
target, to als Zielgruppe nehmen
trade fair Handelsmesse
withdraw a product from the market, to ein Produkt aus dem Markt nehmen, oder nicht mehr anbieten

Sales and distribution

Distribution channels

agency contract Händlervertrag
agent Handelsvertreter/in *(auf Provisionsbasis)*
bulk delivery Großlieferung
buy in bulk, to in großen Mengen einkaufen
chain Kette, Ladenkette
commission Provision
contractual relationship Vertragsverhältnis
department store Kaufhaus
discount store Billigladen
distribution channels Vertriebswege
distributor Lieferant, Händler, Vertragshändler, Vertreiber
distribution chain Absatzkette, Verteilerkette
expenses, to incur Auslagen/Kosten übernehmen
factory outlet Direktverkauf, Fabrikverkauf
franchising Franchising *(Vertriebsform)*
intermediary (= middleman) Zwischenhändler
mail order Versandhaus

mall *(AE)*, shopping centre *(BE)* Einkaufszentrum
outlet Verkaufsstelle
retail outlet Einzelhandelsgeschäft, Einzelhandelsverkaufsstelle
retailer Einzelhändler/in
retailing, retail Einzelhandel
specialty store *(AE)*, speciality shop *(BE)* Fachgeschäft
supply chain Lieferkette
telesales / telemarketing Telefonmarketing
trader (= dealer) Händler
wholesale, wholesaling Großhandel
wholesaler Großhändler

Terms of payment and delivery
at your expense auf Ihre Kosten
cash discount (= early-payment discount) Skonto
cash on delivery (= payment on delivery) Zahlung bei Lieferung
DDP (delivered, duty paid) frei Haus, verzollt geliefert
ex works ab Werk
guarantee, to garantieren
handling charges Abladegebühren, Bearbeitungsgebühren
loyalty rebate Treuerabatt
make an offer, to ein Angebot machen
place an order, to einen Auftrag erteilen, eine Bestellung aufgeben
purchase, to kaufen
quantity discount (= bulk-purchase discount) Mengenrabatt
sales contract Kaufvertrag
to your premises an Ihre Firma / auf Ihr Firmengelände
trade discount Handelsrabatt
trial order Probeauftrag
warranty (= guarantee) Garantie

Transport and shipping
aircraft Flugzeug *(Sammelbegriff)*
bulky goods sperrige Waren
cargo Fracht, Ladung
carrier Frachtführer
commodities Handelswaren, Rohstoffe
consignee Empfänger (einer Warensendung)
consignment Warensendung, Lieferung
consignor Versender (einer Warensendung)
consolidated shipment Sammelladung, Sammeltransport
consulate Konsulat
country of destination Bestimmungsland
country of origin Ursprungsland, Herkunftsland
customs clearance Zollabfertigung
damage Beschädigung, Schaden
delayed verspätet
deliver, to liefern
delivery Lieferung
delivery van Lieferwagen
depot Lager, Warendepot
destination Ziel, Bestimmungsort
dispatch, to versenden
dispatch / despatch Versand
distance Entfernung
docks Hafen
embassy Botschaft
EU single market EU-Binnenmarkt
exporter Exporteur
forwarder, forwarding agent, forwarding agency, freight forwarder Spedition / Spediteur
freight Fracht
freight train Güterzug
haulier, haulage company Lkw-Unternehmer, Lkw-Spediteur
helicopter Hubschrauber
importer Importeur
in stock, to have am Lager führen, vorrätig haben
in time rechtzeitig
in transit auf dem Transportweg
inland waterway Binnengewässer, Wasserstraße
merchandise Waren
modes of transport Transportmittel
on time pünktlich
paperwork Formalitäten, Dokumentation
port of destination Bestimmungshafen
port of shipment Verschiffungshafen
receipt of delivery Empfangsbeleg, Wareneingang
ship goods, to Waren versenden
shipment Warensendung, Lieferung
shipper Versender
shipping (= delivery) Verschiffung, Versand
shipping documents Versanddokumente
stock Lagerbestand, Vorrat
truck *(AE)*, lorry *(BE)* Lastwagen
vehicle Fahrzeug
vessel (≈ ship) Schiff, Wasserfahrzeug
warehouse Lager (≠ Warenhaus)
warehousing Lagerung

Packing and labelling
bar-code Strichcode, Balkencode, Barcode
cardboard box Pappkarton
crate Lattenkiste
fragile zerbrechlich
hazardous gefährlich
inflammable entzündbar, brennbar, feuergefährlich
label Etikett, Bezeichnung
labelled beschriftet, gekennzeichnet, etikettiert, bezeichnet
markings Markierungen
packing (≠ packaging) Versandverpackung
packing list Packliste
pallet Palette
protection Schutz
sell-by-date Haltbarkeitsdatum
shrink wrap Schrumpffolie
sturdy robust
toxic waste Giftmüll

Business travel

Preparation and booking
appointment (≠ date), to book / make an appointment Termin, Verabredung, einen Termin vereinbaren
arrangements, to make arrangements Vorkehrungen
arrival Ankunft
cancel, to stornieren
cancellation Stornierung
change (trains, buses), to umsteigen

Anhang | Glossary

confirm, to bestätigen
confirmation Bestätigung
connection Anschlussflug, -zug
delay Verspätung
departure Abfahrt, Abflug
fare Fahrpreis, Flugpreis
miss a connection, to einen Anschluss verpassen
return ticket *(BE)*, round-trip ticket *(AE)* Rückfahrkarte, Hin- und Rückreise
stopover Zwischenstopp
take out insurance, to eine Versicherung abschließen
travel agent Reisebüro
travel expenses Reisekosten, Spesen
travel insurance Reiseversicherung

Flying and the airline industry
airline Fluggesellschaft
aisle seat Sitzplatz am Gang
baggage / luggage Reisegepäck
baggage / luggage trolley *(BE)*, luggage cart *(AE)* Gepäckwagen
board a flight, to an Bord eines Flugzeugs gehen
boarding pass / card Bordkarte
carrier Fluglinie *(Gesellschaft)*
declare something etwas zollamtlich melden
fasten one's seatbelt, to sich anschnallen
hand luggage *(BE)*, carry on luggage *(AE)* Handgepäck
long-haul flight Langstreckenflug
overhead compartment *(BE)*, bin *(AE)* Gepäckfach
runway Laufbahn
security Sicherheitskontrolle
short-haul flight Kurzstreckenflug
take off, to starten
taxes and charges Steuern und Gebühren
window seat Sitzplatz am Fenster

Hiring a car
car hire / rental Autovermietung
driving licence *(BE)*, driver's license *(AE)* Führerschein
fully comprehensive insurance Vollkaskoversicherung
hire / rental car Mietwagen
left- / right-hand drive Linkssteuerung / Rechtssteuerung
mileage Kilometerstand, Kilometer(leistung)
petrol *(BE)*, gas *(AE)* Benzin
pick up the car, to das Auto abholen
third-party (insurance) Haftpflichtversicherung
vehicle Fahrzeug

Staying in a hotel
breakfast buffet Frühstücksbuffett
complimentary gratis, kostenlos
corporate rates (special prices for companies) Firmentarife
double room with shower Doppelzimmer mit Dusche
ensuite bathroom eigenes Bad *(Hotelzimmer)*
hair dryer Fön, Haartrockner
ironing board Bügelbrett
porter Portier
reception Empfang
registration form Anmeldeformular
room service Zimmerservice
single room Einzelzimmer
spa Wellness-Einrichtung, Kurort

Rail travel
buffet car Speisewagen
carriage *(BE)*, car *(AE)* Wagen
communication cord Notbremse
connection Anschlusszug
forward- / rear-facing seat Sitz in Fahrtrichtung / in entgegengesetzter Fahrtrichtung
late-running train verspäteter Zug
platform Gleis, Bahnsteig
season ticket Saisonticket, Zeitkarte

Conferences, trade fairs and exhibitions
badge, button Namensetikett
booth Messestand
business card (≠ visiting card) Visitenkarte
convention centre Kongresszentrum
delegate Messebesucher/in
demonstration Vorführung
display Anzeigetafel
event Veranstaltung
exhibition Ausstellung, Messe
exhibition hall, exhibit hall Messehalle
exhibitor Aussteller/in
freebies (= giveaways) Werbegeschenke
guide (Messe-) Führer
hospitality Bewirtung, Gastfreundlichkeit
host Gastgeber/in
prospective customer Interessent/in
purchaser (= buyer) Einkäufer/in
register, to sich anmelden
registration Anmeldung
sales literature Verkaufsliteratur
salesperson Standdienst, Vertriebsmitarbeiter/in
sample Muster, Probe
site map Ortsplan, Übersichtsplan
speaker (= presenter) Referent/in
stand (≈ booth) Messestand, Ausstellungsstand
trade fair (= trade show, expo) (Handels-)Messe
venue Veranstaltungsort

Human resources

Hiring and firing
applicant Bewerber/in
application form Bewerbungsformular
application letter Bewerbungsschreiben
apply for a job / a post, to sich bewerben
candidate Kandidat/in
closing date for applications Bewerbungsschluss
covering letter *(BE)*, cover letter *(AE)* Begleitbrief
CV (= curriculum vitae) *(BE)*, résumé *(AE)* Lebenslauf
degree Hochschulabschluss
dismiss, to entlassen
entry requirments Zugangsvoraussetzungen
hand in one's notice, to die Kündigung einreichen, kündigen
interview Vorstellungsgespräch
job advertisement Stellenanzeige, Stellenausschreibung
job description Stellenbeschreibung
job vacancy offene Stelle
lay (someone) off, to (jemanden) entlassen

make (someone) redundant, to (jemanden) entlassen, freisetzen, überflüssig machen
period of notice Kündigungsfrist
recruit, to einstellen, anwerben, rekrutieren
recruitment Personalbeschaffung
reference *(BE)*, **testimonial** *(AE)* Referenzschreiben, Zeugnis
rejection letter Absagebrief
replacement Vertretung, Nachfolger/in
take (someone) on, to jemanden einstellen
vacancy offene Stelle *(Arbeit)*
without notice fristlos

Wages and salaries

annual salary Jahresgehalt
benefits Zusatzleistungen, Sozialleistungen
bonus Gratifikation
commission Provision
expenses Auslagen
expenses claim form Reisekostenabrechnungsformular
fee (for a service) Honorar
holiday pay Urlaubsgeld
hourly rate Stundensatz
lump sum payment Pauschalbetrag
minimum wage Mindestlohn
payment by seniority Zahlung nach Betriebszugehörigkeit
pay rise *(BE)*, **raise** *(AE)* Gehaltserhöhung
pension Rente, Pension
performance-related pay leistungsorientierte Bezahlung
perks (= fringe benefits) Zusatzleistungen des Arbeitgebers *(außer Gehalt/Lohn)*
redundancy pay *(BE)*, **severance pay** *(AE)* Abfindung
reimburse, to (rück)erstatten
salary Gehalt
unemployment benefit Arbeitslosengeld
wage Lohn
weekly wage Wochenlohn

Training and assessment

apprentice Auszubildende/r
apprenticeship Ausbildung, Lehre
assess, to bewerten, evaluieren
assessment Bewertung, Evaluierung
evaluate, to bewerten, evaluieren
job satisfaction Zufriedenheit am Arbeitsplatz
peer pressure Gruppendruck
promote, to befördern
promotion Beförderung
skills Fertigkeiten, Fähigkeiten, Kompetenzen
track record Erfolgsbilanz, (gute) Leistungen am Arbeitsplatz
trainee Auszubildende/r, Praktikant/in, Lehrling
training course Ausbildung
vocational training berufliche Aus-/Weiterbildung, Berufsausbildung

Quality

Standards

below standard, to be unter dem Standard sein
compliance (with) Einhaltung, Übereinstimmung (mit)
comply with, to einhalten
conforming to specifications / requirements genau nach den technischen Vorgaben; den Vorschriften entsprechend
customer satisfaction Kundenzufriedenheit
error Irrtum, Fehler
exceed expectations, to die Erwartungen übertreffen
excellent exzellent
fragile zerbrechlich
fulfil a requirement, to (= to meet a need) eine Voraussetzung/Bedingung erfüllen
improve (in quality), to (sich) verbessern
in compliance with entsprechend, gemäß, in Übereinstimmung mit
International Standards Organisation (ISO) ISO (Internationale Organisation für Normung)
maintain standards, to Standards einhalten
non-compliance Nichteinhaltung
of (a) high / good / top quality, to be von hervorragender Güte/Spitzenqualität sein
of (a) low / poor / varying quality, to be von minderwertiger Güte/Qualität sein
of a high standard, to be hohen Standard erfüllen
of a low standard, to be von niedrigem Standard sein
out of service außer Betrieb
poorly-designed schlecht konstruiert sein
satisfy customers, to Kunden zufriedenstellen
set high standards, to hohe Anforderungen stellen
up to standard, to be den Anforderungen entsprechen
value for money Preis-Leistungs-Verhältnis
waste Verschwendung

Measures and approaches

benchmarking Benchmarking, Vergleichstest
best practice optimaler Geschäftsablauf, bestes Verfahren
carry out checks, to Kontrollmaßnahmen durchführen, kontrollieren
certification Zerfifizierung, Abnahme
customer feedback Kundenbewertung
investigate, to untersuchen, ermitteln
inspection Besichtigung, Prüfung, Kontrolle
external audit außerbetriebliche Revision/Prüfung
internal audit betriebseigene Revision/Prüfung
Just-in-time (JIT) bedarfsorientierte Produktion
peer review Begutachtung, geregelte Kollegenkontrolle
performance appraisal Leistungsbeurteilung
procedure Verfahren
quality audit Qualitätsaudit, Qualitätsmanagement
quality control Qualitätskontrolle
questionnaire Umfrage
random sample Stichprobe, Zufallsauswahl
spot check Stichprobe
verify, to auf Richtigkeit prüfen, kontrollieren
validation Gültigkeitsprüfung, Bewertung, Bestätigung
verification Nachweis, Nachprüfung, Feststellung der Richtigkeit

Business and the economy

Business sectors
automotive Automobil
biotechnology Biotechnologie, Biotechnik
chemicals Chemikalien
civil engineering Hoch- und Tiefbau
construction Bauwesen, Konstruktion
consumer electronics Unterhaltungselektronik
energy Energie, Strom
engineering Maschinenbau, Technik
financial services Finanzdienstleistungen
food and beverages Lebensmittel
furniture and furnishings Möbel und Ausstattung
healthcare Gesundheitsversorgung
household goods Haushaltswaren
insurance Versicherung
manufacturing Herstellung, Produktion, Fertigung
media and publishing Medien- und Verlagsbuchhandel
pharmaceuticals Pharmaindustrie, Arzneimittelindustrie
restaurant and catering Gastronomie
retail Einzelhandel
telecommunications Telekommunikationsbranche
tourism and leisure Touristik
transport and logistics Transport und Logistik
waste and recycling Wiederverwertung
wholesale Großhandel

Cycles and trends
average, to durchschnittlich betragen
boom Hochkonjunktur
business cycle Konjunktur, Konjunkturzyklus
climb, to steigern, klettern
cycle (Konjunktur-)Zyklus
decline, to sinken, fallen
decrease, to sinken, fallen
depression langanhaltende Rezession
dip, to (sich) senken, abfallen
downturn Abschwung
fluctuate, to (fluctuation) schwanken (Schwankung)
go up, to steigern
growth (= expansion) Wachstum
hit a low / a high einen Tiefpunkt / einen Höhepunkt erreichen
improve, to (sich) verbessern
improvement Verbesserung
increase, to steigern
on average im Durchschnitt
reach a peak, to einen Höchststand erreichen
recession Rezession, Tiefkonjunktur
recover, to sich erholen
rise Anstieg
rise, to ansteigen
shrink, to schrumpfen
slowdown (in the economy) Abschwung, Konjunkturrückgang
stand at, to stehen bei, liegen bei
steady gleichbleibend, stabil

Government policy
bail (a company) out, to finanziell retten
base rate / prime rate / minimum lending rate *(BE)*, **discount rate** *(AE)* Diskontsatz
borrowing Verschuldung
business cycle Konjunktur
currency Währung
debt relief Schuldenerlass
default on one's debts, to die Schulden nicht zahlen
deficit spending öffentliche Verschuldung durch Geldaufnahme
deregulation Zahlungsbilanz
devalue, to abwerten
domestic demand Binnennachfrage
economic wirtschafts-, wirtschaftlich, volkswirtschaftlich
economic recovery plans / packages Konjunkturprogramme, Rettungspakete
economic system Wirtschaftssystem
economical wirtschaftlich *(im Sinne von sparsam)*
economist Wirtschaftswissenschaftler/in
economy Wirtschaft
exchange rate Wechselkurs
expenditure on Ausgaben für
fiscal policy Steuerpolitik, Finanzpolitik
globalisation Globalisierung
government policy Regierungspolitik, Politik
impose, to auferlegen, einführen
infrastructure Infrastruktur
legislation Gesetzgebung
monetary policy Geldpolitik
public debt Staatsverschuldung
public opinion öffentliche Meinung
public spending öffentliche Ausgaben, Staatsausgaben
quota (≈ limit on imports) Mengenbeschränkung
regulators Regulierungsbehörde
revaluation (of a currency) Aufwertung (einer Währung)
shorter working hours Arbeitszeitverkürzung
subsidise, to subventionieren
subsidy Subvention
taxation Besteuerung
trade barriers Handelsbeschränkungen
write off a debt, to Schulden abschreiben

Credit control and banking
access, to Zugang (haben)
account Konto
afford, to sich leisten können
affordable erschwinglich, bezahlbar
allocate, to zuteilen, zuordnen
assets Vermögen
ATM (= automated teller machine) Bankautomat
balance Kontostand, Saldo, Bilanz
bank account Bankkonto
bank balance (= account balance) Kontostand, Saldo
bank details Bankverbindung, Kontoverbindung
bank loan Bankkredit, Darlehen
bank statement Kontoauszug
bargain, to handeln *(um Preise)*
bill *(AE)* Banknote, Geldschein, Rechnung
bill, to berechnen, Rechnung senden
borrow, to (sich) ausleihen, borgen
budget Budget, Haushalt
budgeting Budgetierung, Haushaltsplanung
cash Bar, Bargeld
cash flow Cashflow
cash in, to einlösen
cashless payment bargeldlose Zahlung

charge, to berechnen, belasten, in Rechnung stellen
clear a cheque, to einen Scheck verrechnen
coin Münze, Geldstück
compensation Entschädigung, Schadensersatz
credit card Kreditkarte
credit limit Dispolimit
credit period Kreditlaufzeit, Zahlungsziel
credit risk Kreditrisiko
credit transfer Überweisung
creditworthiness Bonität, Kreditwürdigkeit, Zahlungsfähigkeit
creditworthy kreditwürdig
current account Girokonto
debit card Kundenkarte, EC-Karte
debt Schuld
deduct, to abziehen
deposit Einlage, Pfand, Anzahlung
deposit, to einzahlen
discount Rabatt, Skonto
do a deal, to ein Geschäft machen
donate, to spenden
donation Spende
due fällig
earn, to verdienen
earnings Einkommen, Einkünfte
exchange rate Wechselkurs
expenditure Ausgaben
expense Kosten, Aufwand
expensive (= costly) teuer
fare Fahrpreis
fee Gebühr
fine Geldstrafe
fraud Betrug, Hinterziehung
get into debt, to sich verschulden
grant Zuschuss
handling fee Bearbeitungsgebühr
identity theft Identitätsdiebstahl
in advance im Voraus
in return als Gegenleistung
in the black schwarze Zahlen schreiben
in the red rote Zahlen schreiben
income Einkommen, Einkünfte
instalment Rate
interest Zins(en)
interest rate Zinssatz
invest, to (Geld) anlegen
investments Geldanlagen
invoice Rechnung
invoice, to Rechnung senden, berechnen
issue, to ausstellen
late payment Zinsverzug
lease, to pachten, leasen, mieten
lend, to ausleihen
letter of credit Akkreditiv
liquidity Liquidität
loan Darlehen, Kredit
loss Verlust
overdue überfällig
pay off the balance, to den Restbetrag bezahlen
payment terms Zahlungsbedingungen
postage and packing Porto und Verpackung
prepaid card Prepaid Karte
profit(s) Gewinn

purchase, to kaufen
query Rückfrage
rebate Rückerstattung *(falls zu viel bezahlt worden ist)*
receipt Beleg, Quittung
reduction Preisnachlass
refund Rückerstattung
refund, to rückerstatten, vergüten
reminder Zahlungserinnerung, Mahnung
rent Miete
revenue Einkommen, Einkünfte
savings account Sparkonto
settle a debt / an invoice, to Schulden/eine Rechnung begleichen
spend, to (Geld) ausgeben
standing order Dauerauftrag
subtotal Zwischensumme
subtract, to abziehen
terms and conditions Allgemeine Geschäftsbedingungen (AGB)
tip, to Trinkgeld geben
transfer, to überweisen
unit price Stückpreis, Einzelpreis
wealth Wohlstand
welfare Wohlfahrt
withdraw, to (Geld) abheben
withdrawal Abhebung

International issues and policy

apply for a licence, to eine Lizenz beantragen
arrange insurance, to eine Versicherung abschließen
balance of trade (= trade balance) Handelsbilanz
customs clearance Zollabfertigung
deal with customs formalities, to Zollformalitäten bearbeiten
domestic trade Binnenhandel, inländischer Handel
dumping unter Preis anbieten
fair trade fairer Handel
foreign trade Außenhandel
free trade Freihandel
international trade Welthandel, Außenhandel, internationaler Handel
negotiate terms of payment and delivery Zahlungs- und Lieferbedingungen verhandeln
notify the exporter that the goods have arrived, to den Lieferanten über den Empfang der Waren informieren
open an L/C in favour of the supplier, to ein Akkreditiv eröffnen zugunsten des Lieferanten
protectionism Protektionismus, Schutzzollpolitik
quota Kontingent, Quote
sign the sales contract, to den Kaufvertrag unterschreiben
subsidy Subvention
tariff (Einfuhr-)Zoll
trade deficit / surplus Außenhandelsdefizit/-überschuss
trade term Handelsklausel
transfer the invoice amount, to den Rechnungsbetrag überweisen
translate documents, to Unterlagen übersetzen

Acronyms and abbreviations

Abbreviation: shortened form of a word
Acronym: abbreviation formed from the first letters of each word in a term

Short form **Full form** German

a.m. / am ante meridian morgens/vormittags (24 Uhr – 12 Uhr)
approx. approximately ungefähr
asap as soon as possible so schnell wie möglich
ATM automated teller machine Geldautomat
Attn. for the attention of zu Händen (von)
B / E bill of exchange Wechsel
B / L bill of lading Konnossement, Frachtbrief
B2B business to business Business-to-Business
BIC bank identifier code internationaler Bank-Code
BOP balance of payments Zahlungsbilanz
BOT balance of trade Handelsbilanz
BRIC Brazil, Russia, India, China Brasilien, Russland, Indien, China
cc carbon copy, copy circulated, cubic centimeters (Kohlepapier-)Durchschlag, Verteiler, Kubikzentimeter
CEO Chief Executive Officer (etwa:) (Haupt-)Geschäftsführer/in, Firmenchef/in, Vorstandsvorsitzende/r
CFO Chief Financial Officer Finanzleiter/in
CIF cost, insurance and freight (Incoterm) Kosten, Versicherung und Fracht
COD cash on delivery Lieferung per Nachnahme
CPT carriage paid to (Incoterm) frachtfrei, Fracht bezahlt
CRM customer relationship management Kundendienst, Kundenbetreuung
CV curriculum vitae Lebenslauf
CWO cash with order Zahlung bei Auftragserteilung
D / A documents against acceptance Dokumente gegen Akzept
D / P documents against payment Kasse gegen Dokumente
DAP delivery at place (Incoterm) geliefert benannter Ort
DAT delivery at terminal (Incoterm) geliefert Terminal
DDP delivered, duty paid (Incoterm) frei Haus, verzollt geliefert
dept. Department Abteilung
e.g. exempli gratia = for example zum Beispiel (z. B.)
encl. enclosed beiliegend, in der Anlage
etc. etcetera und so weiter (usw.)
EU European Union Europäische Union (EU)
EXW ex works (Incoterm) ab Werk
FAO for the attention of zu Händen von
FAQ frequently asked question häufig gestellte Frage
FAS free alongside ship (Incoterm) frei Längsseite Schiff
FOB free on board (Incoterm) frei an Bord
GDP gross domestic product Bruttoinlandsprodukt (BIP)
GNP gross national product Bruttosozialprodukt (BSP)
HQ headquarters Hauptsitz, Zentrale
HR human resources Personalabteilung, -wesen
i.e. id est (Latin) = that is das heißt (d. h.)
IBAN International Bank Account Number Internationale Kontonummer
ICC International Chamber of Commerce Internationale Industrie- und Handelskammer (ICC)
IMF International Monetary Fund Internationaler Währungsfond
Inc.; inc incorporated (AE) Aktiengesellschaft

ISO International Standards Organisation ISO (Norm)
JIT just-in-time bedarfsorientierte Produktion (gerade rechtzeitig)
L / C letter of credit Akkreditiv
lbs pounds Pfunde (Gewicht)
Ltd. limited mit beschränkter Haftung
MD managing director Geschäftsführer/in
MNC multinational company multinationales Unternehmen
mph miles per hour Meilen pro Stunde (Geschwindigkeit)
NGO non-governmental organisation Nichtregierungsorganisation
no. number Nummer (Nr.)
OPEC Organisation of the Petroleum Exporting Countries Organisation erdölexportierender Länder (OPEC)
P&L Profit and Loss Gewinn und Verlust
p.a. per annum jährlich, pro Jahr
p.m. / pm post meridian nachmittags/abends (12 Uhr – 24 Uhr)
PIN Personal Identification Number PIN (Erkennungsnummer)
plc / PLC public limited company (etwa:) AG
pp paginae = pages Seiten
pp / ppa per procurationem = on behalf of im Auftrag von
PR public relations Öffentlichkeitsarbeit
R&D research and development Forschung und Entwicklung
Re. regarding bezüglich
Re. reply (e-mail) Antwort
Ref. reference Aktenzeichen
ROI return on investment Rentabilität, Kapitalertrag
SME small and medium(-sized) enterprise (BE); small to mid-sized enterprise (AE) Mittelstand; kleines und mittelständisches Unternehmen (KMU)
sq. square Quadrat (Maß), Platz (Ort)
SWOT Strengths, Weaknesses, Opportunities, Threats Stärken, Schwächen, Möglichkeiten, Gefahren/Risiken
WTO World Trade Organisation Welthandelsorganisation

False friends

False friends (= falsche Freunde) sind Wörter, die in Deutsch und Englisch identisch oder ähnlich aussehen, die aber nicht dieselbe Bedeutung haben. Im besten Fall kann das zu bloß lustigen, im schlimmsten Fall aber zu peinlichen oder gefährlichen Missverständnissen führen. Die wichtigsten falschen Freunde sollte man also gut kennen.

Deutsch	Englische Bedeutung	Nicht zu verwechseln mit	Deutsch
aktuell	topical, current(ly)	actual	wirklich, tatsächlich
also	therefore, then	also	auch
bald	soon	bald	kahl, glatzköpfig
bekommen	to receive, to get	to become	werden
Billion	1,000,000,000,000.00	billion	Milliarde
blamieren	to embarrass	to blame	jemanden beschuldigen
Brief	letter	brief	kurz
Chef	boss	chef chief *(adjective)*	Chefkoch haupt-, Haupt-
dezent	discreet, modest	decent	anständig; nett, großzügig
Direktion	management, administration	direction	Richtung
Distanz	detachment, coolness	distance	Entfernung
Dose	can, tin	dose	Dosis
engagiert	involved	engaged	verlobt; besetzt *(Telefon)*
eventuell	possibly, maybe	eventually	endlich, schließlich
Fabrik	factory, works	fabric	Gewebe, Stoff
familiär	family-related	familiar	bekannt
fast	almost	fast	schnell
Fotograf	photographer	photograph	Foto
Gift	poison	gift	Geschenk
Gymnasium	secondary school, high school *(AE)*, grammar school *(BE)*	gym(nasium)	Turnhalle
Handy	cellular / mobile phone	handy *(adjective)*	praktisch
Hochschule	college, university	high school	Gymnasium, Oberschule
irritieren	confuse, distract	irritate	ärgern, auf die Nerven gehen
Kaution	deposit	caution	Vorsicht
Klosett	toilet	closet	Verschlag, Wandschrank
Konkurrenz	competition	concurrence	Übereinstimmung
konsequent	consistent	consequently	infolgedessen
kontrollieren	check, monitor	control	steuern, regulieren
Kritik	criticism	critic	Kritiker / in
Mappe	briefcase, folder	map	Landkarte
Meinung	opinion	meaning	Bedeutung

Anhang | Glossary

Deutsch	Englische Bedeutung	Nicht zu verwechseln mit	Deutsch
Menü	set meal	menu	Speisekarte; Menü (Computer)
Messe	trade fair, show	mess	Unordnung
Note	mark (school)	note	Notiz
ordinär	vulgar, cheap	ordinary	üblich, normal
Pension	small hotel	pension	Rente
plump	tactless, awkward, clumsy	plump	mollig
prinzipiell	on principle	principally	hauptsächlich
Promotion	doctor's exam	promotion	Beförderung, Förderung
Prospekt	brochure, leaflet	prospect	Aussicht
Provision	commission, percentage of price	provision	Vorsorge
prüfen	check	prove	beweisen
rentabel	profitable	rentable	(ver)mietbar
Rente	pension	rent	Miete
Rezept	recipe (cooking) prescription (medical)	receipt	Quittung
Rückseite	back, rear	backside	Hinterteil
selbstbewusst	self-confident	self-conscious	schüchtern, gehemmt
sensibel	sensitive	sensible	vernünftig
seriös	reliable	serious	ernsthaft
spenden	donate	to spend	ausgeben
Sympathie	a liking, a feeling of solidarity	sympathy	Mitleid
sympathisch	likable, nice	sympathetic	mitfühlend
übersehen	overlook, miss something	oversee	überwachen
Unternehmer	businessman, businesswoman, employer	undertaker	Leichenbestatter
Warenhaus	department store	warehouse	Lagerhalle

World map | Anhang

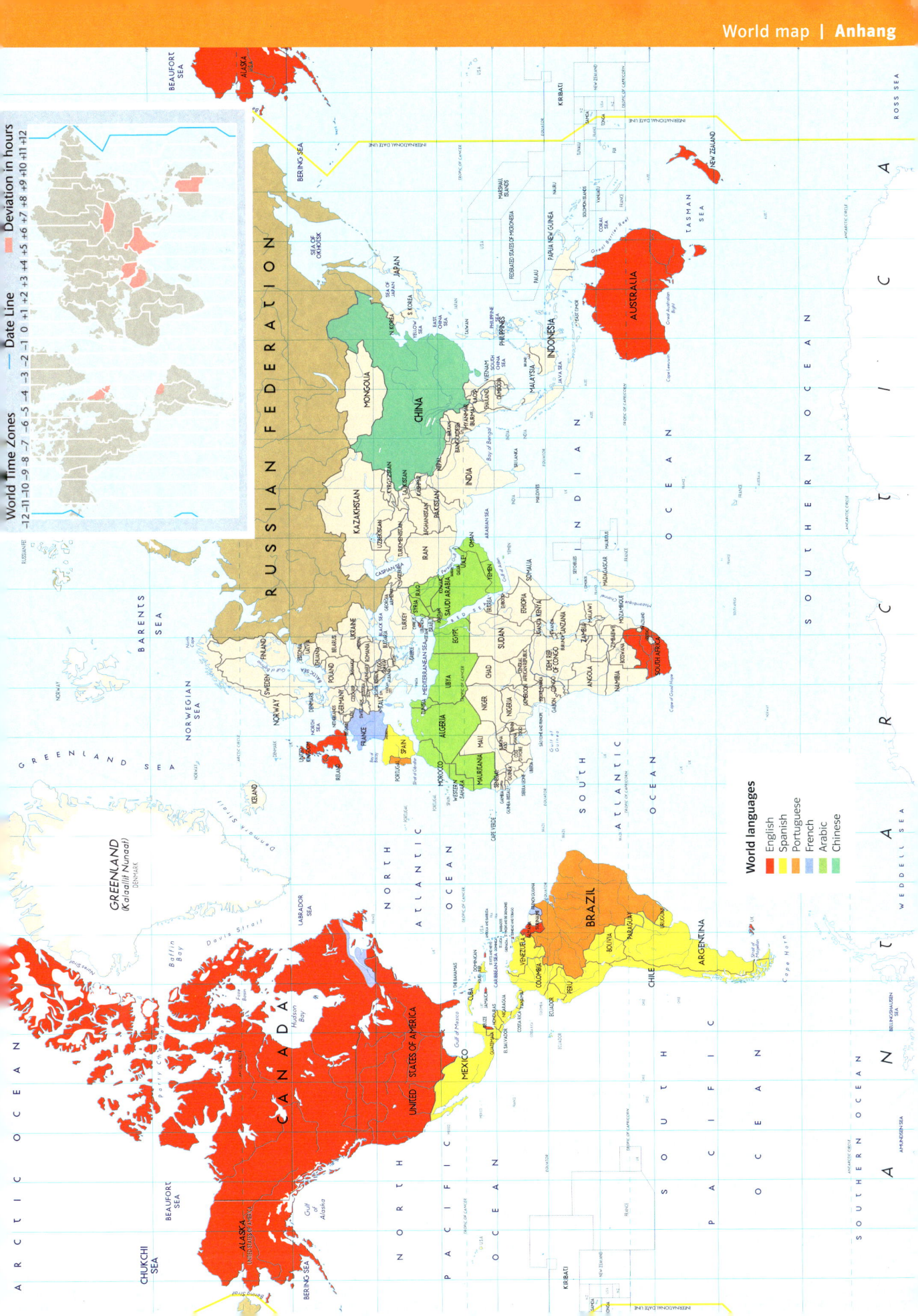

Anhang | Quellenverzeichnis

Bildquellennachweis

4 Thinkstock (Comstock), München; **5** shutterstock (J. Henning Buchholz), New York, NY; **6** Corbis RF (Royalty-Free), Düsseldorf; **6** Getty Images RF (Digital Vision), München; **6** Getty Images (PhotoDisc), München; **6** Fotosearch Stock Photography, Waukesha, WI; **7** JupiterImages photos.com (Photos.com), Tucson, AZ; **8** plainpicture GmbH & Co. KG (Maria Simon), Hamburg; **8** Alamy Images (Janine Wiedel Photolibrary), Abingdon, Oxon; **8** iStockphoto (RF/Locke), Calgary, Alberta; **10** Photothek.net Gbr (Ute Grabowsky), Radevormwald; **11** Robert Bosch GmbH, Stuttgart; **11** Imageshop (Imageshop), Düsseldorf; **11** Mauritius Images (Gilsdorf), Mittenwald; **14** Fotosearch Stock Photography (Banana Stock), Waukesha, WI; **18** www.bilderbox.com, Thening; **18** Corbis (Eric K. K. Yu), Düsseldorf; **18** Joker (Marcus Gloger), Bonn; **18** JupiterImages photos.com (RF/Photos.com), Tucson, AZ; **19** Klett-Archiv (Meyle + Müller/Harter), Stuttgart; **20** Klett-Archiv (Meyle + Müller/Harter), Stuttgart; **21** iStockphoto (RF/artydanmark), Calgary, Alberta; **25** Kartographie Huber, München; **25** images.de digital photo GmbH (Giribas), Berlin; **25** MEV Verlag GmbH, Augsburg; **25** Jahns, Rainer, Siegsdorf; **27** Klett-Archiv (Meyle + Müller/Harter), Stuttgart; **28** Fotolia LLC (Ralf Beier), New York; **28** StockFood GmbH (Newedel), München; **28** StockFood GmbH (Joff Lee Studios), München; **28** obs (ABCEuroRSCG), Hamburg; **28** Getty Images RF (PhotoDisc), München; **31** Dreamstime LLC (Lario Tus), Brentwood, TN; **31** shutterstock (Theos), New York, NY; **32** Corbis (Mark Bolton), Düsseldorf; **32** Dreamstime LLC (Woolfenden), Brentwood, TN; **33** Thinkstock (Photodisc), München; **38** Avenue Images GmbH (Corbis RF/Tom Grill), Hamburg; **38** MEV Verlag GmbH, Augsburg; **39** Picture-Alliance (akg), Frankfurt; **39** Picture-Alliance (epa), Frankfurt; **39** Picture-Alliance (Imaginechina), Frankfurt; **39** Klett-Archiv (Meyle + Müller/Harter), Stuttgart; **41** Dreamstime LLC (Maksim Shmeljov), Brentwood, TN; **43** Klett-Archiv (Meyle + Müller/Harter), Stuttgart; **43** Mauritius Images (Pöhlmann), Mittenwald; **43** MEV Verlag GmbH, Augsburg; **43** Avenue Images GmbH (Ingram Publishing), Hamburg; **43** Ingram Publishing, Tattenhall Chester; **44** Fotosearch Stock Photography, Waukesha, WI; **44** Avenue Images GmbH (Image Source), Hamburg; **44** Avenue Images GmbH (Image Source RF), Hamburg; **44** Bananastock, Watlington/Oxon; **44** Imageshop, Düsseldorf; **44** BBC Information and archives, London; **48** Thinkstock (Goodshoot), München; **49** Thinkstock (Comstock Images), München; **51** shutterstock (Monkey Business Images), New York, NY; **51** Thinkstock (Erik Snyder), München; **51** iStockphoto (Dmitry Kutlayev), Calgary, Alberta; **51** Corbis RF (Image Source), Düsseldorf; **52** Klett-Archiv (Meyle + Müller/Harter), Stuttgart; **53** shutterstock (ArtmannWitte), New York, NY; **54** iStockphoto (Jason Stitt), Calgary, Alberta; **54** iStockphoto (RF/Chen), Calgary, Alberta; **54** iStockphoto (RF/Anna Bryukhanova), Calgary, Alberta; **55** iStockphoto (Anna Bryukhanova), Calgary, Alberta; **55** iStockphoto (Jason Stitt), Calgary, Alberta; **55** iStockphoto (RF/Chen), Calgary, Alberta; **60** iStockphoto (Francesco Ridolfi), Calgary, Alberta; **63** Thinkstock (Jupiterimages), München; **63** Avenue Images GmbH (Corbis RF/Jack Hollingsworth), Hamburg; **63** PhotoAlto, Paris; **63** Getty Images RF (Eyewire), München; **65** Klett-Archiv (Meyle + Müller/Harter), Stuttgart; **65** Fotosearch Stock Photography (Banana Stock), Waukesha, WI; **65** Avenue Images GmbH (Image Source), Hamburg; **67** Klett-Archiv (Meyle + Müller/Harter), Stuttgart; **70** iStockphoto (RF/peter chen), Calgary, Alberta; **70** Fotosearch Stock Photography (Banana Stock), Waukesha, WI; **74** BigStockPhoto.com (RF), Davis, CA; **74** Dreamstime LLC (Ronfromyork), Brentwood, TN; **74** iStockphoto (RF), Calgary, Alberta; **77** iStockphoto (miniature), Calgary, Alberta; **78** shutterstock (Miguel Angel Salinas Salinas), New York, NY; **78** Thinkstock (Stockbyte), München; **84** Thinkstock (Ryan McVay), München; **85** Klett-Archiv (Meyle + Müller/Harter), Stuttgart; **85** Fotosearch Stock Photography (Banana Stock), Waukesha, WI; **86** iStockphoto (RF/Thompson), Calgary, Alberta; **86** Klett-Archiv (Meyle + Müller/Harter), Stuttgart; **88** Klett-Archiv (Meyle + Müller/Harter), Stuttgart; **91** Klett-Archiv (Meyle + Müller/Harter), Stuttgart; **91** BBC Information and archives, London; **92** Klett-Archiv (Meyle + Müller/Harter), Stuttgart; **96** Google Inc. (http://maps.google.de), Mountain View, CA 94043; **100** Thinkstock (IT Stock), München; **105** LinguaTV GmbH, Berlin; **109** Thinkstock (Comstock), München; **112** iStockphoto (Jill Fromer), Calgary, Alberta; **112** Mauritius Images (B. Lehner), Mittenwald; **112** Thinkstock (Hemera/Keith Bell), München; **113** iStockphoto (RF/Hudson), Calgary, Alberta; **117** Thinkstock (Hemera), München; **128** shutterstock (J. Henning Buchholz), New York, NY; **129** Corbis (Ocean), Düsseldorf; **132** Düsseldorfer Messeges. mbH, Düsseldorf; **135** iStockphoto (McDonald), Calgary, Alberta; **136** LinguaTV GmbH, Berlin; **142** Corbis (Talaie), Düsseldorf; **147** MEV Verlag GmbH, Augsburg; **148** Thinkstock (Jupiterimages), München; **149** MEV Verlag GmbH, Augsburg; **153** shutterstock (Ralf Beier), New York, NY; **153** iStockphoto (Bogdan Lazar), Calgary, Alberta; **153** Avenue Images GmbH (Corbis RF/Jose Luis Pelaez, Inc./Blend Images), Hamburg; **153** Fotosearch Stock Photography (Corbis RF), Waukesha, WI; **155** Messe, Stuttgart; **156** shutterstock (Mark Yuill), New York, NY; **156** MEV Verlag GmbH, Augsburg; **156** Fotolia LLC (froto), New York; **156** Thinkstock (Comstock), München; **159** BLG Logistics Group AG, Bremen; **163** MEV Verlag GmbH, Augsburg; **163** Fotosearch Stock Photography (Digital Vision), Waukesha, WI; **163** Corel Corporation Deutschland, Unterschleissheim; **164** MEV Verlag GmbH, Augsburg; **165** Thomas Gremmelspacher, Stuttgart; **167** BBC Information and archives, London; **171** Corbis (Saloutos), Düsseldorf; **172** Fotosearch Stock Photography (PhotoDisc), Waukesha, WI; **172** Flughafen Frankfurt-Hahn, Hahn-Flughafen; **173** iStockphoto (bluenemo), Calgary, Alberta; **173** iStockphoto (RF/Prikhodho), Calgary, Alberta; **173** creativ collection Verlag GmbH, Freiburg; **174** iStockphoto (RF/David Meharey), Calgary, Alberta; **174** iStockphoto (RF/Paul Senyszyn), Calgary, Alberta; **174** iStockphoto (RF/Joe Gough), Calgary, Alberta; **174** iStockphoto (RF/Tschakert), Calgary, Alberta; **174** Thinkstock (Hemera Technologies, Getty Images), München; **174** Klett-Archiv (Ruth Feiertag), Stuttgart; **174** Thinkstock (iStockphoto), München; **176** iStockphoto (Rohde), Calgary, Alberta; **176** Getty Images RF (Annie Reynolds/PhotoLink), München; **177** Klett-Archiv (Meyle + Müller/Harter), Stuttgart; **178** BBC Information and archives, London; **180** iStockphoto (RF/Paul Cowan), Calgary, Alberta; **183** iStockphoto (RF/Hudson), Calgary, Alberta; **183** iStockphoto (RF), Calgary, Alberta; **183** MEV Verlag GmbH, Augsburg; **185** iStockphoto (fazon1), Calgary, Alberta; **186** Fotolia LLC (ExQuisine), New York; **186** iStockphoto (RF/Maureen Perez), Calgary, Alberta; **186** iStockphoto (RF/Caspel), Calgary, Alberta; **186** Mauritius Images (Pöhlmann), Mittenwald; **186** creativ collection Verlag GmbH, Freiburg; **190** Thinkstock (iStockphoto), München; **192** Thinkstock (Hemera), München; **193** Corbis (Ocean), Düsseldorf; **196** Thinkstock (Polka Dot Images), München; **198** Fotolia LLC (Sulamith), New York; **201** Getty Images RF (Photodisc), München; **201** Corel Corporation Deutschland, Unterschleissheim; **202** Klett-Archiv (Meyle + Müller), Stuttgart; **206** iStockphoto (David Hughes), Calgary, Alberta; **208** shutterstock (Iurii Konoval), New York, NY; **211** Thinkstock (Comstock), München; **212** shutterstock (argo74), New York, NY; **215** shutterstock (ary718), New York, NY; **217** MEV Verlag GmbH, Augsburg; **218** Alamy Images (Expuesto - Nicolas Randall), Abingdon, Oxon; **218** Avenue Images GmbH (CorbisRF), Hamburg; **220** BBC Information and archives, London; **221** Alamy Images (Adams Picture Library t/a apl), Abingdon, Oxon; **223** Corbis (Harms), Düsseldorf; **229** iStockphoto (Zorani), Calgary, Alberta; **230** Mercedes Benz, Niederlassung, Stuttgart; **230** MEV Verlag GmbH, Augsburg; **230** iStockphoto (RF/Maier), Calgary, Alberta; **238** BBC Information and archives, London; **239** Thinkstock (Digital Vision), München; **242** Mauritius Images (Simone Fichtl), Mittenwald; **244** creativ collection Verlag GmbH, Freiburg; **245** Thinkstock (Jack Hollingsworth), München; **247** Logo, Stuttgart; **257** Klett-Archiv, Stuttgart; **COVER** shutterstock (StockLite), New York, NY; **COVER** shutterstock (Dmitriy Shironosov), New York, NY; **COVER** Avenue Images GmbH (Fancy), Hamburg

Sollte es in einem Einzelfall nicht gelungen sein, den korrekten Rechteinhaber ausfindig zu machen, so werden berechtigte Ansprüche selbstverständlich im Rahmen der üblichen Regelungen abgegolten.